Get the ebook FREE!

To get a free PDF copy of this book
(sold separately for $29.99) purchase the print
book and register it at the Manning website
following the instructions inside this insert.

That's it!

Thanks from Manning!

Erlang and OTP in Action

Erlang and OTP in Action

MARTIN LOGAN
ERIC MERRITT
RICHARD CARLSSON

MANNING
Greenwich
(74° w. long.)

For online information and ordering of this and other Manning books, please visit
www.manning.com. The publisher offers discounts on this book when ordered in quantity.
For more information, please contact

    Special Sales Department
    Manning Publications Co.
    180 Broad St.
    Suite 1323
    Stamford, CT 06901
    Email: orders@manning.com

Manning Publications Co.   Development editor: Cynthia Kane
180 Broad St.   Copyeditor: Tiffany Taylor
Suite 1323   Proofreader: Katie Tennant
Stamford, CT 06901   Typesetter: Dennis Dalinnik
                                     Cover designer: Marija Tudor

ISBN: 9781933988788
Printed in the United States of America
1 2 3 4 5 6 7 8 9 10 – MAL – 16 15 14 13 12 11 10

To all the great Erlangers,
many of whom we call friends, that we have met along the way.
May this book put an end to the long hard slog through
internet docs that we had to endure to learn OTP.

brief contents

contents

foreword

For a long time, the world of Erlang programming had only one book—The Book,[1] released in 1993 and revised in 1996. Fanatics can still find it in print, at a price of over $100. A decade or so after its publication, The Book was getting long in the tooth, to say the least. The language had evolved to include several new and powerful programming constructs. Higher-order functions, list comprehensions, and the bit syntax are found everywhere in modern Erlang programs but weren't described in The Book. But the most notable omission was the Open Telecom Platform (OTP), Erlang's application development framework, which was first released in 1996. Erlang was rather easy to learn; OTP wasn't, and early adopters like Martin Logan, who started using Erlang in 1999, pretty much had to learn it the hard way through trial and error.

In the past few years, as an indication that Erlang had become interesting enough to justify it, a number of books was released, and we were told that other books were being written. *Erlang and OTP in Action* by Martin Logan, Eric Merritt, and Richard Carlsson was the one most talked about. And now it is here.

I started programming Erlang in 1993, when I was designing disaster response systems in Anchorage, Alaska. I bought a precompiled version of Erlang for HP-UX, delivered on a magnetic QIC tape. The language was smaller back then, as were the number of support libraries. I had to start designing my own data-access structures, database managers, protocol parsers, and error-handling frameworks—but I enjoyed

---

[1] Robert Virding, Claes Wikstrom, and Mike Williams, *Concurrent Programming in Erlang* (Prentice Hall, 1993, 1996).

myself thoroughly. After all, this was a different time: the web was emerging with the release of the Mosaic browser that same year, and the term *open source* wouldn't be used for another five years; if you wanted a programming framework with support for distributed computing and fault tolerance, you had to be prepared to pay dearly, both in time and money. I had scoured the market for such tools and felt well-informed about the commercial alternatives. Erlang was raw and unassuming, with a weird-looking syntax and practically no documentation, but its core concepts felt right in a way that no other tools had.

Three years later, I found myself in Sweden, working for Ericsson and chief designer of the largest Erlang-based project to date. We would build what is known as a *telecom-class ATM switch* using Erlang, as well as a new framework called the Open Telecom Platform. The name was intended to make decision makers in the company feel warm and fuzzy—*Telecom* was our core business, *Open* was the buzzword of the day, and the prevailing wisdom was that if you wanted to build a robust complex product, you had to have a *Platform* that provided things like redundancy, support for remote configuration, live software upgrade, and real-time tracing and debugging.

Ericsson isn't in the business of selling development tools, but it has designed programming languages by necessity since the early 1970s. To its credit (but also to its own benefit), Ericsson released Erlang/OTP as open source in 1998. Enthusiasts across the world picked it up and used it, mainly in the telecom field at first, but later also in other areas. We made several attempts in the '90s to pitch Erlang to web developers, but the challenge facing web developers back then wasn't how to make redundant, scalable, and highly responsive e-commerce sites; the time for such systems hadn't yet come, nor had the time when concurrency would be a conversation topic for mainstream programmers. Concurrency was hard—everyone knew that. Concurrency was something to be avoided. Why, then, choose a programming language where you could hardly even write "hello world" without introducing concurrency?

The explosive growth of the web and the emergence of increasingly interactive web applications eventually brought Erlang in from the cold. Unexpected help also came from the laws of physics, which finally made it impossible to keep cranking up the clock frequency on our CPUs to produce faster and faster single-core chips. The message "The free lunch is over" from the hardware vendors, urging developers to start learning how to make their programs scale across many weaker cores rather than one very fast CPU, was wonderful news for Erlang. This meant many clever programmers would at least look at Erlang, to figure out what supposedly made it so special. Many would simply look, and others would borrow concepts and implement them in their favorite language. This was wonderful too, because it meant the market value of knowing and loving Erlang and the principles behind it would increase rapidly.

OTP has by now been proven in several problem domains other than telecom and is highly regarded by those who have learned to master it. Erlang/OTP is an amazingly powerful platform, but it does take time to learn, not least when you try to apply it to a new niche. Interestingly, even programmers who have worked for years in OTP-based projects may be fairly ignorant of how to build an OTP-based system from scratch, because the application programmer is exposed only to a fairly small part of the total framework. This is exactly what you want in a large project, but the entrepreneur in a small startup can't rely on someone else burning the midnight oil and figuring out the subtleties of OTP release-handling and other dark corners without helpful examples and tutorials.

A good book on OTP has been sorely needed, and it's with great pleasure that we welcome *Erlang and OTP in Action*. Martin Logan, Eric Merritt, and Richard Carlsson represent an enormous amount of experience combined, and they have contributed greatly to the Erlang community. I'm convinced that this book will help boost the already impressive trend of Erlang adoption.

Enjoy!

ULF WIGER
CTO, ERLANG SOLUTIONS LTD

preface

This book is an attempt to distill what we think are the most important things a professional Erlang programmer needs to know in order to use this hugely productive programming language to its full potential. Erlang/OTP gives you a lot of power, but so far it's been a daunting task for budding Erlang programmers to learn the OTP framework on their own by studying the documentation (which goes into a lot of detail but doesn't show you the big picture).

The three of us have worked with Erlang for a long time, but our individual paths have been very different.

Martin: "My first 'real' job introduced me to Erlang programming. I had been doing C and C++, and I thought I was having fun. My first boss, Hal Snyder, who even years ago in the '90s had a passionate dislike for threading, stumbled across Erlang. I was an intern at the time, so he gave me a project to complete with Erlang because, well, I was cheap, and if I failed, the company only lost about $70 on the deal. I didn't fail. I wrote my own 1,000-line monstrosity of a supervisor, because I didn't know what OTP was, and there certainly were no books about it. In the process, I fell in love with the 'right' way to write back-end systems, and I fell in love with Erlang. Erlang gave me the opportunity to see into the future: I wrote complex distributed systems, using advanced algorithms that my imperative language colleagues could only dream about and never implement in less than two years and a million lines of code. Thousands of pages of documentation and tens of thousands of lines of code later, I still love it. Along the way, I've met some great people, and I'm thrilled to be writing this book with two of them. I met Richard while speaking at an ACM conference in 2004, and I met Eric four years later as we formed Erlware—a project in which we're opening new chapters even now. Erlang has been a big part of my professional and personal life for many years and will continue to be so."

Eric: "I started noodling with Erlang as a side issue. I wanted to write a massively multiplayer game, but I knew that one person, even if they had a talent for it, couldn't do the graphics for such a game single-handedly. I decided to concentrate on game play, thinking that I might be able to do this well, given the right tools and the right language. I liked the idea of agents in the game learning on their own over time, having independent concurrent actions. The only realistic way in my mind, at the time, was to model each of these agents as some type of independent concurrent thing, but I didn't know what that was. The languages I knew wouldn't work for one person writing a game like that all by themselves. So, I started exploring languages. I spent five years or so doing this, on and off, in some pretty extreme depth. I came upon Erlang fairly early, and although I liked the concurrency, its syntax and functional nature threw me off. It wasn't until I had explored programming languages in general a lot more that I started to appreciate Erlang and write code in it. I never wrote that game, but after I settled on Erlang as the right choice, I delved deeply into it, explored it thoroughly, and started realizing how useful a language it was for many things. This was back in 2000 or 2001. For the following few years, I experimented and taught myself OTP. Then, in 2005, I introduced Erlang at Amazon.com, released the first version of Sinan, and met Martin Logan, and we founded Erlware. In 2008, I moved to Chicago to get the book project moving and start Erlware in earnest."

Richard: "I was introduced to Erlang around 1995 when I was looking for a subject for my master's thesis in computer science at Uppsala University. This led to me being part of the High-Performance Erlang research group as a PhD student, working on the Erlang compiler and runtime system for many years. I met Martin Logan and Eric Merritt through conferences in Sweden and the U.S. and was impressed by their enthusiasm for Erlang despite it being such a little-known language in those days— particularly in the U.S. During my PhD studies, I also hacked on a few side projects: the Syntax Tools library and the EDoc application were spin-offs from my compiler-related work, and EUnit had its basis in the need for me to check that my students' concurrent programming assignments worked according to spec. After leaving the world of academia, I spent a few years working with non-Erlang-related things, coding mostly in Python, Ruby, and C++. But these days, I'm working full time with Erlang again, in the fast-moving world of high-availability payment systems, at one of Sweden's most successful startup companies."

We've tried to extract as much as we can from our collective experience in order to make your journey toward becoming a master Erlang programmer easier; and we hope that with the help of this book, the OTP framework will finally become something that every Erlang programmer knows how to use—not only those brave few who have read the manuals back to front.

acknowledgments

First, we want to thank Bob Calco for getting this project started—without you, the book wouldn't have happened, and we hope you like the results.

We also want to thank all those readers who bought the Early Access edition and waited so long for us to finish, while we more or less rewrote the book three times. Your interest made us pull through.

Thanks to Jerry Cattell for reviewing the Java code, Francesco Cesarini for his help and promotion, Ulf Wiger for the foreword, Kevin A. Smith for his driver example code, Ryan Rawson for help with Java and HBase, Ken Pratt for the technical proofreading, and Alain O'Dea and all the other Early Access readers who gave us their feedback.

Special thanks to the following peer reviewers who read the manuscript at various stages of development for their invaluable input: Chris Chandler, Jim Larson, Bryce Darling, Brian McCallister, Kevin Jackson, Deepak Vohra, Pierre-Antoine Grégoire, David Dossot, Greg Donald, Daniel Bretoi, James Hatheway, John S. Griffin, Franco Lombardo, and Stuart Caborn.

And a big thank you to the people at Manning for their support and patience, in particular Tiffany Taylor, Katie Tennant, and Cynthia Kane. You didn't lose hope.

Last but not least: Martin wants to thank his wife Veronica for her patience in this marathon book-writing endeavor. Likewise, Richard wants to thank his wife Elisabet for her steadfast support and encouragement despite all the evenings and weekends lost to writing. Eric would like to thank Rossana for listening to his complaints about the workload and teasing him incessantly about the interminable nature of the book.

about this book

This book is focused on getting real, stable, versioned, and maintainable software out into the world. It's less theoretical, and more hands-on practical. We (the authors) have put many systems into production over the years, and in this book we distill that knowledge for use in real software development. Our focus is not just the Erlang programming language by itself—other books out there are more suited as language tutorials. This book is about the practice of writing Erlang code for production.

Because this book is aimed at allowing individual programmers or teams of programmers across a company to write effective code, it covers Erlang/OTP right from the start, not just Erlang the language. Erlang by itself offers the potential for powerful applications to be created, but it's with OTP that it realizes that potential. OTP is simultaneously a framework, a set of libraries, and a methodology for structuring applications; it's really a language extension. To learn Erlang for the real world means learning Erlang/OTP.

This book illustrates how to use Erlang/OTP in practice, through carefully chosen realistic examples. By implementing these examples for yourself, you'll come to understand how to build solid, versioned, production-ready code that is ready to utilize every cycle of that 32-core machine you have sitting in your server rack!

Roadmap

The book is divided into three parts. Part 1 is aimed at getting you past programming in pure Erlang, introducing the basics of OTP:

- Chapter 1 presents the Erlang/OTP platform and the main features that make it tick, such as processes, message passing, links, distribution, and the runtime system.
- Chapter 2 gives a whirlwind tour of the Erlang programming language, both for reference and as a summary of the things every professional Erlang programmer should know.
- Chapter 3 introduces the concept of OTP behaviours, by throwing you headfirst into writing a server in Erlang that communicates over TCP sockets.
- Chapter 4 introduces OTP applications and supervision trees, showing how to package your server from the previous chapter as an application with a supervisor and with documentation generated by EDoc.
- Chapter 5 presents the main GUI tools for finding out what is happening in a running Erlang system: the application monitor, the process manager, the debugger, and the table viewer.

Part 2 of the book gets down to business, giving you a real programming task and adding more advanced OTP features to the code as you move along:

- Chapter 6 starts you off on the main project in this book: implementing a cache system for speeding up accesses to a web server. This will demonstrate a more complicated application with many processes and using a supervisor as a process factory.
- Chapter 7 explains how Erlang/OTP logging and event-handling work, and adds a logging facility to the cache application by means of a custom event handler.
- Chapter 8 introduces distributed Erlang/OTP, explaining what nodes are, how Erlang clusters work, how you communicate between nodes, and how you use job control in the Erlang shell to perform operations on remote nodes. You'll then put this into immediate use by implementing a distributed resource-discovery application that can be used to publish and find information about available resources in a cluster of Erlang nodes.
- Chapter 9 presents the Mnesia built-in distributed database in Erlang and shows how to use a distributed table to make the cache application span multiple nodes in a cluster.
- Chapter 10 talks about how one or more Erlang/OTP applications are packaged for release, either as a standalone minimal installation or as add-ons to a previous installation, and how to deploy such packages.

Part 3 of the book is about making your code work as part of a greater whole, integrating it with other systems and users, and optimizing it as the load increases:

- Chapter 11 shows how to add a RESTful HTTP interface over TCP to the cache application, by taking you through the process of writing your own web server from the ground up as a custom OTP behaviour.

- Chapter 12 explains the basic mechanisms in Erlang for communicating with code written in other languages, by demonstrating how to integrate a third-party C library in three different ways: using plain ports, using a port driver, and as NIFs.
- Chapter 13 shows how to integrate Java code with the help of the Jinterface library, making the Java program appear as a node in the Erlang cluster. This is then used to add a Hadoop HBase database as a backing store for the cache application.
- Chapter 14 talks about performance measurement and optimization in an Erlang/OTP system, explaining how to use the main code profiling tools and discussing some implementation details worth knowing when you're trying to tune your program.

It's worth noting that we don't cover the gen_fsm behaviour in this book. This is intentional; gen_fsm is a behaviour seldom used in practice. The book covers the most important of the OTP behaviours in great detail, and from this you'll come to understand behaviours well enough that learning about gen_fsm from the official documentation on your own will be easy. Among other things, it can be useful for parsing binary protocols; but a plain gen_server and the judicious use of pattern matching is almost always more appropriate and, in particular, more flexible. If you were looking forward to learning about gen_fsm, we're sorry, but overall you're better served by the main behaviours.

Source code

All source code in listings or in text is in a fixed-width font like this to separate it from ordinary text. Code annotations accompany many of the listings, highlighting important concepts. In some cases, numbered bullets link to explanations that follow the listing.

The code for this book is available at http://github.com/erlware/Erlang-and-OTP-in-Action-Source (or go to github.com and search for "Erlang and OTP in Action"). It is also available from the publisher's website at www.manning.com/ErlangandOTP-inAction.

Author Online

The purchase of *Erlang and OTP in Action* includes free access to a private forum run by Manning Publications where you can make comments about the book, ask technical questions, and receive help from the authors and other users. You can access and subscribe to the forum at http://www.manning.com/ErlangandOTPinAction. This page provides information on how to get on the forum once you're registered, what kind of help is available, and the rules of conduct in the forum.

Manning's commitment to our readers is to provide a venue where a meaningful dialogue between individual readers and between readers and the authors can take place. It isn't a commitment to any specific amount of participation on the part of the authors, whose contributions to the book's forum remains voluntary (and unpaid). We suggest you try asking the authors some challenging questions, lest their interest stray!

The Author Online forum and the archives of previous discussions will be accessible from the publisher's website as long as the book is in print.

About the authors

MARTIN J. LOGAN has been heavily involved with the Erlang community since 1999. His great interest in distributed systems and service-based design has made him a constant presence in the community. He has given many talks on the topic, in the U.S. and Canada as well as in Europe, and he is one of the people behind the Chicago ErlangCamp conference. Martin has implemented many complex systems using Erlang in the telecom space, including one of the first call-detail record-collection systems for the SIP protocol; but more recently, he has focused on large-scale e-commerce backing systems. Currently, Martin brings his expertise to Orbitz Worldwide, one of the largest online travel companies in the world. Martin has also taken on a leadership role with Erlware, where he is a core developer and the primary author of the Faxien package-management system. He currently lives in Chicago with his wife Veronica.

ERIC MERRITT is a software engineer who specializes in concurrent languages and distributed systems. For the last nine years, he has been coding Erlang and has also been heavily involved in the Erlang community. Eric has been involved in both professional and open source development for the last ten years. He started his career developing in C and Java on IBM mainframe and midrange hardware. He also provided training and consulting in object-oriented principles and concepts. However, his interest in languages, concurrency, and distributed systems soon drove him to more interesting and challenging work at companies such as Amazon.com. Currently, Eric is a core developer for the Erlware family of open source products and he is the primary author of the Sinan build system. His day job involves hacking Erlang for eCD Market, LLC.

RICHARD CARLSSON has been deeply involved with Erlang since the mid-nineties. He was one of the original members of the High-Performance Erlang group at Uppsala University, and has contributed to many parts of the standard libraries, the Erlang compiler, runtime system, and the language itself. Among other things, he is the author of Erlang's EDoc documentation system and the EUnit unit testing framework. He is currently working for Klarna, one of Sweden's fastest growing companies, which provides payment solutions, all based on Erlang, in Scandinavia, Germany, and the Netherlands.

About the cover illustration

The illustration on the cover of *Erlang and OTP in Action* bears the caption "An Artvinian," a resident of a region called Artvin in northeast Turkey. The image is taken from a collection of costumes of the Ottoman Empire published on January 1, 1802, by William Miller of Old Bond Street, London. The title page is missing from the collection and we have been unable to track it down to date. The book's table of contents identifies the figures in both English and French, and each illustration also bears the names of two artists who worked on it, both of whom would no doubt be surprised to find their art gracing the front cover of a computer programming book...two hundred years later.

The collection was purchased by a Manning editor at an antiquarian flea market in the "Garage" on West 26th Street in Manhattan. The seller was an American based in Ankara, Turkey, and the transaction took place just as he was packing up his stand for the day. The Manning editor did not have on his person the substantial amount of cash that was required for the purchase and a credit card and check were both politely turned down. With the seller flying back to Ankara that evening the situation was getting hopeless. What was the solution? It turned out to be nothing more than an old-fashioned verbal agreement sealed with a handshake. The seller simply proposed that the money be transferred to him by wire and the editor walked out with the bank information on a piece of paper and the portfolio of images under his arm. Needless to say, we transferred the funds the next day, and we remain grateful and impressed by this unknown person's trust in one of us. It recalls something that might have happened a long time ago.

The pictures from the Ottoman collection, like the other illustrations that appear on our covers, bring to life the richness and variety of dress customs of two centuries ago. They recall the sense of isolation and distance of that period—and of every other historic period except our own hyperkinetic present. Dress codes have changed since then and the diversity by region, so rich at the time, has faded away. It is now often hard to tell the inhabitant of one continent from another. Perhaps, trying to view it optimistically, we have traded a cultural and visual diversity for a more varied personal life. Or a more varied and interesting intellectual and technical life.

We at Manning celebrate the inventiveness, the initiative, and, yes, the fun of the computer business with book covers based on the rich diversity of regional life of two centuries ago, brought back to life by the pictures from this collection.

introduction

Erlang is a programming language where *processes* are a fundamental concept. But what is a process? When you run several programs at once on your computer, such as a word processor and a web browser, each one of those programs runs inside its own process. If your word processor should crash, your browser generally stays running as if nothing happened—or vice versa, a crashing web browser will not cause you to lose that document you were writing. Processes are a kind of bubble that provides isolation as well as parallel execution, and Erlang is built entirely around processes.

Erlang makes it easy for you to create processes as you need them—just as easy as it is to create *objects* in a language like Java. Because processes are so cheap, we can start to look at systems in a different manner. Each independent activity in an Erlang program can be coded as a separate process. No unintuitive event loops, no thread pooling, none of those pesky implementation details. If your program needs 10,000 processes running simultaneously to accomplish a job, it can easily be done. As you'll see as you read this book, this fundamentally alters the way we look at systems, presenting a view that is, as we hope to show you, much more intuitive (and much more productive).

Erlang is also what is known as a *functional* programming language. Don't let this intimidate you. Erlang could have been more like the mainstream programming languages you know; the properties described here can be achieved without functional programming. But functional programming and its main characteristics like referential transparency, the use of higher-order functions, and the general avoidance of mutable data structures lend themselves nicely to the fundamental features of Erlang.

Functional programming is the vehicle by which these features were codified, and it allows them to be expressed elegantly and succinctly. The power of Erlang without the clarity of functional code would yield a more complex and much less enjoyable language to program in.

Where Erlang comes from

When you first heard of Erlang, it may have been described to you as a "functional, concurrent programming language," and you may have thought that it sounded like some kind of academic and probably unpractical toy language. But we want to emphasize that Erlang has its roots in real-world, large-scale software engineering problems. To make this clear, we'll here give you the history behind the language in some detail.

A comparison with C

The background of Erlang can be seen as an interesting parallel to that of the C programming language. First, both languages were created by a small group of people working in the relatively relaxed setting of an R&D department deep in the bowels of a large telecom company. The language creators were free spirits, but they were also pragmatic engineers out to solve a concrete problem. In the case of C, the problem was how to write systems software in more high-level language than assembler, but on hardware with limited resources (for that time). For Erlang, it was how to enable programmers to write very large, highly parallel, and extremely fault-tolerant software, while radically improving productivity and reducing the number of software defects— a tall order indeed.

Both languages accumulated followers within the company who used them for internal projects and real products, and gave valuable early feedback to the creators about pragmatic details. In both cases, it took some 10 years before the general public heard about them, and by that time, they had been well and truly battle tested. C was created around 1972 and was popularized during the 1980s. Similarly, Erlang took shape around 1988 and was released as open source in 1998. Both languages also sparked an early outside interest within research organizations and universities. And both certainly have their quirks, for historical reasons, but we're generally willing to forgive them because they get the job done like nothing else.

Let's step back in time.

Stockholm, mid-1980s: an Englishman gets a license to poke around

Erlang was born as the result of a project aiming to find a better way of programming the kind of control systems that were largely limited to the telecom industry in those days: high-traffic, extremely parallel systems with draconic demands on uptime. Joe Armstrong joined this project in 1985, at Ericsson's Computer Science Laboratory in Stockholm, Sweden.

A major part of this project was to implement the same kind of telephony control system in as many different programming languages as possible. This included Ada, CLU, Smalltalk, and others. The results weren't conclusive. Although it became clear that the high-level, declarative style of the functional and logic languages was attractive, no language had a suitable concurrency model.

But what would a good concurrency model look like? In those days (and still almost two decades later), research into concurrency was mostly focused on either pure and abstract process models such as CSP, pi-calculus, and concurrent logic languages, or low-level mechanisms such as semaphores, monitors, and signals.

Meanwhile, engineers had to solve the real problems involved with creating massively parallel and fault-tolerant communication systems. Ericsson already had one such home-made solution in the shape of a proprietary hybrid programming language and operating system called PLEX, for its successful line of AXE telephony switches.

Some perplexing demands

PLEX was a relatively normal imperative programming language, but it had some particular features that defined a kind of baseline for any solution that aimed to replace it:

- Processes had to be an intrinsic part of the language.
- Processes must not be able to corrupt each other's memory spaces, leave dangling pointers, and so on.
- It must be possible to run tens or hundreds of thousands of processes, so process creation and task switching must be fast, and processes must use very little memory.
- Failure of individual processes must be isolated.
- You must be able to do a code upgrade on the fly in a running system.
- You must be able to detect and handle both hardware and software errors.

The only languages that came close to this were concurrent logic languages such as Parlog and Strand, but those had a very different, much more fine-grained process concept, with little control over individual processes.

Erlang comes to life

One day, after discovering the logic programming language Prolog and how well its rule-based programming style matched his hand-written notation for describing the telephony control problem, Joe started writing a Prolog meta-interpreter. This way, he could extend Prolog with simulated process switching, to run multiple concurrent telephone calls.

Pretty soon, the interpreted expressions had grown into a small language, with processes and message passing; and although it was implemented on top of Prolog, it was simpler, was functional, and didn't use Prolog's unification and backtracking features. Not much later, the name *Erlang* was suggested, as a deliberate pun. (A. K. Erlang, a Danish mathematician, was a familiar name to many telecom engineers, due to his contributions to the field of communication system statistics, but the name could also be read as "Ericsson language.")

The initial evolution of Erlang was thus driven by the requirements of writing a small but working telephony control system. In particular, the message-passing primitives were carefully chosen to match the realities of large telecom systems rather than any particular theory of concurrency. This meant using an asynchronous send operator, and with automatic buffering of messages and out-of-order selective receive (strongly influenced by the CCITT SDL notation used for specifying complicated communication protocols).

After an initial experiment on a group of real users during 1988, writing a prototype for a new telephony architecture, it was clear that the new language gave a very large productivity boost but that its current implementation was much too slow. Starting in 1990, Joe, Mike Williams, and Robert Virding began implementing the first abstract machine for Erlang. Its name was JAM; it was a stack-based abstract machine written in C and was 70 times faster than the Prolog implementation.

The first Erlang book was published in 1993, with a second edition in 1996. Erlang could finally be considered a real language.

The in-between years

Over the following years, Erlang accumulated many features, such as distribution, the record syntax, the preprocessor, lambda expressions (*funs*), list comprehensions, the Mnesia database, the binary data type, the bit syntax, and more. The system was ported to other platforms besides UNIX, such as Windows, VxWorks, and QNX.

Erlang got a crucial boost within Ericsson due to the collapse of a gigantic C++-based project in 1995. The project was restarted from scratch, this time using Erlang and "a mere 60" programmers; and a proper language support department—the OTP team—was formed to back them up. The result was the highly successful AXD301 system, containing more than a million lines of Erlang code.

Meanwhile, a couple of students doing their master's thesis on native code compilation of Erlang led to the *High Performance Erlang* research group being founded at Uppsala University in 1998; and eventually, the HiPE native code compiler was integrated in the standard Erlang/OTP distribution. Furthermore, although an Ericsson project to improve efficiency by compiling Erlang to C was unsuccessful due to the greatly increased code size, a spin-off effect was that a faster, register-based, threaded code abstract machine design named BEAM replaced the older JAM.

But in the late 90s, Java was the word of the day. Upper management decided that Ericsson shouldn't commit itself to developing and supporting its own programming language but should instead focus on "globally used languages." Hence, Erlang was banned for new projects. Management was eventually persuaded to release Erlang as open source, to benefit users outside Ericsson. This happened in December 1998. Soon after that, many of the core developers left to form a small startup, using Erlang and their substantial telecom experience to successfully get rich quick.

Getting dressed for success

Slowly, the external user base started growing. At Ericsson, people started to forget about the ban as time passed and it became obvious that Erlang was too useful to ignore and that the existing systems weren't going to be rewritten in anything else. The OTP team kept developing and supporting Erlang, and Ericsson kept sponsoring the HiPE project, with its many spin-off applications such as EDoc and Dialyzer.

In the world of academia, Erlang began to get recognition as a well-established and interesting functional programming language. Since 2002, the annual Erlang Workshop has been an ACM SIGPLAN sponsored event, co-located with ICFP, the International Conference on Functional Programming. As the highest form of flattery, the Erlang concurrency model has been experimentally copied onto several other programming languages; but as many people have found out, this is hard to do as an afterthought.

In 2006, while the hardware industry was beginning to admit that it had hit the uniprocessor performance wall, the first release of Erlang with SMP support was released, as the result of a joint effort between Ericsson's OTP team and the HiPE team. Then, in 2007, Joe's new book *Programming Erlang* (the first Erlang book in a decade) was published—and suddenly, Erlang was getting a lot of attention all over the world. Many companies, both large and small, have picked it up and are putting it to weird and wonderful uses.

That is where this book begins.

Part 1

Getting past pure Erlang: the OTP basics

Part 1 of this book is a dive into the fundamentals. We cover language basics in a whirlwind tour and then explore some of the fundamental OTP building blocks that set things up for the real-world scenarios that play out through the rest of the book.

The Erlang/OTP platform

This chapter covers

- Understanding concurrency and Erlang's process model
- Erlang's support for fault tolerance and distribution
- Important properties of the Erlang runtime system
- What functional programming means, and how it applies to Erlang

If you're reading this book, you probably know already that Erlang is a programming language—and as such it's pretty interesting in itself—but as the title of the book indicates, our focus is on the practical use of Erlang for creating real, live systems. And for that, we also need the OTP framework. This is always included in any Erlang distribution and is such an integral part of Erlang these days that it's hard to say where the line is drawn between OTP and the plain Erlang standard libraries; hence, we often say "Erlang/OTP" to refer to either or both. Despite this close relationship, not many Erlang programmers have a clear idea of what OTP can provide

What does OTP stand for?

OTP was originally an acronym for Open Telecom Platform, a bit of a branding attempt from the time before Erlang went open source. But few people care about that now; these days, it's just OTP. Nothing in either Erlang or OTP is specific to telecom applications: a more fitting name might have been Concurrent Systems Platform.

or how to start using it, even if it has always been just a few keystrokes away. This book is here to help.

The Erlang programming language is already fairly well known for making it easy to write highly parallel, distributed, and fault-tolerant systems, and we give a comprehensive overview of the language in chapter 2 before we jump into the workings of the OTP framework. But why should you learn to use OTP, when you could happily hack away, rolling your own solutions as you go? These are some of the main advantages of OTP:

- *Productivity*—Using OTP makes it possible to produce production-quality systems in a very short time.
- *Stability*—Code written on top of OTP can focus on the logic and avoid error-prone reimplementations of the typical things that every real-world system needs: process management, servers, state machines, and so on.
- *Supervision*—The application structure provided by the framework makes it simple to supervise and control the running systems, both automatically and through graphical user interfaces.
- *Upgradability*—The framework provides patterns for handling code upgrades in a systematic way.
- *Reliable code base*—The code for the OTP framework is rock solid and has been thoroughly battle tested.

Despite these advantages, it's probably true to say that to most Erlang programmers, OTP is still something of a secret art, learned partly by osmosis and partly by poring over the more impenetrable sections of the documentation. We'd like to change this. This is, to our knowledge, the first book focused on learning to use OTP, and we want to show you that it can be a much easier experience than you may think. We're sure you won't regret it.

At the end of this book, you'll have a thorough knowledge of the concepts, libraries, and programming patterns that make up the OTP framework. You'll understand how individual programs and whole Erlang-based systems can be structured using OTP components and principles in order to be fault tolerant, distributable, concurrent, efficient, and easy to control and monitor. You'll probably also have picked up a number of details about the Erlang language, its runtime system, and some of the libraries and tools around it that you weren't already aware of.

In this chapter, we discuss the core concepts and features of the Erlang/OTP platform that everything else in OTP builds on:

- Concurrent programming
- Fault tolerance
- Distributed programming
- The Erlang virtual machine and runtime system
- Erlang's core functional language

The point is to get you acquainted with the thinking behind all the concrete stuff we dive into from chapters 2 and 3 onward, rather than starting by handing you a bunch of facts up front. Erlang is different, and many of the things you'll see in this book will take some time to get accustomed to. With this chapter, we hope to give you an idea of why things work the way they do, before we get into technical details.

1.1 Concurrent programming with processes

Erlang was designed for *concurrency*—having multiple tasks running simultaneously—from the ground up. It was a central concern when the language was designed. Its built-in support for concurrency, which uses the *process* concept to get a clean separation between tasks, allows you to create fault-tolerant architectures and fully utilize the multicore hardware that is available today. But before we go any further, we should explain more exactly what we mean by the terms *concurrency* and *process*.

1.1.1 Understanding concurrency

Is *concurrent* just another word for *in parallel?* Almost but not exactly, at least when we're talking about computers and programming.

One popular semiformal definition reads something like, "Those things that don't have anything that forces them to happen in a specific order are said to be concurrent." For example, given the task to sort two packs of cards, you could sort one first and then the other; or if you had extra arms and eyes, you could sort both in parallel. Nothing requires you to do them in a certain order; hence, they're concurrent tasks. They can be done in either order, or you can jump back and forth between the tasks until they're both done; or, if you have the extra appendages (or perhaps someone to help you), you can perform them simultaneously in true parallel fashion.

This may sound strange: shouldn't we say that tasks are concurrent only if they're happening at the same time? Well, the point with that definition is that they *could* happen at the same time, and we're free to schedule them at our convenience. Tasks that *need* to be done simultaneously aren't separate tasks at all, whereas some tasks are separate but nonconcurrent and must be done in order, such as breaking the egg before making the omelet. The rest are concurrent.

One of the nice things that Erlang does for you is help with the physical execution of tasks. As illustrated in figure 1.1, if extra CPUs (or cores or hyperthreads) are available, Erlang uses them to run more of your concurrent tasks in parallel. If not, Erlang

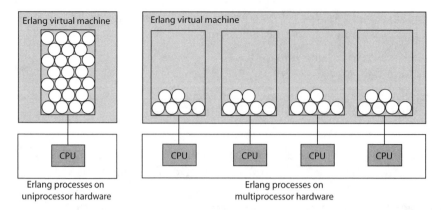

Figure 1.1   Erlang processes running on uniprocessor and on multiprocessor hardware, respectively. The runtime system automatically distributes the workload over the available CPU resources.

uses what CPU power there is to do them all a bit at a time. You won't need to think about such details, and your Erlang programs automatically adapt to different hardware—they just run more efficiently if there are more CPUs, as long as you have things lined up that can be done concurrently.

But what if your tasks aren't concurrent, and your program must first do X, then Y, and finally Z? That is where you need to start thinking about the real dependencies in the problem you're out to solve. Perhaps X and Y can be done in any order as long as they're before Z. Or perhaps you can start working on a part of Z as soon as parts of X and Y are done. There is no simple recipe, but surprisingly often a little thinking can get you a long way, and it gets easier with experience.

Rethinking the problem in order to eliminate unnecessary dependencies can make the code run more efficiently on modern hardware. But that should usually be your second concern. The most important effect of separating parts of the program that don't need to be together is that doing so makes your code less confused, more readable, and allows you to focus on the real problems rather than on the mess that follows from trying to do several things at once. This means higher productivity and fewer bugs. But first, we need a more concrete representation of the idea of having separate tasks.

1.1.2   *Erlang's process model*

In Erlang, the unit of concurrency is the *process*. A process represents an ongoing activity; it's an agent that is running a piece of program code, concurrent to other processes running their own code, at their own pace. Processes are a bit like people: individuals who don't share anything between them. Not that people aren't generous, but if *you* eat food, nobody else gets full; and more important, if you eat *bad* food, only you get sick from it. You have your own brain and internals that keep you thinking and living independently from everyone else. This is how processes behave;

they're separate from one another and are guaranteed not to disturb one another through their own internal state changes.

A process has its own working memory and its own mailbox for incoming messages. Whereas *threads* in many other programming languages and operating systems are concurrent activities that share the same memory space (and have countless opportunities to step on each other's toes), Erlang's processes can safely work under the assumption that nobody else will be poking around and changing their data from one microsecond to the next. We say that *processes encapsulate state*.

> ### Processes: an example
>
> Consider a web server: it receives requests for web pages, and for each request it needs to do some work that involves finding the data for the page and either transmitting it back to the place the request came from (sometimes split into many chunks, sent one at a time) or replying with an error message in case of failure. Clearly, each request has little to do with any other; but if the server accepts only one at a time and doesn't start handling the next request until the previous is finished, there will quickly be thousands of requests on queue if the web site is popular.
>
> If the server instead can begin handling requests as soon as they arrive, each in a separate process, there will be no queue, and most requests will take about the same time from start to finish. The state encapsulated by each process is then the specific URL for the request, who to reply to, and how far it has come in the handling as yet. When the request is finished, the process disappears, cleanly forgetting about the request and recycling the memory. If a bug causes one request to crash, only that process dies, while all the others keep working happily.

Because processes can't directly change each other's internal state, it's possible to make significant advances in fault tolerance. No matter how bad the code is that a process is running, it can't corrupt the internal state of your other processes. Even at a fine-grained level within your program, you can have the same isolation that you see between, for example, the web browser and the word processor on your computer desktop. This turns out to be very powerful, as you'll see later in this chapter when we talk about process supervision.

Because processes can share no internal data, they must communicate by copying. If one process wants to exchange information with another, it sends a message; that message is a read-only copy of the data the sender has. These fundamental semantics of message passing make *distribution* a natural part of Erlang. In real life, you can't share data over the wire—you can only copy it. Erlang's process communication always works as if the receiver gets a personal copy of the message, even if the sender happens to be on the same computer. Although it may sound strange at first, this means network programming is no different from coding on a single machine!

This *transparent distribution* allows Erlang programmers to look at the network as a collection of resources—we don't much care about whether process X is running on a different machine than process Y, because the method of communication is exactly the same no matter where they're located. In the next section, we provide an overview of methods of process communication used by various programming languages and systems, to give you an understanding of the trade-offs involved.

1.1.3 *Four process communication paradigms*

The central problem in all concurrent systems, which all implementers have to solve, is sharing information. If you separate a problem into different tasks, how should those tasks communicate with one another? It may seem like a simple question, but some of the brightest minds out there have wrestled with it, and many approaches have been tried over the years, some of which have appeared as programming language features and some as separate libraries.

We briefly discuss four approaches to process communication that have gained mindshare over the last few years. We won't spend too much time on any single one, but this will give you an overview of the approaches current-day languages and systems are taking and highlight the differences between those and Erlang. These four are shared memory with locking, software transactional memory, futures, and message passing. We start with the oldest but still the most popular method.

SHARED MEMORY WITH LOCKS

Shared memory could reasonably be called the GOTO of our time: it's the current mainstream technique for process communication; it has been so for a long, long time; and just like programming with GOTO, there are numerous ways to shoot yourself in the foot. This has imbued generations of engineers with a deep fear of concurrency (and those who don't fear it haven't tried it yet). Still, we must admit that like GOTO, there is a low-level niche for shared memory where it probably can't be replaced.

In this paradigm, one or more regular memory cells can be read or written to by two or more processes in parallel. To make it possible for a process to perform an *atomic* sequence of operations on those cells, so that no other process is able to access any of the cells before all the operations have completed, there must be a way for the process to block all others from accessing the cells until it has finished. This is done with a *lock*: a construct that makes it possible to restrict access to a single process at a time.

Implementing locks requires support from the memory system, typically hardware support in the form of special instructions. The use of locks requires complete cooperation between processes: all must make sure to ask for the lock before accessing a shared memory region, and they must return the lock when they're done so that someone else gets a chance to use it. The slightest failure can cause havoc; so, generally, higher-level constructs such as semaphores, monitors, and mutexes, are built on these basic locks and are provided as operating system calls or programming language constructs to make it easier to guarantee that locks are properly requested and returned. Although this avoids the worst problems, locks still have a number of drawbacks. To mention only a few:

- Locks require overhead even when the chances of collisions are low.
- They're points of contention in the memory system.
- They may be left in a locked state by failed processes.
- It's extraordinarily hard to debug problems with locks.

Furthermore, locking may work well for synchronizing two or three processes, but as the number grows, the situation quickly becomes unmanageable. A real possibility exists (in many cases, more of a certainty) of ending up with a complex deadlock that couldn't be foreseen by even the most experienced developer.

We think this form of synchronization is best left to low-level programming, such as in the operating system kernel. But it can be found in most current popular programming and scripting languages. Its ubiquitousness is likely due to the fact that it's fairly easy to implement and doesn't interfere with the programming model these languages are based on. Unfortunately, its widespread use has hurt our ability to think about concurrent issues and make use of concurrency on a large scale even though multiprocessor systems have been widely available for several years.

SOFTWARE TRANSACTIONAL MEMORY (STM)

The first nontraditional method we are going to look at is software transactional memory (STM). This mechanism can currently be found in the GHC implementation of the Haskell programming language, as well as in the JVM-based language Clojure. STM treats memory more like a traditional database, using *transactions* to decide what gets written and when. Typically, the implementation tries to avoid using locks by working in an optimistic way: a sequence of read and write accesses are treated as a single operation, and if two processes try to access the shared region at the same time, each in its own transaction, only one of them succeeds. The other processes are told that they failed and should try again after checking what the new contents are. It's a straightforward model and doesn't require anyone to wait for someone else to release a lock.

The main drawback is that you have to retry failed transactions (and they could, of course, fail repeatedly). There is also some significant overhead involved with the transaction system itself, as well as a need for additional memory to store the data you're trying to write until it's decided which process will succeed. Ideally, there should be hardware support for transactional memory just as there typically is support for virtual memory.

The STM approach seems more manageable to programmers than the use of locks, and it may be a good way to take advantage of concurrency as long as transactions don't have to be restarted too often due to contention. We still consider this approach to be at its core a variant of shared memory with locks, and one that may be more help on an operating system level than on an application programming level; but it's currently a lively research topic, and things may turn out differently.

FUTURES, PROMISES, AND SIMILAR

Another more modern approach is the use of so-called *futures* or *promises*. This is a concept with several variants; it can be found in languages like E and MultiLisp and as a library in Java, and it's similar to I-vars and M-vars in Id and Glasgow Haskell, concurrent logic variables in Concurrent Prolog, and dataflow variables in Oz.

The basic idea is that a future is a result of a computation that has been outsourced to some other process, possibly on another CPU or a completely different computer. A future can be passed around like any other object, but if someone wants to read the value and it isn't ready yet, they have to wait for it to be done. Although this is conceptually simple and makes it easy to pass around data in concurrent systems, it also makes the program brittle in case of failure of the remote process or the network in between: the code that tries to access the value of the promise may have no idea what to do if the value is still missing and the connection is dead.

MESSAGE PASSING

As we said in section 1.1.2, Erlang processes communicate by message passing. This means the receiving process effectively gets a separate copy of the data, and nothing it does to that copy is observable by the sender. The only way to communicate information back to the sender is to send another message in the reverse direction. One of the most important consequences is that communication works the same whether the sender and receiver are on the same computer or separated by a network.

Message passing in general comes in two flavors: *synchronous* and *asynchronous*. In the synchronous form, the sender can't do anything else until the message has arrived at the receiving end; in the asynchronous form, senders can proceed immediately after posting the message. (In the real world, synchronous communication between separate machines is only possible if the receiver sends an acknowledgement back to the sender, telling it that it's OK to continue, but this detail can be kept hidden from the programmer.)

In Erlang, the message passing primitives are asynchronous, because it's easy to implement the synchronous form when necessary by making the receiver always send an explicit reply that the sender can wait for. Often, though, the sender doesn't need to know that the message arrived—that knowledge is overrated, because nothing tells you what the receiver did next: it may have died just afterward. This asynchronous "send-and-pray" method of communication also means the sender doesn't need to be suspended while the message is being delivered (in particular if the message is sent over a slow communications link).

Of course, you don't get this level of separation between sender and receiver for free. Copying data can be expensive for large structures and can cause higher memory usage if the sender also needs to keep their copy of the data. In practice, this means you must be aware of and manage the size and complexity of messages you're sending. But in normal, idiomatic Erlang programs, the majority of messages are small, and the overhead of copying is usually negligible.

We hope this discussion has been of use to your understanding of Erlang's place in the concurrent programming landscape of today. Message passing may not be the sexiest of these techniques, but the track record of Erlang shows that from a systems engineering perspective, it seems to be the most practical and flexible.

1.1.4 Programming with processes in Erlang

When you build an Erlang program, you say to yourself, "What activities here are concurrent—can happen independently of one another?" After you sketch out an answer to that question, you can start building a system where every single instance of those activities you identified becomes a separate process.

In contrast to most other languages, concurrency in Erlang is cheap. Spawning a process is about as much work as allocating an object in your average object-oriented language. This can take some getting used to in the beginning, because it's such a foreign concept! But when you do get used to it, magic begins to happen. Picture a complex operation that has several concurrent parts, all modeled as separate processes. The operation starts, processes are spawned, data is manipulated, and a result is produced, and at that moment the processes involved disappear magically into oblivion, taking with them their internal state, their database handles, their sockets, and any other stuff that needs to be cleaned up that you don't want to have to deal with manually.

In the rest of this section, we take a brief look at how easy it is to create processes, how lightweight they are, and how simple it is to communicate between them.

CREATING A PROCESS: SPAWNING

Erlang processes are *not* operating system threads. They're much more lightweight, implemented by the Erlang runtime system, and Erlang is easily capable of spawning hundreds of thousands of processes on a single system running on commodity hardware. Each of these processes is separate from all the other processes in the runtime system; it shares no memory with the others, and in no way can it be corrupted by another process dying or going berserk.

A typical thread in a modern operating system reserves some megabytes of address space for its stack (which means a 32-bit machine can never have more than a few thousand simultaneous threads), and it still crashes if it uses more stack space than expected. Erlang processes, on the other hand, start with only a couple of hundred bytes of stack space each, and they grow or shrink automatically as required.

Erlang's syntax for creating processes is straightforward, as illustrated by the following example. Let's spawn a process whose job is to execute the function call `io:format("erlang!")` and then finish:

```
spawn(io, format, ["erlang!"])
```

That's all. (Although the `spawn` function has some other variants, this is the simplest.) This code starts a separate process, which prints the text "erlang!" on the console and then quits.

In chapter 2, we give an overview of the Erlang language and its syntax, but right now we hope you'll be able to get the gist of our examples without further explanation. One of the strengths of Erlang is that it's generally easy to understand the code even if you've never seen the language before. Let's see if you agree.

HOW PROCESSES TALK

Processes need to do more than spawn and run—they need to exchange information. Erlang makes this communication simple. The basic operator for sending a message is !, pronounced "bang," and it's used in the form "Destination ! Message". This is message passing at its most primitive, like mailing a postcard. The OTP framework takes process communication to another level, and we dive into that in chapter 3; for now, let's marvel at the simplicity of communicating between two independent and concurrent processes, as illustrated in the following listing.

Listing 1.1   Process communication in Erlang

```
run() ->
    Pid = spawn(fun ping/0),
    Pid ! self(),
    receive
        pong -> ok
    end.

ping() ->
    receive                          ❶ From contains
        From -> From ! pong              sender ID
    end.
```

Take a minute or two and look at this code. You can probably understand it without any previous knowledge of Erlang. Points worth noting are a variant of the spawn function that gets a single reference to "the function named ping that takes zero arguments"; and the function self(), which produces the identifier of the current process, which is passed to the new process so that it knows where to reply ❶.

That's Erlang's process communication in a nutshell. Every call to spawn yields a fresh process identifier that uniquely identifies the new child process. This identifier can then be used to send messages to the child. Each process has a mailbox where incoming messages are stored as they arrive, even if the receiving process is currently busy, and the messages are kept there until the process decides to check the mailbox. It can then search and retrieve messages from the mailbox at its convenience using a receive expression, as in the example (which grabs the first available message).

PROCESS TERMINATION

When a process is done with its work, it disappears. Its working memory, mailbox, and other resources are recycled. If the purpose of the process is to produce data for another process, it must send that data explicitly as a message before it terminates.

Crashes (exceptions) can make a process terminate unexpectedly and prematurely, and if this happens, other processes can be informed of the crash. We've previously talked about how processes are independent and the fact that a crash in one can't corrupt another, because they don't share internal state. This is one of the pillars of another of Erlang's main features: fault tolerance, which we cover in more detail in the next section.

1.2 *Erlang's fault tolerance infrastructure*

Fault tolerance is worth its weight in gold in the real world. Programmers aren't perfect, nor are requirements. In order to deal with imperfections in code and data, just like aircraft engineers deal with imperfections in steel and aluminum, we need to have systems that are fault tolerant, that are able to deal with mistakes and don't go to pieces each time an unexpected problem occurs.

Like many programming languages, Erlang has *exception handling* for catching errors in a particular piece of code, but it also has a unique system of *process links* for handling process failures in a effective way, which is what we're going to talk about here.

1.2.1 *How process links work*

When an Erlang process dies unexpectedly, an *exit signal* is generated. All processes that are *linked* to the dying process receive this signal. By default, this causes the receiver to exit as well and propagate the signal on to any other processes it's linked to, and so on, until all the processes that are linked directly or indirectly to each other have exited (see figure 1.2). This cascading behaviour allows you to have a group of processes behave as a single application with respect to termination, so that you never need to worry about finding and killing off any leftover processes before you can restart that entire subsystem from scratch.

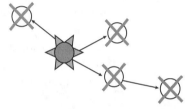

Figure 1.2 An exit signal triggered by a crashing process is propagated to all its linked processes, generally making those terminate as well so that the whole group is cleaned up.

Previously, we mentioned cleaning up complex state through processes. This is basically how it happens: a process encapsulates all its state and can therefore die safely without corrupting the rest of the system. This is just as true for a group of linked processes as it is for a single process. If one of them crashes, all its collaborators also terminate, and all the complex state that was created is snuffed out of existence cleanly and easily, saving programmer time and reducing errors.

> ### Let it crash
> Rather than thrashing around desperately to save a situation that you probably won't be able to fix, the Erlang philosophy is "let it crash"—you drop everything cleanly and start over, logging precisely where things went pear-shaped and how. This can take some getting used to, but it's a powerful recipe for fault tolerance and for creating systems that are possible to debug despite their complexity.

1.2.2   *Supervision and trapping of exit signals*

One of the main ways fault tolerance is achieved in OTP is by overriding the default propagation of exit signals. By setting a *process flag* called `trap_exit`, you can make a process *trap* any incoming exit signal rather than obey it. In this case, when the signal is received, it's dropped in the process's mailbox as a normal message on the form `{'EXIT', Pid, Reason}` that describes in which other process the failure originated and why, allowing the trapping process to check for such messages and take action.

Such a signal-trapping process is sometimes called a *system process* and typically runs code that is different from that run by ordinary *worker processes*, which don't usually trap signals. Because a system process acts as a bulwark that prevents exit signals from propagating further, it insulates the processes it's linked to from each other and can also be entrusted with reporting failures and even restarting the failed subsystems, as illustrated in figure 1.3. We call such processes *supervisors.*

The point of letting an entire subsystem terminate and be restarted is that it brings you back to a state known to function properly. Think of it like rebooting your computer: a way to clear up a mess and restart from a point that ought to be working. But the problem with a computer reboot it's that it isn't granular enough. Ideally, you'd like to be able to reboot only a part of the system, and the smaller, the better. Erlang process links and supervisors provide a mechanism for such fine-grained "reboots."

If that was all, though, you'd still be left to implement supervisors from scratch, which would require careful thought, lots of experience, and a long time shaking out

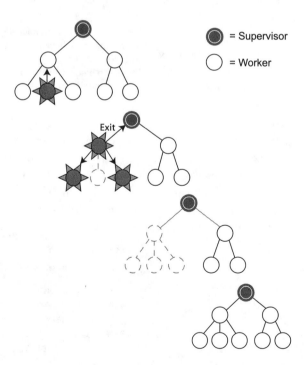

Figure 1.3
Supervisor, workers, and signals: the crash in one of the worker processes is propagated to the other linked processes until the signal reaches the supervisor, which restarts the group. The other group of processes under the same supervisor isn't affected.

the bugs and corner cases. Fortunately, the OTP framework provides just about everything you need: both a methodology for structuring applications using supervision, and stable, battle-hardened libraries to build them on.

OTP allows processes to be started by a supervisor in a prescribed manner and order. A supervisor can also be told how to restart its processes with respect to one another in the event of a failure of any single process, how many attempts it should make to restart the processes within a certain period of time before it ought to give up, and more. All you need to do is to provide some parameters and hooks.

But a system shouldn't be structured as a single-level hierarchy of supervisors and workers. In any complex system, you'll want a *supervision tree* with multiple layers that allows subsystems to be restarted at different levels in order to cope with unexpected problems of varying kinds.

1.2.3 *Layering processes for fault tolerance*

Layering brings related subsystems together under a common supervisor. More important, it defines different levels of working base states that you can revert to. In figure 1.4, you see two distinct groups of worker processes, A and B, supervised separately from one another. These two groups and their supervisors together form a larger group C, under yet another supervisor higher up in the tree.

Let's assume that the processes in group A work together to produce a stream of data that group B consumes. Group B isn't required for group A to function. To make things concrete, let's say group A is processing and encoding multimedia data, and group B presents it. Let's also suppose that a small percentage of the data entering group A is corrupt in some way that wasn't predicted at the time the application was written.

This malformed data causes a process within group A to malfunction. Following the let-it-crash philosophy, that process dies immediately without trying to untangle the mess; and because processes are isolated, none of the other processes are affected by the bad input. The supervisor, detecting that a process has died, restores the base state prescribed for group A, and the system picks up from a known point. The beauty of this is that group B, the presentation system, has no idea what's going on and doesn't care. As long as group A pushes enough good data to group B for the latter to display something of acceptable quality to the user, you have a successful system.

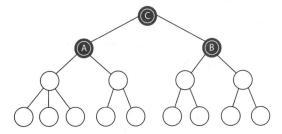

Figure 1.4
A layered system of supervisors and workers. If for some reason supervisor A dies or gives up, any still-living processes under it are killed and supervisor C is informed, so the whole left-side process tree can be restarted. Supervisor B isn't affected unless C decides to shut everything down.

By isolating independent parts of your system and organizing them into a supervision tree, you can create subsystems that can be individually restarted in fractions of a second to keep your system chugging along even in the face of unpredicted errors. If group A fails to restart properly, its supervisor may eventually give up and escalate the problem to the supervisor of group C, which may then, in a case like this, decide to shut down B as well and call it a day. If you imagine that the system is running hundreds of simultaneous instances of C-like subsystems, this could correspond to dropping a single multimedia connection due to bad data, while all the rest keep streaming.

But you're forced to share some things as long as you're running on a single machine: the available memory, the disk drive, the network connection, even the processor and all related circuitry, and, perhaps most significant, a single power cord to a single outlet. If one of these things breaks down or is disconnected, no amount of layering or process separation will save you from inevitable downtime. This brings us to our next topic, which is distribution—the feature of Erlang that allows you to achieve the highest levels of fault tolerance and also make your solutions scale.

1.3   *Distributed Erlang*

Erlang programs can be distributed naturally over multiple computers, due to the properties of the language and its copy-based process communication. To see why, take, for example, two threads in a language such as Java or C++, running happily and sharing memory between them as a means of communication. Assuming that you manage to get the locking right, this is nice and efficient, but only until you want to move one of the threads to a separate machine. Perhaps you want to make use of more computing power or memory, or prevent both threads from dying if a hardware failure takes down one machine. When this moment comes, the programmer is often forced to fundamentally restructure the code to adapt to the different communication mechanism necessary in this new distributed context. Obviously, it will require a large programming effort and will most likely introduce subtle bugs that may take years to weed out.

Erlang programs, on the other hand, aren't much affected by this kind of problem. As we explained in section 1.1.2, the way Erlang avoids sharing of data and communicates by copying makes the code immediately suitable for splitting over several machines. The kind of intricate data-sharing dependencies between different parts of the code that you can get when programming with threads in an imperative language occur only rarely in Erlang. If it works on your netbook today, it could be running on a cluster tomorrow.

The fact that it's usually straightforward to distribute an Erlang application over a network of nodes also means that scalability problems become an order of magnitude easier to attack. You still have to figure out which processes will do what, how many of each kind, on which machines, how to distribute the workload, and how to manage the data, but at least you won't need to start with questions like, "How on Earth do I split my existing program into individual parts that can be distributed and replicated?" "How should they communicate?" and "How can I handle failures gracefully?"

> **A real-life example**
>
> At one employer, we had a number of different Erlang applications running on our network. We probably had at least 15 distinct types of self-contained OTP applications that all needed to cooperate to achieve a common goal. Integration testing this cluster of 15 different applications running on 15 separate virtual machines, although doable, wouldn't have been the most convenient undertaking. Without changing a line of code, we were able to invoke all the applications on a single Erlang instance and test them. They communicated with one another on that single node in exactly the same manner, using exactly the same syntax, as when they were running on multiple nodes across the network.
>
> The concept demonstrated in this example is known as *location transparency*. It basically means that when you send a message to a process using its unique ID as the delivery address, you don't need to know or even care about where that process is located—as long as the receiver is still alive and running, the Erlang runtime system will deliver the message to its mailbox for you.

Now that you know a bit about what Erlang can do for you, we next talk about the engine at the heart of it all, to give you a better idea of what is going on under the hood when your Erlang program is running.

1.4 The Erlang runtime system and virtual machine

So what makes all of the above tick? The core of the standard Erlang implementation is something called the Erlang Run-Time System application (ERTS): this is a big chunk of code written in the C programming language, and it's responsible for all the low-level stuff in Erlang. It lets you talk to the file system and the console, it handles memory, and it implements Erlang processes. It controls how these processes are distributed over the existing CPU resources to make good use of your computer hardware, but at the same time makes it possible to run Erlang processes concurrently even if you only have a single CPU with a single core. ERTS also handles message-passing between processes and allows processes on two different machines, each in its own ERTS instance, to talk to each other as if they were on the same machine. Everything in Erlang that needs low-level support is handled by ERTS, and Erlang runs on any operating system that ERTS can be ported to.

One particularly important part of ERTS is the Erlang virtual machine emulator: this is the part that executes Erlang programs after they have been compiled to byte code. This virtual machine is known as Bogdan's Erlang Abstract Machine (BEAM) and is very efficient: even though it's also possible to compile Erlang programs to native machine code, it isn't usually necessary, because the BEAM emulator is fast enough. Note that there is no clear-cut line between the virtual machine and ERTS as a whole; often, people (including us) talk about the *Erlang VM* when they mean the emulator and runtime system as a whole.

There are many interesting features of the runtime system that you won't know about unless you dig through the documentation or spend a lot of time on the Erlang mailing list. These are at the core of what enables Erlang to handle such a large numbers of processes at the same time and are part of what makes Erlang unique. The basic philosophy of the Erlang language combined with the pragmatic approach the implementers have taken have given us an extraordinarily efficient, production-oriented, stable system. In this section, we cover three important aspects of the runtime system that contribute to Erlang's power and effectiveness:

- *The scheduler*—Handles the running of Erlang's processes, allowing all the ready-to-run processes to share the available CPU resources, and waking up sleeping processes when they get a new message or a timeout happens
- *The I/O model*—Prevents the entire system from stopping just because a single process wants to talk to some external device, making the system run smoothly
- *The garbage collector*—Keeps recycling memory that is no longer used

We start with the scheduler.

1.4.1   *The scheduler*

The process scheduler in ERTS has evolved over the years, and these days it gives you a flexibility matched by no other platform. Originally, it was there to make it possible to have lightweight Erlang processes running concurrently on a single CPU, regardless of what operating system you were using. ERTS generally runs as a single operating system process (usually found under the name `beam` or `werl` in OS process listings). Within this, the scheduler manages its own Erlang processes.

As threads became available in most operating systems, ERTS was changed to run a few things like the I/O system in a different thread from the one running Erlang processes, but there was still only one thread for the main body of work. If you wanted to use a multicore system, you had to run multiple ERTS instances on the same machine. But starting in May 2006 with release 11 of Erlang/OTP, support for symmetric multiprocessing (SMP) was added. This was a major effort, allowing the Erlang runtime system to use, not one, but multiple process schedulers internally, each using a separate operating system thread. The effect can be seen in figure 1.1.

This means there is now an $n{:}m$ mapping between Erlang processes and OS threads. Each scheduler handles a pool of processes. At most m Erlang processes can be running in parallel (one per scheduler thread), but the processes within each pool share their time as they did when there was only one scheduler for all processes. On top of this, processes can be moved from one pool to another to maintain an even balance of work over the available schedulers. In the latest releases of Erlang/OTP, it's even possible to tie processes to schedulers depending on the CPU topology of the machine, to make better use of the cache architecture of the hardware. That means, most of the time, you as an Erlang programmer don't have to worry about how many CPUs or cores you have available: you write your program as normal, trying to keep your program separated into reasonably sized parallel tasks, and let the Erlang runtime system take care of spreading the workload. A single core or 128 cores—it works the same, only faster.

One caveat is that inexperienced Erlang programmers have a tendency to rely on effects of timing, which may make the program work on their laptop or workstation but break when the code moves to a server with multiple CPUs where timings may be much less deterministic. Hence, some testing is always in order. But now that even laptops often have at least two cores, this sort of thing is getting found out much earlier.

The scheduler in Erlang is also involved in another important feature of the runtime system: the I/O subsystem. This is our next topic.

1.4.2   *I/O and scheduling*

One of the things that many concurrent languages get wrong is that they don't think much about I/O. With few exceptions, they make the entire system or a large subset of it block while any process is doing I/O. This is annoying and unnecessary, considering that Erlang has had this problem solved for the last two decades. In the previous section, we talked about the Erlang process scheduler. Among other things, the scheduler allows the system to elegantly handle I/O. At the lowest levels of the system, Erlang does all I/O in an event-based way, which lets a program handle each chunk of data as it enters or leaves the system in a nonblocking manner. This reduces the need to set up and tear down connections, and it removes the need for OS-based locking and context switching.

This is an efficient method of handling I/O. Unfortunately, it also seems to be a lot harder for programmers to reason about and understand, which is probably why we only see these types of systems when there is an explicit need for highly available, low latency systems. Dan Kegel wrote about this problem in his paper "The C10K Problem" back in 2001; it's out of date in some respects now, but it's still relevant and worth reading. It should give you a good overview of the problem and the approaches available to solve it. All of these approaches are complex and painful to implement; that is why the Erlang runtime system does most of it for you. It integrates the event-based I/O system with its process scheduler. In effect, you get all the benefits with none of the hassle. This makes it much easier to build highly available systems using Erlang/OTP.

The last feature of ERTS that we want to explain is memory management. This has more to do with processes than you may think.

1.4.3   *Process isolation and the garbage collector*

As you probably know or assume, Erlang manages memory automatically, like Java and most other modern languages. There is no explicit de-allocation. Instead, a so-called *garbage collector* is used to regularly find and recycle unused memory. Garbage collection (GC) algorithms constitute a large and complicated field of research, and we can't go through any details here; but for those of you who know a bit and are curious, Erlang currently uses a straightforward generational copying garbage collector.

Even with this relatively simple implementation, programs in Erlang don't tend to suffer from pauses for GC, like systems implemented in other languages. This is mostly due to the isolation between processes in Erlang: each has its own areas of memory, allocated when the process is created and de-allocated again when the process dies. That may not sound important, but it is. First, it means that each process can be individually paused for garbage collection while all the others keep running. Second, the memory used by any single process is usually small, so traversing it can be done quickly. (Although some processes use large amounts of memory, those typically aren't the ones that are also expected to respond quickly.) Third, the scheduler always knows when a process was last running, so if it hasn't been doing any work since the last time it was garbage collected, it can be skipped. All this makes life simpler for the Erlang garbage collector and lets it keep pause times small. Furthermore, in some cases it's possible for a process to be spawned, do its job, and die again without triggering any garbage collection at all. In those cases, the process acted as a short-lived memory region, automatically allocated and de-allocated with no additional overhead.

The features of the runtime system that we have described in this section make it possible for an Erlang program to have a large number of processes running that make good use of the available CPUs, perform I/O operations, and automatically recycle memory, all while maintaining soft real-time responsiveness. Understanding these aspects of the platform is important for understanding the behaviour of your systems after they're up and running.

Finally, before this chapter is done, we'll say a few words about the functional programming aspect of Erlang. It won't be much, because we get into much more detail about the Erlang language in the next chapter.

1.5   *Functional programming: Erlang's face to the world*

For many readers of this book, *functional programming* may be a new concept. For others, it isn't. It's by no means the defining feature of Erlang—concurrency has that honor—but it's an important aspect of the language. Functional programming and the mindset that it teaches you are a natural match to the problems encountered in concurrent and distributed programming, as many others have recently realized. (Need we say more than "Google MapReduce"?)

To summarize what functional programming is, the main ideas are that functions are data, just like integers and strings; that algorithms are expressed in terms of function calls, not using loop constructs like `while` and `for`; and that variables and values are never updated in place (see appendix B for a discussion of referential transparency and lists). Those may sound like artificial restrictions, but they make perfectly good sense from an engineering perspective, and Erlang programs can be very natural and readable.

Erlang isn't a "pure" functional language—it relies on side effects. But it limits these to a single operation: message passing by copying. Each message is an effect on the world outside, and the world can have effects on your processes by sending them messages. But each process is, in itself, running an almost purely functional program. This model makes programs much easier to reason about than in traditional languages like C++ and Java, while not forcing you to program using monads as in Haskell.

In the next chapter, we go through the important parts of the Erlang programming language. For many of you, the syntax will feel strange—it borrows mainly from the Prolog tradition, rather than from C. But different as it may be, it isn't complicated. Bear with it for a while, and it will become second nature. After you're familiar with it, you'll be able to open any module in the Erlang kernel and understand most of what it does, which is the true test of syntax: at the end of the day, can you read it?

1.6   *Summary*

In this chapter, we've gone over the most important concepts and features of the Erlang/OTP platform that OTP is built on: concurrent programming with processes and message passing, fault tolerance through links, distributed programming, the Erlang Run-Time System and virtual machine, and the core functional language of Erlang. All these things combine to provide a solid, efficient, and flexible platform on which you can build reliable, low-latency, high-availability systems.

If you have previous experience with Erlang, much of this may not be news to you, but we hope our presentation was of interest and pointed out at least a few aspects you hadn't thought about before. Still, we haven't talked much about the OTP framework yet; we'll wait until chapter 3, but then things will move quickly, so enjoy this background reading while you can. First, chapter 2 will give you a thorough overview of the Erlang programming language.

Erlang language essentials

In the previous chapter, we talked about the underlying platform for Erlang and OTP, but not much about the Erlang programming language. The focus of this book isn't on Erlang in itself; but before can you move on to programming with Erlang/OTP design patterns, we want to go through the language basics to make sure everyone is on the same page. This chapter will also serve as a reference as you work your way through the book.

This is a long chapter. If you already know Erlang, you can skim this chapter, but we try to make sure there are some useful nuggets for you too. These are the things we think every Erlang programmer should be aware of, and we know it's possible for even the most experienced old-timers to have missed some useful detail.

If this is your first contact with Erlang, you may want to read only part of this chapter before you move on, and come back to it later as needed. We hope the material here is enough for you to digest the rest of the book; but before you start using Erlang for a real project, you should also arm yourself with a more thorough guide to Erlang programming. The chapter ends with some pointers to further reading material. We can't teach you general programming techniques and tricks here, only explain how the different parts of the language work. But we give a crash course in using the Erlang shell, show how to compile and run your programs, and help you get a grip on recursion.

To get the most out of this chapter, you should have a working Erlang installation on your computer. If your operating system is Windows, open a web browser and go to www.erlang.org/download.html, and then download and run the latest version from the top of the Windows Binary column. For other operating systems and further details about installing Erlang, see appendix A.

In this chapter, we go through Erlang's basic data types and then talk about modules, functions, and compiling and running code, before we move on to variables and pattern matching. After that, we talk about function clauses and guards, case switches, funs (lambda expressions), exceptions, list comprehensions, and binaries and bitstrings. Finally, we examine records, preprocessor includes and macros, process operations and message passing, and ETS tables, before we finish with a thorough discussion of programming with recursion.

Before we get to all that, though, we begin where you find yourself when you start Erlang: in the shell.

2.1 The Erlang shell

An Erlang system is a more interactive environment than you may be used to. With most programming languages, you either compile the program to an OS executable that you then run, or run an interpreter on a bunch of script files or byte-code compiled files. In either case, this runs until the program finishes or crashes, and then you get back to the operating system again, where you can repeat the process (possibly after editing the code).

Erlang, on the other hand, is more like an operating system within your operating system. Although Erlang starts pretty quickly, it isn't designed for start-stop execution—it's designed for running continuously, and for interactive development, debugging, and upgrading. Optimally, the only reason for restarting Erlang is because of a hardware failure, operating system upgrade, or similar.

Interaction with an Erlang system happens mainly through the *shell*. The shell is your command central. It's where you can try out short snippets to see how they work; it's where you do incremental development and interactive debugging; and it can also be used to control a running system in production. To make you comfortable with working in the shell, the examples are written so that you can try them as you read them. Let's start a shell right away!

2.1.1   *Starting the shell*

We assume that you've downloaded and installed Erlang/OTP. If you're using Linux, Mac OS X, or any other UNIX-based system, open a console window and run the erl command. If you're using Windows, you should click the Erlang icon that the installer created for you; this runs the program called werl, which opens a special console for Erlang that avoids the problems of running erl interactively under the normal Windows console.

You should see something like the following:

```
Erlang (BEAM) emulator version 5.6.5 [smp:2] [async-threads:0]

Eshell V5.6.5  (abort with ^G)
1>
```

1> is the prompt. This will change to 2>, and so on, as you enter commands. You can use the up and down arrows or the Ctrl-P/Ctrl-N keys to move up and down among previously entered lines; and a few other Emacs-style key bindings also exist, but most normal keys behave as expected.

It's also possible to start the Erlang system with the -noshell flag, like this (on your operating system command line):

```
erl -noshell
```

In this case, the Erlang system is running, but you can't talk to it via the console. This is used for running Erlang as a batch job or daemon.

Now that you know how to start the shell, let's talk about what you can do with it.

2.1.2   *Entering expressions*

First, what you enter at the shell prompt aren't commands as such, but *expressions*, the difference being that an expression always has a *result*. When the expression has been evaluated, the shell prints the result. The shell also remembers the result so you can refer to it later, using the syntax v(1), v(2), and so on. For example, type the number 42, followed by a period (.), and then press Enter, and you should see the following:

```
Eshell V5.6.5  (abort with ^G)
1> 42.
42
2>
```

When you pressed Enter, Erlang evaluated the expression 42, printed the result (the value 42), and finally printed a new prompt, this time with the number 2. But why was that period necessary after the number 42?

ENDING WITH A PERIOD

The period or full-stop character before you press Enter must always be used to tell the shell that it has seen the end of the expression. If you press Enter without it, the shell will keep prompting for more characters (without incrementing the prompt number), like this:

```
2> 12
2> + 5
2> .
17
3>
```

If you forget the period character at first, don't worry; all you need to do is type it in and press Enter. As you see, simple arithmetic expressions work as expected. Now, let's try referring back to the previous results:

```
3> v(1).
42
4> v(2).
17
5> v(2) + v(3).
59
6>
```

Before you get ahead of yourself, we show you something that almost all beginners get snagged on: entering strings, and how to get out of them again.

ENTERING QUOTED STRINGS

When you enter double- or single-quoted strings (without going into detail about what that means, for now), a particular gotcha worth bringing up right away is that if you forget a closing quote character and press Enter, the shell will expect more characters and will print the same prompt again, much like the previous example when you forgot the period. If this happens, enter the appropriate quote character to balance the string and follow it with a period; then press Enter again. For example, if you do this

```
1> "hello there.
1>
```

the period doesn't end the expression—it's part of the string. To get the shell out of this state, you need to close the string by adding the following:

```
1> ".
"hello there.\n"
2>
```

Note that this result is a string that contains a period and a newline, which is probably not what you want. You can use the up arrow or Ctrl-P to go back and edit the line, inserting the missing quote character in the right place this time:

```
2> "hello there".
"hello there"
3> v(2).
"hello there"
4>
```

The shell by default keeps the latest 20 results, regardless of whether they're numbers, strings, or any other kind of data. Next, let's get into some more detail about the v(...) function and its cousins.

2.1.3 *Shell functions*

Some functions like v(N) are available only in the shell and nowhere else in Erlang. These *shell functions* usually have short (and somewhat cryptic) names. If you want a list of the available shell functions, enter help() (which is a shell function in itself). It's a confusing list for the beginner, so table 2.1 shows the shell functions you should know about from the start.

Table 2.1   Important Erlang shell functions

Shell function	Summary
help()	Prints the available shell functions
h()	Prints the history of entered commands
v(N)	Fetches the value computed at prompt N
cd(Dir)	Changes the current directory (Dir should be a double-quoted string)
ls() and ls(Dir)	Prints a directory listing
pwd()	Prints the working directory (current directory)
q()	Quits (shorthand for init:stop())
i()	Prints information about what the system is running
memory()	Print memory usage information

Please try a few of these right now—for example, list or change the current directory, print the history, and print the system and memory information. Look briefly at the output from running i(), and note that much like in an operating system, a bunch of things are going on in the background apart from the shell prompt you see.

Now that you know how to start the Erlang system and enter things in the shell, we'll explain the various ways to get out of the shell and return to your operating system.

2.1.4 *Escaping from the shell*

There are some different ways of leaving the shell (and stopping the entire Erlang system). You should be familiar with all of them, because they all have their uses in managing and debugging a system. We start with the most system-friendly.

CALLING Q() OR INIT:STOP()

The safest method is to run the shell function q(), shown in the previous section. This is a shortcut for the function init:stop() (which you can call directly if you like), which shuts down the Erlang system in a controlled manner, telling running applications to stop and giving them time to respond. This usually takes a couple of seconds but can require more time on a running production system with a lot to clean up.

THE BREAK MENU

If you're more impatient and don't have anything important running that you're afraid to interrupt, you can bring up the low-level BREAK menu by pressing Ctrl-C on UNIX-like systems, or Ctrl-Break on Windows in the `werl` console. It looks like this:

```
BREAK: (a)bort (c)ontinue (p)roc info (i)nfo (l)oaded
       (v)ersion (k)ill (D)b-tables (d)istribution
```

The interesting options here are `(a)` to abort the system (hard shutdown), `(c)` to go back to the shell, and `(v)` to print the running Erlang version. The others print a lot of raw information about the system, which you may find useful for debugging after you've become an Erlang master; and `(k)` even lets you browse through the current activities within Erlang and kill off any offenders, if you know what you're doing. Note that the shell as such doesn't know about the BREAK menu, so it won't refresh the prompt when you go back using `(c)`, until you press Enter.

CTRL-G

The third and most useful escape is the User Switch Command menu, which you reach by pressing Ctrl-G. It presents you with this cryptic text:

```
User switch command
 -->
```

Type h or ? and press Enter, and you'll see this list:

```
c [nn]            - connect to job
i [nn]            - interrupt job
k [nn]            - kill job
j                 - list all jobs
s [shell]         - start local shell
r [node [shell]]  - start remote shell
q                 - quit erlang
? | h             - this message
```

Entering `c` at the `-->` prompt gets you back to the shell. Entering `q` causes a hard shutdown, like `(a)` in the BREAK menu—don't confuse `q` here with the system-friendly shell function `q()` described previously! Also note that the BREAK menu is more low-level and can be called up while you're in the Ctrl-G menu, but not the other way around.

The remaining options are for job control, which we briefly introduce in the next section.

2.1.5 *Job-control basics*

Suppose you're sitting at your Erlang shell prompt, and you happen to write something stupid that will run forever (or longer than you care to wait, anyhow). We all do this now and then. You *could* make the Erlang system shut down by one of the methods described earlier, and restart it; but the nicer and more Erlang-like way (especially if some important processes are running on this system that you would prefer not to interrupt) is to kill the current job and start a new one, without disturbing anything else.

To simulate this situation, enter the following at your Erlang shell prompt, followed by a period and newline:

```
timer:sleep(infinity)
```

(That didn't need any explanation, we hope.) Now the shell is locked up. To get out of this mess, you bring up the User Switch Command menu with Ctrl-G, as described in the previous section, and enter j to list current jobs. There should be only one job right now, so you see something like this:

```
User switch command
 --> j
   1* {shell,start,[init]}
 -->
```

Enter s to start a new shell job (on the local system) like the one you had before, and then list your jobs again:

```
 --> s
 --> j
   1  {shell,start,[init]}
   2* {shell,start,[]}
 -->
```

To connect to the new job, you could enter c 2, to be explicit. But because the * marker indicates that job number 2 is already the default choice, it's enough to say c:

```
 --> c
Eshell V5.7.2  (abort with ^G)
1>
```

And you're back at the wheel! But wait, what about the old job? Press Ctrl-G again, and list the jobs, and you see that it's still hanging around. Let's kill it by entering k 1, and then go back to the shell so you can get on with making more mistakes:

```
User switch command
 --> j
   1  {shell,start,[init]}
   2* {shell,start,[]}
 --> k 1
 --> j
   2* {shell,start,[]}
 --> c
```

When you do this sort of thing, be careful about which job you're killing, in case you have several things in progress in different jobs. When you kill a job, all the history, previous results, and other things associated with that shell job will disappear. You'll see more of the Ctrl-G menu in chapter 8 when we talk about distributed Erlang and how to use remote shells. This is as simple as it is powerful and is the single most important tool for remote-controlling and -debugging production systems.

Now that you have a feel for how to work in the Erlang console, it's time to start playing around with the programming language.

2.2   *Data types in Erlang*

Understanding basic data representation conventions is an essential part of learning any programming language. Erlang's built-in data types are straightforward and relatively few, but you can achieve a lot with them. The following list is how we present them here:

- Numbers (integers and floats)
- Binaries/Bitstrings
- Atoms
- Tuples
- Lists (and strings)
- Unique identifiers (pids, ports, references)
- Funs

Data in Erlang is usually referred to as *terms*. Try entering some examples of terms while you read this section. (Don't forget to add a period before you press Enter.) Let's start with the simplest ones.

2.2.1   *Numbers and arithmetic*

Erlang has two numerical data types: integers and floating-point numbers (floats). Conversion is done automatically by most of the arithmetic operations, so you don't usually need to do any explicit type coercion (see the following sections for details).

INTEGERS

Integers in Erlang can be of arbitrary size. If they're small enough, they're represented in memory by a single machine word; if they get larger (so-called *bignums*), the necessary space is allocated automatically. This is completely transparent to the programmer and means you never need to worry about truncation or wraparound effects in arithmetic—those things can't happen.

Normally, integers are written as you would expect (and you can try entering some large numbers just for fun):

```
101
-101
1234567890 * 9876543210 * 9999999999
```

You can also write integers in any base between 2 and 36 (corresponding to digits 0–9 plus characters A–Z/a–z), although bases except 2, 16, and possibly 8 are rarely seen in practice. This notation was borrowed from the Ada programming language:

```
16#FFffFFff
2#10101
36#ZZ
```

Also, the following $-prefix notation yields the character code (ASCII/Latin-1/Unicode) for any character (try it):

```
$9
$z
$\n
```

You'll see a little more of this notation when we discuss strings in section 2.2.6.

FLOATS

Floats are handled using 64-bit IEEE 754-1985 representation (double precision), and the syntax is the same as used by most programming languages, with the exception that whereas many languages allow a floating-point number to begin with a period, as in .01, Erlang requires that it starts with a digit, as in 0.01:

```
3.14
-0.123
299792458.0
6.022137e23
6.6720e-11
```

There are no single precision floating-point numbers in Erlang. This is important to remember if you come from a C/C++/Java background where the word *float* implies single precision.

ARITHMETIC AND BITWISE OPERATIONS

Normal infix notation is used for the common arithmetic operators, and +, -, * work as you'd expect. If either or both of the arguments of a binary arithmetic operation is a float, the operation is made in floating point, and Erlang automatically converts any integer arguments to floating point as necessary. For example, 2 * 3.14 yields the float 6.28.

For division, you have two choices. First, the / operator always yields a floating-point number: for example, 4/2 yields 2.0, not 2. Integer division (truncating) is performed by the div operator, as in 7 div 2, yielding 3.

The remainder of an integer division is given by the rem operator, as in 15 rem 4, yielding 3. (This can differ from what a modulo operator would yield, if negative numbers are involved.)

Other floating-point arithmetic functions are found in the standard library module math; these are named directly after the corresponding functions in the C standard library, such as math:sqrt(2).

There are some additional integer operators for bitwise operations: N bsl K shifts the integer N K steps to the left, and bsr performs a corresponding arithmetic right shift. The bitwise logic operators are named band, bor, bxor, and bnot. For example, X band (bnot Y) masks away those bits from X that are set in Y.

From numerical data, let's move on to something equally primitive: bits and bytes.

2.2.2 *Binaries and bitstrings*

A *binary* is a sequence of unsigned 8-bit bytes, used for storing and processing chunks of data (often data that comes from a file or has been received over a network protocol). A *bitstring* is a generalized binary whose length in bits isn't necessarily a multiple of 8; it can, for instance, be 12 bits long, consisting of one and a half bytes.

Arbitrary bitstrings are a more recent addition to the language, whereas whole-byte binaries have been around for many years; but to a programmer there is little difference on the surface, except that you can do some nifty things these days that used to be impossible. Because the syntax is the same, and the name *binary* is so ingrained, you rarely hear people (including us) talk about bitstrings unless they want to make a point about the more flexible length.

The basic syntax for a binary is

```
<<0, 1, 2, ..., 255>>
```

that is, a comma-separated list of integers in the range 0 to 255, enclosed in << ... >>. There must not be any space between the two delimiter characters on either side, as in < <. A binary can contain any number of bytes; for example, <<>> is an empty binary.

Strings may also be used to make a binary, as in

```
<<"hello", 32, "dude">>
```

This is the same as writing the corresponding sequence of bytes for the 8-bit character codes (ASCII/Latin-1) of the strings. Hence, this notation is limited to 8-bit characters, but it's often useful for things like text-based protocols.

These short examples only show how to create proper binaries, whose length in bits is divisible by eight. Erlang has an advanced and somewhat intricate syntax for constructing new binaries or bitstrings as well as for matching and extracting data from them. We show some examples of this later, in section 2.10.

Our next topic is something almost as primitive as numbers and bits to an Erlang programmer: *atoms*.

2.2.3 *Atoms*

In Erlang, an *atom* is a special kind of string constant that is identified only by the characters in the string, so that two atoms are always considered to be exactly the same if they have the same character representation. But internally, these strings are stored in a table and are referred to by the table index, so that checking atoms for equivalence at runtime amounts to comparing two small integers; and each time you use an atom, it takes up only one word of memory. (The index number used for any particular atom is automatically assigned at runtime and can vary from one run of the system to the next; there is no way, and no need, for the user to know this.)

Atoms in Erlang play a role similar to `enum` constants in Java or C: they're used as labels. The difference is that you don't need to declare them in advance; you can invent them as you go and use them anywhere you like. (Try entering some of the following examples in the shell.) In the Lisp programming language, they're known as *symbols*. Programming with atoms is easier, more readable, and more user friendly than using numeric constants.

Normally, atoms are written starting with a lowercase letter, like the following:

```
ok
error
```

```
foo
undefined
trap_exit
```

After the initial letter, you can use uppercase letters, digits, underscores, and @ characters, like this:

```
route66
atoms_often_contain_underscore
pleaseDoNotUseCamelCaseInAtomsItLooksAwful
vader@deathstar
```

For anything else, you need to use single quotes (and you can of course single-quote the previous atoms as well—this is sometimes done for clarification, such as in documentation):

```
'$%#*!'
'Blanks and Capitals can be quoted'
'Anything inside single-quotes\n is an atom'
```

You should think about atoms as special labels, not as any old strings. Their length is limited to 255 characters, and there is an upper limit on the number of atoms you can have in a system: currently, just over a million (1,048,576, to be exact). This usually isn't a problem, but you should avoid dynamic generation of unique atoms such as 'x_4711', 'x_4712', and so on, in a system that is expected to run for a long time (days, months, years). Atoms aren't removed from the table until the system restarts, even if they're no longer used by anyone.

A few atoms are used in practically all Erlang programs:

- true and false are the values used by all Boolean operators.
- ok is used as the return value in functions that don't produce any value of interest but are called for their effects (where you would use void in C or Java).
- undefined is often used as a placeholder for an unspecified value.

Now that we've gone through the primitive data types, it's time to look at how you can create more complicated data structures, starting with tuples.

2.2.4 *Tuples*

A *tuple* (or *n*-tuple, as generalized from triple, quadruple, and so on) is a fixed-length ordered sequence of other Erlang terms. Tuples are written within curly braces, like this:

```
{1, 2, 3}
{one, two, three, four}
{from, "Russia", "with love"}
{complex, {nested, "structure", {here}}}
{}
```

As you see, they can contain zero ({}), one ({here}), or more elements; the elements may be all of the same type or of wildly different types; and the elements can themselves be tuples or any other data type.

A standard convention in Erlang is to label tuples to indicate what type of data they contain, by using an atom as the first element, as in {size, 42}, or {position, 5, 2}. These are called *tagged tuples*.

Tuples are the main way of constructing compound data structures or returning multiple values in Erlang, like structs in C or objects in Java; but the entries aren't named, they're numbered (from 1 to *N*). Accessing an element of a tuple is a constant-time operation, just as fast (and safe) as accessing an entry in a Java array. The *record syntax*, explained later, allows you to declare names for the entries of tuples, so you don't have to work directly with indices. Also, *pattern matching* makes it easy to refer to the different parts of a tuple using variables, so it's rare that you need to access an entry directly by its index.

The standard library contains modules that implement some more complicated *abstract data types*, such as arrays, sets, dictionaries (that is, associative arrays or hash maps), and so on; but under the hood, they're mostly implemented using tuples in various ways.

Tuples are meant for constant-length sequences. To handle sequences of varying length, you also need lists.

2.2.5 *Lists*

Lists are truly the workhorse of Erlang's data types—as they are in most functional programming languages, for that matter. This has to do with their simplicity, efficiency, and flexibility, but also with the fact that they follow naturally from the idea of *referential transparency*, which basically means that the value to which a name refers isn't allowed to change (see appendix B for details). Lists are used to hold an arbitrary number of items. They're written within square brackets, and in the simplest form they look like this:

```
[]
[1, 2, 3]
[one, two, three]
[[1,2,3],[4,5,6]]
[{tomorrow, "buy cheese"},
 {soon, "fix trap door"},
 {later, "repair moon rocket"}]
```

That is, a list is a sequence of zero or more other Erlang terms (which may be other lists). The empty list, [], is also known as *nil*, a name that comes from the Lisp programming language world; it's more like an atom, in that it's a special value that takes only a single word of memory to represent.

ADDING TO A LIST

What you can do with lists that you can't do as easily and efficiently with tuples is create a new, longer list from an existing list in such a way that the old list is a part of the new one. This is signaled with the | character (a vertical bar). For example:

```
[ 1 |  []  ]
```

This combines the empty list on the right of the | with the additional element 1 on the left, yielding the list [1]. Try typing it in the shell and see for yourself how these examples work. Continuing in the same manner,

```
[ 2 |  [1]  ]
```

yields the list [2,1] (note the order: you're adding to the left). You can even add more than one element at a time, but only on the left side of the |:

```
[ 5, 4, 3 |  [2,1]  ]
```

This gives you [5,4,3,2,1]. This is done by adding first 3, then 4, and finally 5, as with 1 and 2 previously, but the compiler does the job of splitting it into smaller steps for you.

For lists of arbitrary lengths, you can use the ++ operator to append them. For example,

```
[1,2,3,4] ++ [5,6,7,8]
```

yields the list [1,2,3,4,5,6,7,8]. This happens exactly the same way: by starting with [4|[5,6,7,8]], then [3|[4,5,6,7,8]], and so on, and finally [1|[2,3,4,5,6,7,8]]. The list that was on the right side of ++ is never modified—you don't do that sort of destructive update in Erlang—it's included in the resulting list, technically via a pointer. This also means that the ++ operator doesn't care how long the right-side list is, because it never has to do anything with it.

The list on the left side is a different thing, though. To create the resulting list in the way described, you must first find the end of the left-side list (the element 4, in this case) and then start building the result backward from there. This means *the length of the left-side list decides how much time ++ takes.* For this reason, always try to add new (shorter) stuff to the left of the list, even if it means the final list will be in reverse order. It's much cheaper to finish up with a quick call to reverse the list afterward (please trust us here) than it is to repeatedly go through a list that keeps getting longer and longer every time so you can add something to its end.

Erlang also uses lists to represent another common kind of data: strings of text.

2.2.6 *Strings*

A double-quoted string in Erlang is merely an alternative way of writing a list of character codes. For example, these

```
"abcd"
"Hello!"
" \t\r\n"
""
```

are exactly equivalent to

```
[97,98,99,100]
[72,101,108,108,111,33]
[32,9,13,10]
[]
```

which can also be written as

```
[$a, $b, $c, $d]
[$H, $e, $l, $l, $o, $!]
[$\ , $\t, $\r, $\n]
[]
```

(if you recall the $ syntax from the section about integers, a few pages back). This correspondence is reflected in the names of some of the standard library functions in Erlang, such as atom_to_list(A), which returns the list of characters of any atom A.

That strings are lists means that all the tricks you learn for working with lists are equally applicable to strings, and you can do a lot of string programming with basic list-processing techniques. But one of the drawbacks is that it can be hard to tell whether a list was intended as a string.

STRINGS AND THE SHELL

The Erlang shell tries to maintain the illusion that strings are different from plain lists, by checking whether they contain only printable characters. If they do, it prints them as double-quoted strings, and otherwise as lists of integers. This is more user friendly but occasionally doesn't do what you want (for example, when an expression returns a list of numbers that by coincidence look like printable characters, and you see a string of line noise as a result).

A useful trick in that case is to append a zero to the start of the list, to force the shell to print the real representation. For example, even if v(1) is shown as a string, [0 | v(1)] won't be. (You can of course use the string formatting functions in the standard library to pretty-print the value, giving you full control, but how much fun is that?)

Now that you know how to build complex data structures, we quickly go over the remaining primitive data types: identifiers and funs.

2.2.7 Pids, ports, and references

These three *identifier* data types are closely related, so we present them here together.

PIDS (PROCESS IDENTIFIERS)

As you know by now, Erlang supports programming with processes; for any code to run, an Erlang process must be running it. Every process has a unique identifier, usually referred to as a *pid*. Pids are a special data type in Erlang and should be thought of as opaque objects. But when the shell prints them, they show up in the form <0.35.0>—that is, as three integers enclosed in angle brackets. You can't enter this into the shell and create a pid using this syntax; it's only shown for debugging purposes so that you can compare pids easily.

Although pids are expected to be unique for the lifetime of the system (until you restart Erlang), in practice the same identifier may be reused when the system has been running for a long time and some hundred million processes have come and gone. This is rarely considered a problem.

The function `self()` always gives you the pid of the process that is currently running (the one that called `self()`). You can try it in the shell—that's right, the shell is also a process in Erlang.

PORT IDENTIFIERS

A *port* is much like a process, except that it can also communicate with the world outside Erlang (and can't do much else—in particular, it can't run any code). Hence, *port identifiers* are closely related to pids, and the shell prints them on the form `#Port<0.472>`. We get back to ports later in this book.

REFERENCES

The third data type of this family is *references* (often called *refs*). They're created with the function `make_ref()` (try it!) and are printed by the shell on the form `#Ref<0.0.0.39>`. References are used as unique one-off labels or cookies.

2.2.8 *Functions as data: funs*

Erlang is said to be a *functional* programming language, and an expected feature of such a language is that it should be able to handle functions as data—that is, pass a function as input to another function, return a function as the *result* of another function, put a function in a data structure and pick it up later, and so on. Of course, you must also be able to *call* a function that you've gotten that way. In Erlang, such a function-as-data object is called a *fun* (or sometimes a *lambda expression* or *closure*).

We explain funs in more detail in section 2.7, after we've presented functions in general in section 2.5. We note for now that the shell prints them in the form `#Fun<...>`, with some information for debugging purposes between the angle brackets. You can't create a fun using this syntax.

That was the last in our list of built-in data types. We now discuss something that unites them all: the comparison operators.

2.2.9 *Comparing terms*

The different data types in Erlang have one thing in common: they can all be compared and ordered, using built-in operators like `<`, `>`, and `==`. The normal orderings on numbers of course hold, so that `1 < 2` and `3.14 > 3` and so on, and atoms and strings (as well as any other lists) and tuples are ordered lexicographically, so that `'abacus' < 'abba'`, `"zzz" > "zzy"`, `[1,2,3] > [1,2,2,1]`, and `{fred,baker,42} < {fred,cook,18}`.

So far, it all seems pretty normal; but on top of that, you also have an ordering between values of different types, so that, for example, `42 < 'aardvark'`, `[1,2,3] > {1,2,3}`, and `'abc' < "abc"`. That is, all numbers come before all atoms, all tuples come before all lists, and all atoms come before all tuples and lists (strings are lists, remember?).

You don't have to memorize which data types come before which in this order. The important thing to know is that you can compare *any* two terms for order, and you'll get the same result always. In particular, if you sort a list of various terms of different types (a list of mixed numbers, strings, atoms, tuples, ...) by using the standard library function `lists:sort(...)`, you'll always get a properly sorted list as a result, where all the numbers come first, then all atoms, and so on. You can try it in the shell: for example, `lists:sort([b,3,a,"z",1,c,"x",2.5,"y"])`.

LESS-THAN/GREATER-THAN OR EQUALS

One of those little differences in syntax between Erlang and most other programming languages except Prolog is that the less-than-or-equals operator is *not* written <=, for the reason that this looks too much like an arrow pointing to the left (and that symbol is indeed reserved for use as a left arrow). Instead, less-than-or-equals is written =<. The greater-than-or-equals operator is written >= as in most languages. The only thing you need to remember is that *comparisons never look like arrows.*

EQUALITY COMPARISONS

There are two kinds of operators for equality comparisons in Erlang. The first one is the *exact equality*, written =:=, which returns `true` only if both sides are exactly the same. For example, `42 =:= 42`. The negative form (*exact inequality*) is written =/=, as, for example, in `1 =/= 2`.

Exact equality is the preferred kind of equals operator when you're comparing terms in general (and it's also the one used in pattern matching, which we talk about later). But it means that integers and floating-point numbers are considered to be different, even if they're as similar as could be. For instance, `2 =:= 2.0` returns `false`.

If you're comparing numbers in general (or perhaps tuples containing numbers, like vectors) in a mathematical way, you should instead use the *arithmetic equality* operator, written ==. This compares numbers by coercing integers to floating point as necessary. Hence, `2 == 2.0` returns `true`. The negative form (*arithmetic inequality*) is written /=. For example, `2 /= 2.0` returns `false`. Remember, though, that comparing floating-point numbers for equality is always a somewhat suspicious thing to do, because the tiny rounding errors involved in the floating-point representation may cause values that ought to be equal to differ ever so slightly, and then == will return `false`. It's usually a better idea to use <, >, =<, or >= to compare numbers when they may be in floating point. Those operators are also arithmetic, by the way—they always coerce integers to floats when necessary. That's why you could compare 3 and 3.14 using > previously.

If you use == (the coercing, arithmetic equality operator) when it isn't warranted—which is more or less always except when you're doing math—you'll only be making it harder for program analysis tools like Dialyzer to help you find out if your program is doing something it shouldn't. You may also be masking errors at runtime so they aren't detected as early as they could be and instead show up much later, perhaps as weird data in a file or database (like a year showing up as 1970.0 or a month as 2.0).

That said, seasoned Erlang programmers usually avoid using the equality comparison operators at all and do as much as possible through pattern matching, which we talk about in section 2.4.3.

2.2.10 *Understanding lists*

Lists are different enough in Erlang compared to most common programming languages that we need to give them special treatment before we can leave the topic of data types.

THE STRUCTURE OF A LIST

Basically, lists are created from the *empty list* (nil) and so-called *list cells* which add one element at a time on top of an existing list, building a singly linked list in memory. Each such cell uses only two words of memory: one for the value (or a pointer to the value), known as the *head*, and one for a pointer to the rest of the list, called the *tail*; see figure 2.1. List cells are sometimes called *cons cells* (from list constructor) by people with a background in Lisp or functional programming, and the action of adding a cons cell is known as *consing* if you want to be geeky.

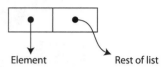

Figure 2.1   A list cell—the primitive building block of lists (two adjacent words in memory)

Although there is no technical difference between the head and the tail elements of a list cell, they're by convention always used so that the first (the head) contains the payload of the cell, and the second (the tail) is the rest of the list. This convention is used in the syntax as well as in all library functions that operate on lists.

A common gotcha for beginners (and even old-timers get snagged on this in the form of a typo sometimes) is to mistakenly write a comma instead of the intended vertical bar. Consider this: what is the difference between the following two expressions?

```
[ 1, 2, [3,4] ]
[ 1, 2 | [3,4] ]
```

(See if you get the point before you read on. Try entering them in the shell if you need more clues.)

The answer is that the first is a list with three elements, the last of which happens to be another list (with two elements). The second expression is a list with four elements, made from stacking two elements on top of the list `[3,4]`. Figure 2.2 illustrates the structure of these two examples. Make sure you understand it before you read on—it's

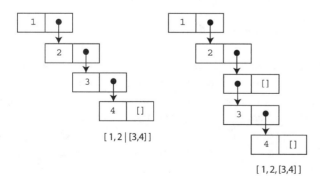

**Figure 2.2
The list cell structures in the example in the text. The left is a simple list, made from adding 2 and 1 on top of `[3,4]`. The right is a list of three elements `[1,2,X]`, where the last element `X` is the list `[3,4]`.**

central to everything you do with lists. Also see appendix B for a deeper discussion about lists and referential transparency.

You should learn to love the list. But remember, lists are mainly good for temporary data (for example, as a collection that you're processing), as a list of results that you're compiling, or as a string buffer. For long-term data storage, you may want to use a different representation when size matters, such as binaries for storing larger amounts of constant string data.

As you'll see moving forward, a large part of the data processing you'll do in Erlang, including string manipulation, comes down to traversing a list of items, much like you traverse collections and arrays in most other languages. Lists are your main intermediate data structure.

IMPROPER LISTS

A final note is on the difference between a *proper list* and an *improper list*. Proper lists are those that you've seen so far. They're built up with an empty list as the innermost tail. This means that starting from the outside, you can peel off one cell at a time and know that you must finally end up with the tail being an empty list.

But an improper list is created by adding a list cell on top on something that isn't a list to begin with. For example:

```
[ 1 |   oops  ]
```

This creates a list cell with a nonlist tail (in this case, an atom `'oops'`). Erlang doesn't forbid it and doesn't check for such things at runtime, but you should generally regard such a thing, if you see it, as a programming error and rewrite the code.

The main problem is that any functions that expect to receive a proper list will crash (throw an exception) if they try to traverse an improper list and end up finding a nonlist as the tail. Don't be tempted to use list cells this way even if you think you have a clever idea—it's bug-prone and confuses both humans and program-analysis tools. That said, there are one or two valid uses for creating improper lists, but they're considered advanced programming techniques and are beyond the scope of this book.

Now that we're done with the basic data types in Erlang, we can move on to the subject of creating programs and how to compile and run them. First, we need to talk about where your code will live: in functions, within modules.

2.3 *Modules and functions*

So far, you've only seen basic Erlang expressions: code snippets that can be evaluated to produce some value. But real Erlang programs aren't one-liners that you can enter in the shell. To give your code some structure in life and a place to call home, Erlang has *modules*, which are containers for program code. Each module has a unique name, which is specified as an atom. Erlang's standard library contains a large number of predefined modules, such as the `lists` module that contains many functions for working with lists.

In this section, we first explain some details about functions in Erlang: how you call them, why the arity of a function is important, the standard library, and what a BIF is. We then show how to create your own modules, compile them, and run the functions in them. We also explain a little about the difference between compiled modules and code that you enter in the shell. First, let's look at how to call a function in a module.

2.3.1 Calling functions in other modules (remote calls)

When you want to call a function that resides in some other module, you need to qualify the function name with the name of the module it's in, using a colon character as separator. For instance, to reverse a list [1,2,3] using the function reverse in the standard library module lists, you write as follows (and you can try this in the shell):

```
lists:reverse([1,2,3])
```

This form is called a *remote call* (calls a function in a different module), as opposed to a *local call* (calls a function in the same module). This shouldn't be confused with a remote procedure call, which is a concept in distributed programming and is a completely different thing (asking another process or computer to run a function for you).

In the previous example, the function took a single argument. When you program in Erlang, it's particularly important to take note of such details. The next section will explain why.

2.3.2 Functions of different arity

The number of arguments a function takes is referred to as its *arity*. For example, a function that takes one argument is a *unary* function, one that takes two arguments is a *binary* function, one that takes three arguments it a *ternary* function, and so on. You've seen a couple of functions already such as self() that are *nullary*—that is, that take no arguments.

The reason we bring this up is that the arity of functions is more important in Erlang than in most other programming languages. Erlang doesn't have function overloading as such; instead, it treats functions of different arities as completely separate even if they have the same atom as identifier. The full name of a function must always include the arity (written with a slash as separator). For example, the earlier list-reversing function is reverse/1; or, if you want to be particular about which module it resides in, you write lists:reverse/1. Note, though, that you can only use this syntax where the language expects a function name; if you write hello/2 as an expression, Erlang will interpret this as an attempt to divide the atom 'hello' by 2 (and won't like it).

To show how this works, there is in fact a function lists:reverse/2 that does almost the same as reverse/1 but also appends the list given as its second argument to the final result; so, lists:reverse([10,11,12], [9,8,7]) results in the list [12,11,10,9,8,7]. In some languages, this function might have had to be called reverse_onto or similar to avoid a name collision, but in Erlang you can get away with using the same atom for both. Don't abuse this power when you write your own functions—naming should be done in a systematic way so that it's easy for your users to remember how to call your functions. If you create functions that differ only in arity but produce wildly different results, you won't be thanked for it. When in doubt, opt for giving the functions clearly different names.

At any rate, always remember that in order to exactly specify which function you're talking about, you need to give the arity, not just the name.

2.3.3 *Built-in functions and standard library modules*

Like any other programming language, Erlang comes with a *standard library* of useful functions. These are spread over a large number of modules, but some standard library modules are more commonly used than others. In particular, the module named erlang contains functions that are central to the entire Erlang system, which everything else builds on. Another useful module that you've seen already is the lists module. The io module handles basic text input and output. The dict module provides hash-based associative arrays (dictionaries), the array module provides extensible integer-indexed arrays, and so forth.

Some functions are involved with things that are so low-level that the functions are an intrinsic part of the language and the runtime system. These are commonly referred to as *built-in functions* (BIFs), and like the Erlang runtime system, they're implemented in the C programming language. (Although some may disagree on the details, this is the most common definition.) In particular, all the functions in the erlang module are BIFs. Some BIFs, like our friend lists:reverse/1 from the previous section, could in principle be written directly in Erlang (like most of the other functions in the lists module) but have been implemented in C for efficiency reasons. In general, though, you don't have to care about how the functions are implemented—they look the same to the eye. But the term *BIF* is used often in the Erlang world, so it's useful to know what it refers to.

A few functions (all found in the module erlang) are both important and commonly used, in Erlang programs as well as in the shell. These are automatically *imported*, which means you don't need to write the module name explicitly. You've already seen the function self(), which returns the process identifier (the pid) of the process that calls it. This is a remote call to erlang:self(), but because it's one of the auto-imported functions, you don't need to prefix it with erlang:. Other examples are spawn(...), which starts a new process, and length(...), which computes the length of a list. Finally, even the operators of the language, such as +, are built-in functions and belong to the erlang module. For example, you can write erlang:'+'(1,2) for 1+2.

So far, we've talked about modules that already exist somewhere in the standard library. But what if you want to create a module of your own? It's finally time for that.

2.3.4 *Creating modules*

To create your own, real, Erlang programs, and not only experiment with expressions in the Erlang shell, the code you write must be housed by one or more modules. In order to make a new module that can be used by you or others, you need to do the following:

1 Write a source file.
2 Compile it.
3 Load it, or at least put it in the load path for automatic loading.

The first step is easy—start your favorite text editor (even if it's Notepad), open a new file, and start typing. Give the module a name, and save the file using the same name as for the module, plus the suffix *.erl*. For example, the following listing shows how such a file (named `my_module.erl`) might look. Create this file using your text editor now.

Listing 2.1 my_module.erl

```
%% This is a simple Erlang module

-module(my_module).

-export([pie/0]).

pie() ->
    3.14.
```

To start with the easiest part, the part that says `pie() -> 3.14.` is a *function definition*. It creates a function `pie` that takes no arguments and returns the floating-point number 3.14. The arrow `->` is there to separate the function *head* (the name and arguments) from its *body* (what the function does). Note that you don't need to say *return* or use any such keyword: *a function always returns the value of the expression in the body.* Also note that you must have a period (`.`) at the end of the function definition, like you had to write a `period` after each expression you entered in the shell.

The second thing to note is the *comment* on the first line. Comments in Erlang are introduced with the % character; and we'll say more about that in a moment.

The first item in a module, apart from any comments, must always be the *module declaration*, in the form `-module(...)`. *Declarations* are basically anything that's not a function or a comment. They always begin with a hyphen (`-`), and like function definitions, they must end with a period character. The module declaration is always required, and the name it specifies must match the name of the file (apart from the .erl suffix).

The line we saved for last is the one that says `-export([...])`.. This is an *export declaration*, and it tells the compiler which functions (separated by commas) should be visible from the outside. Functions not listed here will be kept internal to the module (so you can't call them from the shell). In this example, you have only one function, and you want that to be available, so you put it in the export list. As explained in the previous section, you need to state the arity (0, in this case) as well as the name in order to identify exactly what function you're referring to; hence, `pie/0`.

Before we move on, let's explain a few things about comments.

COMMENTS

There is only one kind of source code comment in Erlang. These comments are introduced with the % character and go on until the end of the line. Of course, % characters within a quoted string or atom don't count. For example:

```
% This is a comment and it ends here.

"This % does not begin a comment"

'nor does this: %'    %<-but this one does
```

You can write comments in the shell, if you like, but there is little point to it, which is why we haven't talked about doing so earlier.

Style-wise, comments that follow code on the same line are usually written with only a single % character, whereas comments that are on lines of their own are typically written starting with two % characters, like this:

```
%% This is your average standalone comment line.
%% Also, longer comments may require more lines.

frotz() -> blah.   % this is a comment on a line of code
```

(Some people even like to start with three % characters on comment lines that describe things on a whole-file level, such as comments at the top of the source file.)

One good reason to stick to these conventions is that syntax-aware editors such as Emacs and erlIDE can be made to know about them, so that they will indent comments automatically according to how many % characters they begin with.

Now that you have a source file that defines a module, you need to compile it.

2.3.5 *Compiling and loading modules*

When you *compile* a module, you produce a corresponding file with the extension .beam instead of .erl, which contains instructions in a form that the Erlang system can load and execute. This is a more compact and efficient representation of the program than the source code, and it contains everything the system needs to load and run the module. In contrast, a source code file might require that additional files be available via include declarations (section 2.12.2). All such files that make up the complete source code for the module have to be read at the time the module is compiled. The single .beam file, then, is a more definite form for a module, although it can't be easily read by a human and can't be edited by hand—you have to edit the source file instead and recompile it.

COMPILING FROM THE SHELL

The simplest way to compile a module when you're playing around and testing things, is to use the shell function `c(...)`, which compiles a module and also loads it (if the compilation worked) so you can try it out immediately. It looks for the source file relative to the current directory of the Erlang shell, and you don't even need to say .erl at the end of the name. For example, if you start Erlang in the same directory as the file you created earlier, you can do the following:

```
1> c(my_module).
{ok,my_module}
2> my_module:pie().
3.14
3>
```

The result {ok,my_module} from the call to c(...) is an indicator that the compilation worked, creating a module called my_module, which has now been loaded. You can call the function pie you exported from it to check that it works.

If you look in the directory of the source file (you can use the shell function ls() to do this), you'll see that there is now a new file called my_module.beam alongside the source file my_module.erl. This is the compiled version of the module, also called an *object file*.

MODULE LOADING AND THE CODE PATH

If you now exit the Erlang shell (using the shell function q(), for example) and then restart Erlang again in the same directory, you can try calling your module directly without compiling it first (assuming the previous compilation worked):

```
1> my_module:pie().
3.14
2>
```

How did this work? It's simple: whenever Erlang tries to call a module that hasn't been loaded into the system yet, it automatically tries to load it from a correspondingly named .beam file, if it can find one. The directories it looks in are listed in the *code path*; and by default, this includes the current directory (where it found your .beam file and loaded it).

To check out the current setting of the code path, call the function code:get_path(). This returns a list, at the start of which you'll see a period (.), meaning the current directory. The default code path also includes all the standard library directories. In addition, you can use the functions in the code module to modify the path as you like.

2.3.6   *The stand-alone compiler, erlc*

In a real software project, you typically want to script your builds using an external build tool, such as GNU Make. In this case, you can use the standalone erlc program to run the compiler from your operating system command line. For example:

```
erlc my_module.erl
```

(You can of course run this by hand if you like. Try it!) This is a bit different from the shell function you used earlier. Here, you need to give the full file name, including the .erl extension. You can also use options much as you would with a C compiler; for instance, to specify the output directory (where to put the .beam file), you can write something like this:

```
erlc -o ./ebin my_module.erl
```

(You may have noticed in the `code:get_path()` example that all the standard library directories in the path had names ending in /ebin. This is the normal convention for Erlang, to keep the .beam files in a subdirectory called ebin. We get back to this in more detail later when we talk about applications.)

If you're on Windows, there is a slight complication: the installation program doesn't set up the PATH environment variable to point to the `erl` and `erlc` programs; you have to do this yourself if you want to run them from your cmd.exe command line. They can be found in the bin subdirectory of the directory where Erlang was installed—the path probably looks something like C:\Program Files\erl5.7.3\bin. Also remember that the `erl` command doesn't play well with cmd.exe—it's good for running Erlang applications from scripts, but as an interactive environment, you want to run `werl` (for example, when you click the Erlang icon).

2.3.7 *Compiled modules versus evaluation in the shell*

There is a difference between what happens with expressions that you enter in the Erlang shell and code that you put in a module (and compile, load, and run). A .beam file, as we said, is an efficient, ready-to-deploy representation of a module. All the code in a .beam file was compiled together at the same time, in the same context. It can do things relating to the module it's in, such as specifying which functions are exported or not, or find out what the name of the module is, or declare other things that should hold for the module as a whole.

But code that you enter in the shell consists basically of one-off expressions, to be forgotten fairly soon. This code is never part of any module. Therefore, it isn't possible to use declarations (like `-export([...]).` or `-module(...).`) in the shell; there is no module context for such declarations to apply to.

The shell parses expressions and evaluates them by interpreting them on the fly. This is much less efficient (by several orders of magnitude) than running compiled code, but that doesn't matter much when all it has to do is to perform a call to a function in some existing compiled module (which will run at normal speed)—for example, when you say `lists:reverse([1,2,3])`. In this case, all the shell does is to prepare the list `[1,2,3]` and then pass it over to the `reverse` function (and print the result afterward). Even if it does this at a comparatively slow speed, it's still much too fast for a human to notice.

It's possible, though, by use of things such as list comprehensions (explained in section 2.9) or clever use of recursive funs (a neat trick, but may cause the brains of novices to implode), to write code in the shell that is more or less entirely evaluated by the shell's interpreter from start to end, and that does some significant amount of work. In that case, it will be notably slower than if you had written it in a module and compiled it. So, remember this: *never measure on code that is interpreted by the shell.* If you want sane numbers from your benchmarks, you must write them as modules, not as shell one-liners. Don't draw conclusions about efficiency from what the shell does.

> **NOTE** It may happen that in some odd corner case, code evaluated in the shell behaves slightly differently from the same code when compiled as part of a module. In such a case, the compiled version is the gold standard. The shell tries its best to do the exact same thing when it interprets the expressions.

One thing has been missing from all our examples so far. Did you notice it? You haven't used any variables yet! The reason is that because they're so intimately connected, we wanted to present variables and pattern matching together. Now that you know about basic data types, modules, and functions, it's time to show how to use variables in your code.

2.4 *Variables and pattern matching*

Variables in Erlang are a bit different from variables in most other programming languages, which is why we've postponed introducing them until now. It isn't that they're more difficult than in other languages; it's that they're so much simpler! So simple, in fact, that your first reaction may be, "How do I do anything useful with them?"

In this section, we start by showing how variables, single assignment, and the = operator work, before we dive into pattern matching and show how to easily extract or make assertions on parts of data structures.

2.4.1 *Variable syntax*

The most visible difference is that in Erlang, variables begin with an uppercase letter! (You've already reserved names that begin with lowercase for writing atoms, remember?) Here are some examples of variables, using CamelCase to separate word parts, which is the normal style for variables in Erlang:

```
Z
Name
ShoeSize12
ThisIsARatherLongVariableName
```

You can also begin a variable with an underscore character. In that case, the second character is by convention usually an uppercase character:

```
_SomeThing
_X
_this_may_look_like_an_atom_but_is_really_a_variable
```

There is a small difference in functionality here: the compiler normally warns you if you assign a value to a variable and then don't use that variable for anything. This catches a lot of silly mistakes, so don't turn off that warning. Instead, when you want to use a variable for something to make the program more readable, you can use one that starts with an underscore. (You'll see how you might want to write variables like this when we talk about pattern matching.) The compiler won't complain if those are unused. Also, any variables that aren't used will be optimized away, so they carry no extra cost: you can use them freely to annotate your program for better readability.

2.4.2 *Single assignment*

The next surprise is that Erlang's variables are strictly *single assignment*. This means that when you assign a value to a variable—or, as we say in Erlang country, *bind* the variable to a value—that variable will hold the same value throughout its entire *scope* (that part of the program code where the variable exists). The same variable name can be reused in different places in the program, but then we're talking about different variables with distinct and non-overlapping scopes (just like Paris can be one thing in Texas and another thing in France).

In most other programming languages, what's called a variable is a kind of box with a name, and you can change the contents of the box from one point in the program to the next. This is odd, if you think about it, and it's certainly not what you learned in algebra class. Erlang's variables, on the other hand, are like those you knew from mathematics: a name for some value, which doesn't change behind your back (which is why you can solve equations). The values are stored somewhere in the computer's memory, but *you* don't have to care about micromanagement issues like creating those little boxes and moving things between them or reusing them to save space. The Erlang compiler handles all of that for you, and does it well.

For more details about single assignment and the concept of *referential transparency*, see appendix B.

THE = OPERATOR AND USING VARIABLES IN THE SHELL

The simplest form of assignment in Erlang is through the = operator. This is a *match operator*, and as you'll see, it can do more than straightforward assignment; but for now, here's an example you can try in the shell:

```
1> X = 42.
42
2> X.
42
3> X+1.
43
4>
```

That probably worked as you expected. Variables in the shell are a bit particular, though. Their scope is "as long as the shell is still running, unless I say otherwise." To forget all bound variables, you can call the shell function f(), like this:

```
4> f().
ok
5> X.
* 1: variable 'X' is unbound
6> X = 17.
17
7> X.
17
8>
```

As you see, once forgotten, X can be reused for something else. What if you try to reuse it without forgetting the old value?

```
8> X = 101.
** exception error: no match of right hand side value 101
9>
```

Oops. The single assignment is enforced, and you get an exception instead. The error message indicates that a match was taking place. What if you try to reassign the same value that X already has?

```
9> X = 17.
17
10>
```

No complaints this time. That's what the match part means: if X already has a value, it checks that the right side is the same (comparing them for *exact equivalence*, look back to section 2.2.9 if you've forgotten what this means). If you want to forget X and not all the other variable bindings you may have made in the shell, use f(X), like this:

```
10> Y = 42.
42
11> f(X).
ok
12> X.
* 1: variable 'X' is unbound
13> Y.
42.
14>
```

Just remember that this is how variable scope works *in the shell*. Within a module, scopes are tied to function definitions and similar things, and there is no way to forget variable bindings prematurely; we get into more detail in section 2.5.2.

VARIABLES AND UPDATES

After you accept that you can't update a variable with a new value, you'll probably wonder how to change anything. After all, much of what a program does is compute new data from old—for instance, adding 1 to a number. The short answer is, if you need to keep track of another value, give it another name. For example, if you have a variable X that holds some integer, and you want to give a name to the value you get if you add 1 to X, you can say something like X1 = X + 1:

```
1> X = 17.
17
2> X1 = X + 1.
18
3>
```

Maybe you can come up with a more descriptive name, like NewX or IncrementedX; and depending on the code at hand, this may or may not be better (overlong names can also be bad for readability). But the normal fallback when you're out of inspiration is to use names like X1, X2, and X3 for modified variants of X. (If you're wondering what to do with variables in a loop, it will have to wait until we discuss recursive functions in section 2.15.)

Usually, you should avoid situations where you need a lot of different variables for almost-the-same-thing-only-modified-a-bit. Try to split the code into separate functions instead, where each function can have its own X and works on only one step of the whole problem. This makes for much more readable and sane code in the long run.

On their own, variables are fairly boring. Single assignment or not, every practical language has them. The real power comes through pattern matching.

2.4.3   *Pattern matching: assignment on steroids*

Pattern matching is one of the utterly indispensible features of Erlang. When you get used to it, you'll wonder how you could ever be without it, and the thought of programming in a language that doesn't have pattern matching will become depressing. (Trust us.)

Pattern matching serves the following important purposes:

- Choosing control flow branches
- Performing variable assignments (bindings)
- Decomposing data structures (selecting and extracting parts)

We start by exposing the dirty secret of the = operator.

THE = OPERATOR IS A PATTERN MATCH

In the previous section, we called = a match operator. This is because what it does is *pattern matching*, rather than assignment. On the left side, you have a *pattern*; and on the right side, you have a plain old expression. To evaluate the match, the right-side expression is evaluated first, to get a value. That value is then *matched* against the pattern (a bit like when you match a string against a regular expression). If the pattern doesn't match, as in 17 = 42, or true = false, the match fails and throws an exception containing the reason code badmatch. In the shell, this is presented to you as the error message "no match of right hand side value ...."

If the match works, the program continues with any expressions that follow after it, but now any variables that occurred in the pattern on the left side have the same values as the corresponding parts of the value from the right side. (If the pattern is only a single variable, as in X = 42, then the corresponding part is the entire right-side value.) To illustrate, try the following in the shell:

```
1> {A, B, C} = {1970, "Richard", male}.
{1970,"Richard",male}
2> A.
1970
3> B.
"Richard"
4> C.
male
5>
```

It shouldn't be hard to see what is happening here. The pattern {A,B,C} matches the right-side tuple; as a result, the variables are bound to the corresponding elements, so you can refer to them afterward. It couldn't be any simpler.

This shows another common kind of match:

```
1> {rectangle, Width, Height} = {rectangle, 200, 100}.
{rectangle,200,100}
2> Width.
200
3> Height.
100
4>
```

Here, the pattern requires that the first element of the tuple be an atom rectangle (used as a label). Because the right-side tuple has a matching atom as its first element and has three elements as required, the match succeeds, and the variables Width and Height become bound.

A variable can occur several times in a pattern, and this is sometimes useful when you want to specify that two fields must have the same value:

```
1> {point, X, X} = {point, 2, 2}.
{point,2,2}
2> X.
2
3>
```

If the fields aren't exactly equal, the match fails:

```
1> {point, X, X} = {point, 1, 2}.
** exception error: no match of right hand side value {1,2}
2>
```

Because of the single-assignment variables, it's impossible to give X both the values 1 and 2, no matter which one you start with.

2.4.4 *More about patterns*

Patterns look like expressions but are more limited. They can only contain variables, constants, and constant data structures like lists and tuples—no operators, function calls, funs, and so on. They can be arbitrarily complicated and nested, though. For example, let's first create a list containing some information about users of some system (only one, right now):

```
1> Users = [{person, [{name, "Martin", "Logan"}, {shoe_size,12},
      {tags,[jujitsu,beer,erlang]}]}].
...
2>
```

(The shell will print back the value of what you just entered; we skipped that for clarity.) Now, let's extract some selected data about the first user in the list:

```
2> [ {person, [{name,_,Surname},_,{tags, Tags}]} | _ ] = Users.
...
```

```
3> Surname.
"Logan"
4> Tags.
[jujitsu,beer,erlang]
5>
```

First, note the use of a single underscore (_) to indicate a *don't-care pattern*. In other words, where you wrote _, you don't care what value the right side has at that point, and you don't want to know. You can have several underscores in the same pattern, as in this example, but they don't have to have the same values in all places (like variables do). These don't-care patterns are sometimes referred to as *anonymous variables*, but they aren't variables at all, just placeholders.

Second, look at the outermost part of the pattern, in particular the last part before the =. This has the form [... | _]. To understand this, you need to recall what we said about lists in section 2.2.10: lists are made up of list cells, forming a chain, and a single list cell is written [...|...]. You can also visualize the cells as layers upon layers, like an onion, with an empty list as the center, and each layer carrying some data.

The previous pattern can then be read out as follows:

Something that consists of an outermost list cell, whose inner layers I don't care about for now (the | _] part of the pattern), but whose payload (in the [... | part of the pattern) has the shape {person, [..., ..., ...]}—that is, is a 2-tuple tagged as person, whose second element is a list of exactly three elements. The first of these elements is a 3-tuple labeled name, and I want the third element of that—let's call it Surname; the third is a 2-tuple labeled tags, and I want the second element of that one—let's call it Tags.

Congratulations if you got through all that. But it does show that what a pattern can express in a single line and less than 50 characters can be a rather long-winded business if you spell it out (which you need to do to get the same effect in most other languages). Patterns are natural, compact, readable, and powerful.

MATCHING STRING PREFIXES USING ++

As you recall, strings in Erlang (written within double quotes) are lists of character codes. This makes matching on string prefixes particularly easy. First, take this example of matching a simple list prefix:

```
[1,2,3 | Rest] = [1,2,3,4,5,6,7]
```

Because the left-side pattern has the same three initial elements as the list on the right side, they match. As a result, the variable Rest is bound to the list cells that follow the 3: that is, Rest = [4,5,6,7].

But strings are lists of character codes, and you can get the code point for a character through the $ syntax (for example, $A yields 65), so the following also works:

```
[$h, $t, $t, $p, $: | Rest] = "http://www.erlang.org"
```

This should give the string "//www.erlang.org" in Rest. This is nice but can be nicer. We said before that operators aren't allowed in patterns. There is one exception: the

++ operator, which is used to append strings. It can be used in patterns if and only if its left argument is a constant string. The example can then be written as

```
"http://" ++ Rest = "http://www.erlang.org"
```

(To make things more interesting, we included the two slashes in the pattern as well, giving `"www.erlang.org"` in `Rest`.) There is no magic behind this; if you say `"abc" ++ SomeString`, the ++ operator creates a list of the form `[$a, $b, $c | SomeString]`, like the pattern you wrote by hand previously. Obviously, for the compiler to be able to do this expansion, the left argument of ++ must be a constant string at compile time.

The ease with which you can do basic string matching is probably the reason why you don't see a lot of regular expressions in Erlang programs. They would be overkill and have more overhead for straightforward matches like this.

We want to encourage you at this point and tell you that by now, you've seen most of that which may seem strange and difficult about Erlang. Concepts like atoms, tuples, and strange lists that are also strings. Variables that start with uppercase and that can only be assigned once. Functions where the arity is part of the name. Well, from now on, it will be much more straightforward. Erlang isn't a difficult language, after you get over the initial culture shock. With those words, let's move on to writing functions that do something interesting.

2.5   *Functions and clauses*

We had to discuss a lot of basics before we could start talking about functions! But we wanted to make sure you understand variables and pattern matching first, because after that, you'll have no trouble understanding how functions work in Erlang. Not that the concept of functions is much different compared to other languages; but in Erlang, functions and pattern matching are intimately connected. Although this can be intuitive, it can also take some getting used to.

You saw a simple function definition already, in section 2.3.4, when we introduced modules. From now on, we won't do many examples in the shell, because you'll be writing your own modules (although you'll use the shell for compiling and running your code). For these initial examples, you'll continue using the module you created back then—the one called `my_module`—and add new functions to it so you can try them. Remember to add the function name (with the correct arity) to the `-export([...])` list and recompile the module using `c(my_module)` before you try to call the function. If you see an error message saying something like "undefined function my_module:xxx/N," it's probably because you forgot to do either of these things. If you get the error message "undefined shell command xxx/N," you forgot to write `my_module:` before the function name when you tried to call it.

2.5.1   *A function with side effects: printing text*

Let's start with something basic: taking some input and printing text to the console. The standard library function `io:format(...)` is the normal way of writing text to the standard output stream in Erlang. It takes two arguments: the first is a format string, and the second is a list of terms to be printed. You'll use this in your own function, called print, which has a variable Term as parameter:

```
print(Term) ->
    io:format("The value of Term is: ~p.~n", [Term]).
```

Write this function in your module, add print/1 to the export list, compile the module again from the shell using c(my_module), and then call my_module:print ("hello"). You should see the following:

```
1> c(my_module).
{ok,my_module}
2> my_module:print("hello").
The value of Term is: "hello".
ok
3>
```

The escape code ~p in the format string means to pretty-print an Erlang term. This means lists of printable characters will be displayed as double-quoted strings, and also that if the term is too large to fit on one line, it will be split over several lines (with suitable indentation). Try calling your new print function with different values from the data types you got to know in section 2.2. What happens if you try to print the list [65,66,67]?

(The escape code ~n means "insert a line break," so you get a new line after the message, but you probably figured that out already.)

If you now change the ~p to ~w (do this!) and recompile, and then call the function again with my_module:print("hello") as before, you'll see this:

```
5> c(my_module).
{ok,my_module}
6> my_module:print("hello").
The value of Term is: [104,101,108,108,111].
ok
7>
```

What's that ugly list? Well, a string is a list of character codes, remember? The escape code ~w means "print an Erlang term in its raw form" without fancy line breaking and without printing lists as double-quoted strings even if they contain only printable character codes.

The function io:format(...) is an example of a function that has *side effects*. It does return a result, as you can see (the atom 'ok'), but its main purpose is to have an effect on the environment around it. (And by extension, the same is true for your print function.) In Erlang, practically all side effects can be seen as *messages* (and they usually are in practice, too). In this case, the io:format function prepares the text to be printed and then sends it as a message to the console driver before it returns 'ok'.

Finally, note that you've already started doing *interactive development* in the Erlang shell: you changed your program, recompiled and loaded the new version, and tried it, without ever stopping and restarting the Erlang environment. If your Erlang system had been doing something of interest in the background (like serving up web pages to customers), it would still be merrily chugging along while you keep fixing things.

2.5.2   *Multiple clauses and pattern matching for choice*

Next, we look at where pattern matching comes in. In Erlang, a function can consist of more than one *clause*. Whereas the example in the previous section had a single clause, the following example has three clauses:

```
either_or_both(true, _) ->
    true;
either_or_both(_, true) ->
    true;
either_or_both(false, false) ->
    false.
```

The function either_or_both/2 here is an example of a Boolean function—one that operates on the values true and false (which are ordinary atoms in Erlang, remember?). As its name indicates, you want it to behave like the built-in or operator: if either of the arguments, or both, are true, the result should also be true; otherwise the result should be false. And no non-Boolean inputs are accepted.

Note that the clauses are separated by semicolons (;) and that only the last clause is terminated by a period (.). All the clauses must begin with the same name and have the same number of arguments, and they must be defined together—you can't put another function definition between two clauses of the same function.

CLAUSE SELECTION

When the function is called, Erlang tries the clauses in top-down order using pattern matching: first, it matches the incoming arguments against the patterns in the first clause; if they don't match, the next clause is tried, and so on. In the example, it means that if the first argument is true, the first clause will always be chosen (no matter what the second argument is—note that the example uses a don't-care pattern in its place).

If the first clause doesn't match, and if the second argument is true, the second clause of the example will be chosen. But if that clause doesn't match either, the third clause is tried, and if that still doesn't match, you'll get a runtime exception of the type function_clause to indicate that the arguments didn't match *any* of the clauses of the function in this call.

Now, take another look at these clauses, and think about what you know at each point. If you ever get to the second clause, you *know* the first argument isn't true (because otherwise the first clause would match). Likewise, if you get as far as the third clause, you know that *neither* of the arguments can be true. The only valid possibility left at that point is that both arguments are false (if the function was called with only true or false as argument values).

It's good programming practice to make this knowledge explicit in the code— that's why you don't accept anything other than (false, false) in the last clause.

If someone calls this function with an unexpected value like foo or 42, they will get a runtime exception (function_clause), which is what you *want*: it means they will *fail early* and get a chance to detect the mistake and fix the code as soon as possible, so bad data doesn't propagate further throughout the system. If you tried to be nice and said (_, _) in the last clause, to return false in all remaining cases, then a call such as either_or_both(foo, bar) would also return false without any hint of a problem.

2.5.3 *Guards*

There is still a possibility of some nonsense slipping through, though. If someone called the previous function as either_or_both(true, 42) or as either_or_both(foo, true), then it would quietly return true as if all was well in the world. You can add extra requirements to the clauses to plug this hole, using *guards*:

```
either_or_both(true, B) when is_boolean(B) ->
    true;
either_or_both(A, true) when is_boolean(A) ->
    true;
either_or_both(false, false) ->
    false.
```

A clause guard begins with the keyword when and ends at the -> arrow. It contains one or more tests, separated by commas if there are more than one, and all of them have to be true for the clause to be selected. As you can see, you need to use variables in the patterns to be able to refer to them in the guard, so this example uses the names A and B instead of don't-care patterns. The is_boolean(...) test is one of those built-in functions that you can call without specifying the module name (they live in the erlang module). There are similar tests for all the primitive data types: is_atom(...), is_integer(...), and so on. The is_boolean(...) test checks that the value is one of the atoms true and false.

Apart from such *type tests*, the number of things you can do within a guard is strictly limited. You can use most of the operators (+, -, *, /, ++, and so on), and some of the built-in functions (like self()), but you can't call your own functions, or functions in another module. This is partly for efficiency reasons—you want to be sure that clause selection is fast—but mostly because of possible side effects. It's important that if a guard *fails* (turns out to be false), you should be able to go on and try the next clause *as if nothing happened*. For example, if you could somehow send a message from inside a guard, but that guard failed, it would be impossible to undo that message—someone might already have seen it and as a consequence performed some visible change to the world, like changing a file or printing some text. Erlang doesn't allow this, and that makes guards (and clauses in general) much easier to reason about, reorder, and refactor.

Make sure you add this function to your module and try it, first the initial version and then the one with guards. Give them some different inputs and check their behaviour. We hope you see how this ability to experiment with functions in Erlang, test them interactively, and incrementally improve them without restarting the runtime environment can be a big boost both for productivity and for creativity.

2.5.4 *Patterns, clauses, and variable scope*

Let's take another example of pattern matching, to show how you use it to both select clauses and extract the interesting data at the same time. The following function assumes that you're using tagged tuples to represent information about different geometric shapes:

```
area({circle, Radius}) ->
    Radius * Radius * math:pi();
area({square, Side}) ->
    Side * Side;
area({rectangle, Height, Width}) ->
    Height * Width.
```

If you, for instance, call `my_module:area({square, 5})`, you should get 25. If you pass it {rectangle, 3, 4}, it returns 12, and so on. Pattern matching decides which clause will be selected, but it also binds the variables to the elements of the data structure so that you can refer to these values in the body of each clause. Note that as opposed to the earlier `either_or_both` function, the order of the clauses in this function doesn't matter, because only one can match at any time; they're *mutually exclusive.*

The *scope*, or lifetime, of a variable that is bound in the head of a function clause is the entire clause, up until the semicolon or period that ends that clause. For example, in the `area` function, you use different variable names for `Radius` (of a circle) and `Side` (of a square), but you could also have called both `X` if you wanted, because they live in separate clauses. On the other hand, the `Height` and `Width` variables (for a rectangle) must have distinct names, because they have overlapping scope. You never need to declare variables in Erlang—you use them as you need them; but this convention means you can't reuse the same name within the same clause.

When a variable goes out of scope, the value that it referred to becomes a candidate for garbage collection (the memory it used will be recycled) if no other part of the program still needs it. That's another thing you rarely need to think about in Erlang.

2.6 *Case and if expressions*

If function clauses were the only way to make control flow branches in Erlang, you'd have to invent a new function name for each little choice to be made in your program. Although it might be pedagogical, it could also be annoying. Fortunately, Erlang provides `case` expressions for this purpose. These expressions also have one or more clauses, but can only have one pattern per clause (so no parentheses are needed).

For example, the `area` function from section 2.5.4 can also be written using a `case` expression:

```
area(Shape) ->
    case Shape of
        {circle, Radius} ->
            Radius * Radius * math:pi();
        {square, Side} ->
            Side * Side;
        {rectangle, Height, Width} ->
            Height * Width
    end.
```

Note that you must give the input to area a name, so you can refer to it as the value the case should switch on (case Shape of ...). Also note that all the clauses are separated by semicolons, as with function clauses, and that the entire case expression must end with the keyword end. (There is no semicolon after the last clause—they're separators, not terminators.) In this particular case, the new version of the function is arguably *less* readable, because of the extra variable and the case/of/end keywords, and most Erlang programmers would prefer the original (even if that repeats the function name three times).

When you want to switch on multiple items using a case expression, you have to group them using tuple notation. For example, the either_or_both function from section 2.5.3 can be written as follows:

```
either_or_both(A, B) ->
    case {A, B} of
        {true, B} when is_boolean(B) ->
            true;
        {A, true} when is_boolean(A) ->
            true;
        {false, false} ->
            false
    end.
```

As you can see, you can use guards (when ...) in case clauses as well. Again, you may or may not prefer the original version of the function as being more succinct.

2.6.1 *Boolean if-then-else switches in Erlang*

Surprise: there aren't any! You use a case expression instead, like the following:

```
case either_or_both(X, Y) of
    true  -> io:format("yes~n");
    false -> io:format("no~n")
end
```

Although it can be tempting to use an underscore as a catch-all pattern in the last case, don't do that. Spell out both the true and the false cases. This ensures that your program fails early, in case the input to the switch happens to be something other than true/false, and also helps program analysis tools like Dialyzer to see what your intention was.

2.6.2 *If expressions*

As a special case, `if` expressions are a stripped-down variant of `case` expressions, without a specific value to switch on and without patterns. You can use an `if` expression when you want to have one or more clauses that only depend on what is in the guards. For example:

```
sign(N) when is_number(N) ->
    if
        N > 0 -> positive;
        N < 0 -> negative;
        true  -> zero
    end.
```

This can also be written using a `case` with a dummy switch value (and using don't-care underscores as patterns in all clauses):

```
sign(N) when is_number(N) ->
    case dummy of
        _ when N > 0 -> positive;
        _ when N < 0 -> negative;
        _ when true  -> zero
    end.
```

We hope that also makes you see why the last catch-all clause in the `if` expression is written `true -> ....` If the guard test is always true, the clause will always match.

The `if` expressions were added to the language a long time ago, a bit on a whim. They aren't used often, because most switches tend to have some kind of pattern involved anyway. Although they come in handy on occasion, a long-standing complaint from Erlang programmers has been that they're mostly a waste of the keyword `if`. It's one of those things that are hard to change in a language in retrospect. As a beginner, what you need to remember is that the conditions you switch on can't be any old expressions—they're *guard tests*, and as such they're limited (see section 2.5.3).

2.7 *Funs*

We introduced funs briefly in section 2.2.8. But it isn't until now, after we've shown how functions and clauses work, that we're ready to talk about how funs are created.

2.7.1 *Funs as aliases for existing functions*

If you have a function in the same module—for example, `either_or_both/2`—and you want to refer to it so you can say to some other part of the program, "please call this function," then you can create a fun by saying

```
fun either_or_both/2
```

Like any value, you can bind it to a variable

```
F = fun either_or_both/2
```

or pass it directly to another function:

```
yesno(fun either_or_both/2)
```

And if you get a fun value from somewhere, you can call it like any old function, like this:

```
yesno(F) ->
    case F(true, false) of
        true  -> io:format("yes~n");
        false -> io:format("no~n")
    end.
```

This means it's simple to parameterize behaviour. The same function (yesno) can be used in different ways depending on which funs you give it. In this example, the input parameter F is expected to be some kind of condition that takes two Boolean arguments, but apart from that, it could be doing anything.

Higher-order functions

The function yesno/1 in the previous example is what is called a *higher-order function*: one that gets a fun as input, or returns a fun as the result, or both. Funs and higher-order functions are useful indeed; they're used for all sorts of things that delegates, adapters, commands, strategies, and so on, are used for in object-oriented languages.

Note that these local alias funs are similar in implementation to *anonymous* funs (explained shortly) and are *tied to the current version of the module*. See "Local funs have a short expiration date" in the next section for more details.

REMOTE ALIAS FUNS

If you want to create a fun that refers to a function which exists in some *other* module, you can use the following syntax (it also works for exported functions in the same module):

```
fun other_module:some_function/2
```

These remote alias funs have a different behaviour with respect to code loading: they aren't tied to any particular version of the function they refer to. Instead, they're always directed to the latest available version of the function whenever the fun is called. Such fun values are merely symbolic references to the function and can be stored for any period of time and/or passed between Erlang systems without problems.

2.7.2 *Anonymous funs*

Although alias funs are useful, the real power comes with the syntax for *anonymous* funs, also known as *lambda expressions*. Like the funs in the previous section, they start with the fun keyword; and like a case expression, they end with the end keyword. Between those keywords, they look like one or more function clauses without any function names. For example, here is the simplest possible anonymous fun. It takes no arguments and always returns zero:

```
fun () -> 0 end
```

Here, on the other hand, is a more complicated one—it does exactly the same thing as the area function from section 2.5.4, but it has no name:

```
fun ({circle, Radius}) ->
        Radius * Radius * math:pi();
    ({square, Side}) ->
        Side * Side;
    ({rectangle, Height, Width}) ->
        Height * Width
end
```

Obviously, to make any use of anonymous funs, you either have to bind them to a variable or pass them directly to some other function, like you did with the yesno/1 function in section 2.7.1:

```
yesno( fun (A, B) ->  A or B  end )
```

> ### Local funs have a short expiration date
> When you create an anonymous fun, or a fun as an alias for a local function, the fun value is tied to that particular version of the code. If you reload the module that it belongs to more than once, the fun will no longer work: it will throw an exception if someone attempts to call it. Hence, it isn't a good idea to keep such fun values around for a long time (for example, by storing them in a database). Also, if you send them in a message to a different Erlang system, then that system must have the exact same version of the code for the fun to work. Remote alias funs are better for such purposes.

CLOSURES

The word *closure* is often used interchangeably with *fun* or *lambda expression*, but more specifically it refers to the common and extremely useful case when you're accessing variables within fun ... end that are bound *outside* the fun. The fun value will then also encapsulate the current values of those variables.

To make it more concrete, let's say you have a list of items as pairs of strings, each pair representing a name and a corresponding description. You also have a function to_html (not shown here) that will create an HTML fragment containing these strings marked up as a definition list or similar—the details could change. Furthermore, for every name string, but not the description strings, to_html will apply a callback fun that you provide, to wrap the name for emphasis using some additional markup of your choice. The callback is applied after to_html has HTML-escaped the string, so you don't need to handle such details.

You can then, for example, make the names bold, like this:

```
to_html(Items, fun (Text) -> "<b>" ++ Text ++ "</b>" end)
```

Note here that `Text` is a parameter of the fun and represents the escaped string passed by `to_html` each time it applies the callback. For example, if `Items` has the value `[{"D&D", "Dungeons and Dragons"}]`, you get something like this as output:

```
... <b>D&amp;D</b> ... Dungeons and Dragons ...
```

(The rest of the HTML markup could be anything, depending on the details of what `to_html` does: a definition list, a table, a bunch of `div`s, and so on.)

Now, suppose you want to make the exact kind of emphasis a parameter: something that is passed to this part of your program from somewhere else, in a variable. You can then use that variable in the fun:

```
render(Items, Em) ->
    to_html(Items,
            fun (Text) ->
                "<" ++ Em ++ ">" ++ Text ++ "</" ++ Em ++ ">"
            end).
```

Such a fun will include, as a snapshot, the current values of those variables that it uses (`Em` in this case) that have been bound outside the fun itself—this is what the word *closure* refers to.

Because Erlang's single assignment and referential transparency properties guarantee that these values can't be changed by anyone, you know that, whether you call the fun right away or not until later, it will have exactly the same values for these variables as when it was created. (Of course, you can create multiple *instances* of the same fun, each with possibly different values for the externally bound variables, but each of those instances lives its own isolated life.)

The previous fun is the meeting place for three different sources of information: the caller of `render`, which says whether to use `"b"` or `"i"` or something else for every name string; the `to_html` function, which does the main job of transforming the items to HTML; and the `render` function, which specifies how the additional markup is added (that is, what the callback fun does). Note that it's a requirement from `to_html` that the callback fun should take one argument, which must be a string. The interface of the callback becomes a part of the interface of `to_html`.

2.8 Exceptions, try, and catch

We've mentioned exceptions without further explanation up until now. What, then, is an exception? You could say that it's an alternative way of returning from a function, with the difference that it keeps going back to the caller, and to the caller's caller, and so on, until either someone catches it or it reaches the initial call of the process (in which case the process dies).

There are three classes of exceptions in Erlang:

- error—This is the runtime error kind of exception, caused by things like division by zero, failing match operations, no matching function clause, and so on. These exceptions also have the property that if they cause a process to die, it's reported to the Erlang error logger.

- exit—This kind of exception is used to signal "this process is giving up." It's generally expected not to be caught, but to cause the process to die and let others know why it quit. exit can also be used for normal termination, to quit and signal "job done, all OK." In either case, process termination due to exit (for whatever reason) isn't considered unexpected, so it isn't reported to the error logger.

- throw—This kind of exception is for user-defined purposes. You can use throws to signal that your function encountered something unexpected (like a missing file or bad input), or to perform a so-called *nonlocal return* or long jump out of a deep recursion. A throw that isn't caught by the process mutates into an error exception with the reason nocatch, terminating the process and logging it.

2.8.1 *Throwing (raising) exceptions*

For each of the exception classes, there is a corresponding built-in function to throw (or *raise*) such an exception:

```
throw(SomeTerm)
exit(Reason)
erlang:error(Reason)
```

Because throw and exit are common, they're auto-imported: you don't need to prefix them with erlang:. In normal code, you typically don't need to raise error exceptions (but it can be a good thing to do if you're writing a library and want to throw errors like badarg, like Erlang's standard library functions).

As a special case, if a process calls exit(normal), and the exception isn't caught, that process terminates as if it had finished the job it was spawned to do. This means that other (linked) processes won't regard it as an abnormal termination (as they will for all other exit reasons).

2.8.2 *Using try...catch*

In modern Erlang, you use a try expression to handle exceptions that occur in a piece of code. In most ways, it works like a case expression, and in the simplest form it looks like this:

```
try
    some_unsafe_function()
catch
    oops          -> got_throw_oops;
    throw:Other   -> {got_throw, Other};
    exit:Reason   -> {got_exit, Reason};
    error:Reason  -> {got_error, Reason}
end
```

Between `try` and `catch`, you have the *body* or *protected section*. Any exception that occurs within the body and tries to propagate out from it will be caught and matched against the clauses listed between `catch` and `end`. If it doesn't match any of the clauses, the exception will continue as if there was no `try` expression around the body. Similarly, if the body is evaluated without raising an exception, its result will become the result of the whole expression, as if the `try` and `catch...end` had not been there. The only difference is when there is an exception, and it matches one of the clauses. In that case, the result becomes whatever the matching clause returns.

The patterns of these clauses are special—they may contain a colon (:) to separate the exception class (`error`, `exit`, or `throw`) from the thrown term. If you leave out the class, it defaults to `throw`. You shouldn't normally catch `error` and `exit` unless you know what you're doing—it goes against the idea of failing early, and you could be masking a real problem. Sometimes, though, you want to run some code that you don't trust too much and catch anything that it throws. You can use the following pattern for catching *all* exceptions:

```
_:_ -> got_some_exception
```

(Or you can use `Class:Term -> ...` if you want to inspect the data in the exception.)

Also, note that after you get to the `catch` part, the code is no longer protected. If a new exception happens in a `catch` clause, it will propagate out of the entire `try` expression.

2.8.3   *try...of...catch*

A longer form of `try` is useful when you need to do different things in the successful cases and the exception cases. For instance, if you want to continue doing some work with the value you got in the successful case, but you want to print an error message and give up in the exception case, you can add an `of...` section, like this:

```
try
    some_unsafe_function(...)
of
    0 -> io:format("nothing to do~n");
    N -> do_something_with(N)
catch
    _:_ -> io:format("some problem~n")
end
```

Because it's common that the thing you immediately want to do in the successful case (apart from giving a name to the result) is to switch on the value you got, you write one or more clauses between `of` and `catch`, like those in a `case` expression, for what should happen if the `try...of` part succeeds. Just note that the `of...` part, like the `catch` clauses, is no longer protected—if an exception occurs there, it won't be caught by this `try` expression.

2.8.4   *after*

Lastly, you can add an `after` section to any `try` expression. Its purpose is to guarantee that a piece of code is executed for the sake of its side effects, no matter what happens in the rest of the `try` expression, before you're about to leave it. This usually involves de-allocating a resource in some way or other—for example, to guarantee that a file is closed, as in this example:

```
{ok, FileHandle} = file:open("foo.txt", [read]),
try
    do_something_with_file(FileHandle)
after
    file:close(FileHandle)
end
```

Here, if the match `{ok,FileHandle}=...` works, you know you've successfully opened the file. You then immediately enter a `try` expression whose `after` section ensures that the file will be closed, even if an exception occurs.

Note that if you have an `after` part, you don't need a `catch` part (but you can of course have that, and an `of` part too if you like). In either case, the `after` part isn't executed until the entire `try` expression is ready, and this includes the situation where a new exception is thrown from the `of` part or from one of the `catch` clauses. If so, that exception is temporarily put on hold while the `after` part runs and is then rethrown. If the `after` part throws an exception, that takes over, and any suspended exception is forgotten.

2.8.5   *Getting a stack trace*

Normally, the execution stack trace isn't included in the part of the exception that you can see; it's stored internally. You can inspect the stack trace of the latest thrown exception of the current process by calling the built-in function `erlang:get_stacktrace()`.

The *stack trace* is a list, in reverse order (last call first), of the calls nearest the top of the stack when the exception occurred. Each function is represented as `{Module, Function, Args}`, where `Module` and `Function` are atoms, and `Args` is either the arity of the function or the list of arguments to the call, depending on what information was available at the time. Typically, only the topmost call might have an argument list.

Note that if you call `erlang:get_stacktrace()` and get an empty list, it means that no exception has been caught by this process yet.

2.8.6   *Rethrowing*

It may happen that you need to examine an exception more closely before you decide whether to catch it. Although this is unusual, you can then catch it first and rethrow it if necessary, using the built-in function `erlang:raise(Class, Reason, Stacktrace)`. Here, `Class` must be one of `error`, `exit`, or `throw`, and `Stacktrace` should be what you got from `erlang:get_stacktrace()`. For example:

```
try
  do_something()
catch
    Class:Reason ->
        Trace = erlang:get_stacktrace(),
        case analyze_exc(Class, Reason) of
            true  -> handle_exc(Class, Reason, Trace);
            false -> erlang:raise(Class, Reason, Trace)
        end
end
```

Here, you catch *any* exception, analyze it, and either handle it or rethrow it. But this is both messy and inefficient (because it requires creating the symbolic stack trace as a list of tuples) and should only be done if you see no better solution.

2.8.7 *Plain old catch*

Before `try` expressions were added to the language, there was `catch`. You'll see a lot of this in older code, because it was the only way of handling exceptions. It works like this: `catch Expression` evaluates `Expression` (which can be any expression); and if it produces a result (doesn't throw an exception), you get that result. Otherwise, if there is an exception, it's caught and presented as the result of the `catch`, using different conventions depending on the exception class. This shell dialog demonstrates the different cases:

```
1> catch 2+2.
4
2> catch throw(foo).
foo
3> catch exit(foo).
{'EXIT',foo}
4> catch foo=bar.
{'EXIT',{{badmatch,bar},[{erl_eval,expr,3}]}}
```

In brief, for `throw` you get the thrown term as it is; for `exit` you get the reason in a tagged tuple (`'EXIT'` is an atom in all uppercase, to be hard to fake by mistake); and for `error`, you get it tagged and packed up along with the stack trace. This may look handy, but there is a lot of confusion going on that makes it hard or impossible to tell exactly what has happened and how to proceed. You should avoid plain `catch`, but you'll likely need to understand what it's doing when you see it in older code.

2.9 *List comprehensions*

A *comprehension* is a compact notation for describing operations on sets or sequences of items (like lists). You may already know it from ordinary mathematical set notation, where, for example, $\{x \mid x \in N, x > 0\}$ is read as "all values x such that x comes from the natural numbers (denoted by N), and x is greater than zero"—in other words, all positive natural numbers.

If you're not already familiar with set notation, take a close look at this example, and you'll quickly see how it works. The vertical bar | separates the *template* part, which describes how the individual elements are made up, from the *generators and conditions* part that specifies what the sources for elements are and what restrictions you have. In this example, the template is *x*, you have a generator that says "for all values *x* in *N*," and a condition that only those *x* that are greater than zero may be part of the result. Pretty simple stuff, really, but it's an efficient way of expressing these kinds of operations.

2.9.1   *List comprehension notation*

Erlang is a programming language, and not pure mathematics. You can use the same ideas in your notation, but you must be more concrete. In particular, the order of elements becomes more important, as well as what data structures you use. In Erlang, the first choice for representing a sequence of items is of course a *list*, so you get a *list comprehension*. The notation must be adapted a bit. For example, if you have an existing list of integers, both positive and negative, you can easily create a new list containing only the positive ones (preserving their relative order in the list), like this:

```
[ X || X <- ListOfIntegers, X > 0 ]
```

Note that you must use double vertical bars ||, because the single vertical bar is already used for plain list cells. Apart from that, you write [...] as usual for a list. You don't have ∈ on your keyboard, so a left arrow <- is used to denote a generator; anything else to the right of the || that's not a generator must be a conditional, such as X > 0. The template part can be any expression and can use any variables that are bound to the right of the vertical bars (such as X, which is bound by the generator) or that are bound outside the list comprehension.

Furthermore, if you have more than one generator in the comprehension, it will cause it to go through all combinations of elements, as if you had nested loops. This is rarely useful, but on occasion it can turn out to be what you need.

2.9.2   *Mapping, filtering, and pattern matching*

A single list comprehension can perform any combination of *map* and *filter* operations, where *map* means you perform some operation on the elements before you put them in the resulting list. For example, the following list comprehension selects only positive even numbers from the source list (rem is the remainder operation) and squares them:

```
[ math:pow(X,2) || X <- ListOfIntegers, X > 0, X rem 2 == 0 ]
```

But the greatest power comes via pattern matching. In a generator, the left side of the <- arrow doesn't have to be a variable—it can be any pattern, like in a match operation (=). This means generators already have a built-in condition: *only those elements that match the pattern are considered*; any others are silently skipped. Furthermore, patterns let you extract parts of the elements for use in conditions or in the template section. For example, assume that you have a list of tuples representing geometric shapes, as in the `area` function of section 2.5.4. You can then select, say, only those rectangles whose area is at least 10 (and no other shapes) and create a corresponding list of areas, like this:

```
[ {area, H*W} || {rectangle, H, W} <- Shapes, H*W >= 10 ]
```

You should learn to use list comprehensions when you can. Apart from being efficient, they're generally the most compact and readable way of expressing this type of operation.

2.10 *Bit syntax and bitstring comprehensions*

We introduced binaries and general bitstrings in section 2.2.2, but we only showed examples of how to create plain binaries (whose length in bits is divisible by 8—that is, that can be viewed as a sequence of whole bytes). But in modern Erlang, bitstrings can be of any length. The so-called *bit syntax* allows you to form new bitstrings of exactly the size and layout you want; conversely, it can be used in patterns to match and extract segments from a bitstring (for example, binary data read from a file or from a socket). In combination with *comprehensions*, this notation becomes extremely powerful.

2.10.1 *Building a bitstring*

A bitstring is written as `<<Segment1, ..., SegmentN>>`, with zero or more segment specifiers between the double less-than/greater-than delimiters. The total length of the bitstring, in bits, is exactly the sum of the lengths of the segments.

A segment specifier can be on one of the following forms:

```
Data
Data:Size
Data/TypeSpecifiers
Data:Size/TypeSpecifiers
```

`Data` must be an integer, a floating-point number, or another bitstring. You can specify the size of the segment as an integer number of units, and you can specify the segment type, which decides what `Data` is expected to be and how it should be encoded or decoded. For example, a simple binary like `<<1,2,3>>` has three segments that all have plain integers as data and no size or type specifiers. In this case, the type defaults to be `integer`, and the default size for integers is 1. The unit for the `integer` type is 8 bits, so each segment is encoded as an 8-bit unsigned byte. Similarly, `<<"abc">>` is shorthand for `<<$a,$b,$c>>`—that is, a sequence of 8-bit integer character codes (in Latin-1). If an integer needs more bits than the segment has room for, it's truncated to fit, so `<<254,255,256,257>>` becomes `<<254,255,0,1>>`.

The type of a segment depends only on what you've specified; it doesn't depend on what the `Data` happens to be from one time to the next. You may think that would be handy, but it goes against the fail-early philosophy and could land you in some nasty situations—for example, with bogus binary data written to a file. This means that you can't, for instance, concatenate two bitstrings like this:

```
B1 = <<1,2>>,
B2 = <<3,4>>,
<<B1, B2>>
```

because, by default, it's assumed that `B1` and `B2` are integers. But if you say that `B1` and `B2` are bitstrings, it works:

```
<<B1/bits, B2/bits>>
```

This yields `<<1,2,3,4>>`, as you want.

You can control the details of the encoding and decoding of a segment through the `TypeSpecifiers` part (after the `/`). It consists of one or more atoms separated by a hyphen (`-`), as in `integer-unsigned-big`. The order of the atoms isn't significant. The current set of specifiers you can use is as follows:

- `integer, float, binary, bytes, bitstring, bits, utf8, utf16, utf32`
- `signed, unsigned`
- `big, little, native`

As a special case, you can include `unit:`*Integer*. These specifiers can be combined in various ways, picking at most one from each group in the previous list. (`bits` is an alias for `bitstring`, and `bytes` is an alias for `binary`). For the types `integer`, `float`, and `bitstring`, the size unit is 1 bit, whereas for `binary` the unit is 8 bits (whole bytes).

There are a lot more details that we don't have room to go through here, so you'll need to check up on the official documentation or read another book about Erlang programming if you want to start working with binaries. This should be enough to give you the idea.

UTF encodings in bitstrings

As a recent addition to Erlang, you can specify one of `utf8`, `utf16`, and `utf32` as the type of a bitstring segment, as you probably noted in the earlier list. These let you work with UTF-encoded characters in bitstrings. For example:

```
<<"Motörhead"/utf8>>
```

You can't specify a size for such a segment, because the size is determined by the input. In this example, the result uses 10 bytes to encode 9 characters.

2.10.2 *Pattern matching with bit syntax*

Just as you can both construct and deconstruct tuples with the same syntax, you can deconstruct the data in a bitstring by using the same bit syntax. This makes parsing funny file formats and protocol data a much simpler task and is much less error prone than doing manual bit shifting and masking. To show a classic example, here is how you can parse the contents of an IP packet header, using a pattern in a function clause:

```
ipv4(<<Version:4, IHL:4, ToS:8, TotalLength:16,
    Identification:16, Flags:3, FragOffset:13,
    TimeToLive:8, Protocol:8, Checksum:16,
    SourceAddress:32, DestinationAddress:32,
    OptionsAndPadding:((IHL-5)*32)/bits,
    RemainingData/bytes >>) when Version =:= 4 ->
    ...
```

Any incoming packet that is large enough to match, and whose `Version` field is 4, is decoded into these variables; most are decoded as integers, except for `OptionsAnd-Padding` (a bitstring whose length depends on the previously decoded IHL field) and the `RemainingData` segment, which contains all the data following the header. Extracting a binary from another like this doesn't involve copying the data, so it's a cheap operation.

2.10.3 *Bitstring comprehensions*

The idea of list comprehensions, which exists in many functional programming languages, has been extended in Erlang to work with the bit syntax. A *bitstring comprehension* looks much like a list comprehension but is enclosed in `<<...>>` rather than in `[...]`. For example, if you have a list of small numbers, all between 0 and 7, you can pack them into a bitstring using only 3 bits per number, like this:

```
<< <<X:3>> || X <- [1,2,3,4,5,6,7] >>
```

This returns a bitstring that the shell prints as `<<41,203,23:5>>`. Note the `23:5` at the end—it means the total length is 8 + 8 + 5 = 21 bits, which makes sense because you had 7 elements in the input list.

How can you decode such a bitstring? With another bitstring comprehension, of course! The difference is that you need to use a generator written with a `<=` to pick out parts of the input (which is now a bitstring), instead of `<-`, which only picks elements from lists:

```
<< <<X:8>> || <<X:3>> <= <<41,203,23:5>> >>
```

This yields the binary `<<1,2,3,4,5,6,7>>`, so you've successfully recoded a 3-bit-per-number format into an 8-bit-per-number format. But if you want the result as a list, not as another bitstring? You can use a list comprehension with a bitstring generator!

```
[ X || <<X:3>> <= <<41,203,23:5>> ]
```

This produces the corresponding list `[1,2,3,4,5,6,7]`. We invite you to play a little with the bit syntax in the shell to get the hang of it. You can do many interesting things with the bit syntax and a little creativity.

2.11 *Record syntax*

In order to keep down the amount of strange syntax in the previous sections, we've postponed explaining one of the more important parts of Erlang: the record syntax.

Tuples are the main building blocks in Erlang for most kinds of structured data; but software-engineering wise, they aren't as flexible as we'd like. Imagine that you write a whole program (perhaps many modules) around the fact that your representation of a customer (for example) is a tuple with five elements. If you then find that you need to add another field, which is pretty likely as these things happen, you'll be forced to go through all the code and edit every occurrence of such tuples, both where they're created and in any patterns that match on them. Not to mention that this process is error prone: what if you write a 4-tuple instead of a 5-tuple somewhere, or forget to add a field to one instance when you update all the others? To remedy this problem (but without sacrificing the speed and small memory footprint that you get with tuples), the *record syntax* was invented.

2.11.1 Record declarations

The record syntax lets you work with *records*, which are tagged tuples, in a way that avoids most of the problems with adding or removing fields and remembering in which order they occur in the tuple. The first thing you need to do is to write a *record declaration*, which looks like this:

```
-record(customer, {name="<anonymous>", address, phone}).
```

This tells the compiler that you'll be working with 4-tuples (three fields plus the tag), where the first element is always the atom `customer`. The other fields will be in the same order as in the record declaration, so `name` is always the second field.

2.11.2 Creating records

To create a new record tuple, you use some variant of the following syntax:

```
#customer{}
```

```
#customer{phone="55512345"}
```

```
#customer{name="Sandy Claws", address="Christmas Town", phone="55554321"}
```

You always need to give the record name after the #, so the compiler can match it to the record declaration. Within the {...}, you can choose to give values for any of the fields (or none) and in any order. (The compiler will make sure they're ordered as in the declaration.) Those fields that you didn't give values for will be set to the default, which is the atom `undefined` unless you've specified a default value in the declaration.

2.11.3 Record fields and pattern matching

Assume that you bind the variable R to the second of the previous examples. You can now access the individual fields by using a dot notation:

```
R#customer.name      →    "<anonymous>"
R#customer.address   →    undefined
R#customer.phone     →    "55512345"
```

As before, you need to specify the record name in order to tell the compiler, "Treat the tuple in R as a customer record." But the most common way of extracting fields from a record is to use pattern matching. The following function takes a customer record as input and checks that the phone number isn't `undefined`:

```
print_contact(#customer{name=Name, address=Addr, phone=Phone})
        when Phone =/= undefined ->
    io:format("Contact: ~s at ~s.~n", [Name, Phone]).
```

It's like matching on a tuple, except that you don't need to care about the exact number of fields and their order. If you add or reorder fields in the record declaration, you can recompile the code, and it will work as it did before.

2.11.4 *Updating record fields*

As we've pointed out before, you don't update parts of existing data structures in Erlang, at least not in place. What you do is create a new, slightly modified copy of the old data. For instance, if you want to update a tuple with four elements, you create a new 4-tuple and copy those elements that should be kept unchanged. That may sound expensive, but you never copy more than a single word per element—a shallow copy. And tuple creation is a fast operation: Erlang is optimized for creating (and recycling) large amounts of small tuples and list cells at high speed—they're scratchpad data as much as they're used to represent more permanent data structures.

The notation for updating fields is similar to that for creating new records, except that you need to say where the old record comes from. Suppose you have the second customer record from the previous section in R. The following creates a copy of R with the name and address fields updated:

```
R#customer{name="Jack Skellington", address="Hallowe'en"}
```

It's important to keep in mind that R itself isn't changed in any way by this, and you can't reassign R to hold the new value; if you want to put it in a variable, you must use another name, such as R1. On the other hand, if it turns out that no part of the program is using the tuple in R anymore after the creation of R1, then R will be recycled automatically. (A clever compiler can sometimes see that it's safe to reuse the existing tuple in R to create the new R1, if it's going to become garbage anyway after that.)

2.11.5 *Where to put the record declarations*

For records that are only used within a single module, you usually write the record declarations at the top of the module, along with the export declarations and similar things that belong in the header of the module. But if you need to use the exact same record declaration in several modules, you have to do something different. Because you don't want multiple definitions of the same records spread over several source files (making it hard to remember to keep them all in sync), you should put those definitions that need to be shared in a separate so-called *header file*, which will then be read by all the modules that need it. This is handled by the preprocessor, which is the next topic.

2.12 *Preprocessing and include files*

Erlang has a preprocessor similar to the one used in C and C++, which means it's a *token-level* preprocessor. It works on the sequence of tokens produced by splitting the source file into separate words and symbols, rather than on the characters of the text. This makes it easier to reason about but also limits what it can do.

The preprocessor always runs as part of the compilation process and performs three important tasks: *macro expansion, file inclusion*, and *conditional compilation*. We look at these in order.

2.12.1 *Defining and using macros*

You can define a macro with or without parameters using the `define` directive, as in the following examples:

```
-define(PI,  3.14).
-define(pair(X,Y),  {X, Y}).
```

Macro names can be written as Erlang variables or atoms, but it's traditional to use all-uppercase for constants and mostly lowercase for other macros. To expand a macro at some point in the source code (following its definition), you must prefix it with a question mark:

```
circumference(Radius) -> Radius * 2 * ?PI.
```

```
pair_of_pairs(A, B, C, D) -> ?pair( ?pair(A, B), ?pair(C, D) ).
```

This code is expanded to the following, just before proper compilation starts:

```
circumference(Radius) -> Radius * 2 * 3.14.
```

```
pair_of_pairs(A, B, C, D) -> { {A, B}, {C, D} }.
```

Macros aren't a substitute for using proper functions but are an escape route when normal functions won't do for the kind of abstraction you want to perform: when you need to be absolutely sure the expansion is performed at compile time, or the syntax doesn't allow you to use a function call.

UNDEFINING A MACRO

The `undef` directive can be used to remove a macro definition (if there is one). For example, after the following lines

```
-define(foo, false).
-undef(foo).
-define(foo, true).
```

the `foo` macro is defined to `true`.

USEFUL PREDEFINED MACROS

The preprocessor predefines certain macros for your convenience, and the most useful of them is probably the `MODULE` macro. It always expands to the name of the module that is being compiled, in the form of an atom. You can also use the `FILE` and `LINE` macros to get the current position in the source file. For example:

```erlang
current_pos() -> [{module, ?MODULE}, {file, ?FILE}, {line, ?LINE}].
```

Macro definitions, like record declarations (as we mentioned in section 2.11), should be placed in a header file when the same definition needs to be shared between multiple source files. This brings us to the next feature.

2.12.2 Include files

An Erlang source code file can include another file by using an *include directive*, which has the following form:

```erlang
-include("filename.hrl").
```

The text of the included file is read by the preprocessor and is inserted at the point of the include directive. Such files generally contain only declarations, not functions; and because they're typically included at the top of the source file for the module, they're known as *header files*. By convention, an Erlang header file has the file name extension .hrl.

To locate a file specified by a directive such as `-include("some_file.hrl").`, the Erlang compiler searches in the current directory for the file called `some_file.hrl`, and also in any other directories that are listed in the *include path*. You can add directories to the include path by using the `-I` flag to `erlc`, or by an option `{i,Directory}` to the `c(...)` shell function, as in

```erlang
1> c("src/my_module", [ {i, "../include/"} ]).
```

THE INCLUDE_LIB DIRECTIVE

If your code depends on a header file that is part of some other Erlang application or library, you have to know where that application is installed so you can add its header file directory to the include path. In addition, the install path may contain a version number, so if you upgraded that application, you might need to update the include path as well. Erlang has a special include directive for avoiding most of this trouble: `include_lib`. For example:

```erlang
-include_lib("kernel/include/file.hrl").
```

This looks for the file relative to the locations of the installed applications that the Erlang system knows about (in particular, all the standard libraries that came with the Erlang distribution). For example, the path to the `kernel` application could be something like C:\Program Files\erl5.6.5\lib\kernel-2.12.5. The `include_lib` directive matches this path (stripping the version number) to the leading kernel/ part of the file name and looks for an include subdirectory containing file.hrl. Even if the Erlang installation is upgraded, your source code doesn't need to be modified.

2.12.3 *Conditional compilation*

Conditional compilation means that certain parts of the program may be skipped by the compiler, depending on some condition. This is often used to create different versions of the program, such as a special version for debugging. The following preprocessor directives control which parts of the code may be skipped, and when:

```
-ifdef(MacroName).
```

```
-ifndef(MacroName).
```

```
-else.
```

```
-endif.
```

As the names indicate, `ifdef` and `ifndef` test whether a macro is defined or isn't defined. For each `ifdef` or `ifndef`, there must be a corresponding `endif` to end the conditional section. Optionally, a conditional section may be divided in two halves by an `else`. For example, the following code exports the function `foo/1` only if the DEBUG macro is defined (to any value):

```
-ifdef(DEBUG).
-export([foo/1]).
-endif.
```

To control this from the command line or from your build system, you can define a macro by giving an option `{d,MacroName,Value}` to the shell c function, or you can pass the option `-Dname=value` to the `erlc` command. Because the macro value doesn't matter here, `true` is usually used.

Because Erlang's parser works on one period-terminated declaration (called a *form*) at a time, *you can't use conditional compilation in the middle of a function definition*, because the period after the `ifdef` would be read as the end of the function. Instead, you can conditionally define a macro, and use the macro within the function, like this:

```
-ifdef(DEBUG).
-define(show(X), io:format("The value of X is: ~w.~n", [X])).
-else.
-define(show(X), ok).
-endif.

foo(A) ->
    ?show(A),
    ...
```

If this is compiled with DEBUG defined, the `foo` function prints the value of A on the console before it continues with whatever the function is supposed to do. If not, the first thing in the function will be the atom ok, which is a constant; and because it isn't used for anything, the compiler will optimize it away as if it hadn't been there.

2.13 *Processes*

In chapter 1, we introduced processes, messages, and the concept of process links and signals; and we presented process identifiers (pids) in section 2.2.7. In this section, we go through the most important things you should know about working with Erlang processes.

2.13.1 *Operating on processes*

In section 1.1.4, we showed how to spawn a process, send a message from one process to another with !, and extract a message from the mailbox using `receive`. At that point, we didn't explain further about modules, function names, and function arities, but by now that stuff should be pretty clear to you.

SPAWNING AND LINKING

There are two types of spawn functions: the ones that take a (nullary) fun as the starting point for the new process, and the ones that take a module name, a function name, and a list of arguments:

```
Pid = spawn(fun() -> do_something() end)
Pid = spawn(Module, Function, ListOfArgs)
```

The latter require that the named function is exported from its module, and initial data can only be passed through the argument list. On the other hand, they always look up the latest version of the module and are generally better for starting a process on a remote machine that may not have the exact same version of the module as you do on your local machine. For example:

```
Pid = spawn(Node, Module, Function, ListOfArgs)
```

There is also a version named `spawn_opt(...)` that takes a list of additional options, as in

```
Pid = spawn_opt(fun() -> do_something() end, [monitor])
```

One of the options you can give to `spawn_opt(...)` is `link`. There is also a simple function alias for this:

```
Pid = spawn_link(...)
```

Using `spawn_link(...)` ensures that the link is created along with the new process as an atomic operation, preventing race conditions that can occur if you spawn the process first and try to link to it afterward using `link(Pid)`.

All these spawn functions return the process identifier of the new process, so that the parent process can communicate with it. But the new process doesn't know its parent process unless this information is passed to it somehow.

When a process wants to find its own pid, it can call the built-in function `self()`. For example, the following code spawns a child process that knows its parent:

```
Parent = self(),
Pid = spawn(fun() -> myproc:init(Parent) end)
```

This assumes that `myproc:init/1` is the entry point for the child process that you want to start, and that it takes a parameter that is the parent process ID. Note in particular that the call to `self()` must be made outside of `fun...end`, because otherwise it will be executed by the new child process (which is definitely not its own parent). This is why you capture the parent pid first and pass it in to the child process via a variable. (Recall what we said about closures in section 2.7.2; this spawn function gets a closure and runs it in a new process.)

MONITORING A PROCESS

There is also an alternative to links, called *monitors*. These are a kind of unidirectional link and allow a process to monitor another without affecting it.

```
Ref = monitor(process, Pid)
```

If the monitored process identified by `Pid` dies, a message containing the unique reference `Ref` is sent to the process that set up the monitor.

THROWING AN EXCEPTION TO END THE PROCESS

The `exit` class of exception is meant for terminating the running process. This is thrown using the BIF `exit/1`:

```
exit(Reason)
```

Unless this is caught by the process, it will terminate and pass on `Reason` as part of its exit signal to any processes that are linked to it.

SENDING AN EXPLICIT EXIT SIGNAL TO A PROCESS

In addition to the signals sent automatically when processes die unexpectedly, it's also possible to send an exit signal explicitly from one process to another. The processes don't have to be linked for this:

```
exit(Pid, Reason)
```

Note that this uses `exit/2`, not `exit/1`—they're different functions (unfortunately, both called `exit`). This doesn't terminate the sender, but rather the receiver. If `Reason` is the atom `kill`, the signal can't be trapped by the receiver.

SETTING THE TRAP_EXIT FLAG

By default, a process dies if it gets an exit signal from another linked process. To prevent this and trap exit signals, the process can set its `trap_exit` flag:

```
process_flag(trap_exit, true)
```

Incoming exit signals will then be converted to harmless messages. The only exception is untrappable signals (`kill`).

2.13.2 *Receiving messages, selective receive*

The receiving process can extract messages from the mailbox queue using a `receive` expression. Although incoming messages are queued up strictly in order of arrival, the receiver can decide which message to extract and leave the others in the mailbox for later. This ability to selectively ignore messages that are currently irrelevant (for example, may have arrived early) is a key feature of Erlang's process communication. The general form for `receive` is

```
receive
    Pattern1 when Guard1 -> Body1;
    ...
    PatternN when GuardN -> BodyN
after Time ->
    TimeoutBody
end
```

The `after...` section is optional; if omitted, the `receive` never times out. Otherwise, `Time` must be an integer number of milliseconds or the atom `infinity`. If `Time` is 0, the receive will never block; in all other cases, if no matching message is found in the process's mailbox, the `receive` will wait for such a message to arrive or the timeout to occur, whichever happens first. The process will be suspended while it's waiting and will only wake up in order to inspect new messages.

Each time a `receive` is entered, it starts by looking at the oldest message (at the head of the queue), tries to match it against the clauses as in a `case` expression, and, if no clause matches it, moves on to the next message. If the pattern of a clause matches the current message, and the guard succeeds (if there is one), the message is removed from the mailbox, and the corresponding clause body is evaluated. If no message is found and a timeout occurs, the timeout body is evaluated instead, and the mailbox remains unchanged.

2.13.3 *Registered processes*

On each Erlang system, there is a local process registry—a simple name service, where processes can be registered. The same name can be used by only one process at a time, which means this can only be used for singleton processes: typically, system-like services, of which there is, at most, one at a time on each runtime system. If you start the Erlang shell and call the built-in function `registered()`, you see something like the following:

```
1> registered().
[rex,kernel_sup,global_name_server,standard_error_sup,
 inet_db,file_server_2,init,code_server,error_logger,
 user_drv,application_controller,standard_error,
 kernel_safe_sup,global_group,erl_prim_loader,user]
2>
```

A bunch, as you can see. An Erlang system is much like an operating system in itself, with a set of important system services running. (One is even called `init`...) You can find the pid currently registered under a name using the built-in `whereis` function:

```
2> whereis(user).
<0.24.0>
3>
```

You can even send messages directly to a process using only the registered name:

```
1> init ! {stop, stop}.
```

(Did you try it? It's a dirty trick, relying on knowledge about the format of messages between system processes. There are no guarantees that it won't change some day.)

If you start your own processes, you can register them with the `register` function:

```
1> Pid = spawn(timer, sleep, [60000]).
<0.34.0>
2> register(fred, Pid).
true
3> whereis(fred).
<0.34.0>
4> whereis(fred).
undefined
5>
```

(Note that in this example, the process you start will be finished after 60 seconds, and the name will then automatically go back to being undefined again.)

Furthermore, to talk to a registered process that you think should exist on another Erlang node, you can write

```
6> {some_node_name, some_registered_name} ! Message.
```

One major point with registered processes is this: Suppose a registered process dies, and the service it performed is restarted. The new process will then have a different process identifier. Instead of individually telling every process in the system that the service `rex` (for example) has a new pid, you can update the process registry. (But there is a period during which the name doesn't point anywhere, until the service has been restarted and reregistered).

2.13.4 *Delivery of messages and signals*

The messages sent between Erlang processes with the ! operator are a special case of a more general system of signals. The *exit signals* that are sent from a dying process to its linked neighbors are the other main kind of signal; but there are a few others that aren't directly visible to the programmer, such as the *link requests* that are sent when you try to link two processes. (Imagine that they're on different machines, and you'll see why they need to be signals. Because the link is bidirectional, both sides must know about the link.)

For all signals, there are a couple of basic delivery guarantees:

- If a process P1 sends out two signals S1 and S2, in that order, to the same destination process P2 (regardless of what else it does between S1 and S2, and how far apart in time the signals are sent), then they will arrive in the same relative order at P2 (if both arrive). This means, among other things, that an exit signal can never overtake the last message sent before the process dies, and that a message can never overtake a link request. This is fundamental for process communication in Erlang.

- A best effort attempt is made to deliver all signals. Within the same Erlang runtime system, there is never a danger of losing messages in transit between two processes. But between two Erlang systems connected over a network, it may happen that a message is dropped if the network connection is lost (somewhat depending on the transport protocol). If the connection is then restored, it's possible that S2 in the previous example will eventually arrive, but S1 will be lost.

For the most part, this means you don't have to think much about message ordering and delivery—things tend to work much as you expect.

2.13.5 *The process dictionary*

Each process has, as part of its state, its own private *process dictionary*, a simple hash table where you can store Erlang terms using any values as keys. The built-in functions `put(Key, Value)` and `get(Key)` are used to store and retrieve terms. We won't say much about the process dictionary except give you some reasons why you should avoid using it, no matter how tempting it may seem:

- The simplest point is that it makes programs harder to reason about. You can no longer look at the code and get the whole story. Instead, it suddenly depends on which process is running the code and what its current state is.

- A more important point is that it makes it hard or impossible to do a handover from one process to the next, where you do half of the work in one process and the rest in another. The new process won't have the correct data in its own dictionary unless you make sure to pack it up and ship it from the first process to the second.

- If you write some kind of library, and you use the process dictionary to store certain information between calls from the client (much like a web server uses cookies), you force the client to use a single process for the duration of the session. If the client tries to call your API from a second process, it won't have the necessary context.

Using the process dictionary can in some cases be justified, but in general, there is a better solution to the problem of storing data (that even lets you share the information between processes if you like). It goes by the strange name of ETS tables.

2.14 *ETS tables*

ETS stands for Erlang Term Storage. An ETS table, then, is a table containing Erlang terms (that is, any Erlang data) that can also be shared between processes. But that sounds like it goes against the fundamental ideas of referential transparency and avoiding sharing. Are we suddenly smuggling in destructive updates through the back door? Two words: process semantics.

2.14.1 *Why ETS tables work like they do*

The main design philosophy behind the ETS tables in Erlang is that such tables should look and feel almost exactly as if they were separate processes. They could have been implemented as processes and still have the same interface. In practice, though, they're implemented in C as part of the Erlang runtime system, so they're lightweight and fast, and the interface functions are BIFs. This extra focus on efficiency is warranted because so many other things in Erlang are built on top of these ETS tables.

You should still avoid sharing data (when you can), and you particularly want to avoid the situation where things unexpectedly change behind someone's back. On the other hand, if you can implement a form of storage based on the normal semantics of processes and message passing, you know that nothing fundamentally fishy is going on, so why shouldn't you use it? In particular when it's something you'll always need in one form or another: efficient hash tables for storing data.

An ETS table basically works like a simplistic database server: it's isolated from everything else and holds information that is used by many. The difference compared to arrays in Java, C, or similar is that the clients are aware that they're talking to a separate entity with a life of its own and that what they read right now may not be what they read from the same table index later. But at the same time, they can be assured that the data they *have* read isn't subject to mysterious changes. If you look up an entry in the table, you get the currently stored tuple. Even if someone immediately afterward updates that position in the table with a new tuple, the data you got won't be affected. By comparison, if you look up a stored object in a Java array, it may be possible for another thread to look up the same object moments later and modify it in some way that will affect you. In Erlang, we try to keep it obvious when we're referring to data that is subject to change over time and when we're referring to plain immutable data.

2.14.2 *Basics of using ETS tables*

ETS tables are created and manipulated via the standard library `ets` module. To create a new table, use the function `ets:new(Name, Options)`. The name must be given as an atom, and `Options` must be a list. Unless the `named_table` option is specified, the name isn't used for anything in particular (and you can reuse the same name in as many tables as you like); but it can be a useful indicator when you're debugging a system and find a mysterious table lurking somewhere, so it's better to, for instance, use the name of the current module, rather than `table` or `foo`, which won't be of much help.

The function `ets:new/2` returns a table identifier that you can use to perform operations on the table. For example, the following creates a table and stores a couple of tuples:

```
T = ets:new(mytable,[]),
ets:insert(T, {17, hello}),
ets:insert(T, {42, goodbye})
```

Another similarity with databases is that an ETS table only stores rows—that is, tuples. If you want to store any other Erlang data, you need to wrap it in a tuple first. This is because one of the tuple fields is always used as the index in the table, and by default it's the first field. (This can be changed with an option when you create the table.) Thus, you can look up rows in your table by their first elements, like this:

```
ets:lookup(T, 17)
```

This returns [{17, hello}]. But hang on, why is it in a list? Well, a table doesn't need to be a *set* of rows (where every key is unique), which is the default; it can also be a *bag* (where several rows can have the same key, but there can't be two completely identical rows) or even a *duplicate bag*, where there can be several identical rows as well. In those cases, a lookup may return more than one row as the result. In any case, you always get an empty list if no matching row is found.

There is a lot to learn about what you can do with ETS tables. You can specify many parameters when you create them, and many powerful interface functions are available for searching, traversing, and more. You'll meet them again later, in chapter 6.

2.15 *Recursion: it's how you loop*

You may have noted that apart from list comprehensions, there has been a notable lack of iterative constructs in this presentation of the language. This is because Erlang relies on recursive function calls for such things. Although it's not difficult, only different, there are some details and techniques that you should know about, both to make your path easier if you aren't used to this way of thinking and to help you produce solid code that avoids the common pitfalls.

To get started with recursion, let's take something simple, like adding up the numbers from 0 to N. This is easily expressed as follows: to sum the numbers from 0 to N, you take the sum from 0 to N-1, add the number N, and you're done. Unless N is already 0, in which case the sum is 0. Or, as an Erlang function (add it to my_module.erl):

```
sum(0) -> 0;
sum(N) -> sum(N-1) + N.
```

Couldn't be simpler, right? Never had to do recursion before? Don't worry; it's a natural concept for a human. (Reasoning about nested for loops with break and continue and whatnot—now *that* often requires superhuman attention to detail.) But to understand how you can write all kinds of iterative algorithms using recursion, we need to go through some basics. This is important stuff, so please bear with us.

2.15.1 *From iteration to recursion*

All problems that can be expressed recursively can also be written as loops (if you do your own bookkeeping). Which approach you choose is a question of how easy your programming language makes it to write your code depending on the choice, and how efficient the result is. Some languages, like old Basic dialects, Fortran-77, or machine language assembler, don't have any support for recursion as a programming technique. Many, like Pascal, C/C++, Java, and so on, allow you to write recursive functions; but because of limitations and inefficiencies in the implementation, recursion isn't as useful as it could be. This situation is probably what most programmers are used to. But Erlang is different: it *only* uses recursion to create loops, and the implementation is efficient.

A PLAIN OLD LOOP

Sometimes, you start out with a loop-style piece of code (maybe in your head), and you want to implement it in Erlang. Perhaps you have something like the following typical code in C or Java for computing the sum from 0 to n, where n is the input parameter:

```
int sum(int n) {

  int total = 0;
  while (n != 0) {
      total = total + n;
      n = n - 1;
  }
  return total;

}
```

This code is a procedural way of expressing the algorithm: mentally, you can go through the program step by step and see how it keeps changing state until it's finished.

But let's think about how you would *describe* that algorithm to someone else using plain text, as concisely as you can. You'd probably come up with something like this:

1 You have the number N already. Let Total be zero, initially.
2 If N isn't zero yet:
    a Add N to Total.
    b Decrement N by one.
    c Repeat step 2.
3 You're done; the result is in Total.

LOOPING IN A FUNCTIONAL WAY

Now, consider this alternative way of stating step 2:

2 If N isn't zero yet, repeat this same step with
    a Total+N as the new value for Total
    b N-1 as the new value for N

Seen this way, point 2 is a *recursive function* with two parameter variables, N and Total. It doesn't use any other information. On each recursive call, you pass the values for the next iteration, and you can forget the previous values. This way of saying "and then you do the same thing again, but with different values" is a natural way for humans to reason about iteration. (Kids don't usually have a problem with it; it's us grown-ups, perhaps damaged by years of procedural coding, who can find it mind-bending.) Let's see how this step looks if you write it in Erlang, much to the letter:

```
step_two(N, Total) when N =/= 0  ->  step_two(N-1, Total+N) .
```

Pretty readable, don't you think? (Add this function to `my_module.erl`.) Note that you never say `N = N-1` or similar—that doesn't work in Erlang: you can't demand that a number should be the same as itself minus one. Instead, you say "call `step_two` with `N-1` for the new `N` and `Total+N` for the new `Total`." But you're missing something, right? What do you do when you're done? Let's add another clause to this function (and give it a better name):

```
do_sum(N, Total) when N =/= 0 -> do_sum(N-1, Total+N);
do_sum(0, Total) -> Total.
```

This incorporates step 3 from the verbal description into the code. When the first clause no longer matches (when the guard test turns `false`), the second clause is used instead, and all it has to do is return the result that's found in `Total`.

INITIALIZING THE LOOP

Now you have to do something about step 1: giving an initial value of 0 to `Total`. This obviously means calling `do_sum(N, 0)` from somewhere. But where? Well, you have a step zero, which is the problem description: "to compute the sum of the numbers from 0 to *N*." That would be `do_sum(N)`, right? To compute `do_sum(N)`, you have to compute `do_sum(N, 0)`, or

```
do_sum(N) -> do_sum(N, 0).
```

Note what you're doing here: you're creating one function called `do_sum/1` (note the period that ends the definition) that takes a single argument. It calls your other function `do_sum/2`, which takes two arguments. Recall that to Erlang, these are completely different functions. In a case like this, the one with fewer arguments acts as a front end, whereas the other shouldn't be directly accessed by users; hence, you should only put `do_sum/1` in the export list of the module. (We named these functions `do_sum` so they don't clash with the `sum` function from the start of this chapter. You should try typing in both and check that `sum/1` and `do_sum/1` give the same results for the same values of `N`.)

FINAL TOUCHES

Let's summarize this two-part implementation and improve it a little:

```
do_sum(N) -> do_sum(N, 0).

do_sum(0, Total) -> Total;
do_sum(N, Total) -> do_sum(N-1, Total+N).
```

Can you see what happens here? Rather that following the literal translation from the text that says "*N* is not zero" in the recursive case, you change the order of the clauses so that the *base case* (the clause that doesn't do any recursion) is tested first each time around. For this particular algorithm, that makes the code even simpler: in the first clause, try to match `N` against 0. If it doesn't match, then `N` isn't zero, so you can use the second case without any guard test.

That was a long section, but we still have some postmortem to do, to help you understand a couple of important points and give names to the techniques you just used. We start by discussing the two kinds of recursion used in `sum` and `do_sum`.

2.15.2 *Understanding tail recursion*

Recursive calls can be divided into two categories: *tail recursive* and *non-tail recursive* (or *body recursive* as they're sometimes called). The function sum at the start of the chapter is an example of a non-tail recursive function (it contained a non-tail recursive call). In many other programming languages, this is the only kind of recursion you ever think about, because in other cases you typically use some kind of loop construct instead.

But the function do_sum/2, which you got from reasoning about loops, is a *tail recursive function.* All its recursive calls are so-called *tail calls.* The thing about tail calls is that they can easily be spotted; in particular, the compiler can always tell by looking at the code whether a call is a tail call or not, so it can treat them specially.

What is this difference? It's that a tail call is one where there is nothing left for the function to do when that call is done (except return). Compare the bodies of these two function clauses of sum and do_sum, respectively:

```
sum(N) -> sum(N-1) + N.

do_sum(N, Total) -> do_sum(N-1, Total+N).
```

In sum, after the call to sum(N-1) is done, there is still some work left to do before it can return: namely, adding N. On the other hand, in do_sum, when the call to do_sum(N-1, Total+N) is done, no more work is needed—the value of that recursive call is the value that should be returned. *Whenever that is the case, the call is a tail call, or "last call."* It doesn't matter if the call is recursive (back to the same function again) or not—that's a special case, but it's the most important one. Can you spot the last call in the body of sum? (That's right, it's the call to +.)

YOU CAN RELY ON TAIL CALL OPTIMIZATION

You're probably aware that behind the scenes, each process uses a *stack* to keep track of what it needs to go back and do later while it's running the program (such as "remember to go back to this spot and add *N* afterward"). The stack is a last-in-first-out data structure, like a heap of notes stacked on top of each other; and of course, if you keep adding more things to remember, you'll run out of memory. That's not a good thing if you want your server to run forever, so how can Erlang use only recursive calls for loops? Doesn't that add more stuff to the stack on each call? The answer is no, because Erlang guarantees *tail call optimization.*

Tail call optimization means that when the compiler sees that a call is a tail call (the last thing that needs to be done before returning), it can generate code to throw away the information about the current call from the stack *before* the tail call is performed. Basically, the current call has no more real work to do, so it says to the function that it's about to tail call: "Hey! When you're finished, hand over your result directly to my parent. I'm going to retire now." Hence, *tail calls don't make the stack grow.* (As a special case, if the tail call is a recursive call back to the *same* function, it can reuse much of the info on top of the stack rather than throwing away the note to re-create it.) Essentially, a tail call becomes "clean up if needed, and then jump."

Because of this, tail recursive functions can run forever without using up the stack, *and* they can be as efficient as a `while` loop.

2.15.3 *Accumulator parameters*

If you compare the behaviour of `sum` and `do_sum` earlier, for the same number `N`, `sum` will do half of the work counting down to zero and making notes on the stack about what numbers to add later, and the other half going back through the notes adding up the numbers until the stack is empty. `do_sum`, on the other hand, uses a single note on the stack, but keeps replacing it with newer information until it sees that `N` is zero; then it can throw away that note as well and return the value `Total`.

In this example, `Total` is an example of an *accumulator parameter*. Its purpose is to accumulate information in a variable (as opposed to keeping information on the stack and returning to it later). When you write a tail-recursive version of a function, you usually need at least one such extra parameter, and sometimes more. They must be initialized at the start of the loop, so you need one function as a front end and one as the main loop. At the end, they're either part of the final return value or are thrown away if they only hold temporary information during the loop.

2.15.4 *Some words on efficiency*

A tail recursive solution is often more efficient than the corresponding non-tail recursive solution, but not always; it depends a lot on what the algorithm does. Whereas the non-tail recursive function can be sloppy and leave it to the system to handle the stack and remember everything necessary to come back and finish up, the tail recursive version needs to be pedantic and keep everything it needs to complete the job in its accumulator variables, often in the form of data structures like lists. If non-tail recursive functions are drunkards who drop papers behind themselves so they can find their way back home, tail recursive functions are travelers who push everything they own in front of them on a cart. If everything you need for the final result is a number, as in the `sum`/`do_sum` example, the traveler wins big, because the load is light and she can move quickly. But if the result requires tracking essentially the same information that the drunkard gets for free, then the traveler has to do complicated data management and may turn out to be a bit slower.

In general, some problems are more straightforward to solve using a non-tail recursive implementation, whereas some problems are more obvious to solve in a tail-recursive fashion. It can be a nice intellectual exercise to try both variants, but for production code our advice is that if you have a choice between writing a tail recursive or a non-tail recursive implementation of a function, pick the approach that will be more readable and maintainable and that you feel sure that you can implement correctly. When that is working, leave it and go do something else. Don't spend time on premature optimization, in particular at the cost of readability.

Of course, in many cases, the choice is obvious: a function that must loop forever has to be tail recursive. We say that it runs in *constant space*: that is, it doesn't use more memory as time passes, even if it never returns.

2.15.5 *Tips for writing recursive functions*

When you're new to programming with recursion, it can often feel as though your mind goes blank when you try to see how to solve a problem—like you don't know where to start. A couple of methods can help you get going.

To demonstrate, let's use a concrete problem that you'll often need to solve in one form or another: to go through the elements of a data structure. We look at lists here, but the same thinking applies to all recursive data structures, such as trees of tuples. Your task is to *reverse a list*, or rather, to create a new, reversed version of a given list (which can be of any length). For this, you'll obviously have to visit all the elements of the original list, because they need to be in the result.

LOOK AT EXAMPLES

The first thing you can do, if you're unsure about where to start, is to write down a couple of simple examples of inputs and the desired results. For reversed lists, you might have these examples:

```
[]        →  []
[x]       →  [x]
[x,y]     →  [y,x]
[x,y,z]   →  [z,y,x]
```

Trivial, indeed, but having something written down is often better for seeing recurring patterns than mulling it over in your head, and it makes the problem more concrete. It may also make you remember some special cases. If you're into test-driven development, you can write the examples as unit tests right away.

BASE CASES

The next thing you can do is write down the base cases and what should happen in those. (The base cases are those cases that won't require any recursive calls. Usually there is only one such case, but sometimes there are more.) For reversing lists, you can consider the first two of the previous as base cases. Let's write a couple of clauses to get started with your new function (in my_module), rev/1:

```
rev([])  -> [];
rev([X]) -> [X].
```

This is far from complete, but at least you can try it right away for simple cases like rev([]), rev([17]), rev(["hello"]), and rev([foo]). That is, it shouldn't matter what type of elements you have in the list; it's only the order that matters.

After this step, it gets more difficult: you must get the recursive cases right.

THE SHAPE OF THE DATA

You now have to look at the remaining cases and how they're constructed. If you have a list that isn't one of the earlier base cases, it must have at least a couple of elements—that is, it has the shape [A, B, ...]. Recall that a list is made up of list cells: [...|...] (look back at section 2.2.5 for reference if you need to). If you write out the individual cells, your list here has the following form:

```
[ A |  [B | ...]  ]
```

In other words, it has a cell for each element. Suppose you write this down in Erlang as the first clause of your rev function (do this!):

```
rev([A |  [B | TheRest]  ]) -> not_yet_implemented;
```

Recall that the function head is a pattern that will be matched against the actual arguments in order to decompose them (see section 2.5.4). You may get some warnings about unused variables A, B, and TheRest, and the body of the clause doesn't do anything useful except return an atom saying "this isn't implemented yet"; but at least you can check that your rev function now accepts lists with two or more elements.

Next, you need to figure out what to do in this case. It's going to be something with a recursive call to rev, you know that much.

IMAGINE YOU HAVE A WORKING FUNCTION ALREADY

If you can't see a solution from the examples and the structure of the data (this gets much easier after a little practice), or you can almost see it but can't get the details right, then a useful trick is to say to yourself, "I have a working version of this function already, somewhere, and I'm writing a new version that does the same thing (but better)." While you're working on your new function, you're allowed to use the old one for experimenting.

Suppose you try to think like this: you have a function old_rev/1 that you can use. Great! To replace not_yet_implemented with something useful, what could you do? You have the variables A, B, and TheRest, and you want to end up with the same list only backward. If you could reverse TheRest (using old_rev) and then put B and A at the end (recall that ++ appends two lists), you should get the correct result, right? Like this:

```
rev([A |  [B | TheRest]  ]) -> old_rev(TheRest) ++ [B, A];
```

That was easy enough. Now, it looks like your function should be computing the right result for all lists, regardless of length. But if it's fully working, that means it's as good as old_rev, so let's use your own rev instead! The entire function then becomes

```
rev([A |  [B | TheRest]  ]) -> rev(TheRest) ++ [B, A];
rev([])   -> [];
rev([X]) -> [X].
```

It works on its own, as you can see if you call my_module:rev([1,2,3,4]). Nice! Next, let's think about how you can know that it will work correctly on all lists.

PROVING TERMINATION

It may be easy to see at a glance that a function must sooner or later terminate—that is, that it won't loop forever, regardless of input. But for a more complicated function, it can be harder to see that it will *always* eventually reach a point where it will return a result.

The main line of reasoning that you can follow to convince yourself that your function will terminate is that of *monotonically decreasing arguments.* This means that, assuming that your base cases are the smallest possible inputs that your function will accept and the recursive cases handle all inputs that are larger than that, then, if each recursive case always passes on a smaller argument to the recursive call than what it got as input, you know that the arguments must therefore eventually end up as small as the base cases, so the function *must* terminate. The thing that should make you suspicious and think twice is if a recursive call could pass on arguments that were as large as the inputs, or larger. (If a function is recursive over several arguments, which happens, then in each step, at least one of these should be getting smaller and none of them should be getting larger.) Of course, arguments that aren't part of the loop condition can be disregarded, such as accumulator parameters.

In the rev example, no lists can be smaller than those in the base cases. And if we look at the recursive case, you see that when you call rev(TheRest) recursively, TheRest will have fewer elements than the list you got as input, which started with A and B. Hence, you're working on successively smaller lists, so you know you can't loop forever.

When you're recursing over numbers, as in the sum example from the start of this chapter, it can be easy to miss the fact that there is no smallest possible integer. If you look back at the definition of sum, you see that the recursive case is always passing on a smaller number than its input, so it must eventually become zero or less. But if it was already smaller than zero to begin with—for example, if you called sum(-1)—it will keep calling itself with -2, -3, -4, and so on, until you run out of memory trying to represent a huge negative number. To prevent this from happening, you can make sure no clause matches if the input is negative, by adding a guard when N > 0 to the recursive case.

You may also need to reinterpret what *small* and *large* mean in the context of your function. For instance, if you recurse over a number N starting at 1 and ending at 100, you need to think of 100 as the smallest case and of N+1 as smaller than N. The important thing is that on each recursive call, you keep moving toward the base cases.

MINIMIZE THE BASE CASES

Although it doesn't do any harm for the functionality to have unnecessarily many base cases, it can be confusing for the next person working on the code. If you have more than one base case, try to see if some of them can be easily eliminated. You started out with two: [] and [X], because it seemed easiest. But if you look at what [X] means in terms of list cells, you see that it can be written as

```
[ X | [] ]
```

And because `rev` already can handle the empty list, you see that you could handle `rev([X])` by doing `rev([])` `++` `[X]`, even if it looks a little redundant. But that means you don't need two separate cases for lists of one element and lists of two or more elements. You can join those two rules into a single recursive case, to give a cleaner solution:

```
rev([X | TheRest]) -> rev(TheRest) ++ [X];
rev([]) -> [].
```

(Note that the order of these clauses doesn't matter: a list is either empty or it isn't, so only one clause can match. But it's useless to check for empty lists first, because if you recurse over a list of 100 elements, it will be nonempty 100 times and empty once.)

RECOGNIZING QUADRATIC BEHAVIOUR

So, you have a working function that reverses a list. All fine? Not quite. If the input is a long list, this implementation will take much too long. Why? Because you've run into the dreaded *quadratic time* behaviour. It's quadratic in the sense that if it takes T units of time (for whatever unit you like to measure it in) to run the function on some list, then it will take $4T$ units of time to run it on a list that's twice as long, $9T$ units for a list that's three times as long, and so on. You may not notice it for shorter lists, but it can quickly get out of hand. Say you have a function that gets a list of all the files in a directory and does something with that list. It's working fine, but you've never tried it on directories with more than 100 files. Doing so took 1/10th of a second, which didn't seem like a problem. But if the algorithm is quadratic in time, and you one day use it on a directory containing 10,000 files (100 times larger than before), that will take 100 x 100 = 10,000 times as long time (over 15 minutes), rather than the 10 seconds it would have taken if the algorithm had been proportional, or linear, in time. Your customers won't be happy.

Why is your implementation of `rev` quadratic in time? Because for each recursive call (once for every element in the list), you also use the `++` operator, which in itself takes time in direct proportion to the length of the list on its left side (if you recall from section 2.2.5). Let's say `++` takes time T if the left list has length 1. In your `rev`, the left side of `++` is the list returned by the recursive call, which has the same length as the input. This means that if you run `rev` on a list of length 100, the first call will take time $100T$, the second $99T$, the third $98T$, and so on, until you're down to 1. (Each call will also take a little time to pick out X and `TheRest` and perform the recursive call, but that's so small in comparison to $100T$ that you can ignore it here.)

What does $100T + 99T + 98T + ... + 2T + 1T$ amount to? It's like the area of a right triangle whose legs have length 100: the area is 100 x 100 / 2, or half of a square of side 100. In general, then, the time for `rev` on a list of length N is proportional to N x N / 2. Because we're mostly interested in how it grows when N gets larger, we say that it's *quadratic*, because it grows like N x N. The divided-by-two factor pales in comparison to the main behaviour of the function (figure 2.3).

Note that this sort of thing can happen in *any language*, using any kind of loop or iteration over some kind of collection; it isn't because of recursion, it's because you have to do something *N* times, and for *each* of those times you do something else that takes time proportional to *N*, so that the times add up in a triangle-like way. The only consolation is that it could be worse: if your algorithm takes *cubic* time, you'll be looking at a 28-hour wait in the previous example. If it takes *exponential* time, waiting probably isn't an option.

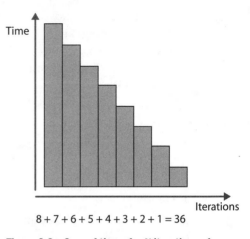

$$8 + 7 + 6 + 5 + 4 + 3 + 2 + 1 = 36$$

Figure 2.3   Sum of times for *N* iterations of a quadratic function = area of triangle

AVOIDING QUADRATIC TIME

What can you do with the rev function to avoid the quadratic-time behaviour? You can't use ++ with the varying list on the left side, at any rate. What if you tried a tail-recursive approach? You go through the list, but at each step, you push all the stuff you need in front of you in the arguments so that when you reach the end of the list, you're finished: there is nothing on the stack to go back to, like you did with do_sum in section 2.15.1. How would that look for recursion over lists? You can use the same basic division into base case and recursive case as rev, but you'll call the new function tailrev, and you'll need an accumulator parameter that will contain the final result when you reach the end, like this:

```
tailrev([X | TheRest], Acc) -> not_yet_implemented;
tailrev([], Acc) -> Acc.
```

Now for the not_yet_implemented part: you want it to do a tail call, so it should have the shape tailrev(TheRest, ...), and the second argument should be something to do with Acc and the element X. You know that a cons operation (adding an element to the left of a list) is a cheap and simple operation to do, and you know you want Acc to become the final reversed list. Suppose you do [X | Acc], adding the element to the left of Acc, basically writing the new list from right to left as you traverse the old list:

```
tailrev([X | TheRest], Acc) -> tailrev(TheRest, [X | Acc]);
tailrev([], Acc) -> Acc.
```

For each element you see, as long as the list isn't yet empty, you tack the element on to the left side of Acc. But what should Acc be initialized to? The easiest way to see this is to look at what should happen with the simplest case that isn't already a base case. Suppose you call tailrev([foo], Acc), to reverse a list of one element. This matches the first clause, binding X to foo and TheRest to [], so the body of the clause becomes tailrev([], [foo | Acc]). In the next step, the base case tailrev([], Acc) matches, and it should return the final Acc. This means the original Acc must be an empty list, so that [foo | Acc] = [foo]. The complete implementation is then the following, with tailrev/1 as the main entry point:

```
tailrev(List) -> tailrev(List, []).

tailrev([X | TheRest], Acc) -> tailrev(TheRest, [X | Acc]);
tailrev([], Acc) -> Acc.
```

Why is this implementation linear in time (in proportion to the length of the list) rather than quadratic? Because for each element of the list, you only perform operations that have fixed cost (such as adding to the left of the list); therefore, if the list has L elements, the total time is L times C, for some small constant C, and the algorithm never blows up in your face like the quadratic version when the input gets big.

LOOK OUT FOR LENGTH

A common beginners' mistake made by many who are used to programming in languages like Java, where it's a fixed-cost operation to get the length of a list, is to use the built-in function length in guards, as in the following listing.

Listing 2.2 Don't do this: `length(List)` traverses the whole list!

```
loop(List) when length(List) > 0 ->
    do_something;
loop(EmptyList) ->
    done.
```

A function like this uses quadratic time in proportion to the length of the list, because it has to *traverse the list from start to end* to count the number of elements each time. This adds up like a triangle, like the time for ++ in the previous section. But if all you want to know is whether the list is nonempty, you can easily do it with pattern matching, as shown in the following listing.

Listing 2.3 Do this: pattern match to check for nonempty lists

```
loop([SomeElement | RestOfList]) ->
    do_something;
loop([]) ->
    done.
```

A match like this takes a small, fixed amount of time. You can even use matching to check for lists that are at least of a certain length, as in the following listing.

Listing 2.4 Checking for lists of various lengths using pattern matching

```
loop([A, B, C | TheRest]) -> three_or_more;
loop([A, B | TheRest]) -> two_or_more;
loop([A | TheRest]) -> one_or_more;
loop([]) -> none.
```

Note that you need to check for the longer lists first, because if you check for two or more before the others, all lists of length three match as well, and so on. We say that you check for the *most specific* patterns first.

2.16 Erlang programming resources

To learn more about the Erlang language, get a better grasp of functional and concurrent programming techniques, and learn more about the available libraries and tools, the following are the most important resources.

2.16.1 Books

There are, as of this writing, two modern books about Erlang, the programming language. The first, which kicked off a new wave of interest in Erlang all over the world, is *Programming Erlang—Software for a Concurrent World* by Joe Armstrong (Pragmatic Bookshelf, 2007). It's a good introduction to the language and to concurrent programming in general, and it gives a number of interesting examples of the kinds of programs you can write easily in Erlang.

The second, more recent addition, is *Erlang Programming* by Cesarini and Thompson (O'Reilly, 2009). It dives deeper into the language details, conventions, and techniques for functional programming and concurrent programming, and the libraries and tools that are part of the Erlang ecosystem.

Finally, and mainly of historical interest, you may be able to find a copy of *Concurrent Programming in Erlang*, 2nd ed., by Armstrong, Virding, Wikström and Williams (Prentice Hall, 1996), but it's outdated with regard to language features, libraries, and tools.

2.16.2 Online material

The main website for Erlang is www.erlang.org, where you can download the latest release of open source Erlang, read online documentation, find official news from the OTP development team at Ericsson, subscribe to mailing lists, and so on.

There is also a community website at www.trapexit.org, with mailing list archives, a wiki for tutorials, articles, cookbooks, links, and more. To help you keep up to date, the site www.planeterlang.org summarizes Erlang-related feeds from various sources.

The main mailing list for Erlang is erlang-questions@erlang.org, where you can generally find answers to the most complicated questions from experienced and professional users. The archives go back more than 10 years and are a treasure trove of information.

Finally, searching for "erlang" at www.stackoverflow.com is a good complement to the erlang-questions mailing list for finding answers to various questions.

2.17 Summary

We have covered a huge number of things in this chapter, from the Erlang shell, via data types, modules and functions, pattern matching, guards, funs and exceptions, to list comprehensions, the bit syntax, the preprocessor, processes, ETS tables, recursion, and more. Although there is much more to learn about the finer points of writing Erlang programs, what we've covered here provides a solid footing for you to move on with. If you skimmed this part, even if you're not that familiar with Erlang, don't worry; you can come back here for reference when and if you need it.

In the following chapters, we explain new concepts as they're brought up, assuming that you have some previous knowledge to stand on. We now dive straight into OTP, where we remain for the rest of this book and where you as an Erlang programmer will (we hope) choose to stay longer.

Writing a TCP-based RPC service

3

This chapter covers

- Introduction to OTP behaviors
- Module layout conventions and EDoc annotations
- Implementing an RPC server using TCP/IP
- Talking to your server over telnet

What!? No "hello world"?

That's right, no "hello world." In chapter 2, we provided a review of the Erlang language, and now it's time to do something concrete. In the spirit of getting down and dirty with real-world Erlang, we say *no* to "hello world"! Instead, you'll create something that is immediately useable. You're going to build a TCP-enabled RPC server!

In case you don't know what that is, let us explain. RPC stands for *remote procedure call*. An RPC server allows you to call procedures (that is, functions) remotely from another machine. The TCP-enabled RPC server will allow a person to connect to a running Erlang node, run Erlang commands, and inspect the results with no more than a simple TCP client, like good old Telnet. The TCP RPC server will be a nice first step toward making your software accessible for post-production diagnostics.

> **Source code**
>
> The code for this book is available online at GitHub. You can find it by visiting http://github.com/ and entering "Erlang and OTP in Action" in the search field. You can either clone the repository using `git` or download the sources as a zip archive.

This RPC application, as written, would constitute a security hole if included in a running production server because it would allow access to run any code on that server, but it wouldn't be difficult to limit the modules or functions that this utility could access in order to close that hole. But you won't do that in this chapter. We use the creation of this basic service as a vehicle for explaining the most fundamental, most powerful, and most frequently used of the OTP *behaviours*: the generic server, or `gen_server`. (We stick to the British spelling of *behaviour*, because that's what the Erlang/OTP documentation uses.) OTP behaviours greatly enhance the overall stability, readability, and functionality of software built on top of them.

In this chapter, we cover implementing your first behaviour, and you'll learn about basic TCP socket usage with the `gen_tcp` module (which isn't a behaviour, despite the name). This book is mainly intended for intermediate-level Erlang programmers, and so we start in the thick of it. You'll need to pay strict attention, but we promise the chapter will be gentle enough to fully understand. When you're done, you'll have taken a great leap forward in terms of being able to create reliable software.

By the end of this chapter, you'll have a working Erlang program that will eventually be a part of a production-quality service. In chapter 4, you'll hook this program deeper into the OTP framework, making it an Erlang application that can be composed with other Erlang applications to form a complete deliverable system (also known as a *release*). Much later, in chapter 11, you'll integrate a similar server into the simple cache application that you'll also build. That will be a more robust and scalable version of this TCP server and will show a few interesting twists on the subject. For now, though, let's get more explicit about what you'll be building in this chapter.

3.1 *What you're creating*

The RPC server will allow you to listen on a TCP socket and accept a single connection from an outside TCP client. After it's connected, it will let a client run functions via a simple ASCII text protocol over TCP. Figure 3.1 illustrates the design and function of the RPC server.

The figure shows two processes. One is the supervisor, as we described in chapter 1; it spawns a worker process that is the actual RPC server. This second process creates a listening TCP socket and waits for someone to

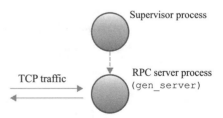

Figure 3.1 RPC server process connected through a socket to the world outside. It accepts requests over TCP, performs them, and returns the results to the client.

connect. When it receives a connection, it reads ASCII text in the shape of normal Erlang function calls, and it executes those calls and returns the result back over the TCP stream. This kind of functionality is useful for any number of things, including remote administration and diagnostics in a pinch. Again, the RPC server understands a basic text protocol over the TCP stream, which looks like standard Erlang function calls. The generic format for this protocol is

```
Module:Function(Arg1, ..., ArgN).
```

For example:

```
lists:append("Hello", "Dolly").
```

(Note that the period character is required.) To interpret these requests, the RPC server parses the ASCII text and extracts the module name, function name, and arguments, transforming them into valid Erlang terms. It then executes the function call as requested and finally returns the results as Erlang terms formatted as ASCII text back over the TCP stream.

Accomplishing this will require an understanding of a number of fundamental Erlang/OTP concepts, all of which we get into in the next couple of sections.

3.1.1 *A reminder of the fundamentals*

You should already have a basic grasp of modules, functions, messaging, and processes, because we addressed these concepts in chapters 1 and 2. We cover them again here, before we introduce the new concept of behaviours. First, in Erlang, functions are housed in modules, and processes are spawned around function calls. Processes communicate with each other by sending messages. Figure 3.2 illustrates these relationships.

Let's take a second to review these concepts:

- *Modules*—Modules are containers for code. They guard access to functions by either making them private or exporting them for public use. There can be only one module per object file (.beam file). If a module is named `test`, it must reside in a source file called test.erl and be compiled to an object file called test.beam.
- *Functions*—Functions do all the work; all Erlang code in a module must be part of a function. They're the sequential part of Erlang. Functions are executed by processes, which represent the concurrent part. A function must belong to some module.

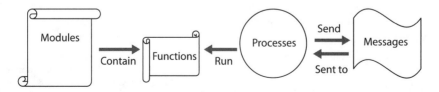

Figure 3.2   The relationships between modules, functions, processes, and messages

- *Processes*—Processes are the fundamental units of concurrency in Erlang. They communicate with each other through messages. Processes are also the basic containers for program state in Erlang: data that needs to be modified over time can be kept inside a process. Any process can create (spawn) another process, specifying what function call it should perform. The new process executes that call and terminates itself when it has finished. A process spawned to perform a simple call to `io:format/2` will be short-lived, whereas one spawned to execute a call like `timer:sleep(infinity)` will last forever, or until someone else kills it.

- *Messages*—Messages are how processes interact. A message can be any Erlang data. Messages are sent asynchronously from one process to another, and the receiver always gets a separate copy of the message. Messages are stored in the mailbox of the receiving process on arrival and can be retrieved by executing a `receive`-expression.

After that quick refresher, let's move on to the concept of behaviours.

3.1.2　*Behaviour basics*

Behaviours are a way of formalizing common patterns in process-oriented programming. For example, the concept of a server is general and includes a large portion of all processes you'll ever need to write. All those processes have a lot in common—in particular, whether they should be made to follow OTP conventions for supervision and other things. Rewriting all that code for every new server-like process you need would be pointless, and it would introduce minor bugs and subtle differences all over the place.

Instead, an OTP behaviour takes such a recurring pattern and divides it into two halves: the generic part and the application-specific implementation part. These communicate via a simple, well-defined interface. For example, the module you'll create in this chapter will contain the implementation part of the most common and useful kind of OTP behaviour: a generic server, or `gen_server`.

COMPONENTS OF A BEHAVIOUR

In daily use, the word *behaviour* has become rather overloaded and can refer to any of the following separate parts:

- The behaviour interface
- The behaviour implementation
- The behaviour container

The behaviour *interface* is a specific set of functions and associated calling conventions. The `gen_server` behaviour interface contains six functions; `init/1`, `handle_call/3`, `handle_cast/2`, `handle_info/2`, `terminate/2`, and `code_change/3`.

The *implementation* is the application-specific code that the programmer provides. A behaviour implementation is a callback module that exports the functions required by the interface. The implementation module should also contain an attribute

-behaviour(...). that indicates the name of the behaviour it implements; this allows the compiler to check that the module exports all the functions of the interface. The listing that follows shows those parts of the module header and the interface functions that must be implemented for a valid gen_server.

Listing 3.1 Minimal gen_server behaviour implementation module

```
-module(...).

-behaviour(gen_server).

-export([init/1, handle_call/3, handle_cast/2, handle_info/2,
        terminate/2, code_change/3]).

-record(state, {}).

init([]) ->
    {ok, #state{}}.

handle_call(_Request, _From, State) ->
    Reply = ok,
    {reply, Reply, State}.

handle_cast(_Msg, State) ->
    {noreply, State}.

handle_info(_Info, State) ->
    {noreply, State}.

terminate(_Reason, _State) ->
    ok.

code_change(_OldVsn, State, _Extra) ->
    {ok, State}.
```

If any of these functions are missing, the behaviour implementation isn't fully conforming to the gen_server interface, in which case the compiler issues a warning. We get into detail about what each of these functions do in the next section, when you implement them in order to build your RPC server.

The third and final part of a behaviour is the *container*. This is a process that runs code from a library module and that uses implementation callback modules to handle application-specific things. (Technically, the container could consist of multiple processes working closely together, but usually there is only one process.) The name of the library module is the same as that of the behaviour. It contains the generic code for that behaviour, including functions to start new containers. For example, for a gen_server behaviour, the code sits within the gen_server module that can be found in the stdlib section of the Erlang/OTP libraries. When you call gen_server:start(...,foo,...), a new gen_server container is created that uses foo as a callback module.

Behaviour containers handle much of what is challenging about writing canonical, concurrent, fault-tolerant OTP code. The library code takes care of things like synchronous messaging, process initialization, and process cleanup and termination, and also provides hooks into larger OTP patterns and structures like code change and supervision trees.

> ## Containers
>
> The word *container* as used here is our own choice of terminology, but we find it fitting. The OTP documentation tends to talk only about the process, but that doesn't convey the division of responsibility in a behaviour and can be unclear at times. (If you have some familiarity with J2EE containers in Java, there are many similarities here, but also some differences: an OTP container is lightweight, and the container is the only real object in this context.)

INSTANTIATING A BEHAVIOUR

The whole point of a behaviour is to provide a template for processes of a particular type. Every behaviour library module has one or more API functions (generally called `start` and/or `start_link`) for starting a new container process. We call this *instantiating* the behaviour.

> ## Process type
>
> The informal notion of process *type* (regardless of whether behaviours are involved) lets us talk about things like a `gen_server` process. Processes are of the same type if they're running mainly the same code, which means that they understand mainly the same kind of messages. The only difference between two processes of the same type is their individual state. Processes of the same type generally have the same *spawn signature* or *initial call*; that is to say, they had the same function as starting point.

In some cases, you'll write a behaviour implementation module so that there can only be one instance at a time; in other cases, you may want to have thousands of simultaneous instances that all run the same code but with different data. The important thing to keep in mind is that when your callback code is running, it's executed by a container, which is a process with identity and state (including its mailbox). This is a lot like objects in object-oriented programming, but with the addition that all these containers are living things that are running code in parallel.

To summarize, the behaviour interface is the contract that allows the behaviour implementation (your code) to leverage the power of the behaviour container. The purpose is to make it simple to implement processes that follow typical concurrent programming patterns. Working with OTP behaviours has a number of advantages:

- Developers get more done with less code—sometimes much less.
- The code is solid and reliable because it has well-tested library code at its core.
- The code fits into the larger OTP framework, which provides powerful features such as supervision for free.
- The code is easier to understand because it follows a well-known pattern.

With this basic understanding of behaviours, we can now move on to the implementation of the RPC server, which will utilize all of what we've described. Everything you do from here on is related to implementing the TCP RPC server. This exercise will cover a lot. At one level, it's about how to use behaviours. You'll be coding up a behaviour implementation that conforms to a behaviour interface, and you'll see how the gen_server behaviour provides all the functionality you're looking for. At another level, what you'll be doing here is even more fundamental: starting to use Erlang within the framework of OTP.

3.2   *Implementing the RPC server*

If you're an intermediate-level Erlang programmer, you already have some familiarity with modules, processes, functions, and messaging. But it's likely that your experience is from a more informal, plain Erlang context. We revisit these concepts in this chapter in the context of OTP. If you're new to Erlang and this is your first book, you're probably an experienced programmer from a different background. In that case, you don't need any prior knowledge of these things to grasp what we cover in this chapter.

It's our opinion that writing pure Erlang code with processes and message passing (and getting everything right) *without* OTP is an advanced topic and is something you should resort to only when you must. Perhaps not having done this sort of programming in pure Erlang is a blessing, because you'll pick up the right OTP habits straight away—maybe even the strict approach we take to module structure and layout, inline documentation, and commenting.

Because you'll need a module to contain your behaviour implementation, we start with a little about module creation and layout.

3.2.1   *Canonical module layout for a behaviour implementation*

One of the nice things about behaviours is that they give you a great amount of consistency. When looking at a behaviour implementation module, you'll recognize aspects that are common to all such modules, like the behaviour interface functions and the customary start or start_link function. To make the files even more recognizable, you can adopt the canonical behaviour implementation module layout that we elaborate on here.

This standard layout consists of four sections. Table 3.1 details them in the order that they appear in the file.

Table 3.1   Source code sections of a canonical behaviour implementation module

Section	Description	Functions exported	EDoc annotations
Header	Module attributes and boilerplate	N/A	Yes, file level
API	Programmer interface; how the world interacts with the module	Yes	Yes, function level

Table 3.1   Source code sections of a canonical behaviour implementation module *(continued)*

Section	Description	Functions exported	EDoc annotations
Behaviour interface	Callback functions required by the behaviour interface	Yes	Optional
Internal functions	Helper functions for the API and behaviour interface functions	No	Optional

We'll now look at the details of implementing each of these sections in turn, starting with the module header.

3.2.2   *The module header*

Before you can create the header, you need to create a file to hold it. Because you'll be building a TCP-based RPC server, let's create a file named tr_server.erl where you'll place this code. Use your favorite text editor.

> ### Module naming conventions and the flat namespace
> Erlang has a flat namespace for modules. This means module names can collide. (There exists an experimental Java-like package system in Erlang, but it hasn't caught on and isn't fully supported.) If modules are given names like `server`, it's easy to end up with two modules from different projects that have the same name. To avoid such clashes, the standard practice is to give module names a suitable prefix. Here, we've taken the first two letters of the acronyms TCP and RPC: `tr_server`.

The first thing you need to enter is the file-level header comment block:

```
%%%-------------------------------------------------------------------
%%% @author Martin & Eric <erlware-dev@googlegroups.com>
%%%  [http://www.erlware.org]
%%% @copyright 2008-2010 Erlware
%%% @doc RPC over TCP server. This module defines a server process that
%%%      listens for incoming TCP connections and allows the user to
%%%      execute RPC commands via that TCP stream.
%%% @end
%%%-------------------------------------------------------------------
```

Note that each comment line begins with three % characters, although a single % is sufficient. This is a convention used for file-level comments, whose contents apply to the file as a whole. Furthermore, this may be the first time you've seen comments containing EDoc annotations. EDoc is a tool for generating documentation directly from source code annotations (similar to Javadoc) and comes with the standard Erlang/OTP distribution. We don't have room in this book to get too deep into how to use EDoc: you can read more about it in the tools section of the OTP documentation. We'll spend a little time on it here, because it's the de facto standard for in-code

Erlang documentation. We suggest that you familiarize yourself with EDoc and make a habit of using it in your own code.

All EDoc tags begin with an @ character. Table 3.2 describes the tags in this header. We return to this subject at the end of chapter 4, after we've explained how OTP applications work; there, we show briefly how to run EDoc to generate the documentation.

Table 3.2   Basic EDoc tags

EDoc tag	Description
@author	Author information and email address.
@copyright	Date and attribution.
@doc	General documentation text. First sentence is used as a summary description. Can contain valid XHTML and some wiki markup.
@end	Ends any tag above it. Used here so that the line %%%----... isn't included in the text for the previous @doc.

The first thing in your file that isn't a comment is the -module(...) attribute. The name supplied must correspond to the file name; in this case, it looks like

```
-module(tr_server).
```

(Remember that all attributes and function definitions must end with a period.) After the module attribute, the next thing to add is the behaviour attribute. This indicates to the compiler that this module is intended to be an implementation of a particular behaviour and allows it to warn you if you forget to implement and export some behaviour interface functions. You'll implement a generic server, so you want the following behaviour attribute:

```
-behaviour(gen_server).
```

Next come the export declarations. You'll typically have two. (The compiler combines them, but grouping related functions helps readability.) The first is for your API section, and the second is for the behaviour interface functions that must also be exported. Because you haven't yet designed the API, a placeholder will suffice for now. But you know which the behaviour interface functions are, so you can list them right away:

```
%% API
-export([]).

%% gen_server callbacks
-export([init/1, handle_call/3, handle_cast/2, handle_info/2,
        terminate/2, code_change/3]).
```

Note the comment above the second declaration. The behaviour interface functions are often referred to as *callbacks*. This is because at startup, the name of the behaviour implementation module is passed to the new container, which then calls back into the implementation module through these interface functions. We go into more detail about the use of each of the interface functions later in the chapter.

Following the exports, there may be a number of optional application-specific declarations and/or preprocessor definitions. They're highlighted in the following listing, which shows the complete header for the tr_server module.

Listing 3.2 Full tr_server.erl header

```
%%%-------------------------------------------------------------------
%%% @author Martin & Eric <erlware-dev@googlegroups.com>
%%%   [http://www.erlware.org]
%%% @copyright 2008 Erlware
%%% @doc RPC over TCP server. This module defines a server process that
%%%      listens for incoming TCP connections and allows the user to
%%%      execute RPC commands via that TCP stream.
%%% @end
%%%-------------------------------------------------------------------
-module(tr_server).

-behaviour(gen_server).

%% API
-export([
        start_link/1,
        start_link/0,
        get_count/0,
        stop/0
        ]).

%% gen_server callbacks
-export([init/1, handle_call/3, handle_cast/2, handle_info/2,
        terminate/2, code_change/3]).

-define(SERVER, ?MODULE).
-define(DEFAULT_PORT, 1055).

-record(state, {port, lsock, request_count = 0}).
```

❶ Sets SERVER to module name
❷ Defines default port
❸ Holds state of process

Macros are commonly used for various constants, to ensure that you only need to modify a single place in the code to change the value (see section 2.12). Here, you use them to define which default port to use ❷ and to set up SERVER as an alias for the name of your module ❶ (you may want to change that at some point, so you shouldn't assume that the server name will always remain the same as the module name). After the macros, you define the name and the format of the record (see section 2.11) that will hold the live state of your server process while it's running ❸.

Now that the header is complete, the next section of your behaviour implementation module is the API.

3.2.3 *The API section*

All the functionality that you want to make available to the users of your module (who don't care much about the details of how you implemented it) is provided through the application programming interface (API) functions. The main things that a user of a generic server wants to do are

- Start server processes
- Send messages to these processes (and receive the answers)

To help you implement this basic functionality, there are three primary gen_server library functions. These are listed in table 3.3.

Table 3.3   gen_server library functions for implementing the API

Library function	Associated callback function	Description
gen_server:start_link/4	Module:init/1	Starts a gen_server container process and simultaneously links to it
gen_server:call/2	Module:handle_call/3	Sends a synchronous message to a gen_server process and waits for a reply
gen_server:cast/2	Module:handle_cast/2	Sends an asynchronous message to a gen_server process

Basically, your API functions are simple wrappers around these library calls, hiding such implementation details from your users. The best way to illustrate how these functions work is to use them to implement the API for the tr_server module, as shown in the following listing.

Listing 3.3   API section of tr_server.erl

```
%%%====================================================================
%%% API                                                                ◁──┐
%%%====================================================================   │
                                                                          │
%%-------------------------------------------------------------------     │
%% @doc Starts the server.                                  Banner at start│
%%                                                             of section  │
%% @spec start_link(Port::integer()) -> {ok, Pid}                         │
%% where                                                                  │
%%   Pid = pid()                                                          │
%% @end                                                                   │
%%-------------------------------------------------------------------
start_link(Port) ->
    gen_server:start_link({local, ?SERVER}, ?MODULE, [Port], []).     ◁──┐
                                                                          │
%% @spec start_link() -> {ok, Pid}                                        │
%% @doc Calls `start_link(Port)' using the default port.                  │
start_link() ->                                            Spawns server  │
    start_link(?DEFAULT_PORT).                                process     │
```

```
%%-------------------------------------------------------------------
%% @doc Fetches the number of requests made to this server.
%% @spec get_count() -> {ok, Count}
%% where
%%  Count = integer()
%% @end
%%-------------------------------------------------------------------
get_count() ->
    gen_server:call(?SERVER, get_count).
```
◄━❶ **Makes caller wait for reply**

```
%%-------------------------------------------------------------------
%% @doc Stops the server.
%% @spec stop() -> ok
%% @end
%%-------------------------------------------------------------------
stop() ->
    gen_server:cast(?SERVER, stop).
```
◄━❷ **Doesn't wait for reply**

A query like ❶ uses gen_server:call/2, which makes the caller wait for a reply. A simple command like stop ❷ typically uses the asynchronous gen_server:cast/2.

Only one process type per module

The same module may be used to spawn many simultaneous processes but should contain code for only one type of process (apart from the API code, which by definition is executed by the clients, who could be of any type). If various parts of the code in a single module are meant to be executed by different types of processes, it becomes hard to reason about the contents of the module, as well as about the system as a whole, because the role of the module isn't clear.

Briefly, the API in listing 3.3 tells you that a tr_server can do three things:

- It can be started using start_link() or start_link(Port).
- It can be queried for the number of requests it has processed, using get_count().
- It can be terminated by calling stop().

Before we get into the details of how these functions work, and the communication between the caller and the server process (the container), let's refresh your memory with regard to messaging in Erlang.

QUICK REMINDER ABOUT PROCESSES AND COMMUNICATION

Processes are the building blocks of any concurrent program. Processes communicate via messages that are posted asynchronously; on arrival, they're queued up in the mailbox of the receiving process. Figure 3.3 illustrates how messages enter the process mailbox, where they're kept until the receiver decides to look at them.

This ability of processes to automatically buffer incoming messages and selectively handle only those messages that are currently relevant is a crucial feature of Erlang (see section 2.13.2 for more about selective receive).

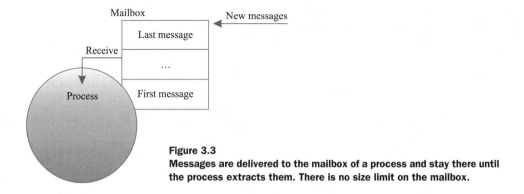

Figure 3.3
Messages are delivered to the mailbox of a process and stay there until the process extracts them. There is no size limit on the mailbox.

With this in mind, we now look at how the OTP libraries take away a lot of the fiddly details of message passing between clients and servers, instead handing you a set of higher-level tools for process communication. These tools may not be as supremely flexible as hacking your own communication patterns, but they're solid, straightforward, and fit most everyday situations. They also guarantee several important properties like timeouts, supervision, and error handling, which you would otherwise have to code manually (which can be boring, verbose, and hard to get completely right).

HIDING THE PROTOCOL

The set of messages that a process will accept is referred to as its *protocol*. But you don't want to expose the details of these messages to your users, so one of the main tasks of the API is to hide this protocol from the rest of the world.

Your `tr_server` process will accept the following simple messages:

- `get_count`
- `stop`

These are plain atoms, but there's no need for users of the `tr_server` module to know this implementation detail; you'll keep all that hidden behind the API functions. Imagine a future extension of your server that requires users to log in before they're allowed to send requests. Your API might then need a function to create a user on the server, which could look something like this:

```
add_user(Name, Password, Permissions) ->
  gen_server:call(?SERVER, {add_user, [{name, Name},
                                       {passwd, Password},
                                       {perms, Permissions}]}).
```

Such a complex message format is something you don't want to leak out of your module; you might want to change it in the future, which would be hard if clients were depending on it. By wrapping the communication with the server in an API function, the users of your module remain oblivious to the format of these messages.

Finally, on a primitive level, all messages in Erlang are sent asynchronously (using the `!` operator), but in practice you often have to block when you can't do

> ### Double blind
> Another level of hiding is going on here: the OTP libraries are hiding from you the details of the real messages going back and forth between processes. The message data that you pass as arguments to `call/2` and `cast/2` is only the payload. It's automatically wrapped up along with a bit of metadata that allows the `gen_server` container to see what kind of message it is (so it knows which callback should handle the payload) and to reply to the right process afterwards.

anything useful before some expected answer arrives. The `gen_server:call/2` function implements this synchronous request-reply functionality in a reliable way, with a default timeout of 5 seconds before it gives up on getting the answer (in addition, the version `gen_server:call/3` lets you specify a timeout in milliseconds, or `infinity`).

Now that we've explained the purpose behind the API functions and the `gen_server` library functions used to implement them, we can get back to the code.

API FUNCTIONS IN DETAIL

Listing 3.3 showed the implementation of the API, and it's time that we explain exactly what it does. First, table 3.4 summarizes the four API functions.

> ### Singleton process
> To keep things simple, we've designed this particular server to be a singleton: you can have only one instance running at a time. When it starts, the new `gen_server` container process is registered under the name specified by the `SERVER` macro defined in listing 3.2 (that's what the argument `{local, ?SERVER}` means in listing 3.3). This makes it possible for the functions `get_count()` and `stop()` to communicate with it by name. If you want to run several server instances simultaneously, you must modify the program a bit, because processes can't have the same registered name (see section 2.13.3 for details about the process registry). On the other hand, it's common to have servers that provide a system-level service, of which there can be only one per Erlang node (or even one per Erlang cluster); so, a singleton server like this isn't an unrealistic example.

Table 3.4 The `tr_server` API

API function	Description
`start_link/1`	Starts the `tr_server` listening on a specific port
`start_link/0`	Alias for `start_link/1`, using the default port
`get_count/0`	Returns the number of requests processed so far
`stop/0`	Shuts down the server

This is how the API functions work:

- `start_link(Port)` and `start_link()`—Start your server process and at the same time link to it. This is done by calling `gen_server:start_link/4` and is where you indicate (in the second argument) to the behaviour container which callback module contains the implementation to be used. The normal thing to do is to pass the value of the built-in macro `MODULE`, which always expands to the name of the current module (see section 2.12.1):

```
gen_server:start_link({local, ?SERVER}, ?MODULE, [Port], [])
```

When this call is executed, it spawns a new `gen_server` container process, registers it on the local node using the name that the `SERVER` macro expands to, and waits until it has been initialized by running the `init/1` callback function of the implementation module (more on this in section 3.2.4) before returning to the caller. At that point, the server is up and running, fully initialized and ready to accept messages.

The third argument, in this case `[Port]`, provides data to the server on startup. This is passed as is to the `init/1` callback function, where you can use it to set up the initial process state. The fourth argument is a list of extra options, which you'll leave empty for now. Note that from the API user's point of view, all these details are hidden; there is only a single argument: the port that the server should listen on.

- `get_count()`—Uses `gen_server:call/2` to send the atom `get_count` as a synchronous request to the server. This means the call waits for the reply from the server, temporarily suspending the calling process:

```
gen_server:call(?SERVER, get_count)
```

The first argument in the call is either the registered name or the process ID of the server process; here, you use the same name (the `SERVER` macro) that was used to register the process in the `start_link/1` function. The second argument in the call is the message to be sent. When the server has received and handled this message, it sends a reply back to the calling process. The `gen_server:call/2` function takes care of receiving this reply and returning it as the result from the function call, so the caller doesn't need to know anything about how to send or receive messages.

Also note that the atom `get_count` used in the message (as part of the server protocol) has the same name as the API function; this is helpful when you're reading the code or debugging—don't make the internal server protocol cryptic just because you can.

- `stop()`—Uses `gen_server:cast/2` to send the atom `stop` as an asynchronous message (meaning that the function returns immediately without waiting for a reply):

```
gen_server:cast(?SERVER, stop)
```

After you've sent this message, you assume that the container will shut itself down as soon as it receives the message. You don't need a reply; hence cast, rather than call.

That's all the functions you need for this simple server. After all, most of its real functionality will be provided via the TCP connection, so these API functions are only needed for starting, stopping, and checking the status.

THE @SPEC TAG

Before we move on to define the behaviour interface callback functions, we want to explain briefly the new EDoc tag you used in the documentation before each function (listing 3.3). It's highly recommended that you have at least a @doc annotation for each and every API function, as well as for the module as a whole (listing 3.2). The additional @spec tag can be used to describe the type of data that the function accepts as input and what type of values it can return. For example, the @spec for start_link/1

```
%% @spec start_link(Port::integer()) -> {ok, Pid}
%% where
%%   Pid = pid()
```

indicates that the function takes a single argument that is an integer and returns a tuple {ok, Pid}, where Pid is a process identifier. Type names always look like function calls, as in integer(), so that they aren't confused with atoms. Types can be attached directly to variables with the :: notation as with Port, or they can be listed at the end of the specification as with where Pid = ...

You're finished with the user API section, so it's finally time to begin implementing the behaviour interface functions—the callbacks, where most of the real work is done.

3.2.4 *The callback function section*

Each of the gen_server library functions you use in your API corresponds to a specific callback function specified by the gen_server behaviour interface. These callbacks now need to be implemented. To refresh your memory, table 3.5 repeats table 3.3, with the addition of handle_info/2, which doesn't correspond to any of the library functions used for the API.

First, look back at the tr_server:start_link/1 function in listing 3.3. That function hides that fact that you're calling gen_server:start_link/4; and as you can see from table 3.5, the new container then calls back to tr_server:init/1 (which must be exported by the tr_server module, as required by the gen_server behaviour interface) in order to perform the initialization. Similarly, tr_server:get_count/0 shields the user from having to worry about your protocol and the fact that the communication is performed by gen_server:call/2. When such a message is received by the container, it calls back to tr_server:handle_call/2 in order to handle the message; in this case, the only possible message of this kind is the atom get_count. Analogously, tr_server:stop/0 uses gen_server:cast/2 to dispatch a message to the

Table 3.5 `gen_server` library functions and callbacks

Library function	Associated callback function	Description
`gen_server:start_link/4`	`Module:init/1`	Starts a `gen_server` container and simultaneously links to it.
`gen_server:call/2`	`Module:handle_call/3`	Sends a synchronous message to a `gen_server` container and waits for a reply.
`gen_server:cast/2`	`Module:handle_cast/2`	Sends an asynchronous message to a `gen_server` container.
N/A	`Module:handle_info/2`	Handles messages sent to a `gen_server` container that were not sent using one of the `call` or `cast` functions. This is for out-of-band messages.

container asynchronously; and on receiving such a message, the container calls back to `tr_server:handle_cast/2`.

But notice that the `handle_info/2` callback doesn't correspond to any `gen_server` library function. This callback is an important special case. It's called to handle any messages that arrive in the mailbox of a `gen_server` that weren't sent using one of the `call` or `cast` library functions (typically, naked messages sent with the plain old `!` operator). There can be various reasons for such messages to find their way to the mailbox of a `gen_server` container—for example, that the callback code requested some data from a third party. In the case of your RPC server, you'll receive data over TCP, which will be pulled off the socket and sent to your server process as plain messages.

After all this talk, the next listing shows what your callback functions do.

Listing 3.4 `gen_server` callback section for `tr_server`

```
%%%===================================================================
%%% gen_server callbacks
%%%===================================================================
init([Port]) ->                                                     ❶ Initializes
    {ok, LSock} = gen_tcp:listen(Port, [{active, true}]),            server
    {ok, #state{port = Port, lsock = LSock}, 0}.

handle_call(get_count, _From, State) ->                             ❷ Returns request
    {reply, {ok, State#state.request_count}, State}.                  count

handle_cast(stop, State) ->                                         ❸ Shuts down
    {stop, normal, State}.                                            gen_server
```

Upon initialization of the server, the `init` function creates a TCP listening socket, sets up the initial state record, and also signals an immediate timeout. Next, the code returns the current request count to the calling client process. A special return value stop tells the gen_server process to shut down.

As you can see in listing 3.4, the first three callback functions are almost trivial. (We leave handle_info/2 and the other two for later, in listing 3.5.) The most complicated thing about these three functions is the format of the values they return to communicate back to the gen_server container. Let's go through them in detail:

- init/1, *initialization callback*—This function is called whenever you start a new gen_server container, for example, via gen_server:start_link/4. These are the first examples of how OTP helps you write industrial-strength code with a minimum of effort. The start_link library function sets you up to be hooked into the powerful process-supervision structures of OTP. It also provides critical initialization functionality, blocking the caller until the process is up and running and registered (if requested), and the init/1 callback has completed. This ensures that your process is fully operational before it starts to process requests.

  Breaking this function down line by line, the first thing you see is init([Port]) ->, meaning that init takes one argument, which must be a list containing a single element that you call Port. Note that this matches exactly what you passed from the start_link/1 function in listing 3.3. (Always passing a list, even with a single element, is a common convention for init/1.)

  Next, you create your TCP listening socket on the specified port ❶, using the standard library gen_tcp module:

  ```
  {ok, LSock} = gen_tcp:listen(Port, [{active, true}]),
  ```

  A *listening socket* is a socket that you create and wait on to accept incoming TCP connections. After you accept a connection, you have an active socket from which you can receive TCP datagrams. You pass the option {active, true}, which tells gen_tcp to send any incoming TCP data directly to your process as messages.

  Last, you return from init/1 with a 3-tuple containing the atom ok, your process state (in the form of a #state{} record), and a curious 0 at the end:

  ```
  {ok, #state{port = Port, lsock = LSock}, 0}.
  ```

  The 0 is a timeout value. A timeout of zero says to the gen_server container that immediately after init/1 has finished, a timeout should be triggered that forces you to handle a timeout message (in handle_info/2) as the first thing you do after initialization. The reason for this will be explained shortly.

- handle_call/3, *callback for synchronous requests*—This function is invoked every time a message is received that was sent using gen_server:call/2. It takes three arguments: the message (as it was passed to call), From (let's not worry about that yet), and the current state of the server (which is whatever you want it to be, as set up in init/1).

You have a single synchronous message to handle: `get_count`. And all you need to do is extract the current request count from the state record and return it. As earlier, the return value is a 3-tuple ❷, but with slightly different content than in `init/1`:

```
{reply, {ok, State#state.request_count}, State}.
```

This indicates to the `gen_server` container that you want to send a reply to the caller (you should, because it's expected); that the value returned to the caller should be a tuple `{ok, N}`, where `N` is the current number of requests; and finally that the new state of the server should be the same as the old (nothing was changed).

■ `handle_cast/2`, *callback for asynchronous messages*—Your API function `stop()` uses `gen_server:cast/2` to dispatch an asynchronous message `stop` to the server, without waiting for any response. Your task is to make your server terminate when it receives this message. Any message sent using `cast` is handled by the `tr_server:handle_cast/2` callback; this is similar to `handle_call/3`, except that there is no `From` argument. When your `handle_cast` function sees the message `stop`, it only has to return the following 3-tuple:

```
{stop, normal, State}.
```

This tells the `gen_server` container that it should stop ❸ (that is, terminate), and that the reason for termination is `normal`, which indicates a graceful shutdown. The current state is also passed on unchanged (even though it won't be used further). Note here that the atom `stop` returned in this tuple instructs the container to shut down, whereas the `stop` message used in the protocol between the API and the server could have been any atom (such as `quit`), but was chosen to match the name of the API function `stop()`.

By now, we've covered most of the important points regarding the `gen_server` behaviour: the interface, the callback functions, the container, and how they interact. There is certainly more to learn about `gen_server`, but we return to that throughout the book. There is one thing left to discuss regarding the server you implement here: handling out-of-band messages. In many typical servers, there are no such messages to handle; but in this particular application, it's where you do all the heavy lifting.

HANDLING OUT-OF-BAND MESSAGES

As we explained, any messages to a `gen_server` process that weren't sent using `call` or `cast` are handled by the `handle_info/2` callback function. These are considered *out-of-band messages* and can happen when your server needs to communicate with some other component that relies on direct messages rather than on OTP library calls—for example, a socket or a port driver. But you should avoid sending out-of-band messages to a `gen_server` if you can help it.

In the `init/1` function, you set up a TCP listening socket for the server, and then you mysteriously return a timeout value of `0` from that function, which you know will trigger an immediate timeout (see listing 3.4).

gen_server timeout events

When a gen_server has set a timeout, and that timeout triggers, an out-of-band message with the single atom timeout is generated, and the handle_info/2 callback is invoked to handle it. This mechanism is usually used to make servers wake up and take some action if they have received no requests within the timeout period.

Here, you're abusing this timeout mechanism slightly (it's a well-known trick) to allow the init/1 function to finish quickly so that the caller of start_link(...) isn't left hanging; but at the same time, you're making sure the server immediately jumps to a specific piece of code (the timeout clause of handle_info/2) where it can get on with the more time-consuming part of the startup procedure—in this case, waiting for a connection on the socket you created (see end of listing 3.5). Because you're not using server timeouts for anything else in this application, you know it won't return to that point again afterward.

But back to TCP sockets: an active socket like this forwards all incoming data as messages to the process that created it. (With a passive socket, you'd have to keep asking it if there is more data available.) All you need to do is to handle those messages as they're arriving. Because they're out-of-band data as far as the gen_server container is concerned, they're delegated to the handle_info/2 callback function, shown in listing 3.5.

Listing 3.5 handle_info/2, terminate/2, and code_change/3 callback functions

```
handle_info({tcp, Socket, RawData}, State) ->
    do_rpc(Socket, RawData),
    RequestCount = State#state.request_count,
    {noreply, State#state{request_count = RequestCount + 1}};     ◁──  Increments
handle_info(timeout, #state{lsock = LSock} = State) ->                  request
    {ok, _Sock} = gen_tcp:accept(LSock),                               count after
    {noreply, State}.                                                  RPC
                                                                       requests
terminate(_Reason, _State) ->
    ok.                                    Obligatory but
                                           uninteresting
code_change(_OldVsn, State, _Extra) ->     for now
    {ok, State}.
```

Let's go through this function like we did with the three previous callbacks. handle_info/2 is the callback for out-of-band messages. This function has two clauses; one for incoming TCP data and one for the timeout. The timeout clause is the simplest, and as we explained earlier, it's also the first thing the server does after it has finished running the init/1 function (because init/1 set the server timeout to zero): a kind of deferred initialization. All this clause does is use gen_tcp:accept/1 to wait for a TCP connection on your listening socket (and the server will be stuck here until that happens). After a connection is made, the timeout clause returns and signals to the gen_server container that you want to continue as normal with an unchanged state.

(You don't need to remember the socket handle returned by `accept`, because it's also included in each data package.)

That finally brings you to the clause that matches messages on the form `{tcp, Socket, RawData}`. This is the kind of message that an active socket sends to its owner when it has pulled data off the TCP buffer. The `RawData` field is what you're interested in; it's the ASCII text that the client has sent to you. (You're finally getting back to the purpose of the program: to handle RPC requests over TCP!) The bulk of the code is in a helper function `do_rpc/2` that's shown in listing 3.6; all you need to do here after the RPC has been executed is to update the request count in the server state (see section 2.11.3 for details about updating record fields) and return control to the `gen_server` container.

THE INTERNAL FUNCTIONS

If you've come this far in the chapter, you're excused if you aren't too interested in how you implement the `do_rpc/2` function. In that case, you can skip directly to section 3.3 (perhaps stopping to type in the code from listing 3.6 first) and look at how you run this server and talk to it over TCP. But if you want to see a few techniques for handling input, parsing, and performing meta-calls, keep reading.

Listing 3.6 Internal functions

```
%%%===================================================================
%%% Internal functions
%%%===================================================================

do_rpc(Socket, RawData) ->
    try
        {M, F, A} = split_out_mfa(RawData),                          ❶ Performs
        Result = apply(M, F, A),                                       requested call
        gen_tcp:send(Socket, io_lib:fwrite("~p~n", [Result]))
    catch                                                            ❷ Outputs
        _Class:Err ->                                                   result
            gen_tcp:send(Socket, io_lib:fwrite("~p~n", [Err]))
    end.

split_out_mfa(RawData) ->                                           ❸ Strips
    MFA = re:replace(RawData, "\r\n$", "", [{return, list}]),          CRLF
    {match, [M, F, A]} =
        re:run(MFA,
               "(.*):(.*)\s*\\((.*)\s*\\)\s*.\s*$",                  ❹ Parses request
               [{capture, [1,2,3], list}, ungreedy]),                  string
    {list_to_atom(M), list_to_atom(F), args_to_terms(A)}.

args_to_terms(RawArgs) ->
    {ok, Toks, _Line} = erl_scan:string("[" ++ RawArgs ++ "]. ", 1),
    {ok, Args} = erl_parse:parse_term(Toks),
    Args.
```

To give a quick overview, the code in listing 3.6 has four main parts: splitting the input, parsing the function arguments, executing the requested call, and sending back the result. First, notice that the inner workings of the `do_rpc/2` function are

> **Check the borders**
>
> Checking data as it passes from the untrusted world into the trusted inner sanctum of your code is a fundamental design principle of Erlang programs. After you verify that the data conforms to your expectations, there is no need to check it repeatedly: you can code for the correct case and let supervision take care of the rest. The reduction in code size from using this technique can be significant, and so can the reduction in number of programming errors, due to the improved readability. Any remaining errors, because you aren't masking them, show up as process restarts in your logs, which allows you to correct the problems as they occur. Let it crash!

wrapped in a `try` expression (section 2.8.2). Because you're working on data from the outside world, several things could go wrong, and this is an easy way to ensure that if the code crashes (throws an exception), you print the error message and continue rather than crashing the entire server process. On the other hand, this doesn't protect against correct but malignant requests, as you'll see in section 3.3.

First you use the standard library `re` module (Perl-compatible regular expressions) to strip the trailing carriage return and line feed ❸. This should leave only text on the form `Module:Function(Arg1,...,ArgN).` according to the protocol defined at the start of section 3.1. (Otherwise, you'll crash at some point, and the `try` expression will handle it.)

Next, you use the `re` module again ❹ to extract the `Module`, `Function`, and `Arg1,...,ArgN` parts. The details of using regular expressions are beyond the scope of this book, so check the standard library documentation for more information. The module and function names should have the form of Erlang atoms, so all you need to do is convert them from strings to atoms.

But the arguments could be much more complicated. They're a comma-separated list of terms, and there could be zero, one, or more. You handle them in `args_to_terms/1`, where you use a couple of standard library functions to first tokenize the string (placed within angle brackets to make a list, and ended with a period character) and then parse the tokens to form a real Erlang list of terms.

> **I/O lists: easy scatter/gather**
>
> It's worth noting that the result from `io_lib:fwrite/2` might not be a normal string (that is, a flat list of characters). It can still be passed directly to a socket, though; it's what is known as an *I/O list*: a possibly nested, deep, list that may contain both character codes and chunks of binary data. This way, no intermediate concatenated lists need to be created in order to output a number of smaller I/O lists in sequence: make a list of the segments, and pass the entire thing to the output stream. This is similar to the scatter/gather techniques found in modern operating systems.

The module name, function name, and list of argument terms are then passed to the built-in function `apply/3` ❶. This looks much like `spawn/3` (see section 2.13) but doesn't start a new process—it executes the corresponding function call. (It's what we call a *meta-call* operator.) The value returned from this function call is finally formatted as text by `io_lib:fwrite/2` ❷ and sent back over the socket as the response to the user—a remote procedure call has been performed!

Your RPC server is now done and ready to try out. In the next section, you'll give it a trial run and see if it works.

3.3   *Running the RPC server*

The first step in getting this running is compiling the code. (As we said at the start of the chapter, the complete source files are available online, at GitHub.com.) Run the command `erlc tr_server.erl`. If it completes without any errors, you have a file named tr_server.beam in your current directory. Start an Erlang shell in the same directory, and start the server, as follows:

```
Eshell V5.6.2  (abort with ^G)
1> tr_server:start_link(1055).
{ok,<0.33.0>}
```

We picked port 1055 arbitrarily here because it's easy to remember (10 = 5 + 5). The call to `start_link` returns a tuple containing `ok` and the process identifier of the new server process (although you don't need that now).

Next, start a telnet session on port 1055. On most systems (not all Windows versions, however—download a free telnet client such as PuTTY if needed), you can do this by entering `telnet localhost 1055` at a system shell prompt (*not* in your Erlang shell). For example:

```
$ telnet localhost 1055
Trying 127.0.0.1...
Connected to localhost.
Escape character is '^]'.
init:stop().
ok
Connection closed by foreign host.
```

The first session was a success! Why? Let's inspect the dialog and see exactly what happened.

First, you use telnet to connect via TCP on port 1055 to the running `tr_server`. After you connect, you enter the text `init:stop().`, which is read and parsed by the server. You expect this to result in the server calling `apply(init, stop, [])`. You also know that `init:stop/0` returns the atom `ok`, which is exactly what you see printed as the result of your request. But the next thing you see is "Connection closed by foreign host." This was printed by the telnet utility because the socket it was connected to suddenly closed at the remote end. The reason is that the call to `init:stop()` shut down the entire Erlang node where the RPC server was running. This demonstrates both that your RPC server works *and* just how dangerous it can be to give someone

> **A server should not call itself**
>
> With your RPC server, you can try calling any function exported from any module available on the server side, except one: your own `tr_server:get_count/0`. In general, a server can't call its own API functions. Suppose you make a synchronous call to the same server from within one of the callback functions: for example, if `handle_info/2` tries to use the `get_count/0` API function. It will then perform a `gen_server:call(...)` to itself. But that request will be queued up until after the current call to `handle_info/2` has finished, resulting in a circular wait—the server is deadlocked.

unrestricted access to run code on your node! In an improved version, you might want to limit which functions a user can call and even make that configurable.

To conclude, in not that many lines of code, you've built an application that can (with a bit of tweaking) be useful in the real world. And more important, it's a stable application that fits into the OTP framework.

3.4 A few words on testing

Before you're done, there is one more thing that you as a conscientious developer should do: add some testing. Many would argue that you should have started with testing, writing your tests first to guide your development. But adding test code to the examples would clutter the code and distract from the main points we're trying to make; this is, after all, a book about the OTP framework, not about testing. Also, the art of writing tests for concurrent, distributed systems like the ones you're creating here could easily be the subject of a book or two.

Two levels of testing are of immediate interest to a developer: unit testing and integration testing. Unit testing is focused on creating tests that are ready to run at the press of a button and that test specific properties of a program (preferably, at most one property per test). Integration testing is more about testing that a number of separately developed components work together and may require some manual work to set up everything before the tests can run.

The Erlang/OTP standard distribution includes two testing frameworks: EUnit and Common Test. EUnit is mainly for unit testing and focuses on making it as simple as possible to write and run tests during development. Common Test is based on the so-called OTP Test Server and is a more heavy-duty framework that can run tests on one or several machines while the results are being logged to the machine that is running the framework; it's something you might use for large-scale testing like nightly integration tests. You can find more details about both these frameworks in the Tools section of the Erlang/OTP documentation.

We show briefly here what you need to do to write a test case using EUnit, because it's so simple. First, put this line of code in your source code, just after the `-module(...)` declaration:

```
-include_lib("eunit/include/eunit.hrl").
```

That was the hard part. Next, think of something to test; for example, you can test that you can successfully start the server. You must put the test in a function, which takes no arguments and whose name must end with _test. EUnit detects all such functions and assumes they're tests. A test succeeds if it returns some value and fails if it throws an exception. Hence, your test can be written

```
start_test() ->
    {ok, _} = tr_server:start_link(1055).
```

Recall that = is the match operator, which throws a badmatch error if the value of the right side doesn't match the pattern on the left. This means the only way this function can return normally is if the start operation succeeds; in every other case, start_test() results in an exception. Simple as that!

To run this test, you have to recompile the module. Then, from the Erlang shell, you can say either

```
eunit:test(tr_server).
```

or

```
tr_server:test().
```

This has the same effect: it runs all the tests in the tr_server module. Note that you never wrote a function called test(): EUnit creates this automatically, and it also ensures that all your test functions are exported.

Many more features in EUnit help you write tests as compactly as possible, including a set of useful macros that you get automatically when you include the eunit.hrl header file as you did earlier. We suggest that you read the EUnit Users Guide in the Erlang/OTP documentation for more information.

3.5   Summary

We've covered a lot of material in this chapter, going through all the basics of OTP behaviours and the three parts that make them what they are: the interface, the container, and the callback module. We've specifically covered the gen_server behaviour at some depth, through a real-world example.

In the next chapter, you'll hook this little stand-alone generic RPC server into a larger structure that will make it an enterprise-grade OTP application. When that's complete, your server will be part of an application that is versioned, fault tolerant, ready for use by others in their projects, and ready to go to production. This will add another layer to your basic understanding of Erlang/OTP as a framework by teaching you the fundamental structure for fault tolerance (the supervisor) and by teaching you how to roll up your functionality into nice OTP packages.

OTP applications and supervision

4

This chapter covers

- An introduction to OTP applications
- Fault tolerance with OTP supervisors
- Generating documentation with EDoc

The entire purpose of the Erlang/OTP ecosystem is building stable, fault-tolerant systems. We introduced the core concepts of this ecosystem in chapter 3, building a simple RPC server; we now take it further and teach you how to pack this up properly and make it a fault-tolerant, production-quality service. We do this by introducing two new fundamental concepts:

- *Applications* are the way you package related modules in Erlang. The focus here isn't on packaging for distribution but on being able to treat a bunch of modules as a single entity. Although OTP applications can be merely some library code for others to call, more often they're like creatures with a life of their own: they start up, do what they're designed to do, and shut down. Some can have multiple running instances, and some are limited to one instance at a time.
- *Supervisors* are one of the most important features of OTP. They monitor other processes and take action if anything goes wrong, restarting the failed

119

process or possibly escalating the problem to a higher level. Layering supervisors into *supervision trees* allows you to create highly fault-tolerant systems.

In this chapter, we don't go too deeply into the theory and practice of applications and supervisors. We mostly concentrate on how to armor the module you created in chapter 3, wrapping it up as an OTP application and setting up a supervisor for it. We go over the most basic aspects of these tasks and explain what you're doing at each step. Later, in part 2 of this book, we go into more detail and talk about all the interesting options that are available for advanced supervision, for handling code within applications, and even for packaging multiple applications into a larger structure called a *release*.

4.1   OTP applications

We start by talking about how to organize your code and get it to fit nicely into a normal Erlang/OTP system. For many reasons, this topic tends to cause a lot of confusion for people who are new to the system. When we first started working with Erlang, OTP was dark magic, poorly documented and with few examples. We all traveled similar paths to gain knowledge of this powerful system, involving a lot of trial and error and a few helpful hints from various old-timers on the Erlang mailing list. Fortunately, when you get your mind around the basic concepts, it's pretty simple.

> **Terminology: applications**
>
> In the context of OTP, the word *application* has a specific meaning: an application is a software component consisting of a number of modules bundled together with a few additional metadata files, and organized on disk according to certain conventions. This allows the system to know which applications are currently installed, and, for example, lets you start or stop an application by its name.
>
> From now on, you can assume that we're talking about applications in the OTP sense, except when otherwise clear from the context.

Superficially, OTP applications are just groups of related code. They can be what we refer to as *library applications*: nothing but a collection of modules to be used by other applications. (The Erlang/OTP `stdlib` is an example of a library application.) More often, OTP applications are living things that are started, run for some time, and eventually shut down. We refer to these as *active applications*. An active application has a *root supervisor* whose job is to manage the processes of the application. We explain supervisors in more detail in section 4.2.

4.1.1   The organization of an OTP application

Creating an OTP application consists mostly of setting up a standard directory structure and writing some application metadata. This metadata tells the system what it

> ### Active versus library applications
> Both active applications and library applications use the same directory layout and metadata files, and both fit into the overall OTP application framework. The main difference is that active applications have a life cycle and must be started in order to be useful. By contrast, library applications are a passive collection of modules to be used by other applications, and they don't need to be started or stopped. Because the focus of this book is on writing active applications, when we say *application* you can assume that is what we mean unless otherwise clear from the context.

needs to know to start and stop the application. It also specifies the dependencies of the application, such as what other applications need to be present or started beforehand. For active applications, there is also a little coding involved, but we get to that in section 4.1.3.

Erlang/OTP applications use a simple directory layout, shown in figure 4.1. Most people who are familiar with Erlang but know nothing else about OTP still use this structure for their applications, but without any metadata.

You should of course replace <application-name> with the name of your application; in this case it will be tcp_rpc. The [-<version>] part is optional: it isn't used in development, but when you ship an application you usually give the directory a name like tcp_rpc-1.0.2 to make code upgrades easier. The names of the subdirectories in figure 4.1 are somewhat self-explanatory, but table 4.1 describes them in more detail.

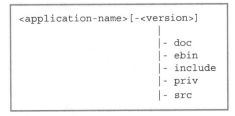

```
<application-name>[-<version>]
             |
             |- doc
             |- ebin
             |- include
             |- priv
             |- src
```

Figure 4.1 Directory layout of an OTP application. The directory name may include a version number. The standard subdirectories are doc, ebin, include, priv, and src. Only ebin is strictly required.

Table 4.1 Subdirectories of the application directory

Directory	Description
doc	Documentation. If you generate documentation from EDoc, you put your overview.edoc file here, and the remaining files are autogenerated.
ebin	Compiled code (the .beam files). It's also the location of the .app file, which contains the application metadata.
include	Public header files. Any .hrl file that is part of your public API should be kept in this directory. Private .hrl files that are only used within your code and aren't intended for public consumption should be kept under src with the rest of your source code.

Table 4.1   Subdirectories of the application directory *(continued)*

Directory	Description
priv	Odd bits that need to be distributed along with your application. These range from template files to shared objects and DLLs. The location of an application's priv directory is easy to find: call the function `code:priv_dir` (`<application-name>`), which returns the full path of the priv directory as a string.
src	Source code related to your application. That means your Erlang .erl files and internal .hrl files, but also any ASN.1, YECC, MIB, and other source files. (If you don't distribute your source code along with your application, this directory is omitted or left empty in your deliverables.)

Go ahead and create this directory structure now, moving your source code from chapter 3 into the src directory.

4.1.2   *Adding the application metadata*

Now that you have the expected directory layout for your application, you can work on adding the metadata that OTP requires. This is expressed as plain Erlang terms, in a text file called <application-name>.app stored in the ebin directory. The following listing shows the metadata for your tcp_rpc application, in the file ebin/tcp_rpc.app.

Listing 4.1   Application metadata file: ebin/tcp_rpc.app

```
%% -*- mode: Erlang; fill-column: 75; comment-column: 50; -*-

{application, tcp_rpc,
 [{description, "RPC server for Erlang and OTP in action"},
  {vsn, "0.1.0"},
  {modules, [tr_app,
             tr_sup,
             tr_server]},
  {registered, [tr_sup]},
  {applications, [kernel, stdlib]},
  {mod, {tr_app, []}}
 ]}.
```

This .app file is used by OTP to understand how the application should be started and how it fits in with other applications in the system. To repeat what we said earlier, the focus here isn't first and foremost on making distribution packages, but on creating larger units of functionality that can be started, stopped, supervised, and upgraded.

The format of this .app (pronounced "dot app") file is straightforward. Apart from normal Erlang comments, it contains a single Erlang term terminated by a period: a 3-tuple {application, ..., ...}.. The second element is the name of the application, as an atom; in this case tcp_rpc. The third element is a list of parameters expressed as pairs {Key, Value}, some of which are required and others of which aren't. Those included here are the most important ones you need in

Table 4.2 Main parameters of a .app file

Part	Description
description	A short description of your application. Usually a sentence or two, but it can be as long as you like.
vsn	The version of your application. The version string can be anything you like, but we suggest that you try to stick with the normal numbering schema `<major>.<minor>.<patch>`: even if Erlang/OTP has no problems with any version string you use, some programs try to parse this string for their own purposes and may get hiccups otherwise.
modules	A list of all the modules in your application. It's tedious to maintain, but there are some tools available to help you. The order of the list doesn't matter, but it can be easier to maintain if it's kept alphabetically ordered.
registered	Recall that Erlang processes can be registered (section 2.13.3), allowing them to be addressed by name. This is typically done for system services and similar. Including a list of registered names in this entry in the .app file doesn't perform the actual registration, but it allows the OTP system to know which applications register what names, which helps with things such as system upgrades and makes it possible to give early warnings for duplicate registered names.
applications	All the applications that need to be started before this application can start. Applications usually have dependencies. Because they're living systems, active applications expect these dependencies to be available and running when they themselves start. The order of the list doesn't matter—OTP is smart enough to look at the entire system and understand what needs to be started when.
mod	Tells the OTP system how to start your application. The value is a tuple containing the module name along with some optional startup arguments. (Don't use these arguments for general configuration—use a proper config file instead.) The module named here must implement the `application` behaviour, as explained in section 4.3.1.

most applications. We get back to these parameters in more detail in part 2 of this book. Table 4.2 describes the parameters used here, in the order they appear in listing 4.1.

So far, you've created the directory structure and put the metadata in place. (If you didn't create the ebin/tcp_rpc.app file yet, do that before you go on.) But you haven't done everything you need to make a complete application. As mentioned in the description of the `mod` parameter in table 4.2, you also need a launching point for your application, in the form of a module that implements the `application` behaviour. This will be your task in the next section.

4.1.3 *The application behaviour*

Every active application needs one module that implements the `application` behaviour. This module provides the startup logic for the system. At a minimum, it provides the point from which the *root supervisor* is started; that supervisor is the grandparent

> **Naming the application behaviour module**
>
> Using the name `<application-name>_app` is a common convention for the module that implements the application behaviour.

of all the processes that will be part of the application. The application behaviour module may also do other things depending on the needs of your system. We explain more about supervisors in section 4.2. Right now, we concentrate on the application behaviour implementation in the file src/tr_app.erl, as shown (stripped of comments) in the following listing.

Listing 4.2   Application behaviour: src/tr_app.erl

```
-module(tr_app).                          Behaviour
                                          declaration
-behaviour(application).

-export([
    start/2,                              Callbacks of application
    stop/1                                behaviour
    ]).

start(_Type, _StartArgs) ->
    case tr_sup:start_link() of           Starts root
        {ok, Pid} ->                      supervisor
            {ok, Pid};
        Other ->
            {error, Other}
    end.

stop(_State) ->
    ok.
```

This small module should be easy to understand, but look back to chapter 2 if you need a refresher on behaviour implementation modules. In this case, you're implementing the `application` behaviour, which requires you to export the callbacks `start/2` and `stop/1`. (This module has no user API apart from those callbacks, so there are no other exports.)

The `stop/1` callback is simple in this case: you don't need to do anything special on shutdown, so you ignore the input parameter and return the atom `ok`. The only real work you need to do is in the `start/2` function. This is called when the OTP system wants to start your application, and it must perform the actual startup and return the process ID of the root supervisor as `{ok, Pid}`. You can do any other startup tasks here as well, such as read a configuration file, initialize an ETS table, and so on. For this simple tcp_rpc application, all you need to do is start the root supervisor; you do that here by calling the function `tr_sup:start_link()`, which we haven't shown yet. (You'll implement the supervisor module `tr_sup` shortly, in section 4.2.) Afterward, you check the form of the value returned by `start_link()` and signal an error if it doesn't look right. The input parameters to `start/2` can be ignored for now; but in case you're curious, `Type` is usually `normal` but can also be `{failover, ...}` or `{take-over, ...}`, and `StartArgs` is whatever arguments you specify in the `mod` parameter in the .app file.

4.1.4 Application structure summary

To conclude, you need to do three things to create an OTP application:

1. Conform to the standard directory structure.
2. Add the application metadata in the form of the .app file.
3. Create a module that implements the `application` behaviour, which is responsible for starting your application.

The one detail that we've left out is how to start a root supervisor, as required for the `start/2` function of the application behaviour. The purpose of an active application is to run one or more processes to do some work. In order to have control over those processes, they should be spawned and managed by *supervisors*: processes that implement the `supervisor` behaviour.

4.2 Adding fault tolerance with supervisors

Supervisors are one of the core things that make Erlang/OTP what it is. An active OTP application consists of one or more processes that do the work. Those processes are started indirectly by supervisors, which are responsible for supervising them and restarting them if necessary. A running application is essentially a tree of processes, both supervisors and workers, where the root of the tree is the root supervisor. Figure 4.2 illustrates a possible process structure for a hypothetical application.

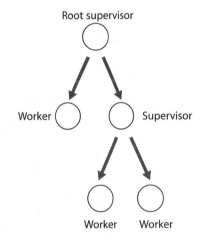

Figure 4.2　Process tree for a hypothetical application. This example has a root supervisor with one immediate worker process and one subsystem supervisor, the latter with two workers.

You create supervisors by writing modules that implement the `supervisor` behaviour. If your worker processes are already based on OTP behaviours (like tr_server), then setting up a supervisor is pretty easy. What the standard OTP worker behaviours `gen_server`, `gen_event`, and `gen_fsm` do in order to be easily hooked in to a supervision tree isn't deep magic—it mostly involves conforming to some interfaces and return-value conventions and setting up process links properly.

Fortunately, it's something you don't need to know about; if you occasionally need to include code that isn't based on a standard behaviour in the supervision tree, you can do so via the `supervisor_bridge` adapter in the standard library.

> **Naming the root supervisor behaviour module**
> Using the name *<application-name>_sup* is a common convention for the module that implements the root supervisor behaviour for an application.

4.2.1   *Implementing a supervisor*

The implementation of the root supervisor for the tcp_rpc application, in the file src/tr_sup.erl, is shown in listing 4.3. It's slightly more complicated than the tr_app module. In particular, this module has an API function, not just callbacks for the behaviour interface. This is so you can start the supervisor from the tr_app module. (In principle, the tr_sup:start_link() function could be part of tr_app:start/2, but we prefer to separate the responsibilities like this, rather than including details about the supervisor in the _app module.)

Listing 4.3   Root supervisor implementation

```
-module(tr_sup).

-behaviour(supervisor).

%% API
-export([start_link/0]).

%% Supervisor callbacks
-export([init/1]).

-define(SERVER, ?MODULE).

start_link() ->                                          ❶ Starts supervisor
    supervisor:start_link({local, ?SERVER}, ?MODULE, []).

init([]) ->                                              ❷ Says how to start and
    Server = {tr_server, {tr_server, start_link, []},       managing children
                permanent, 2000, worker, [tr_server]},
    Children = [Server],                                 ❸ Says how supervisor
    RestartStrategy = {one_for_one, 0, 1},                  should behave
    {ok, {RestartStrategy, Children}}.                   ◁ Returns supervisor specification
```

All that the start_link() API function has to do launch the supervisor is to call the library function supervisor:start_link/3, passing it the name of this module ❶. (Note that this is similar to how you start your tr_server in listing 3.3, by calling gen_server:start_link/4.) The tuple {local, ?SERVER} in the first argument to the call tells the library to automatically register the supervisor process on the local node under the name tr_sup (because you define SERVER to be the same as MODULE). The third argument is passed to the init/1 callback function on startup. Because your init/1 doesn't need any input, you leave this as an empty list.

Most of the interesting stuff in this case is in the function init/1. The value you return from this function tells the OTP supervisor library exactly how the child processes should be started and managed ❷ and how the supervisor process itself should behave ❸.

You can do a lot with supervisors, and we go into more detail about that in part 2 of this book; but for the moment, you only need you to understand what you're doing in this particular instance. Let's start with the easy part: the restart strategy.

4.2.2　*The supervisor restart strategy*

The value that should be returned from the `init/1` callback function (unless there is a problem) has the form `{ok, {RestartStrategy, Children}}`, where `Children` is a list of child specifications; these can get complicated, and we explain them in the next section. The `RestartStrategy` is easier: it's a 3-tuple `{How, Max, Within}`. In this case, you write

```
RestartStrategy = {one_for_one, 0, 1}
```

You choose a `one_for_one` strategy here for the How. That means if a child process dies, that process—and only that one—is restarted. If other children are still running, they aren't involved in the restart, as illustrated in figure 4.3. (Other strategies are available, which we return to later in this book. For example, they allow the child processes to be restarted as a group if any one of them should die.)

The values Max and Within (here set to 0 and 1, respectively) are related: together, they specify the allowed *restart frequency*. The first number indicates the maximum number of restarts, and the second number indicates the timeframe. For instance, if Max=10 and Within=30, you allow at most 10 restarts within any period of 30 seconds. If this limit is exceeded, the supervisor terminates itself and all its child processes and propagates the failure up the supervision tree. These numbers are highly dependent on your application, and it's hard to recommend good all-round defaults, but 4 restarts per hour (3600 seconds) is often used in production systems. Picking 0 and 1 as you do here means you allow no automatic restarts for now, because doing so would make it harder to see any problems in your code. In chapter 7, we talk about error logs and observing restarts.

Next, you get to the `Children` part of the value returned from `init/1`. This is a list of tuples, one per supervised child process. In this case, you have a single child: your server. But you can list as many here as you like; it's not uncommon to have half a dozen or so child processes under a single supervisor. It's also possible to add and remove children dynamically after startup, but in the majority of cases you only need a static list like this.

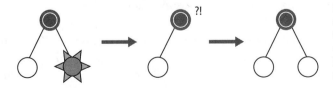

Figure 4.3　One-for-one restart strategy: The supervisor treats its children as independent when any of them needs to be restarted. Healthy children aren't affected by a crashing sibling.

4.2.3   Writing the child specification

A *child specification* is a tuple that describes a process you want the supervisor to manage. In most supervisors, the child processes are started when the supervisor starts and exist only for the life of the supervisor. The init/1 function gives the following description for the single process you want to supervise:

```
Server = {tr_server, {tr_server, start_link, []},
          permanent, 2000, worker, [tr_server]}
```

A child specification has six elements: {ID, Start, Restart, Shutdown, Type, Modules}:

- The first element, ID, is a term that the supervisor uses to identify the specification internally. Here you use the atom tr_server, the name of your module, to keep things simple.

- The second entry, Start, is a triple {Module, Function, Arguments} that is used to start the process. That is, the first element is the name of the module, the second is the name of the function, and the third element is the list of arguments to the function, just like when you call the built-in function spawn/3. In this case, you want the supervisor to call tr_server:start_link() in order to start the child process (that is, your tr_server).

- The third element, Restart, says whether this is a child that should be restarted upon failure. You specify permanent, because you want this to be a long-lived service that should always be restarted if it terminates for any reason. (The other options are temporary for processes that should never be restarted, and transient for processes that should be restarted only if they terminate abnormally but not upon normal termination.)

- The fourth element, Shutdown, says how the process may be killed. Here you use an integer (2000), indicating that this is a soft shutdown and the process has that many milliseconds to shut itself down before it's unconditionally killed. The alternatives are brutal_kill, meaning that the process will always be terminated immediately upon shutdown; and infinity, which is used mainly when the child itself is a supervisor and should be given all the time it needs.

- The fifth value, Type, indicates whether the process is a supervisor or a worker. A worker process is any process in a supervision tree that doesn't implement the supervisor behaviour. You can chain supervisors together into a hierarchy as you see fit (see figure 4.2), providing more fine-grained process control as your applications get more complex. The Type field allows a supervisor to know if one of its children is also a supervisor. In this case, the server process is clearly a worker.

- The sixth option lists the modules that this process depends on. This information is used only during hot code upgrades and indicates to the system in what order modules should be upgraded. Generally, you only need to list the main module for the child processes, in this case tr_server.

That was a lot; but thankfully, after you've done it once, you'll have a template to look at when you create your next supervisor. You can come back here if you forget how to write a child specification. The advantage is that you get a lot of functionality out of those two lines of code.

With that, you're done! There was a lot of explanation for those two tiny modules, but now you're over the greatest threshold. We hope you have a clearer picture of how all these things fit together and what they can do for you.

4.3 *Starting the application*

Your application is complete: you have the directory structure laid out, your metadata in place, you've written an application launching point, and you've implemented a root supervisor. It's time to try running your first proper OTP application.

First, you need to compile all the code in the src directory, generating .beam files that should go in the ebin directory. If your system is set up properly with `erlc` in the search path, the following command line does the trick, assuming that the application root directory tcp_rpc is your current directory:

```
$ erlc -o ebin  src/*.erl
```

(See section 2.3.6 for more details about using `erlc`.) You can also compile the modules from within the Erlang shell with src as the current directory and move the .beam files manually to the ebin directory afterward; but it's time that you learn to use `erlc` (preferably in combination with a build tool like Make, Cons, SCons, or Rake, but that is beyond the scope of this book).

When the .beam files are in place, start Erlang and ensure that the ebin directory is in its code path, like this:

```
$ erl -pa ebin
```

(-pa stands for *path add*, adding a directory to the beginning of the code path.) On Windows, use `werl` instead of `erl`; see section 2.1.1.

With the Erlang shell up and running, you have to do only one thing to launch the application: call the standard library function `application:start/1`, passing it the application name tcp_rpc, like this:

```
Eshell V5.5.5  (abort with ^G)
1> application:start(tcp_rpc).
ok
```

Looks like it started without a hitch. It's not surprising—you did everything by the book. To convince yourself that it's up and running and doing what it should, try it by talking to it over telnet as you did in section 3.3.

The thing you may be wondering right now is how it found the modules, when all you told it was to start the tcp_rpc application, and you have no module with that name. Remember the .app file (listing 4.1)? Just as Erlang searches the code path for .beam files in order to load modules, the `application:start/1` function searches the code path for .app files; and because you added the ebin directory to the path, it found your metadata file ebin/tcp_rpc.app, which told it all it needed to know—in particular, which module to use (tr_app) to kick start the entire application.

You've created your first OTP application! Not all that difficult, was it? Before we leave this subject, you can do one more thing: generate the documentation.

4.4   *Generating documentation with EDoc*

In section 3.2.2, we explained how you can annotate your code with EDoc comments to create documentation from the source code. Now that you've defined your application, generating the documentation files is easy. If you've started erl, run the following in the Erlang shell:

```
2> edoc:application(tcp_rpc, ".", []).
ok
```

Now, you should be able to open the file doc/index.html in a web browser and check out the results. You'll find a bunch of other generated files if you look under doc, but they can all be accessed via the index.html file.

Note that this works even if you haven't written any EDoc annotations in the source code. The documentation will be basic, showing what modules you have and what functions are exported from those modules; but even that is usually much better than nothing.

The empty list [] is for additional options to EDoc (none right now), and the period (.) means the application is supposed to be found in the current directory. You have to specify this because the relative path ebin that you used with the -pa flag doesn't provide enough clues to the system. But if you exit the Erlang shell, change directory to the level above the application directory, and then start Erlang again like this

```
$ erl -pa tcp_rpc/ebin
```

you should be able to use a simpler form of the function you used earlier:

```
Eshell V5.5.5  (abort with ^G)
1> edoc:application(tcp_rpc).
ok
```

The system is now able to figure out on its own which path is associated with the tcp_rpc application name. (See the standard library function code:lib_dir/1 for details.) Note that this works even if the directory name contains a version number (see figure 4.1). Typically, your code path will contain mainly absolute paths to the ebin directories of all installed applications; the three-argument version of the function is mostly used in build scripts.

Now you have a complete, working application, which also has some basic documentation that you can build on by adding more EDoc comments. Time to wrap up this chapter!

4.5 Summary

In this chapter, we've gone over the basics of OTP applications, how they're structured, and what you need to do to turn your code into a full-fledged application. We hope you've tried the examples as you've worked your way through the material; you should at least download the source code as described at the start of chapter 3, and compile and run it.

Conforming to these structures and basing your code on the industrial-grade libraries of OTP will increase the basic level of fault tolerance for your system by an order of magnitude and help you produce consistent, reliable, and understandable software. But creating applications isn't all there is to packaging in OTP. In chapter 10, we cover another type of software package called a *release*. Releases aggregate a number of applications to form a complete software service in Erlang. When we're done with that, you'll know how to boot a full Erlang system the proper way; and you'll understand why the way you started your application earlier by calling `application: start/1` is only for manual testing, and not for production systems.

That said, having read the last two chapters, you've taken the most important step towards creating production-quality Erlang/OTP software. Before we continue on the topic of how to build industrial-grade Erlang services in part 2 of the book, we'll take a short break in the next chapter in order to show you a few useful standard tools that you can use to visualize what's going on in your Erlang system.

Using the main graphical introspection tools

5

This chapter covers

- Monitoring applications with Appmon and WebAppmon
- Managing processes with Pman
- Using the source-level debugger
- Inspecting tables with the Table Viewer
- Using the Erlang Toolbar

You've learned a lot about Erlang and OTP at this point. In the last chapter, we introduced OTP applications and supervisors. We've talked about how these are living things in an Erlang system. In this chapter, we show you. Erlang provides a number of graphical tools for inspecting a running system that are a great help for understanding what's going on. They're really good at helping you visualize things like processes, applications, and supervisor hierarchies. The first tool we introduce is called Appmon; it's specifically made for looking at things from an application and supervision perspective.

5.1 *Appmon*

As the name indicates, Appmon is a tool for monitoring OTP applications. It lets you visualize the applications that are running in the system, as well as their supervisor hierarchies; see the current status of the processes; and perform some basic operations on them.

5.1.1 The Appmon GUI

Before we do too much explaining, let's get Appmon running. Start an Erlang shell, and enter `appmon:start()`:

```
Eshell V5.7.4  (abort with ^G)
1> appmon:start().
```

After a second or two, a window similar to figure 5.1 should pop up. This is Appmon's main window, which shows all the running applications in the system. Right now, that is just the kernel application. The window also shows the overall system load in the bar on the left.

Across the top is a row of menu items. You can use the File menu options to exit Appmon or close the window. You'll also find a Show List Box menu item, which opens another window that lists all the applications in a more compact way. This can make it easier to select a particular application when you have a lot of things running in your system and the main window gets cluttered.

The Actions menu options let you restart the system (stops all applications and cleans up before starting the applications again), reboot the entire system (restarts the Erlang VM—you have to configure a heart command for this to work), or stop the system. There's also an item labeled Ping, which reestablishes a lost connection in a distributed setting. (We discuss distributed Erlang in chapter 8.)

The Options menu lets you select whether the system load should be measured in terms of CPU time or in terms of the number of processes queued up to get access to the CPU. In a distributed Erlang system, it also lets you decide whether you want a single window showing one node at a time or multiple windows showing one node each. The Nodes menu lists the available known nodes: currently, only nonode@nohost, which is your local system running in nondistributed mode. These things will all be

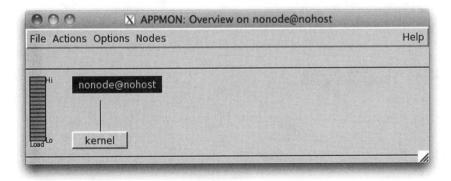

Figure 5.1   The Appmon main window. On the left is a system load bar (currently at zero). On a default Erlang system, only the kernel application is started.

clear to you after chapter 8, but what it boils down to is that you can easily observe and control applications that are running on a different machine in your network.

To have something familiar to study, let's start the `tcp_rpc` application that you created in the previous chapter. Do that now, just as you did in section 4.3. Your main Appmon window should change to show `tcp_rpc` beside the kernel application, as shown in figure 5.2.

The application names are buttons that you can click to open a separate window with information about that particular application. Click the `tcp_rpc` button. The new window should be similar to that in figure 5.3, showing the supervision structure of the `tcp_rpc` application. You may need to resize the window manually to see the whole structure.

Those two topmost, mysterious, unnamed processes are the *application master processes*. They're part of the `application` behaviour container and were spawned by the system when the application started. You don't need to know anything more about them except that they call the `start` function of your application behaviour: in this case, `tr_app:start/2` (see section 4.1.3). When the application is shutting down, they similarly call `tr_app:stop/1` as the last thing they do after all the other application processes have been stopped.

The third process from the top is more interesting: this is your root supervisor, which was started by `tr_sup:start_link()` (listing 4.3). You can see that it in turn has a child `tr_server`, which is the name you gave it in the child specification in `tr_sup:init/1`.

A row of buttons appears across the top of the application window. You use them to specify what should happen if you click one of the processes shown in the window. You first click a button to choose a specific mode of action (by default, the mode is Info), and then you click the process on which you want to perform the action. Click Info for the `tr_server` process: doing so brings up a new window like the one in figure 5.4, showing a number of details about the process and what it's currently doing.

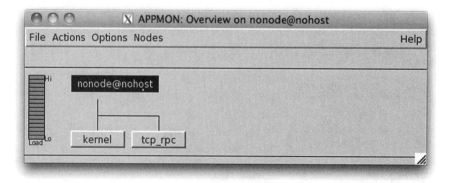

Figure 5.2   The Appmon main window after starting the `tcp_rpc` application. You can click an application's name to view the application in more detail.

APPMON: tcp_rpc on nonode@nohost
File Options
Help
Info
Send
Trace
Kill
<0.51.0>
<0.52.0>
tr_sup
tr_server

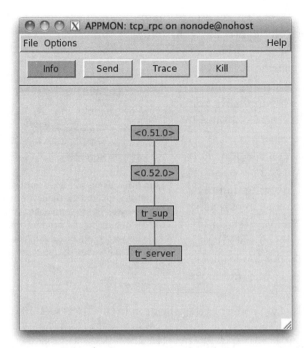

Figure 5.3 The Appmon application window, showing the supervision structure of the running `tcp_rpc` application. Buttons let you select an action to perform: Info, Send, Trace, or Kill.

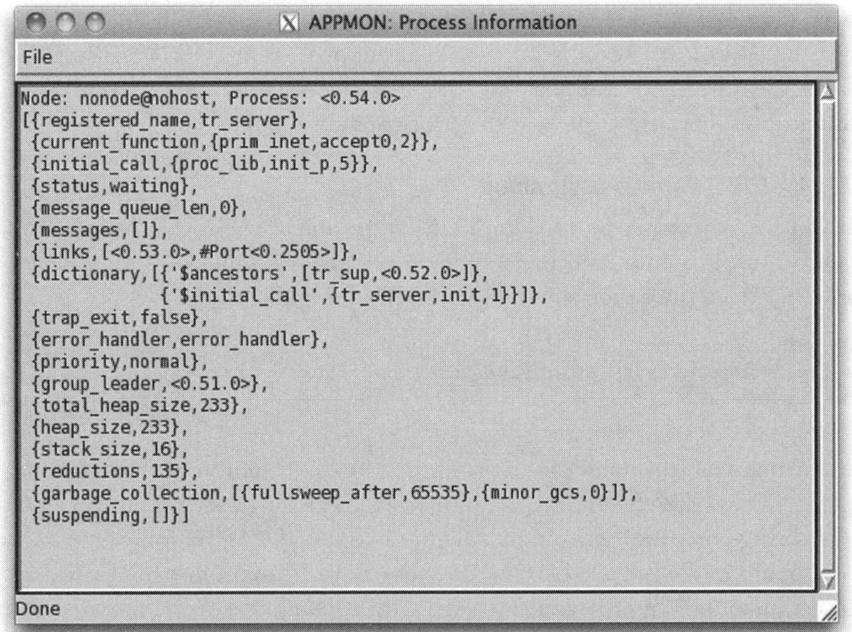

APPMON: Process Information
File
Node: nonode@nohost, Process: <0.54.0>
[{registered_name,tr_server},
{current_function,{prim_inet,accept0,2}},
{initial_call,{proc_lib,init_p,5}},
{status,waiting},
{message_queue_len,0},
{messages,[]},
{links,[<0.53.0>,#Port<0.2505>]},
{dictionary,[{'$ancestors',[tr_sup,<0.52.0>]},
{'$initial_call',{tr_server,init,1}}]},
{trap_exit,false},
{error_handler,error_handler},
{priority,normal},
{group_leader,<0.51.0>},
{total_heap_size,233},
{heap_size,233},
{stack_size,16},
{reductions,135},
{garbage_collection,[{fullsweep_after,65535},{minor_gcs,0}]},
{suspending,[]}]
Done

Figure 5.4 Appmon process information window. It shows details about a specific process, such as the length of its message queue, its memory usage, and the function it's currently running.

Particular points of interest for debugging are the message queue length, the memory usage, and which function the process is currently executing.

When you click the Send button and then click a process, a small window pops up that lets you send arbitrary Erlang terms to the selected process (see figure 5.5). You may enter any term you like here, and it will be sent to the process.

The next button is the Trace action. This allows you to put a trace on the process that you click next. Visually, nothing happens here, but in the background it enables tracing for the selected process. You can read more about the tracing facility in the official Erlang/ OTP documentation, both the low-level API provided by `erlang:trace/3` and the more user-friendly interface provided by the `dbg`

Figure 5.5   **Using the Send action in an Appmon application window to send an arbitrary message to a process. You can use Send for debugging, to see that the process reacts correctly; or, in a pinch, you can use it to unblock a process that is stuck waiting for a message.**

module, which is part of the `runtime_tools` application in the Tools section of the documentation. We get back to tracing in section 5.2 when we discuss the Pman tool.

Finally, you have the Kill action. It sends an untrappable `kill` signal to the process that you click. You can test this by clicking first Kill and then the `tr_sup` process, to see what happens. All the processes of the `tcp_rpc` application should disappear, leaving an empty window. (Recall what we said about process links, OTP supervisors, and automatic cleanup in section 1.2—by killing the root supervisor, you can kill the entire application, because of the way the processes are linked.)

5.1.2   *The WebTool version of Appmon*

If you prefer (or maybe you don't have a graphical environment on your machine), you can use Appmon another way, via the WebTool application. If you call `webtool: start()` from the Erlang shell, you see something like this:

```
2> webtool:start().
WebTool is available at http://localhost:8888/
Or  http://127.0.0.1:8888/
{ok,<0.62.0>}
```

After that, you can point a web browser to http://localhost:8888/ (or whatever name or IP address the machine is using, if you run the browser on a separate computer). This brings up a web page that welcomes you to the WebTool, where you can select one or more tools to start. One of these is WebAppmon, which provides an interface similar to the GUI you've seen in the previous section, but presented via the web browser.

You can use the WebTool version of Appmon even if the Appmon application isn't installed on the system you want to monitor, such as an embedded system with a minimal Erlang environment on it. Currently, the WebTool version doesn't allow you to stop applications or kill processes.

The various graphical tools in Erlang have different world views, so to speak. Appmon has a view based around applications. The next tool we look at is called Pman, and its world view is focused only on processes; it doesn't know anything about applications.

5.2 Pman

Pman, which is short for *process manager*, takes a process-oriented view of the Erlang world. This tool allows you to view all the processes that are running in your system and perform various actions on those processes.

Let's start over with a fresh Erlang system and launch the `tcp_rpc` application as you did in the previous section. After that, launch the Pman application by entering `pman:start()`:

```
Eshell V5.7.4  (abort with ^G)
1> application:start(tcp_rpc).
ok
2> pman:start().
<0.42.0>
3>
```

When Pman starts, you should see a window similar to figure 5.6. It lists the processes that are currently running, along with some information about whether they're registered under a name, how many messages are in their mailboxes, and their estimated

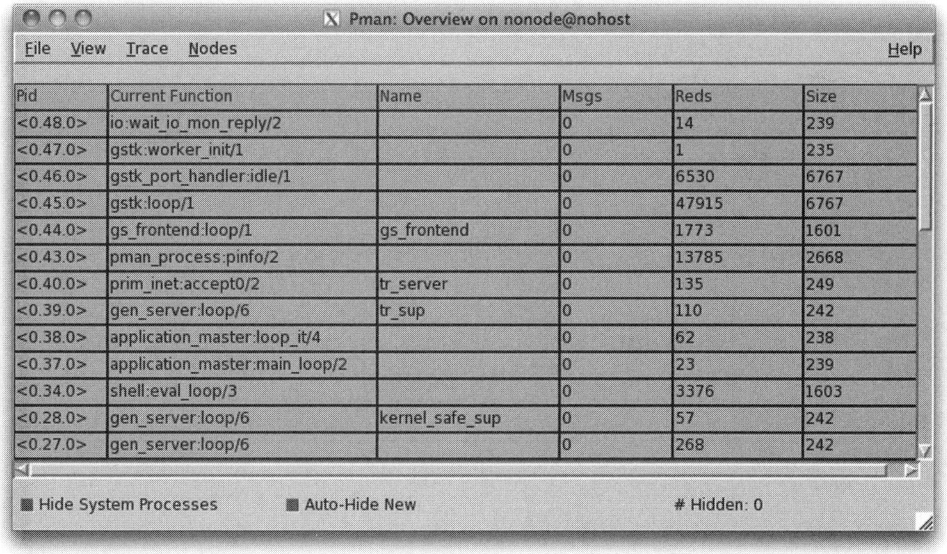
Pman: Overview on nonode@nohost
File View Trace Nodes
Help
Pid | Current Function | Name | Msgs | Reds | Size
<0.48.0> | io:wait_io_mon_reply/2 | | 0 | 14 | 239
<0.47.0> | gstk:worker_init/1 | | 0 | 1 | 235
<0.46.0> | gstk_port_handler:idle/1 | | 0 | 6530 | 6767
<0.45.0> | gstk:loop/1 | | 0 | 47915 | 6767
<0.44.0> | gs_frontend:loop/1 | gs_frontend | 0 | 1773 | 1601
<0.43.0> | pman_process:pinfo/2 | | 0 | 13785 | 2668
<0.40.0> | prim_inet:accept0/2 | tr_server | 0 | 135 | 249
<0.39.0> | gen_server:loop/6 | tr_sup | 0 | 110 | 242
<0.38.0> | application_master:loop_it/4 | | 0 | 62 | 238
<0.37.0> | application_master:main_loop/2 | | 0 | 23 | 239
<0.34.0> | shell:eval_loop/3 | | 0 | 3376 | 1603
<0.28.0> | gen_server:loop/6 | kernel_safe_sup | 0 | 57 | 242
<0.27.0> | gen_server:loop/6 | | 0 | 268 | 242
Hide System Processes
Auto-Hide New
Hidden: 0

Figure 5.6 The Pman main window showing all processes in the Erlang system, along with some basic information about registered names, message queue lengths, and memory usage (in words)

total sizes in memory (measured in machine words, not bytes). The Reds column shows the number of *reductions* performed by each process, which is an approximate measure of how much CPU time they have used.

Note that a lot of processes appear in the list. That's because you're seeing every process, including all the system processes that are part of the normal Erlang environment. Normally, you only care about the processes that are part of the applications you're currently running. To shorten the list, select the Hide System Processes check box in the lower-left corner of the window. Figure 5.7 shows how this leaves you with primarily the processes you care about. In particular, you see the tr_sup and tr_server processes. Compare this to the view in figure 5.3—here, nothing indicates how these two are related.

Look at the second row (the process registered as tr_sup). At what program point was that process last seen? The Current Function column says gen_server:loop/6. That doesn't look like the code you wrote for the tr_sup supervisor, so what's going on? Well, that program point belongs to the code for the behaviour container that we talked about in section 3.1.2. Your tr_sup module in section 4.2 was an implementation of the supervisor behaviour, and supervisors are based on the gen_server behaviour. Any process that is based on gen_server usually hangs around in the main loop of the gen_server module waiting for another message when it has nothing else to do. This is important to keep in mind when you're debugging: the current function for a process is often part of some generic framework code, and in many cases, the registered name of the process is more important for identifying the process you're looking for.

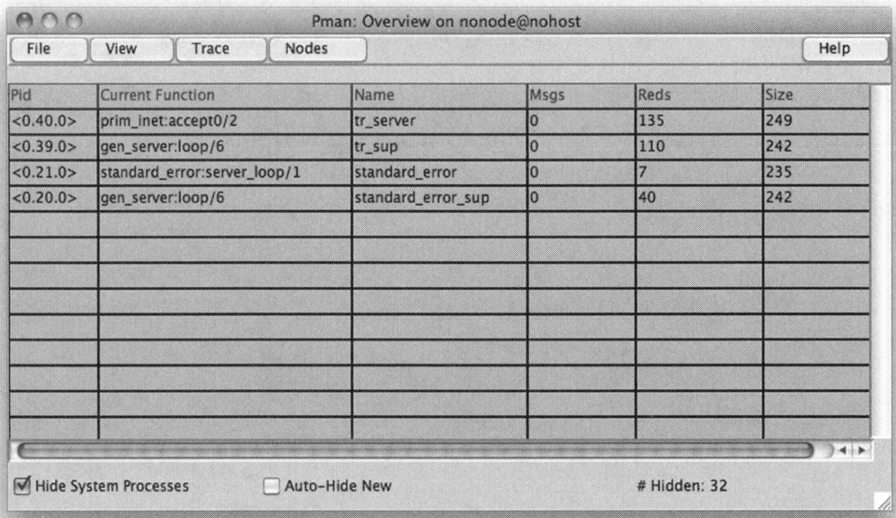

Pid	Current Function	Name	Msgs	Reds	Size
<0.40.0>	prim_inet:accept0/2	tr_server	0	135	249
<0.39.0>	gen_server:loop/6	tr_sup	0	110	242
<0.21.0>	standard_error:server_loop/1	standard_error	0	7	235
<0.20.0>	gen_server:loop/6	standard_error_sup	0	40	242

Figure 5.7   The Pman main window after hiding system processes. This is a more manageable list. You can shorten the list even further by using the Hide Selected Process option in the View menu.

You can use the File menu to exit Pman or set options for tracing. As in Appmon, there's a Nodes menu for working with distributed Erlang. The Trace menu lets you enable tracing for processes and is also where you'll find the menu item for killing a process.

The View menu is the one of most interest right now. It lets you select in more detail which processes you want to see or refresh the information in the window. You can either start by hiding all processes and then selecting the specific ones that you want to show, or by showing all processes and then hiding a few selected ones. You can also choose to hide processes based on the module they're currently executing, or bring up a window with information about the module that a process is in.

If you double-click a process in the list or choose Trace > Trace Selected Process, a Trace window for the process pops up. It first prints some basic information and then starts to trace the process according to the current options. Figure 5.8 shows the window for setting default trace options, which you can open via File > Options. These options can also be controlled individually for each open trace window.

The most important options are those in the Trace Output section. Here, you can decide whether you want to see messages sent or received, function calls, and other events such as processes being spawned, linked, or terminated. You can specify how to treat new processes spawned by the currently traced process (or linked to it), and you can dump the trace output to a file instead of to the GUI window.

A word of warning: tracing can be heavy on the system, if the traced process is doing a lot of work. In particular, you don't want to trace a system process that is involved with displaying the results of the trace itself. Like a logger trying to log its

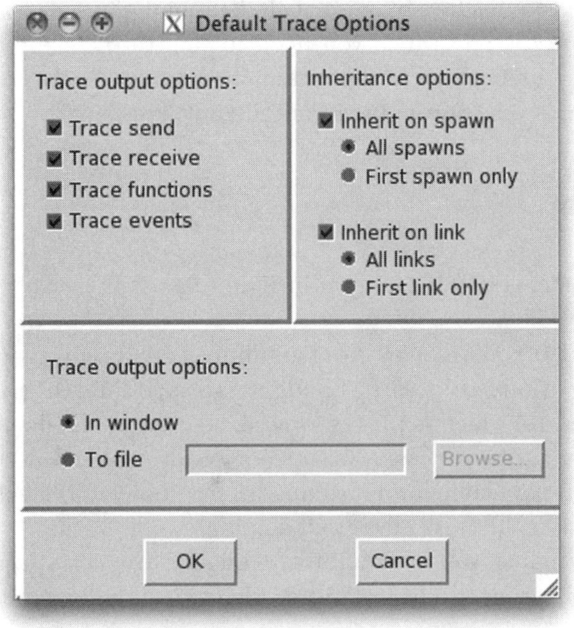

Figure 5.8
Setting default tracing options in Pman. You can choose which actions you want to trace and whether to trace any new processes spawned or linked by the current process. It's also possible to dump the trace output to a file.

own actions, it will quickly flood itself with an enormous amount of information, which can cause the system to run out of memory and crash. Randomly double-clicking a system process in the list is a very bad idea in a production system. (Feel free to play around with it here.)

For this example, try to do some simple tracing on your `tr_server` and `tr_sup` processes while interacting with the server over telnet as you did in section 3.3. Then use the Kill action in the main window's Trace menu to kill the `tr_server` process while tracing the `tr_sup` process, to see how the supervisor reacts when the child dies. There is quite a lot to learn about tracing, but this should give you an idea of how it works.

So far, you've seen the application world view through Appmon and the process-specific world view through Pman. Next, you'll see the module-oriented view with the Debugger.

5.3   *Debugger*

A graphical source–level debugger is one of the quintessential developer tools, although you'll probably find yourself using Erlang's debugger much less than you may be used to from programming in other languages. Partly, this is because you have other sources of information, such as logs and crash reports; and given a crash report, the source code is often so clear (and free from side effects) that you can find the error right away. Another reason is that when crash reports aren't enough, it's usually because the problem lies in a complicated interaction of multiple communicating processes, timing effects, network issues, and general system load. For those situations, good logs are what you need; reproducing the situation in a graphical debugger can be impossible or may give you no clues because of changes in timing.

But there will be some cases in which you need to step through the code—for example, when you're developing a tricky algorithm or protocol. To start the debugger, you can call `debugger:start()` from the Erlang shell:

```
Eshell V5.7.4  (abort with ^G)
1> debugger:start().
{ok,<0.46.0>}
2>
```

This opens the main debugger window, shown in figure 5.9. It's probably not quite what you were expecting.

This doesn't look like DDD, Eclipse, or any of a hundred other debuggers that you may have seen. There are two reasons. First, Erlang uses a very different architecture than you're probably used to, which is process-oriented—even in the debugger: the large empty area is for listing the processes that are currently attached to the debugger. Second, modules aren't available for debugging until you specifically select them: the small area on the left lists the currently selected modules.

To make a module available, you must tell the debugger to *interpret* it. There are two parts to this: the debugger needs the .erl source file (so it can show you the actual

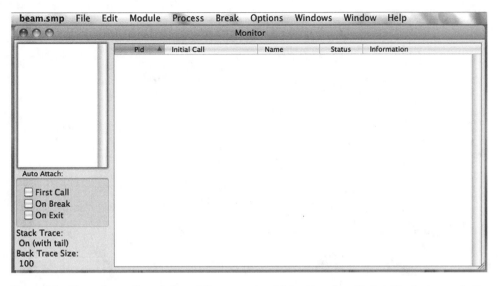

Figure 5.9 **The main monitor window of the source-level debugger when started. The large area to the right shows processes running under the debugger, and the small area to the left lists interpreted modules.**

code), and it needs a corresponding .beam file that contains debugging information. The compiler must be told explicitly to add this, using the debug_info flag. Let's recompile the tcp_rpc code as you did in section 4.3, but with this flag added. (Because this flag should be passed directly to the compiler, it must be prefixed with + instead of – when you give it to erlc.)

```
$ erlc +debug_info -o ebin  src/*.erl
```

Selecting Module > Interpret opens a file-selection dialog box that lets you pick a source file. The debugger automatically finds the corresponding .beam file by looking in the same directory as the source file or in a nearby ebin directory. For this example, locate your tr_server.erl file and select it. You should see tr_server in the module list in the main debugger window. Double-clicking a name in the list opens a new window for viewing the module's source code, as shown in figure 5.10.

First, let's set a breakpoint. Locate the do_rpc/2 function in your code, and double-click the line that calls split_out_mfa(RawData). A red circle appears in the space between the line number and the code. Now, call application:start(tcp_rpc) as before, and try to perform a remote call over telnet as in section 3.3. Unsurprisingly, there is no answer. If you look back to the main debugger window, you should see that it now shows that the process named tr_server has halted at the breakpoint, as in figure 5.11.

If you now double-click the tr_server process in the main window, a new window will open, similar to the one shown in figure 5.12. This allows you to interact with the attached process. As you can see, there are buttons for single-stepping, continuing, and so on, as you expect in a normal source-level debugger. Current variables are

```
View Module tr_server
125    %%
126    %% @spec handle_info(Info, State) -> {noreply, State} |
127    %%                                   {noreply, State, Timeout} |
128    %%                                   {stop, Reason, State}
129    %% @end
130    %%--------------------------------------------------------------
131    handle_info({tcp, Socket, RawData}, State) ->
132        RequestCount = State#state.request_count,
133        try
134            {M, F, A} = split_out_mfa(RawData),
135            Result = apply(M, F, A),
136            gen_tcp:send(Socket, io_lib:fwrite("~p~n", [Result]))
137        catch
138            _C:E ->
139                gen_tcp:send(Socket, io_lib:fwrite("~p~n", [E]))
140        end,
141        {noreply, State#state{request_count = RequestCount + 1}};
142    handle_info(timeout, #state{lsock = LSock} = State) ->
143            {ok, _Sock} = gen_tcp:accept(LSock),
144            {noreply, State}.
145    |
146    %%--------------------------------------------------------------
147    %% @private
148    %% @doc
```

Find: [   ]   ⦿ Next ○ Previous ☐ Match Case   Goto Line: [   ]

Figure 5.10 The debugger window showing the source code for a module. This window lets you search in the code or jump to a particular line. Double-clicking a line sets or removes a breakpoint.

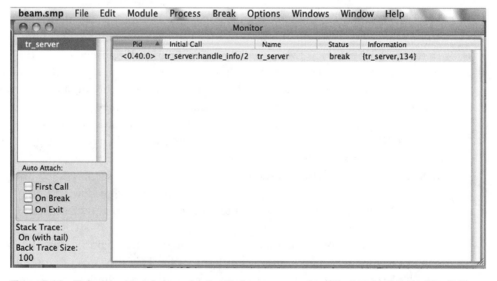

Figure 5.11 Main debugger window, showing that `tr_server` has hit a breakpoint. Double-clicking a process in the list brings up a new window in which you can interact with the process.

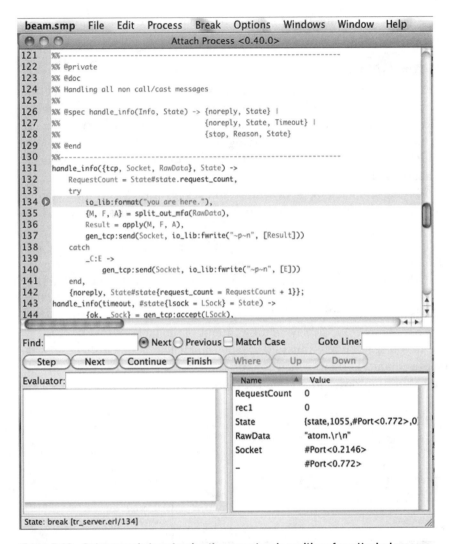

Figure 5.12   Debugger window showing the current code position of an attached process. This window lets you single-step through the code, add or remove breakpoints, view variables, and so on.

shown at lower right in the window; click a variable in the list to display its full value at lower left. You can double-click a source code line to add or remove a breakpoint. Feel free to step through the code to see what is happening.

Using the menus, you can set conditional breakpoints, inspect the message queue, and do other things. We don't have room to go through these options in detail here, but we suggest you play around with the debugger to get an idea of what you can do. We hope this quick tour of the debugger has been enough for you to get over the initial hurdle and start using it for real.

Now, over to something slightly different: a tool for inspecting data, rather than code.

5.4   *TV, the Table Viewer*

The TV application is a bit different from the other tools we've discussed; whereas Appmon, Pman, and the debugger are all about looking at the code running in your system, TV is for looking at the data. TV stands for Table Viewer. You can use it to view the two main types of tables in Erlang: ETS tables and Mnesia tables. We explained about ETS tables in section 2.14, and you'll use them in the next chapter. The Mnesia database will be introduced in chapter 9.

We take a quick look at viewing ETS tables for now. ETS is the default view when you start TV. Entering tv:start() in the Erlang shell brings up the TV main window, as shown in figure 5.13.

In an Erlang system with no user applications running, you initially see few or no tables listed. To make things more interesting, choose Options > System Tables to see a much longer list of tables. At the top of the list, you should find an entry named ac_tab, owned by the application_controller process. Double-click this entry (or click it once and then select File > Open Table) to open a new window like the one shown in figure 5.14, displaying the contents of the table.

As you see, TV lets you view a table much like a spreadsheet. The key symbol (above column 1) shows which column is the primary key. You can adjust the width of the columns in order to see the contents better. This example shows a system table

Terminal Shell Edit View Window Help				
[TV] ETS tables on nonode@nohost				
File View Options				Help
Table Name	**Table Id**	**Owner Pid**	**Owner Name**	**Table Size**
shell_records	8207	<0.26.0>		0
wx_debug_info		<0.43.0>	wxe_master	3931
wx_non_consts		<0.43.0>	wxe_master	53

Figure 5.13   The main window of TV, the Table Viewer. By default, system tables aren't shown.

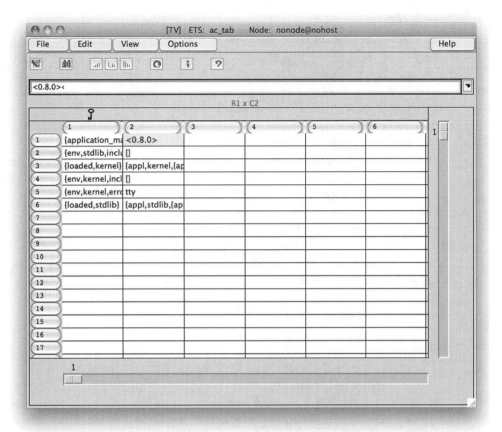

Figure 5.14   TV table window. This example shows the contents of the `ac_tab` system table.

that belongs to the top-level application controller of the Erlang system. It contains some information about the two core applications in Erlang: kernel and stdlib (and possibly more, depending on your system).

The TV application is mostly self-explanatory, so we leave it to you to play around with it and figure it out. The menus and icons provide options for sorting and polling, and you can also get more detailed information about a table, search for entries, and edit or delete entries on the fly. Keep TV in mind when you start using ETS tables and Mnesia in the coming chapters, if you want an easy way to see what's going on with your data.

That concludes our tour of these four GUI tools. Although they're quite different in their features, they all have one thing in common: they can be started from the Erlang Toolbar.

5.5   *Toolbar*

The Toolbar application is a small window with a
button for each of the available applications. If
you use these tools often, for example, during a
debugging session, it may be easier to start Toolbar
right away and keep it somewhere on your
desktop, rather than starting the applications
individually as you did earlier. Call `toolbar:`
`start()` from the Erlang shell, and you'll get a
window similar to the one shown in figure 5.15.

**Figure 5.15   The Erlang Toolbar. This
is handy if you often start TV, Pman,
Debugger, or Appmon. It's even
possible to add your own custom tool
icons to the toolbar.**

The first button starts TV, the next starts
Pman, the third Debugger, and the fourth Appmon. Although it's not likely that you'll do so,
you can add buttons to the toolbar to launch other custom tools: select Tools > Create
Tool File, and you're asked to fill in the details of your new tool, including the icon
file to use and the module and function used to start the tool when the icon is clicked.
For example, specifying `mymod` and `myfun` causes `mymod:myfun()` to be called. (The
tool-start function can't take any arguments.)

5.6   *Summary*

The applications we've introduced here are the primary visual tools for introspection
and interaction with a running Erlang system. We hope that we've shown you enough
about them to make them part of your everyday toolkit; you can now continue exploring on your own. You can find out more in the Tools section of the official Erlang/
OTP documentation.

Part 2

Building a production system

Welcome to the real world, which is what OTP is all about. In this section of the book, we follow the Erlware team as they solve some of the problems they're facing with the help of Erlang and, most especially, OTP. We cover behaviours, monitoring, packaging, and a host of other critical techniques and technologies necessary to build industrial-grade Erlang software.

Implementing a caching system

6

Now that you're familiar with the basics of Erlang/OTP, it's time to move on to more advanced and realistic examples. Starting in this chapter, you'll spend part 2 of this book building up a useful, distributed application in Erlang. To help you understand the motivations for what you're doing, we couch this development within the narrative of an open source project called Erlware that is facing some fictional, but realistic, challenges that you'll solve.

6.1 The background story

The Erlware project is focused on making Erlang applications easily accessible, so that others may run them either as end-user applications or as components in their own projects. Erlang is gaining popularity quickly, so the demand for easy access to open source applications and build tools has grown quickly as well. This has caused quite a bit of growth in the Erlware project, and the project administrators are starting to hear users complain about the responsiveness of the website. Most of the complaints are related to how quickly pages can be served. The Erlware team is naturally concerned about their users, not to mention that search engines like Google are rumored to punish sites that are slow to serve up pages.

The page that has garnered the most complaints is the package search page. This page allows users to search for a particular piece of Erlang/OTP software among the many in the Erlware repository. To produce this page, the web server must go out to a disjoint set of package servers and request a list of packages from each such server. The package servers are independent, and there is no central database for all packages across all servers. This was fine when Erlware was small and had only one package server; it was even fine with up to three servers, but it didn't scale beyond that. The structure of the system is illustrated in figure 6.1.

The team at Erlware sits down and decides that one way to speed things up would be to extend the web servers with local caching. This way, when a package listing is requested, the list will be cached using the URL as key; then, the next time the same URL is asked for, the list of packages can be pulled quickly from the cache and used to render the page. This architecture is illustrated in figure 6.2.

You'll implement this cache as a separate OTP application. This chapter is centered on the basic functionality your cache will offer, which boils down to a few functions:

- Start and stop the cache.
- Add a key/value pair to the cache.
- Retrieve a value for a given key.
- Update the value for a given key.
- Delete a key/value pair.

With these in place, you'll have a working cache in its simplest form. The initial version of the cache that you construct in this chapter won't have any advanced features; it'll be a standalone cache for the purpose of speeding up a single web server on a single machine, easily accessible via plain Erlang function calls. More advanced features, such as distribution, will be added in subsequent chapters. Before we get into the nitty-gritty parts of implementing a basic cache, it's a good idea to go over the proposed design.

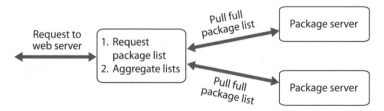

Figure 6.1   The current Erlware architecture: each request to the web server results in a full listing being fetched from every package server.

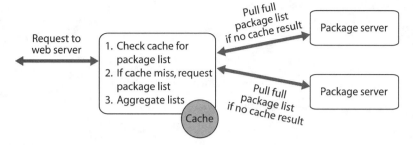

Figure 6.2 The new architecture being planned. The web server caches package listings locally, so it doesn't have to fetch them for each request.

6.2   *The design of your cache*

Your simple cache will store key/value pairs, where the keys are unique and each key maps to a single value. The core idea behind the design of this cache is that you'll use a separate process to store each value you insert and map each key to its corresponding process. You may consider it strange, even unbelievable, that you would use a process for each value like this; but for something like a cache, it makes sense, because every value may have its own life cycle. Erlang's support for large numbers of lightweight processes makes this approach possible.

To build this cache, you'll need to create some basic subsystems. Each of these will be housed in a separate module. Figure 6.3 illustrates the different pieces of the simple cache.

As figure 6.3 shows, you'll be creating five separate modules, listed in table 6.1.

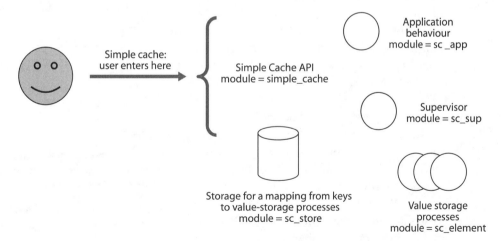

Figure 6.3 The different parts of the Simple Cache implementation. There will be an API front end, a main application module, a number of value-storage processes with a single supervisor module, and a mapping from keys to corresponding storage processes.

Table 6.1   Modules of the Simple Cache application

Module	Purpose
simple_cache	The user API; the application's face to the outside
sc_app	The application behaviour implementation
sc_sup	The root supervisor implementation
sc_store	A module to encapsulate your key-to-pid mapping
sc_element	Code for the individual processes that store the cached data

Module naming conventions

Remember what we said in section 3.2 about naming conventions for modules? This application uses the prefix sc_ (for *Simple Cache*) for all modules, except the main user API module, which is named simple_cache. This is a common pattern, to have a single module acting as a front end that uses the same name as the application.

Users of the cache will interact solely through the simple_cache API module. This will communicate directly with the sc_store module that maps keys to processes, and with the sc_element module for creating storage elements, updating them, and deleting them. All the elements are supervised by the sc_sup supervisor, and there is an application behaviour, sc_app, for starting and stopping the whole cache system. Figure 6.4 illustrates this architecture from a process and dataflow perspective.

The supervisor will be able to spawn sc_element processes on demand at runtime, upon the insertion of a key/value pair. When a process has been spawned to hold the value for a particular key, a mapping from the key to the process ID will be kept in the sc_store. This creates an indirect mapping from the key to the value. To retrieve the value for a key, you first

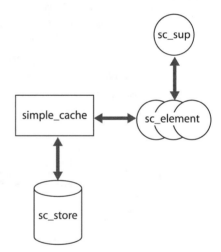

Figure 6.4   The data flow between modules and their corresponding processes. The user API module simple_cache only communicates directly with the sc_store and sc_element modules.

look up the process ID of the storage element and then query it for the current value. Figure 6.5 illustrates this indirect mapping.

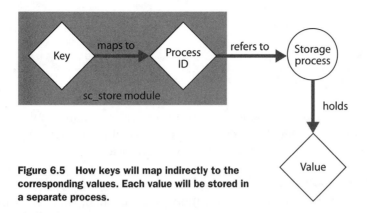

Figure 6.5   How keys will map indirectly to the corresponding values. Each value will be stored in a separate process.

All this may seem strange right now, but this architecture will leverage many powerful mechanisms in OTP. By the end of this chapter, you'll realize how much functionality you get for free and how few lines of code it takes to implement the whole thing. Let's get started by creating the application infrastructure for the cache.

6.3   *Creating the basic OTP application skeleton*

The starting point for any good Erlang project is creating a proper OTP application. Often, a project can be broken down into multiple applications, but for now your simple cache will be a single application (although it's intended to work as part of a larger group).

This section will follow closely what you did in chapter 4 to make an application out of the tr_server. The difference here is that you begin from the other end: having no real functionality, only a design, you'll first set up an application skeleton that you add code to.

To recapitulate, setting up the application structure consists of the following steps:

1   Create a standard application directory layout.
2   Write the .app file.
3   Write the application behaviour implementation module, sc_app.
4   Implement the top-level supervisor, sc_sup.

Because you're making an active application, something that's alive and running, you'll need an application behaviour implementation and a root supervisor implementation. Following the same conventions as in chapter 4, these modules will have the suffixes _app and _sup, respectively. But first, you need to create some directories.

6.3.1   *Laying out the application directory structure*

Start by creating a top-level application directory called simple_cache. Under it, create the subdirectories doc, ebin, include, priv, and src, just like you did in section 4.1.1. The directory tree should look like this:

```
simple_cache
        |
        | - doc
        | - ebin
        | - include
        | - priv
        | - src
```

(You won't use the doc, include, and priv directories in this example, but there's no harm in having them from the beginning in case you need them later.) After you've created the layout, the next step is to put the .app file in place.

6.3.2   *Creating the application metadata*

As explained in section 4.1.2, OTP needs a little metadata about your application in order to be able to do things like start the application or perform safe hot-code upgrades at runtime. The name of the .app file should match the application name (which isn't necessarily the name of any particular module); in this case, the file is ebin/simple_cache.app. The following shows what to put in the .app file for now:

```
{application, simple_cache,
 [{description, "A simple caching system"},
  {vsn, "0.1.0"},
  {modules, [
            sc_app,
            sc_sup
           ]},
  {registered, [sc_sup]},
  {applications, [kernel, stdlib]},
  {mod, {sc_app, []}}
 ]}.
```

Compare this with listing 4.1, and you'll see that they're similar. You know you'll write the sc_app and sc_sup modules, so you can list them right away; you'll add other modules to the list as you go. You also know that you'll register the name of the root supervisor under the name sc_sup.

Next, you'll flesh out the application behaviour implementation.

6.3.3   *Implementing the application behaviour*

The file src/sc_app.erl implements the application behaviour, as shown in listing 6,1; compare this to tr_app.erl in section 4.1.3. Recall in particular that the mod tuple in the .app file points out the name of the application behaviour module, so the system knows how to start and stop the application.

> **Listing 6.1   src/sc_app.erl**

```
-module(sc_app).

-behaviour(application).            Behaviour
                                    declaration

-export([start/2, stop/1]).         Exported behaviour
                                    callbacks
```

```
start(_StartType, _StartArgs) ->
    case sc_sup:start_link() of           ◁─┐ Starts root
        {ok, Pid} ->                          supervisor
            {ok, Pid};
        Other ->
            {error, Other}
    end.

stop(_State) ->
    ok.
```

The only real job to be done by the `sc_app` module is to start the root supervisor when the application is started (you'll modify this slightly in section 6.4.2). You don't need it to do anything special when it stops.

6.3.4 *Implementing the supervisor*

The file src/sc_sup.erl (see listing 6.2) implements the root supervisor. The supervisor you'll use here is different from the one you created in chapter 4; it doesn't have any statically specified permanent child processes, but it can have any number of dynamically added temporary children that will all be of the same type.

SIMPLE-ONE-FOR-ONE SUPERVISION

This supervisor is set up for `simple_one_for_one` supervision. With the other restart strategies, such as `one_for_one`, which you used in section 4.2.1, a supervisor typically manages a number of children that all start when the supervisor starts and usually run for as long as the supervisor is running. A `simple_one_for_one` supervisor can start only one type of child, but can start any number of them; all its children are dynamically added at runtime, and no child process is started when the supervisor starts up.

Listing 6.2 src/sc_sup.erl

```
-module(sc_sup).

-behaviour(supervisor).

-export([start_link/0,             ┐ Starts children
         start_child/2        ◁────┘ dynamically
        ]).

-export([init/1]).                                    Arguments for
                                                sc_element:start_link/2 ┐
-define(SERVER, ?MODULE).                                               │
                                                                        │
start_link() ->                                                         │
    supervisor:start_link({local, ?SERVER}, ?MODULE, []).              │
                                                                        │
start_child(Value, LeaseTime) ->                                       │
    supervisor:start_child(?SERVER, [Value, LeaseTime]).    ◁──────────┘

init([]) ->
    Element = {sc_element, {sc_element, start_link, []},
               temporary, brutal_kill, worker, [sc_element]},
    Children = [Element],
    RestartStrategy = {simple_one_for_one, 0, 1},
    {ok, {RestartStrategy, Children}}.
```

The init/1 function of the supervisor in listing 6.2 still looks much like the one back in listing 4.3. There, you also had a single child specification, but in this case it's a requirement: init/1 for a simple_one_for_one supervisor must specify exactly one child process, but it isn't started along with the supervisor. Instead, the supervisor can be asked to start new child processes at any time, using a simplified form of the function supervisor:start_child/2. For other kinds of supervisors, if you want to add children dynamically, you must give a full child specification to start_child/2. With a simple_one_for_one supervisor, all children have the same specification, and the supervisor already knows it, so you only have to say "please start another one." This is what you want to have here.

THE SUPERVISOR MODULE

You have two API functions in the sc_sup module, compared to just one in tr_sup in listing 4.3. The new start_child/2 function does exactly what we described earlier: it asks the running supervisor (identified by ?SERVER) to start a new child, passing it the extra arguments Value and LeaseTime (because these will be different for each child process). You make this an API function to keep the implementation details encapsulated within this module.

The init/1 function has some subtle differences from the one in listing 4.3, so take a close look and refer to section 4.2.3 for details. The central difference is of course the restart strategy, which is defined as simple_one_for_one with zero restarts allowed within any 1 second. In this supervisor, the children are marked as temporary rather than permanent, meaning that if they die, they should not be restarted. This supervisor is in many ways just a factory for sc_element processes. You also set the shutdown type to brutal_kill, indicating that the children should be terminated immediately when the supervisor shuts down. (For a simple_one_for_one supervisor, the supervisor won't do anything to actively shut down the children; instead, they're expected to terminate when they receive the exit signal triggered by the death of the supervisor. If the children are normal OTP behaviours, this is guaranteed. Specifying brutal_kill here is mostly to show intent.)

When someone calls the start_child/2 API function, it results in a message being sent to the supervisor process, asking it to start a new child process using the start_link function in sc_element with the extra arguments Value and LeaseTime. The following tuple in the child spec

```
{sc_element, start_link, []}
```

which indicates the module name, function name, and arguments of the start function for the child process, gets the list [Value, LeaseTime] appended to the argument list [] before the call is made, resulting in a call to sc_element:start_link(Value, LeaseTime).

Each time sc_sup:start_child/2 is called, a new sc_element process is started, each with its own value and lease time. This results in a dynamically generated supervision tree, as shown in figure 6.6.

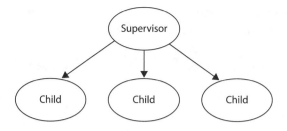

Figure 6.6
A simple-one-for-one supervisor hierarchy.
All the child processes are of the same
type and are added or removed dynamically.
There can be any number of them.

At this point, you have a working application skeleton; you can start it from within the Erlang shell and see it run. Of course, you can't do anything with it, apart from starting and stopping it, because your application has no real functionality and no user interface. As of now, when the supervisor starts, it doesn't start any child processes because it's a `simple_one_for_one` supervisor; but because you haven't implemented `sc_element` yet, you'll get a runtime error if you try to call `sc_sup:start_child/2`. The rest of this chapter will be about adding this functionality to get a fully functioning `simple_cache` application.

6.4 *From application skeleton to a working cache*

Before you go on, look back at figure 6.3 to recall the design of the application, with the modules you'll implement listed in table 6.1. Of these, you've written `sc_app` and `sc_sup`, which were part of the basic application structure. The following remain:

- `simple_cache`—The user API
- `sc_element`—The processes that store cached values
- `sc_store`—The code for mapping keys to processes

First, you'll implement the `sc_element` module so that your top-level supervisor will have something to start. After that, you'll implement `sc_store` to map keys to processes, and finally you'll create the API module to wrap everything up in a nice user interface.

6.4.1 *Coding the sc_element processes*

Recall that `sc_element` is the module that holds the code for the child processes of `sc_sup` and that a new such process will be spawned each time new data is entered into the cache, to hold the data associated with a particular key. The plan is to let the processes be based on the `gen_server` behaviour (like `tr_server` from chapter 3) and keep the data in the `gen_server` state. Refer back to chapter 3 if you need a refresher on how `gen_server` works; we don't repeat the details here.

THE HEADER
The module header, shown in listing 6.3, should look familiar by now; it's similar to the one in listing 3.2. The main difference is the API, which is natural—although the servers are based on the same framework internally, they have different uses. You have

four major functions: creating a new element, fetching the value of an element, replacing the value of an element, and deleting an element.

Listing 6.3   Header of src/sc_element.erl

```erlang
-module(sc_element).

-behaviour(gen_server).

-export([
        start_link/2,
        create/2,
        create/1,                              Exported API
        fetch/1,                               functions
        replace/2,
        delete/1
        ]).

-export([init/1, handle_call/3, handle_cast/2, handle_info/2,
        terminate/2, code_change/3]).

-define(SERVER, ?MODULE).                      One day in
-define(DEFAULT_LEASE_TIME, (60 * 60 * 24)).   seconds
                                                              State
-record(state, {value, lease_time, start_time}).              record
```

You define the macro DEFAULT_LEASE_TIME as the default number of seconds that a key/value pair can live in the cache without being evicted. The purpose of the lease time is to keep the content of the cache fresh; after all, it's a cache, not a database. You'll make it possible to override this value via the API when creating a new sc_element process.

The last thing in the header is the definition of a record to represent the gen_server state. It contains three fields: the value the process is holding on to, the lease time, and a timestamp from when the process was started.

THE API SECTION AND PROCESS STARTUP

The next section of the module is the API implementation, shown in the following listing.

Listing 6.4   API section of src/sc_element.erl

```erlang
start_link(Value, LeaseTime) ->
    gen_server:start_link(?MODULE, [Value, LeaseTime], []).

create(Value, LeaseTime) ->
    sc_sup:start_child(Value, LeaseTime).               Delegates start
                                                         to sc_sup
create(Value) ->
    create(Value, ?DEFAULT_LEASE_TIME).

fetch(Pid) ->
    gen_server:call(Pid, fetch).

replace(Pid, Value) ->
    gen_server:cast(Pid, {replace, Value}).

delete(Pid) ->
    gen_server:cast(Pid, delete).
```

As we explained in section 6.3.4, starting a child process should be done by asking the supervisor; you created the supervisor API function sc_sup:start_child/2 to hide the details of how this is done. But users of sc_element shouldn't have to know about an implementation detail such as the existence of a supervisor. Therefore, you add an API function called create/2, which hides the delegation to sc_sup. You also include the short form create/1, for when you just want the default lease time. Later, if you want to change the underlying implementation drastically, your interface need not change.

Also recall from section 6.3.4 that you set up the child specification for the simple_one_for_one supervisor so that when you ask for a new child process via sc_sup:start_child/2, it calls back to sc_element:start_link(Value, LeaseTime). This API function, it its turn, is implemented in a more standard way, much like tr_server:start_link/1 in listing 3.3. The differences are that in this case, end users shouldn't call start_link/2 directly (because then the process won't be supervised), and that you don't ask the gen_server library to register the process for you (because there will be many such processes, not a singleton).

To make sure you understand this convoluted call flow, let's go over it again. When a new element is to be inserted, you call sc_element:create(...), which delegates to the supervisor API function sc_sup:start_child/2, which in turn calls the library function super-visor:start_child/2. Using the child specification and the extra arguments Value and LeaseTime, the supervisor code calls back to sc_element:start_link/2. Nothing has been said about how an sc_element process is implemented; but because you're basing it on gen_server, this is where you hand over to the library function gen_server:

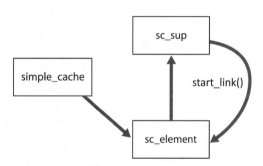

Figure 6.7   Call flow when a new storage element is added. The sc_element API keeps simple_cache from knowing about sc_sup. At the same time, sc_sup knows no details about what an sc_element does.

start_link/3 to kick off a new child process for real. The call flow is illustrated in figure 6.7.

The remaining API functions—fetch/1, replace/2, and delete/1—are simple, much like the ones in tr_server in listing 3.3. All they do is send a request to the process, using either call or cast. Only fetch/1 needs to wait for an answer, so the other two can do an asynchronous cast and return to the caller immediately. A small but important difference from the tr_server is that there is no registered name for any of these sc_element processes. (There can, after all, be any number of them.) This means the API functions must include the process identifier, so that the gen_server functions know where to send the messages. Of course, that means it's the client's problem to keep track of these identifiers. We get back to that when you implement the sc_store module in section 6.4.2.

THE GEN_SERVER CALLBACK SECTION

The first thing that happens when your sc_element process starts is that the gen_server callback function init/1 is called to initialize the process; see section 3.2.4 if you need a reminder about how the gen_server callbacks work. This function should return a fully initialized state record. The call to gen_server:start_link/3 blocks until init/1 returns. The callback section of src/sc_element.erl is shown in the following listing.

Listing 6.5 `gen_server` callback section of src/sc_element.erl

```erlang
init([Value, LeaseTime]) ->
    Now = calendar:local_time(),
    StartTime = calendar:datetime_to_gregorian_seconds(Now),
    {ok,
     #state{value = Value,                          ◁── Initializes
            lease_time = LeaseTime,                      server state
            start_time = StartTime},
     time_left(StartTime, LeaseTime)}.              ◁── Sets timeout on
                                                        initialization
time_left(_StartTime, infinity) ->
    infinity;
time_left(StartTime, LeaseTime) ->
    Now = calendar:local_time(),
    CurrentTime = calendar:datetime_to_gregorian_seconds(Now),
    TimeElapsed = CurrentTime - StartTime,
    case LeaseTime - TimeElapsed of
        Time when Time =< 0 -> 0;
        Time                -> Time * 1000
    end.

handle_call(fetch, _From,  State) ->
    #state{value = Value,
           lease_time = LeaseTime,
           start_time = StartTime} = State,
    TimeLeft = time_left(StartTime, LeaseTime),         ❶  Returns value
    {reply, {ok, Value}, State, TimeLeft}.             ◁─   from state

handle_cast({replace, Value}, State) ->
    #state{lease_time = LeaseTime,
           start_time = StartTime} = State,
    TimeLeft = time_left(StartTime, LeaseTime),
    {noreply, State#state{value = Value}, TimeLeft};
handle_cast(delete, State) ->
    {stop, normal, State}.                              ❷  Signals
                                                       ◁─   shutdown
handle_info(timeout, State) ->
    {stop, normal, State}.

terminate(_Reason, _State) ->                           ❸  Removes key
    sc_store:delete(self()),                           ◁─   for process
    ok.

code_change(_OldVsn, State, _Extra) ->
    {ok, State}.
```

Setting server timeouts

Remember that if you forget to return a new timeout value in one of the callback functions, the timeout will revert to `infinity`. When you're using server timeouts, it's important to remember to set them in every clause of every callback function.

We now go through each of these callback functions in detail:

- `init/1`—The `init/1` function isn't complicated. You use a couple of standard library functions to get the time when the process started and convert it to Gregorian seconds: a useful uniform representation of time as the number of seconds since year 0 (year 1 BC) according to the normal Western/International Gregorian calendar. See the documentation for the standard library `calendar` module for more details. The rest is just filling in the fields of the server state with the value you want to store, the lease time, and the start time.

  Note that you use the third position in the returned tuple to specify the server timeout after initialization. If you recall, you did the same in `tr_server` in chapter 3, but that was for a different purpose. Here, you use it to manage lease times. As you'll see, the decision to use a separate process for every stored value in the cache makes lease management trivial and spares you an implementation headache. If the server process isn't accessed within the lease period, a `timeout` message is sent to the server and passed to the `handle_info/2` function, which shuts down the process.

  The utility function `time_left/2` computes the number of milliseconds left of the lease, which is what the system wants—not seconds. It also allows the use of the atom `infinity` instead of an integer and ensures that you never return a negative number.

- `handle_call/3: fetch`—Because you want to get a value from the `fetch/1` API function, you use a synchronous `call` to talk to the server process. This is passed to the `handle_call/3` callback function.

  All you need to do is match the value from the state and return it to the caller ❶ (the `{ok, Value}` part of the return tuple is returned by `fetch/1`). The only thing that makes the code a little messy is that you need to also get the start time and lease time and compute the new timeout. You return the state unchanged to `gen_server`, because nothing should be modified here.

- `handle_cast/2: replace`—The API function `replace/2` is used to update an existing `sc_element` process with a new value. This needs no particular reply to the client, so you use an asynchronous `cast`, which is passed to `handle_cast/2`. As usual, the message is tagged with the same name as the function that sends the message. Sticking to this simple idiom will save you lots of confusion later when you create servers with more complicated interfaces.

The first clause of handle_cast in listing 6.5 takes care of {replace,Value} messages. The code is similar to the fetch case, but you don't need to extract the old value, there is no reply to be sent, and you return a modified state to gen_server in which you've substituted the new value for the old (see section 2.11.3 for more about record updates).

- handle_cast/2: delete—The delete/1 API function similarly doesn't need a return value and so uses cast, ending up in the second clause of handle_cast/2. The only thing delete needs to do is to terminate this sc_element process, removing it from the cache.

    Note the difference between the tuple returned from delete and the one returned from replace. The latter returns noreply, meaning that the server doesn't reply but stays alive, whereas the former returns stop, which causes the gen_server to shut itself down ❷. The reason for stopping is given as normal. This is a special value that signals to the OTP system that the server shut down normally: it shouldn't be restarted unless it was marked as permanent, and it shouldn't be logged as an abnormal shutdown.

- terminate/2—When a gen_server shuts down, it calls the terminate/2 callback to give you a chance to clean things up. In this case, you need to remove all traces of the key associated with the process ❸. When the process dies, the server state vanishes, which takes care of the stored value but doesn't handle the mapping from the key to the process ID. As we mentioned, this mapping is handled by the sc_store module, which you'll implement in the next section. All you need to do here is call sc_store:delete(Pid), passing it the pid of this particular sc_element process.

You've finished implementing sc_element and its API functions:

- start_link/2
- create/2 (and create/1)
- fetch/1
- replace/2
- delete/1

Together, these functions allow you to store data in an sc_element process and retrieve it, update the value, and delete it. As part of the delete operation, you saw your first interaction with the key-to-pid mapping in the sc_store module, which is what you'll implement next.

6.4.2 *Implementing the sc_store module*

By now, you've implemented the basic application structure and the backing storage for your cache, including lease handling. You now need to build a complete storage system on top of this. The main thing you're missing is the mapping from keys to process identifiers (shown in figure 6.5) so that you can access the value stored for a given key. To implement this mapping, you'll use an ETS table (Erlang Term Storage; see section 2.14); as we go along, we explain some details about ETS tables.

The fact that your storage is implemented with ETS should be hidden from the rest of the system. The `sc_store` module will serve as an abstraction layer for whatever storage mechanism you're using to store the key-to-pid mapping. Instead of using ETS, this could be done with a `gen_server` process that keeps the mapping data in its state, it could be a file on disk that you write to on each insert and delete, or it could be a relational database. Whatever the implementation, you want to decouple the application from the choice of storage system, allowing you to change your mind later and use a different solution. You could even move to a replicated database solution with no change to the rest of the application code.

To quickly recapture what we said in chapter 2, ETS tables are fast, in-memory hash tables for Erlang data. They're implemented in C as a part of the Erlang Run-Time System (ERTS) and are accessed using a set of built-in Erlang functions. Every entry must be a tuple, where one of the tuple columns (normally the first or second) is the key. ETS tables are particularly useful for data that

- Doesn't need to be shared between virtual machines
- Needs to be persistent, but only as long as the VM is alive
- May need to be shared by a number of different processes on the VM
- Needs fast access times
- Is mainly flat and preferably without foreign key relationships to other tables

The example's storage requirements match these criteria well: the mapping needs to persist for as long as the cache is running, but doesn't need to persist if the VM dies, and doesn't need to be shared between multiple VMs; you may need to share the table between processes; the data needs to be fetched quickly because the lookup operation is in the critical path of your cache; and the data is flat and has no relationships to other tables. It's a single table of pairs of keys and process identifiers.

Listing 6.6 shows the code for src/sc_store.erl. For once, this module won't implement an OTP behaviour, and no specific process will be associated with the module—it just contains a set of library functions for other processes to call. (But this could change in the future.)

Listing 6.6   src/sc_store.erl

```erlang
-module(sc_store).

-export([
         init/0,
         insert/2,
         delete/1,
         lookup/1
        ]).

-define(TABLE_ID, ?MODULE).
```

```
init() ->
    ets:new(?TABLE_ID, [public, named_table]),
    ok.

insert(Key, Pid) ->
    ets:insert(?TABLE_ID, {Key, Pid}).

lookup(Key) ->
    case ets:lookup(?TABLE_ID, Key) of
        [{Key, Pid}] -> {ok, Pid};
        []           -> {error, not_found}
    end.

delete(Pid) ->
    ets:match_delete(?TABLE_ID, {'_', Pid}).
```

The API consists of an `init/1` function for initializing the storage system and three functions that handle the basic CRUD operations (*create, read, update,* and *delete*), where the `insert/2` function is used both to create new entries and to update existing ones. All the functions are small. We look at the initialization first.

INITIALIZING THE STORE

In `init/1`, you need to create the ETS table that'll represent the mapping. This is simple: call `ets:new/2`. Because you want the table to be accessible to many different processes, you need to mark it as `public`; and to make it easy for these processes to find the table, you make it a `named_table`. The name is given by the `TABLE_ID` macro, which is defined here to be the same as the module (`sc_store`).

First things first

As a point of style, an initialization or startup function like this should be placed first in the API section. (You did the same with the `start_link` and `init` functions in the other modules.) This kind of predictability makes modules easier to read.

An ETS table can be accessed in two ways. The first and most common is to use the table handle returned by the `ets:new/2` function; this uniquely identifies a table much like a pid identifies a process. The second way is to use the table name. The ETS interface requires that each table is given a name; but unless `named_table` is specified, the name can't be used to access the table, and multiple such tables can have the same name. You use a named table here because you don't want to force users of your library to keep track of the table handle—that would require you to pass the handle to all processes that want to use `sc_store`, and the table handle would have to be included in every `sc_store` API call.

Here is a question for you: from where should you call the `sc_store:init/0` function? Think about it for a moment. You have essentially two options: from your application behaviour module `sc_app`, or from your root supervisor `sc_sup`. As we've said before, it's a good design principle to limit the amount of application code in supervisors in order to keep them small and reliable. Inserting code into the `init/1` function of a top-level supervisor is somewhat forgivable, because if it breaks, the application can't start. We still don't like doing that on principle; and while we may do it on occasion, we prefer placing this sort of initialization code in the application behaviour file. You should modify the start/2 function in src/sc_app.erl (listing 6.1) to look as follows:

```
start(_StartType, _StartArgs) ->
    sc_store:init(),                    Initializes
    case sc_sup:start_link() of         storage
        {ok, Pid} ->
            {ok, Pid};
        Other ->
            {error, Other}
    end.
```

With this in place, sc_store is initialized first thing when the application starts. If you were to initialize it later (for example, after starting the top-level supervisor), you'd run the risk that you somewhere would try to access an ETS table that doesn't yet exist.

Next, to be able to resolve a mapping from a key to a pid, you need to be able to store such a mapping.

CREATING AND UPDATING ENTRIES

The sc_store:insert/2 function in listing 6.6 handles both inserting new mappings and updating existing ones, through a simple call to ets:insert/2, identifying the table by its name. The second argument to ets:insert/2 must always be a tuple, as we explained in section 2.14.2. By default, the first element of the stored tuples is used as the key, and the other elements (any number of them) are the payload. When you look up a particular key, the entire tuple is returned. The default behaviour for an ETS table is to be a *set*: there can only be one entry at a time for any specific key, so if you insert a new tuple using an existing key, it overwrites the previous entry—just what you want for this function.

Note that this function doesn't check any data types; it doesn't seek to ensure that what is being inserted is a pid. This is internal code that trusts its callers. The code that eventually performs the insert will be code that you write. You'll check for sanity at the borders of your system, but not afterward. If you have a problem somewhere, you'll discover it through testing. This philosophy keeps your code clean and makes it easier to maintain.

Now that you can insert data, you want to be able to look it up again.

READING DATA

A lookup on the key element of an ETS table is a fast, constant-time operation if the table is a set (the default type), because this uses a hash table representation internally. As we explained in section 2.14.2, ets:lookup/2 returns a list of all the tuples that have this key. Because the table is a set, the result is either one tuple or none, as you can see in the lookup/1 function in listing 6.6.

If you find an entry for a given key, you transform the return value from ETS into a more palatable {ok, Pid}. If the key isn't in the table, you return {error, not_found} instead. This is another example of encapsulation: there is no reason to leak the exact return value from ETS to the world outside, when the fact that your implementation uses ETS tables is incidental and unimportant to the callers of this function.

All you need to be able to do now is delete entries. How this is done (using a single short line of code) will need a bit of explanation.

DELETING AN ENTRY USING MATCH PATTERNS

The problem is that you want to delete entries based on the value (the process identifier), rather than on the key. This is to make the function `sc_element:terminate/2` from section 6.4.1 (listing 6.5) as simple as possible: when the process dies, it says, "please remove my entry from the table." Note that the way the code is structured ensures that there is exactly one distinct process per key. There are a couple of approaches to solving this problem: you can maintain a separate inverted index table, so that you first look up the key for a particular pid and then use the key to delete the entry, but that requires twice as much code and two write operations instead of one for each insert or delete operation. You can also traverse the table key by key until you find the entry with that specific pid, which is pretty slow (but feasible, if deletion is a rare operation). But ETS tables have a powerful mechanism for using patterns to search through tables without extracting every entry. This still scans the whole table but is fast because it's all done from C code with minimal copying of data.

The `delete/1` function in listing 6.6 generally won't be performed as often as the `insert/2` operation and not nearly as often as `lookup/1`, so this implementation should serve well enough (and you can add an inverted index later to speed it up if necessary). The scan is performed using the function `ets:match_delete/2` with the simple pattern `{'_',Pid}`. We only have space to cover a little about matching here. A full explanation of the matching functions in ETS is beyond the scope of this book and we recommend that you read the Erlang/OTP documentation for more information, because these functions are quite powerful.

The delete operation uses the simple pattern `{'_',Pid}`. This will match against any 2-tuple that contains the given process ID as the second element. Because this pattern is used with `ets:match_delete/2`, any matching entry will be deleted from the table. (You know there will be at most one such entry.) That's all you need to do.

Match patterns

These are patterns expressed as Erlang terms, and they can consist of three things:

- Normal Erlang terms and already-bound variables.
- An underscore as a single-quoted atom (`'_'`). This has the same meaning as an underscore in a regular Erlang pattern—that is, a don't-care pattern or wildcard.
- Pattern variables of the form `'$<integer>'` (for example, `'$1'`, `'$2'`, `'$3'`, ...).

> **(continued)**
> For example, given a stored tuple of the form {erlang,number,1}, a pattern like {erlang,'_',1} will match it. The '_' wildcard indicates that you don't care what is in this position. This pattern will match any 3-tuple with the atom erlang as the first element and the integer 1 as the last. You can also use pattern variables to retrieve values selectively from matched tuples; for instance, a match pattern like {'$2','$1','_'} (on the same stored tuple) will yield the list [number, erlang] because of how the fields line up and because the values of the pattern variables are always returned in the order they're numbered. See the documentation for ets:match/2 for details.

This completes the sc_store module. You have all the operations you need for the key-to-pid mapping, including initialization. You've done this in a way that abstracts away the underlying implementation (using ETS tables) from the rest of your application. You have only one thing left to do: create the user API as a front end to the application.

6.4.3 *Rounding off with the application-level API module*

The convention for application-level API modules is to give them the same name as the application. (Note that the server application in chapter 4 didn't need any API.) In this case, you're creating the simple_cache module as the API to the simple_cache application. This module will contain the interface functions for end users of your cache:

- insert/2—Stores a key and corresponding value in the cache
- lookup/1—Uses a key to retrieve a value
- delete/1—Uses a key to delete the key/value pair from the cache

This API doesn't include any functions for starting or stopping the application; that will be handled via system functions such as application:start/1, as in section 4.3. The previous functions, shown in the following listing, put all the functionality you've created previously in this chapter to use.

Listing 6.7   src/simple_cache.erl

```erlang
-module(simple_cache).

-export([insert/2, lookup/1, delete/1]).

insert(Key, Value) ->                          ❶ Checks if key is
    case sc_store:lookup(Key) of                  already present
        {ok, Pid} ->
            sc_element:replace(Pid, Value);
        {error, _} ->
            {ok, Pid} = sc_element:create(Value),
            sc_store:insert(Key, Pid)
    end.
```

```
lookup(Key) ->
    try
        {ok, Pid} = sc_store:lookup(Key),
        {ok, Value} = sc_element:fetch(Pid),
        {ok, Value}
    catch
        _Class:_Exception ->
            {error, not_found}
    end.

delete(Key) ->
    case sc_store:lookup(Key) of
        {ok, Pid} ->
            sc_element:delete(Pid);
        {error, _Reason} ->
            ok
    end.
```

❷ Fetches pid for key

❸ Cleans up

We now explain the implementation of these API functions in more detail:

- simple_cache:insert/2—This function takes a key and a value and stores the pair in the cache. To do this, you first call sc_store:lookup/1 to determine if you already have an entry for the key ❶. If that is the case, you use the sc_element:replace/2 function to replace the value in the existing storage element with the new value. If there's no entry for the key, you must create a new sc_element process to store the value and then insert a mapping from the key to the process ID in the sc_store. Note that for now, you aren't exposing the lease-time functionality in the API and are relying on the default lease time of 1 day. If you ever want to change that in the user API, it would be a simple matter of adding an extra parameter (and providing a default for backward compatibility).

- simple_cache:lookup/1—Lookup is straightforward: you use sc_store: lookup/1 to fetch the pid for the given key; and if that works, you query the identified sc_element process for the value it holds ❷. In any other case (if the key isn't present, or the process dies before you get an answer) you return {error, not_found}. Using a try expression like this can be useful whenever you have a sequence of things that must be done in order and the result should be the same if any of the steps fails. (See section 2.8 for details of exceptions and try/catch.)

- simple_cache:delete/1—To delete the entry for a given key, you first use sc_store:lookup/1 as in the insert/2 function to find out whether the key is present. If not, you return ok. Otherwise, you delegate the operation to sc_element:delete/1 ❸, which takes care of calling sc_store:delete/1 for you (see the implementation of sc_element:terminate/2 in listing 6.5). You make sc_element responsible for its own cleanup to ensure that it's always done no matter how the element is removed—particularly in the case that the expiry time passes, but also if a bug triggers an exception in sc_element and causes it to terminate unexpectedly.

That's it! Your simple cache is ready and functioning. To give it a try (and we recommend that you do), compile all the modules in the src directory, placing all the resulting .beam files in the ebin directory as you did in section 4.3. Then run Erlang like this (from the root directory of the application), and start the application:

```
$ erl -pa ebin

Eshell V5.5.5  (abort with ^G)
1> application:start(simple_cache).
ok
2>
```

Try the three `simple_cache` API functions you just created. You should be able to store any kind of value using any kind of key. If you want to experiment, you can change the default lease time for src/sc_element.erl (listing 6.3) to something reasonably short, like 60 seconds, to convince yourself that entries do disappear by themselves when the lease time is up. (If you do, don't forget to recompile the module to replace the previous .beam file under ebin.)

6.5   Summary

You have a cache; and although the way you implemented it took a lot of explanation, it was pretty easy when you look back at how few lines of code you had to write. The cache has the expected CRUD functions, is completely memory resident, and even has automatic lease-based eviction of old entries. We put together quite a few concepts in this chapter, using all that you learned in the first part of this book.

You started with a basic design and with setting up the application framework and the application behaviour module. The next step was the top-level supervisor `sc_sup`, which was a different take on supervision compared to what you saw in part 1 of the book: it acts more like a factory for worker processes. With your application skeleton in place, you set about creating the `sc_element` module to store values and handle lease times, the `sc_store` module to handle the key-to-pid mapping, and the application API module `simple_cache` that tied everything together.

You should by now be familiar with how to create an OTP application, and you should also be getting a good idea of how to encapsulate protocols, manage state, structure your program in terms of OTP components, and write clean and readable modules. From here, we delve deeper into more Erlang/OTP technology in order to improve your cache application—because as nice as it is, the Erlware developers have raised the issue that it isn't suitable for the job of speeding up the website. Fundamentally, it's not up to production standards: if a problem occurs in production, you won't know a thing about it—you don't have even the most basic form of logging. Furthermore, monitoring and event handling haven't been considered, so you'll have no idea whether your cache lives or dies unless you probe it manually. These issues will be addressed in the next chapter.

Logging and event handling the Erlang/OTP way

This chapter covers

- Erlang/OTP logging facilities and the SASL application
- Event handling and the gen_event behaviour
- Creating a custom event stream

So, you have the great little cache application you wrote in the previous chapter. It can store key/value pairs for quick retrieval, and it even evicts old entries automatically. It does this in a nice, clean way using various processes, supervisors, and tables. Although the implementation is tidy, a lot is going on within it: the application and the supervisor start up, worker processes come and go, data is stored and fetched, leases time out, and tables are manipulated. But to a user of the application, all this is taking place under the hood, and there is no simple way to find out more. If you were to ask, say, how many inserts took place over the last hour, you'd have no way of knowing. What's more, if something went wrong, you'd have very little information about what happened.

In this chapter, we introduce you to the concept of event handling. Events are continuously being generated in the system, and Erlang/OTP provides a framework for creating event streams and for hooking up handlers to act on the generated events. This framework is the foundation of the standard OTP logging system. We show you how to use that system and how to modify it using custom event handlers. We also show you how to generate your own application-level event stream so you can provide your users with a way to hook into your system. This chapter covers the following topics:

- The logging system
- Event handling and hooking into to the logging system with a custom handler
- Creating and handling custom events

Let's now entertain the question, "What if something goes wrong inside the Simple Cache?" and use that as a starting point for talking about the OTP logging system.

7.1 Logging in Erlang/OTP

What if something *does* go wrong within the Simple Cache while it's running? Right now, you probably wouldn't even notice unless the entire service crashed. (For example, you made the storage element processes clean up after themselves if they die, and the supervisor was told not to worry about it, because the workers were marked as `temporary`.)

You need to put an end to the silent treatment the cache is currently giving you, and Erlang/OTP has pretty good facilities for doing so. These facilities are the logging application, the SASL application, and the event handling infrastructure that the `gen_event` behaviour provides. Together, they give you a powerful tool for communicating various types of information to the world at large. The `gen_event` system even gives you a way to allow other applications to hook into your system.

> ### OTP SASL isn't SASL
> As you may know, SASL is also the name of a common framework for authentication in network protocols. But the SASL application in Erlang/OTP has absolutely nothing to do with that (it was named long before RFC 2222 was written). Here, it stands for *System Architecture Support Libraries*, and it's one of the five basic applications that the rest of Erlang/OTP builds on (`erts`, `kernel`, `stdlib`, `sasl`, and `compiler`). It consists of a small collection of important services for system management.

We get back to SASL and `gen_event` later in this chapter; right now, we want to give you an overview of logging.

7.1.1 Logging in general

You may have used logging systems such as log4j (log4c, log4r, and so on) or similar. Every programming language tends to have a flavor of logging that is the de facto standard for that language, because logging is such an essential part of the software development toolbox. Typically, any logging system has several *severity levels*. These indicate the importance of the information being logged. One common scheme is to have up to five levels: critical (or severe), error, warning, info, and debug. The exact names used may vary between systems. Although they're mostly self-explanatory, it may not always be obvious when to use what level, so here are brief descriptions:

- *Critical or severe*—Indicates that manual action should be taken immediately because the system has failed catastrophically or is unusable by its customers. You should use this level rarely; it should be reserved for the kind of emergency that people need to be dragged out of bed at 3 A.M. to fix.
- *Error*—Notifies the operator of the system that something bad but not critical has happened. For example, a subsystem crashed and was restarted, or a session with a customer was terminated due to bad data. The problem needs to be fixed, but it can probably wait until tomorrow. You shouldn't use this level too often, or people may start to ignore the messages.
- *Warn*—Tells the operator that something potentially bad, but not terrible, has happened. You use this when something occurs that can be ignored or worked around for now but probably should be fixed so it doesn't cause more problems later or put an unnecessary load on the system.
- *Info*—Represents an informational message. You use this when you want to let the operator know that something happened. This event may be good, as in "backup job finished"; or it may be slightly bad, as in "couldn't send mail; will retry in five minutes." You can use this level as much as you like, but don't go crazy with it to avoid swamping your operations people with useless details.
- *Debug*—Provides details about what is happening. This level is mostly for you, the developer. It will help you debug problems in a running system; the more you log, the better (up to a point). Debug messages aren't expected to be seen by anyone who hasn't explicitly asked for them.

Most logging systems allow operators to set the minimum severity level of messages they're interested in. If they want to see everything, they set the level to *debug*, which will show them all message types. If they want to see mostly everything except debug messages, they set the level to *info*. If they only want to be told if there are problems, they set the level to *warn*, and so on.

Logging systems also do other things, like provide adjustable output formats, add timestamps to log messages, and so on. We skip those details for now and go directly into how logging works in Erlang/OTP.

7.1.2 *Erlang/OTP built-in logging facilities*

Logging is a common enough system requirement that a facility for it is included in the basic Erlang/OTP distribution. The primary functionality is provided by the `error_logger` module found in the `kernel` application in the standard library, and extended logging for OTP behaviours is provided by the SASL application. Not only does it give you a way of emitting log messages, but it also gives you a framework for doing your own logging and event handling in general.

That said, the default logging format is a bit unusual and not something you can feed directly to common log-parsing tools. You have to decide whether to use the native logging system, and that decision largely depends on whether you're fitting it into an existing, mainly non-Erlang infrastructure, or if you're creating a new OTP-based system from scratch. You also need to know what you may be trading away if you decide to use an external logging system. Let's start by looking at the main logging API.

7.1.3 *The standard logging functions*

The standard API for posting log messages is straightforward, but it provides only three log levels: error, warning, and info. As we show you, this isn't a huge limitation, because it's easy to add your own report types and event handlers; but for starters, you'll make do with what you get. You can find the API functions in the `error_logger` module (which is part of the `kernel` application). The following are the most basic functions:

```
error_logger:error_msg(Format) -> ok.
error_logger:error_msg(Format, Data) -> ok.

error_logger:warning_msg(Format) -> ok
error_logger:warning_msg(Format, Data) -> ok.

error_logger:info_msg(Format) -> ok.
error_logger:info_msg(Format, Data) -> ok.
```

These functions have the same interface as the standard library functions `io:format/1` and `io:format/2` (see section 2.5.1): the first argument is a format string that can contain escape codes starting with a tilde (~) character, such as ~w, and the second argument is a list of values to be used with the escape codes.

Let's play with these and write some log messages. For example, the following calls `info_msg/1` with a simple message string:

```
2> error_logger:info_msg("This is a message~n").

=INFO REPORT==== 4-Apr-2009::14:35:47 ===
This is a message
ok
```

Here you send an info message to the logger, which formats it and adds a heading with the severity level and a timestamp. By default, log messages are printed to the console, but the system can be reconfigured to log to a file or turn off logging. (The `ok` in the example is the value returned to the shell by the function call; it isn't a part of the message.)

To format some data as part of the message, try `info_msg/2`:

```
3> error_logger:info_msg("This is an ~s message~n", ["info"]).

=INFO REPORT==== 4-Apr-2009::14:39:23 ===
This is an info message
ok
```

The ~s escape code inserts another string in the format string. Check the documentation for io:format/2 for details on format strings; just remember that the second argument must always be a list of terms. There should generally be as many elements in the list as format specifiers in the format string (except for ~n, which generates a newline).

These functions are a little more tolerant of errors than io:format(...). If you write a bad format specification, you still get a message, rather than a crash. For example, if you pass the wrong number of elements in the second argument, you get this report:

```
4> error_logger:info_msg("This is an ~s message~n", ["info",
➡this_is_an_unused_atom]).

=INFO REPORT==== 4-Apr-2009::14:42:37 ===
ERROR: "This is an ~s message~n" - ["info", this_is_an_unused_atom]
ok
```

This is so you always get what may be critical information even if you've screwed up the coding of the log message. It may not seem like a big deal, but it's an awesome feature of the system.

Let's write a more realistic log message:

```
5> error_logger:info_msg("Invalid reply ~p from ~s ~n", [<<"quux">>,
➡"stockholm"]).

=INFO REPORT==== 4-Apr-2009::14:53:06 ===
Invalid reply <<"quux">> from stockholm
ok
```

Of course, in a real system, the data would be passed in via variables, not hardcoded like this. Note the ~p: this is a useful format specifier. As we explained in section 2.5.1, it pretty-prints the given value, making things easier for humans to read—in particular, lists or binaries that contain character data.

Also try these examples calling error_msg and warning_msg instead of info_msg, and note the differences. You should see that the warning messages and the error messages look the same; this is because, by default, warnings are mapped to errors. (Historically, there were only info and error messages. You can change this mapping by starting erl with the option +W w.)

A set of slightly more complicated (but more modern) API functions lets you specify the report in a more flexible way and also lets you add a *type* to the report. You'll see these again in section 7.2.3, in the form of the log events they generate; for now, check the Erlang/OTP documentation for details about how they're used:

```
error_logger:error_report(Report) -> ok.
error_logger:error_report(Type, Report) -> ok.

error_logger:warning_report(Report) -> ok
error_logger:warning_report(Type, Report) -> ok.

error_logger:info_report(Report) -> ok.
error_logger:info_report(Type, Report) -> ok.
```

Now that you know about the basic `error_logger` facility in Erlang, we talk about the SASL application and what it adds to the logging system.

7.1.4 SASL and crash reports

To have something to play with, let's create a little `gen_server`, shown in the following listing, whose only job is to start up, run for a while, and shut down.

> **Listing 7.1 Error report example: die_please.erl**

```
-module(die_please).

-behaviour(gen_server).

-export([start_link/0]).

-export([init/1, handle_call/3, handle_cast/2, handle_info/2,
         terminate/2, code_change/3]).

-define(SERVER, ?MODULE).
-define(SLEEP_TIME, (2*1000)).

-record(state, {}).

start_link() ->
    gen_server:start_link({local, ?SERVER}, ?MODULE, [], []).

init([]) ->
    {ok, #state{}, ?SLEEP_TIME}.                        ➊ Set server
                                                           timeout
handle_call(_Request, _From, State) ->
    Reply = ok,
    {reply, Reply, State}.

handle_cast(_Msg, State) ->
    {noreply, State}.

handle_info(timeout, State) ->                         ➋ Causes an
    i_want_to_die = right_now,                            exception
    {noreply, State}.

terminate(_Reason, _State) ->
    ok.

code_change(_OldVsn, State, _Extra) ->
    {ok, State}.
```

This is a straightforward `gen_server` like the ones you've seen in previous chapters. Again, you use the server timeout functionality ➊, letting the `init/1` function specify a timeout limit in milliseconds. If the server receives no requests within that time (and it shouldn't), `handle_info/2` is called with the atom `timeout` as argument. (Recall that the purpose of the `handle_info/2` callback function is to handle out-of-band messages.) There, you do something that you wouldn't do in a normal application: you write some code ➋ that you know will cause an exception and result in the process dying (the two atoms can never match). Because your purpose here is to play with the SASL logging functionality, that's fine.

BASIC ERROR REPORTS

When you compile the module, the compiler tries to warn you about this glaring error, but you'll ignore its cries. After all, the code compiled successfully, as you see from the {ok, ... } result:

```
$ erl
Eshell V5.7  (abort with ^G)
1> c("die_please.erl").
./die_please.erl:29: Warning: no clause will ever match
{ok,die_please}
```

(Make sure you start a fresh Erlang shell for this example and that you have the source file in the current directory.) After the module has been compiled, start it up using the start_link/0 function, like this:

```
2> die_please:start_link().
{ok,<0.40.0>}
3>
=ERROR REPORT==== 4-Apr-2009::15:18:25 ===
** Generic server die_please terminating
** Last message in was timeout
** When Server state == {state}
** Reason for termination ==
** {{badmatch,right_now},
     [{die_please,handle_info,2},
      {gen_server,handle_msg,5},
      {proc_lib,init_p_do_apply,3}]}
** exception error: no match of right hand side value right_now
       in function  die_please:handle_info/2
       in call from gen_server:handle_msg/5
       in call from proc_lib:init_p_do_apply/3
```

The server process comes up just fine, and 2 seconds later it terminates with some reasonably useful error information. Next, you'll start SASL and see how things change.

STARTING SASL

Fire up the SASL application manually, like this:

```
4> application:start(sasl).
ok
...
```

In addition to the ok shown here, you'll also see a lot of weird text flowing across your screen. That's all right; they're only SASL info messages. The SASL application provides more than just logging, and what you see scrolling past are info messages from various services that are starting. As each process starts up, information about what is happening is printed to the log (and the log in this context is the console). We omit this output from the examples, because it's pretty verbose.

The standard log messages—the ones you can write using the basic functions we showed you in section 7.1.3—are always available in any Erlang system. But applications can also define their own report types, which the system ignores unless an event handler has been added to act on them. SASL adds such a handler, which listens for reports sent by the standard OTP behaviours when supervisors start or restart a child process, if a child process dies unexpectedly, or if a behaviour-based process like a gen_server crashes. When you started SASL, you saw the main SASL supervisor starting some worker processes.

Let's see what happens if you run the same example while SASL is running:

```
5> die_please:start_link().
{ok,<0.53.0>}
6>
=ERROR REPORT==== 4-Apr-2009::15:21:37 ===
** Generic server die_please terminating
** Last message in was timeout
** When Server state == {state}
** Reason for termination ==
** {{badmatch,right_now},
    [{die_please,handle_info,2},
     {gen_server,handle_msg,5},
     {proc_lib,init_p_do_apply,3}]}
6>
=CRASH REPORT==== 4-Apr-2009::15:21:37 ===
  crasher:
    initial call: die_please:init/1
    pid: <0.53.0>
    registered_name: die_please
    exception exit: {{badmatch,right_now},
                     [{die_please,handle_info,2},
                      {gen_server,handle_msg,5},
                      {proc_lib,init_p_do_apply,3}]}
      in function  gen_server:terminate/6
    ancestors: [<0.42.0>]
    messages: []
    links: [<0.42.0>]
    dictionary: []
    trap_exit: false
    status: running
    heap_size: 377
    stack_size: 24
    reductions: 132
  neighbours:
    neighbour: [{pid,<0.42.0>},
                {registered_name,[]},
                {initial_call,{erlang,apply,2}},
                {current_function,{shell,eval_loop,3}},
                {ancestors,[]},
                {messages,[]},
                {links,[<0.27.0>,<0.53.0>]},
                {dictionary,[]},
                {trap_exit,false},
                {status,waiting},
                {heap_size,1597},
                {stack_size,6},
                {reductions,3347}]
```

```
** exception error: no match of right hand side value right_now
     in function  die_please:handle_info/2
     in call from gen_server:handle_msg/5
     in call from proc_lib:init_p_do_apply/3
```

You get the same error report as before, but you also get a crash report from SASL with a lot of additional information about the process that failed. This kind of information is useful when you're debugging a crash in a live system.

WHEN SASL DOESN'T HELP

Another example is in order. Let's create a simple module that doesn't use `gen_server` and see what happens. The code, shown in the following listing, basically does the same thing as in the previous example, but in a much more direct and non-OTP way.

> **Listing 7.2 Non-OTP crash example: die_please2.erl**

```
-module(die_please2).

-export([go/0]).

-define(SLEEP_TIME, 2000).

go() ->
    %% just sleep for a while, then crash
    timer:sleep(?SLEEP_TIME),              ❶ Causes
    i_really_want_to_die = right_now.         process to die
```

Compile and run this module, and see what happens:

```
6> c("die_please2.erl").
./die_please2.erl:10: Warning: no clause will ever match
{ok,die_please2}
6> spawn(fun die_please2:go/0).
<0.79.0>
7>
...
```

The process should start and then die with a `badmatch` error ❶ after 2 seconds. The error information (not shown here) is much less copious than in the previous example, even though you started SASL. The reason is straightforward: to use SASL, a little work is needed. When you build your application on behaviours like `gen_server` and `supervisor`, this work is already done for you. When you roll your own processes, you don't get that—at least not without some extra effort.

If you do things a bit differently, you can get some of the behaviour you expect. Let's try it again, but this time kick off the process using the function `proc_lib:spawn/1` instead of plain `spawn/1`:

```
7> proc_lib:spawn(fun die_please2:go/0).
<0.83.0>
8>
=CRASH REPORT==== 4-Apr-2009::15:34:45 ===
  crasher:
    initial call: die_please2:go/0
    pid: <0.83.0>
```

```
    registered_name: []
    exception error: no match of right hand side value right_now
      in function  die_please2:go/0
    ancestors: [<0.77.0>]
    messages: []
    links: []
    dictionary: []
    trap_exit: false
    status: running
    heap_size: 233
    stack_size: 24
    reductions: 72
  neighbours:
```

This time, you get a crash report from SASL. The `proc_lib` module is part of the Erlang `stdlib` application, and it supports starting processes the OTP way so they're properly set up to follow all the necessary conventions. In the (for now) unlikely event that you want to write processes that aren't built on existing behaviours, you should typically start them via `proc_lib`. You'll be doing yourself a favor in the long run.

Now that you understand basic Erlang/OTP logging, both without and with SASL, the next section will explain how the event-handling system works and how you can hook in your own custom event handlers to get more control over logging.

7.2 A custom event handler with gen_event

Let's say you don't like the format of the logs being output by default by the error logger. After all, it's different from what the rest of the world uses. It may also be that you work at a company that already has a wealth of tools written around its own log format, and the Erlang format doesn't fit in. What can you do? Well, the error logger allows you to plug into the logging system and output your own error information.

7.2.1 Introducing the gen_event behaviour

The logging facility is based on Erlang's event handling framework, which uses the `gen_event` behaviour. This behaviour wraps up pretty much everything you need from an event handler in a nice, easy-to-use interface. To plug into the logging infrastructure, you need to write a new `gen_event` behaviour implementation module. Fortunately, that's simple. The `gen_event` behaviour interface is similar to that of the `gen_server` behaviour: it has the familiar `init`, `code_change`, and `terminate` callback functions, and it also requires the `handle_call` and `handle_info` callbacks. (There are some subtle differences when it comes to arguments and return values, so don't assume too much without checking the documentation.) But the `gen_event` interface replaces `handle_cast/2` with `handle_event/2`; and as you may be able to guess, that's where you receive your error-logger events.

An important difference between `gen_event` and `gen_server` is that when you start a new `gen_server` container, you tell it which callback module to use (and that's it); but when you start a `gen_event` container (sometimes referred to as the *event manager*), it initially has no callback module. Instead, one or several handlers

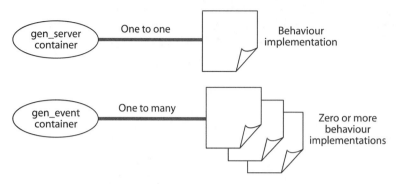

**Figure 7.1   Use of callback modules in `gen_server` and `gen_event`. A
`gen_server` container is always tied to a particular implementation (callback)
module, whereas a `gen_event` container can have any number of callback
modules that are added and removed dynamically.**

may be added (and removed again) dynamically after the container has been initialized. When an event is posted to an event manager, all the currently registered
handler modules are called individually to handle the event. Figure 7.1 illustrates
this difference.

Because of this one-to-many relationship, you typically won't find a `start_link`
function in callback modules that implement the `gen_event` behaviour; if you do,
you'll probably see that the function first checks whether the container is already
started (which of course only works if it's supposed to be a singleton, registered under
some name). Furthermore, keep in mind that the code in your particular callback
module generally isn't the only code that the event manager calls; you should avoid
doing strange things to the process state (and hope that any other added handlers will
be just as nice).

Like a `gen_server`, a `gen_event` process can be registered under a name when it
starts (like the `tr_server` back in chapter 3), to make it easy to talk to. You'll be adding a handler to the standard system process that is registered under the name
`error_logger` and that always exists in any Erlang/OTP system. (This is exactly what
SASL does when it starts.) When you use one of the logging functions in the
`error_logger` module, this is the process to which those log events are sent. There is
even an API function in the `error_logger` module for adding a report handler, so you
don't have to know the details of how the event handler process is found; it delegates
the call to the function `gen_event:add_handler/3` along with the registered name
of the process that should be told to add the handler.

7.2.2   *Event handler example*

The skeleton for your simple log event handler is shown in listing 7.3. This is a bare-
bones implementation of a `gen_event` behaviour for the error logger. It doesn't do
anything yet except receive events and say "OK, go on."

Listing 7.3   Custom logging plug-in module: custom_error_report.erl

```erlang
-module(custom_error_report).

-behaviour(gen_event).

%% API
-export([register_with_logger/0]).

-export([init/1, handle_event/2, handle_call/2,
         handle_info/2, terminate/2, code_change/3]).

-record(state, {}).

register_with_logger() ->
    error_logger:add_report_handler(?MODULE).          ◁── Adds this module
                                                            as callback
init([]) ->
    {ok, #state{}}.

handle_event(_Event, State) ->
    {ok, State}.

handle_call(_Request, State) ->
    Reply = ok,
    {ok, Reply, State}.

handle_info(_Info, State) ->
    {ok, State}.

terminate(_Reason, _State) ->
    ok.

code_change(_OldVsn, State, _Extra) ->
    {ok, State}.
```

There's no stopping

You saw earlier that the callback functions of a gen_server can return a stop value, telling the server process to shut down. A gen_event callback can't do that (because other registered handlers may not be happy if you kill the entire service). Instead, the callback can return a remove_handler value, which causes the gen_event process to remove that handler, calling its terminate callback function as a last favor.

All you need to do now is compile the module as normal and then call its API function custom_error_report:register_with_logger() to make it hook itself into the error-logger event stream.

7.2.3   Acting on error events

You want to do something interesting with the events you receive. In this case, you want to write them out to the screen; and to present them nicely, you need to know what they mean. The error_logger functions generate a specific set of events. These are described in the Erlang/OTP documentation and listed in table 7.1.

Table 7.1   Error logger events

Event tuple			Generated by
{error,	Gleader,	{Pid,Format,Data}}	error_msg()
{error_report,	Gleader,	{Pid,Type,Report}}	error_report()
{warning_msg,	Gleader,	{Pid,Format,Data}}	warning_msg()
{warning_report,	Gleader,	{Pid,Type,Report}}	warning_report()
{info_msg,	Gleader,	{Pid,Format,Data}}	info_msg()
{info_report,	Gleader,	{Pid,Type,Report}}	info_report()

For the events tagged error_report, warning_report, or info_report, the type field is std_error, std_warning, or std_info, respectively, if one of the report functions was called without a specified type. Apart from these, any other type identifiers can be used for user-defined report types. You can ignore the Gleader (group leader) field for now; it can be used to specify where to send standard output.

As a slightly contrived example, listing 7.4 shows how you can change the handle_event/2 callback function from listing 7.3 to use this knowledge.

Listing 7.4   Handling error_logger events

```
handle_event({error, _Gleader, {Pid,Format,Data}}, State) ->
    io:fwrite("ERROR <~p> ~s", [Pid, io_lib:format(Format, Data)]),
    {ok, State};
handle_event({error_report, _Gleader, {Pid, std_error, Report}}, State) ->
    io:fwrite("ERROR <~p> ~p", [Pid, Report]),
    {ok, State};
handle_event({error_report, _Gleader, {Pid, Type, Report}}, State) ->
    io:fwrite("ERROR <~p> ~p ~p", [Pid, Type, Report]),
    {ok, State};
handle_event({warning_msg, _Gleader, {Pid, Format, Data}}, State) ->
    io:fwrite("WARNING <~p> ~s", [Pid, io_lib:format(Format, Data)]),
    {ok, State};
handle_event({warning_report,_Gleader,{Pid,std_warning,Report}}, State) ->
    io:fwrite("WARNING <~p> ~p", [Pid, Report]),
    {ok, State};
handle_event({warning_report,_Gleader,{Pid, Type, Report}}, State) ->
    io:fwrite("WARNING <~p> ~p ~p", [Pid, Type, Report]),
    {ok, State};
handle_event({info_msg, _Gleader, {Pid, Format, Data}}, State) ->
    io:fwrite("INFO <~p> ~s", [Pid, io_lib:format(Format, Data)]),
    {ok, State};
handle_event({info_report, _Gleader, {Pid, std_info, Report}}, State) ->
    io:fwrite("INFO <~p> ~p", [Pid, Report]),
    {ok, State};
handle_event({info_report, _Gleader, {Pid, Type, Report}}, State) ->
    io:fwrite("INFO <~p> ~p ~p", [Pid, Type, Report]),
    {ok, State};
```

```
handle_event(_Event, State) ->
    {ok, State}.
```

All this code does is print the data directly to the standard output in a slightly different format, but it should give you an idea of what you need to do to write your own custom plug-ins. Note that you may receive events that don't match the earlier list of formats; these are typically system messages that you can safely ignore, but you still need a last catch-all clause to handle them and say "OK."

We suggest that you compile the code in listing 7.4, hook it into the system, and call a few of the logging examples from section 7.1.3 to see what happens. You can also try the custom report functions in the `error_logger` module, such as `info_report(Type, Report)` (see the Erlang/OTP documentation for details).

At this point, we've covered the most important aspects of the logging infrastructure in Erlang. You should have a good idea of how the following works:

- The `error_logger` API
- SASL progress reports and crash reports
- The `gen_event` behaviour
- Customizing the error logger with your own `gen_event` implementation

That means you're ready to take all that and apply it to the Simple Cache application from the previous chapters. This is the topic of the next section, where you'll also learn how to create a custom application-level event stream.

7.3   *Adding a custom event stream to the Simple Cache*

As we said at the start of this chapter, a lot is going on inside the Simple Cache system. In the previous sections, we've shown how you can add standard error-logger messages to your code and how the SASL application can give you more information about what your OTP servers and supervisors are doing. We also showed how the event handling system works and how to write a custom event handler. But what if you want to create your own application-specific event stream, separate from the error logger?

For the cache system, you can publish a number of specific events to notify about insertion, deletion, lease timeouts, lookups, and other things. Creating your own event stream will let users of the system easily plug in event handlers to answer questions like "How many lookups did the cache have in the last hour?" and "How often are entries being deleted because they weren't accessed within the lease time?"

In this section, you'll use the `gen_event` behaviour to create a custom event stream. You'll integrate it with the Simple Cache application, hooking it into the supervision structure and instrumenting the code to post events at key points. Finally, we demonstrate how to create an event handler to intercept those events. First, you'll design an API for this event stream.

7.3.1   *The event stream API*

The `sc_event` module will constitute the API for the application-specific event system. As usual, you should encapsulate as many implementation details as possible and only provide a set of easy-to-use functions for any clients who want to subscribe to the event stream. It's a straightforward module, shown in the following listing.

> **Listing 7.5   Simple Cache event stream API: src/sc_event.erl**

```
-module(sc_event).

-export([start_link/0,
         add_handler/2,
         delete_handler/2,
         lookup/1,
         create/2,
         replace/2,
         delete/1]).

-define(SERVER, ?MODULE).

start_link() ->
    gen_event:start_link({local, ?SERVER}).          ❶ Hides gen_event
                                                        start function
add_handler(Handler, Args) ->
    gen_event:add_handler(?SERVER, Handler, Args).    ❷ Hides gen_event
                                                        handler registration
delete_handler(Handler, Args) ->
    gen_event:delete_handler(?SERVER, Handler, Args).

lookup(Key) ->
    gen_event:notify(?SERVER, {lookup, Key}).

create(Key, Value) ->
    gen_event:notify(?SERVER, {create, {Key, Value}}).    ❸ API functions

replace(Key, Value) ->
    gen_event:notify(?SERVER, {replace, {Key, Value}}).

delete(Key) ->
    gen_event:notify(?SERVER, {delete, Key}).
```

As you can see, this API module doesn't implement any specific OTP behaviour. But it does provide a `start_link()` function similar to what you're used to. In this case, it hides a call to the function `gen_event:start_link/1` ❶, starting a new `gen_event` container and registering it locally using the same name as the module.

As we mentioned in section 7.2.1, many `gen_event` behaviour implementation modules don't provide a `start_link` API function. Normally, the `gen_event` container (also called the *event manager*) is instead started directly from a supervisor, as illustrated by the following child specification example:

```
{my_logger,
 {gen_event, start_link, [{local, my_logger}]},
 permanent, 1000, worker, [gen_event]}
```

(Compare this with the specification for the init/1 function in listing 4.3.) After it's started, the process can be referenced by the name my_logger in order to add handlers.

But such an implementation detail shouldn't leak into the rest of the code. And you want to let users add event handlers without having to know what name the manager process is using. Toward that end, you provide not only a start_link function but also wrapper functions ❷ for the standard gen_event registration functions add_handler/3 and delete_handler/3, similar to the wrapper you made for the error_logger registration function add_report_handler/1 in listing 7.3. This makes the user interface completely independent of the registered name.

The four functions that follow are the actual event handling API. The gen_event module provides the function notify/2 for posting events asynchronously, similar to the cast/2 function in gen_server. The API functions ❸ are wrappers around the protocol, the way the API of the tr_server in chapter 3 (listing 3.3) hides the protocol between the server and the clients. But for event handlers, the encapsulation isn't as complete as for servers: the protocol you define in this API module must be understood by every callback module you want to add, and so it should be documented (possibly as internal documentation, depending on the scope of the event system). The terms used in the protocol shouldn't be allowed to leak into any other part of the code, on either side. Table 7.2 summarizes the protocol for the custom event stream.

Table 7.2   Simple Cache application-specific events

Event tuple	Posted by
{lookup, Key}	sc_event:lookup/1
{create, {Key, Value}}	sc_event:create/2
{replace, {Key, Value}}	sc_event:replace/2
{delete, Key}	sc_event:delete/1

With this API in place, when you want to do something like post a lookup event, all you need to do is call sc_event:lookup(Key). If you need to change the event protocol or any other detail of the implementation, you won't have to go back and modify every line that posts such an event throughout your code base.

Next, you'll hook up this module so the event system starts and stops along with the Simple Cache application as a whole.

7.3.2   *Integrating the handler with Simple Cache*

The first thing to realize is that the gen_event container that the sc_event module starts is a service that should be managed by a supervisor. Furthermore, an OTP application always has a single root supervisor that starts everything else. Your problem is that the root supervisor you created in chapter 6 used the simple_one_for_one restart strategy (see section 6.3.4). This fitted the problem well, but such a supervisor

> ### Supervisor naming
>
> It's common practice to use the name *<mod>_sup* for a module that implements a supervisor of a service implemented in the module *<mod>*. For example: `sc_element_sup`.

can have only one type of child process; thus you can't add your `gen_event` process to the supervisor.

Fortunately, you don't need to rewrite the existing supervisor. (A large part of the cache architecture depended on it.) You only need to rename it: it will no longer be the root supervisor, and you'll create a new `sc_sup` module to take over that task. You'll start by renaming the file src/sc_sup.erl to src/sc_element_sup.erl and editing its module declaration to match the new name. Also be sure to update sc_element.erl, changing the `create(Value, LeaseTime)` function to call `sc_element_sup:start_child(…)` instead of `sc_sup:start_child(…)`.

Your old supervisor, now under the name `sc_element_sup`, will be a child process of the new top-level supervisor, and so will your `gen_event` process. Doing all this becomes a simple matter of writing a basic supervisor and a couple of child specifications. The new supervisor is shown in the following listing.

Listing 7.6   New root supervisor: src/sc_sup.erl

```
-module(sc_sup).

-behaviour(supervisor).

%% API
-export([start_link/0]).

%% Supervisor callbacks
-export([init/1]).

-define(SERVER, ?MODULE).

start_link() ->
    supervisor:start_link({local, ?SERVER}, ?MODULE, []).

init([]) ->
    ElementSup = {sc_element_sup, {sc_element_sup, start_link, []},
                permanent, 2000, supervisor, [sc_element]},

    EventManager = {sc_event, {sc_event, start_link, []},
                permanent, 2000, worker, [sc_event]},     ◁—❶ New sc_event process

    Children = [ElementSup, EventManager],
    RestartStrategy = {one_for_one, 4, 3600},      ◁—❷ one_for_one supervisor
    {ok, {RestartStrategy, Children}}.
```

As you see, this is similar to the `tr_sup` supervisor you wrote in chapter 4 (listing 4.3). They're both simple `one_for_one` supervisors ❷ that treat their child processes as separate beings of different types that are restarted individually as necessary. This one has two static children, each with its own child specification: the old renamed supervisor for sc_element processes and the new sc_event process ❶. That one of these children is in itself a supervisor isn't a big deal to the root supervisor; but to help it make better decisions in some situations, you tag the sc_element_sup child as supervisor and the sc_event child as worker. (See section 4.2.3 if you need a reminder of what the fields of a child specification mean.) Following this pattern, you can nest supervisors to any depth you want to give your application a suitably fine-grained supervision structure.

Now that you've set up the event service to run as part of the application, all you have to do is instrument your code so there are events to look at. This means going back and modifying the source code in suitable places, to post events when something of interest happens.

We don't want to repeat all the code here; we look at one function and how to instrument it. The following is the code for simple_cache:insert/1 as it looked back in listing 6.7:

```
insert(Key, Value) ->
    case sc_store:lookup(Key) of
    {ok, Pid} ->
        sc_element:replace(Pid, Value);
    {error, _} ->
            {ok, Pid} = sc_element:create(Value),
            sc_store:insert(Key, Pid)
    end.
```

You want to post a create event when a new storage element is created. To do this, change the code as follows:

```
insert(Key, Value) ->
    case sc_store:lookup(Key) of
    {ok, Pid} ->
        sc_element:replace(Pid, Value);
    {error, _} ->
            {ok, Pid} = sc_element:create(Value),
            sc_store:insert(Key, Pid),
            sc_event:create(Key, Value)          ◁⊐ **Posts create event**
    end.
```

All it takes is inserting a call to sc_element:create(Key, Value) at the right point. In general, you may have several choices of where to post an event; here, for example, you could do it somewhere in sc_element:create/1. We chose to put it at a point where the entire creation operation is known to have completed. Adding the remaining three event notifications from table 7.2 is similar and is left as an exercise. Beware of changing the expected return value from a function like lookup/1.

Now you have an instrumented application that continuously chats about what it's doing to anyone who wants to listen. To do that, they plug into your event stream, exactly as you did to subscribe to error-logger events in section 7.2. The next section will demonstrate handling such custom events.

7.3.3   *Subscribing to a custom event stream*

As an example of how to tap into a custom event stream defined by an application (like the one you've implemented), you'll create an event handler and attach it to the Simple Cache event stream. This is similar to the event handler example for the error logger in section 7.2.2: both are `gen_event` behaviour implementations, and the only real difference is the set of events they handle and what they do with them.

To make the example do something useful, you'll funnel the custom events to the error logger so you can inspect them. In a real-life situation, you could just as easily pass the events on to a statistics system or a remote monitoring system.

Listing 7.7 shows the logging handler for the custom cache events. It's similar to the module in listing 7.3; for the sake of brevity, we've left out all callback functions except `handle_event/2`.

> **Listing 7.7   Custom event handler example: src/sc_event_logger.erl**

```
-module(sc_event_logger).

-behaviour(gen_event).

-export([add_handler/0, delete_handler/0]).

-export([init/1, handle_event/2, handle_call/2,
         handle_info/2, code_change/3, terminate/2]).

add_handler() ->                                          ❶ add_handler/0 and
    sc_event:add_handler(?MODULE, []).                      delete_handler/0
                                                            functions
delete_handler() ->
    sc_event:delete_handler(?MODULE, []).

handle_event({create, {Key, Value}}, State) ->
    error_logger:info_msg("create(~w, ~w)~n", [Key, Value]),   ❷ error_logger
    {ok, State};                                                 message
handle_event({lookup, Key}, State) ->
    error_logger:info_msg("lookup(~w)~n", [Key]),
    {ok, State};
handle_event({delete, Key}, State) ->
    error_logger:info_msg("delete(~w)~n", [Key]),
    {ok, State};
handle_event({replace, {Key, Value}}, State) ->
    error_logger:info_msg("replace(~w, ~w)~n", [Key, Value]),
    {ok, State}.
```

`add_handler/0` and `delete_handler/0` ❶ are convenience functions that make it easy to start and stop the logging. As soon as the handler is added, every event posted via `sc_event` results in a corresponding call to `handle_event/2`, until you delete the handler.

The format of the events you need to handle was shown in table 7.2. All you do here is write a corresponding standard `error_logger` message ❷, nicely formatted, to show what is happening.

We encourage you to try this: instrument the Simple Cache application, write the event handler, compile the new and modified modules, and start the application as you've done before. Make a couple of calls to the cache's insert and lookup functions. Then, call `sc_event_logger:add_handler()` and do some more cache operations to see the log messages. Also check that they go away when you delete the handler. For bonus points, add a new event that is posted when a lease times out in the cache, and make all the necessary changes to observe it working. Finally, make `sc_app:start/2` add the event logger handler automatically, after `sc_sup` has been successfully started.

7.4 *Summary*

You've learned a lot about event handling in Erlang/OTP. You probably know more after reading this than many people who have been programming Erlang for years! You've seen how to use the Erlang/OTP standard logging system, how it's built on the `gen_event` behaviour (and how that works), and how to write event handlers to tap into the logger stream, allowing you to customize the output. Finally, you took all that knowledge and used it to create your own application-level event stream, along with a custom handler that passed those events to the error logger.

If you're anything like us, you found this chapter exciting and perhaps a little overwhelming, and you probably need to take a few moments and get your breath back before you read on. You'll need it, because the next chapter will knock your socks off (we hope). We introduce Erlang's distribution mechanisms and show you how to make good use of them. This is one of the most powerful aspects of Erlang/OTP, and we know you've been looking forward to learning about it.

Introducing distributed
Erlang/OTP

This chapter covers

- The basics of distributed Erlang
- Working with Erlang nodes and clusters
- Implementing a simple resource discovery system

In this chapter, we take a break from adding functionality to the cache application. Instead, we explore the distributed programming capabilities of Erlang, in order to prepare you for the next chapter. Although Erlang/OTP makes distribution a lot simpler than it is in most other languages, it's still a complex topic. This chapter will teach you the basics of working with distributed Erlang, but it can take a lot of experience to get the hang of it and realize how few of the lessons from traditional sequential programming remain valid. But don't worry—above all, it's a lot of fun!

8.1 The fundamentals of Erlang distribution

Let's say you have an instance of the Simple Cache application running on machine A and another instance running on machine B. If would be great if, when you insert a key/value pair into the cache on machine A, it would automatically become available on machine B as well. Obviously, machine A would somehow have to communicate that information to machine B. There are many ways you can go about propagating this information, some easier and more straightforward than others. All of them, however, imply distribution, because you need to communicate between separate computers.

Erlang makes certain types of distributed programming extremely easy; in no time at all, and with very little code, you can have a number of machines across a network happily chatting with one another. Two fundamental features of Erlang make this possible:

- Process communication by copying
- Location transparency

We presented this briefly in chapter 1. Here, we take a much deeper look at both of these properties and talk about how they make distribution possible. We also explain what Erlang *nodes* are and how they can be connected to form a cluster and tell you a little about the basic security model, how to communicate between nodes, and how to work with remote shells. Finally, you'll take all of that and implement a nontrivial distributed application that you can use in later chapters. But first, let's talk about why Erlang's communication model is such a good fit for distributed programming.

8.1.1 *Process communication by copying*

To recapitulate what we said in chapter 1, the most widespread models for communicating between two concurrently executing pieces of code involve sharing certain areas of the memory on the machine where they're both running. This model is illustrated in figure 8.1. But it has many problems, one of which is that if you want to modify the program to run each piece of code on a separate computer, you usually need to change communication strategy completely. This forces you to rewrite a large part of the code.

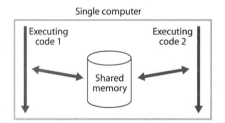

Figure 8.1 Traditional process communication through shared memory. This requires that both processes run on the same machine, or alternatively that some form of distributed shared memory is used.

This sort of problem was one of the things the creators of Erlang wanted to solve from the start. In order to make communication *transparent* and at the same time build *fault-tolerant* systems where one computer doesn't come to a halt just because its neighbor crashes or the network between them dies, sharing must be taken out of the picture.

Instead, Erlang processes communicate strictly by *asynchronous* message passing (so that sending a message doesn't require waiting for acknowledgement over the network), and the data is transferred in such a way that the receiver effectively gets a separate copy; nothing that the sender does to the data afterward can be observed by the receiver, and vice versa. Any further communication must happen through further messages. This is a pragmatic model that works well between processes on the same machine (see figure 8.2) and that keeps working even when processes are on separate machines connected by a network (see figure 8.3).

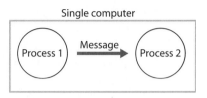

Figure 8.2   **Erlang processes communicating by message passing on a single machine. This is always done so that the receiver effectively gets a private copy of the data. In practice, read-only shared memory may be used for efficiency, but to the processes the result is the same.**

As you can see, the differences between figures 8.2 and 8.3 are trivial. You can change your program from one model to the other, but the way your processes communicate doesn't need to be modified.

In Erlang, you're always using message passing, never sharing, so the distributed case is practically identical to the local case. Much of the code can be written with complete disregard to where the processes will eventually be running.

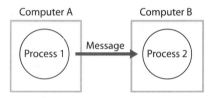

Figure 8.3   **Erlang processes communicating by message passing between different machines. In this case, it's obvious that data must be copied from one computer to another. Apart from the transfer time added by the network layer, nothing is different from figure 8.2.**

That said, you need to be aware of many things when communicating over a network. With local communication, you know that a sent message will be delivered to the receiving process as long as it's still alive, and you know that nothing can delay the transfer. When you have a network between the machines, it's possible that routing will delay the message or that the network will go down. To the sender, this will usually be no different from the case when the receiver dies or has a bug that causes it to not reply; a robust sender should be prepared for that even if the communication is expected to be local. But there are still many more sources for nondeterministic behavior in a distributed system.

But just because the communication mechanism is the same for machines in a network as it is on a single machine, you can't just move code from one machine to another, can you? You must still specify where the messages should be sent and, in particular, to which machine, right?

8.1.2   *Location transparency*

We said that the method of communication between processes is the same regardless of whether the recipient is on the local machine or a remote machine. This applies also on the syntactical level. The following is the syntax for sending a message (a string, in this case) to a process on the same machine as the sender:

```
Pid ! "my message"
```

Now, here is how you send the same message to a process on a different machine:

```
Pid ! "my message"
```

Sorry, couldn't resist that one. Yes, they're exactly the same: the ! (send) operation is *location transparent*—the recipient can be on any machine, and all the information needed to guide the message to the right location is encoded in the process identifier. Erlang guarantees that process identifiers are unique on the network, even across machines. This property means you can write programs in Erlang that don't need to be changed at all when you decide to go from one machine to a dozen; what's more, you can take a program made to run on a dozen machines and test it on your laptop.

Location transparency may seem like a small thing until you realize how much it liberates your programming style. When you no longer think about communication between computers as a huge threshold that you may one day find the strength to cross, and instead consider it the normal state of things—your processes may well be on separate machines unless there is a particular reason for them not to be—you can start designing systems that would previously have been too complicated for thought.

These two properties—communication by copying and location transparency—combine to make distributed programming in Erlang a real pleasure to work with. In the next chapter, you'll apply this to the cache application. But right now, your cache is without networking capabilities. If you start another cache on another machine, neither of them will have a clue that the other exists. That's the first thing you need to change to add distribution to the cache: you must make the machines aware of one another.

8.2 Nodes and clustering

We've been deliberately vague about one thing above: what is a machine in this context? In many cases, you have one Erlang VM (see section 1.4) running on each piece of hardware; but sometimes—particularly when testing and developing—you run several VM instances on a single computer. Given the way you've started erl (or werl) up until now, those instances wouldn't know or care about each other, because they haven't been set up for networking. That can be useful if you want to have multiple standalone Erlang-based programs (for example, the Yaws web server and the CouchDB database) running on the same computer. When an Erlang VM is running with networking enabled, things definitely get more interesting. Such a VM instance is called a *node*.

When two or more Erlang nodes become aware of each other, we say that they form a *cluster*. (The official Erlang/OTP documentation usually refers to it as a network of nodes, but we want to avoid any confusion with computer networks.) An Erlang cluster is by default *fully connected*, as shown in figure 8.4. In other words, every node in the cluster knows about every other node, and they communicate directly with each other.

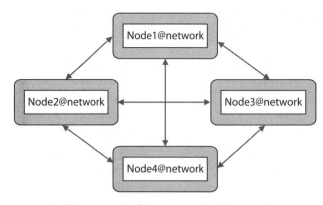

Figure 8.4
Erlang nodes on the network forming a cluster. Each node in the cluster is connected directly to every other node: the network is fully connected.

Nodes

A node is a running Erlang VM that has been configured to work in distributed mode. A node always has a name, which allows other nodes to find it and talk to it. The built-in function `node()` returns the current local node name, which is an atom of the form *nodename@hostname*. (This is always `nonode@nohost` for a VM that isn't running in distributed mode.) There can be multiple nodes running on a single host machine.

8.2.1 *Starting a node*

To start an Erlang node in distributed mode, you run `erl` (or `werl`) with one of the flags `-name` or `-sname`. The first is used in a normal network environment, with a working DNS, where you can use fully qualified domain names. For example:

```
erl -name simple_cache
```

The second form is used where fully qualified names don't work; this may often be the case in certain production environments. It can also happen, for example, on a wireless LAN, where you may be able to connect two computers to the network but they still can't find each other via DNS. In those cases, you must use short node names instead:

```
erl -sname simple_cache
```

Short names work as long as the nodes are on the same subnet.

Long and short names can't be mixed

Nodes with short names and long names work in different communication modes and can't be part of the same Erlang cluster. All connected nodes must use the same mode.

When an Erlang VM is running as a node, the node name is shown in the shell prompt:

```
Eshell V5.6.2  (abort with ^G)
(simple_cache@mybox.home.net)1>
```

This node is named `simple_cache@mybox.home.net`. From that, you can see that it's using long (fully qualified) names—it was started with `-name simple_cache`. If you start a shell with `-sname simple_cache` instead, it looks like this, without periods in the host part of the node name:

```
Eshell V5.6.2  (abort with ^G)
(simple_cache@mybox)1>
```

Try both variants on your computer. If you're running Windows, one way to do this is to right-click the Erlang icon, select Properties, and edit the target command (`C:\...\werl.exe`) to include the `name` or `sname` flag. You can also make a couple of copies of the icon on your desktop and edit each of them to start Erlang nodes with different names at the click of a button.

Now that you can start one or more nodes, the next step is of course to make them communicate.

8.2.2 Connecting nodes

A cluster of Erlang nodes can consist of two or more nodes. As a practical limit, you may have a couple of dozen, but probably not hundreds of nodes. This is because the cluster is a fully connected network, and the communication overhead for keeping machines in touch with each other increases quadratically with the number of nodes.

> **Hidden nodes**
>
> It's possible to connect clusters via special nodes to form a larger, not fully connected cluster. Such nodes are configured not to propagate information about other nodes, or even to be invisible to the other nodes, which can be useful for non-intrusive inspection of a cluster.

Nodes don't actively try to find each other. You have to give them a reason to go look for another node; but after they find each other, they keep track of each other and also exchange information about any other nodes they're connected to so they can form a complete network. For example, if nodes A and B form one cluster, and C and D make up another cluster, then if A and D find each other, they will exchange information about B and C, and all four will be connected to form a larger cluster, as shown earlier in figure 8.4.

Let's try it in practice. You'll start three nodes (each in its own window) with the names a, b, and c, and connect them as follows: first a to b, and then b to c. Start them on the same computer for this example; they could equally well be running on separate machines, but we need to talk a little about the security model before you try that. With multiple computers, you may also run into firewalls blocking your nodes from communicating; for now, let's make it simple and run on just one machine:

```
> erl -name a
Erlang (BEAM) emulator version 5.6.2 [source] [smp:2] [async-threads:0]
[kernel-poll:false]

Eshell V5.6.2  (abort with ^G)
(a@mybox.home.net)1>
```

Do the same for nodes b and c. You can now run the built-in function nodes() in each of these, to see the list of connected nodes. Right now, they should all show an empty list:

```
(b@mybox.home.net)1> nodes().
[]
```

The next step is to start connecting them. The simplest way, if connecting is all you want to do, is to use the standard library function net_adm:ping/1, as follows:

```
(a@mybox.home.net)2> net_adm:ping('b@mybox.home.net').
pong
```

This will either return the atom pong if the communication was successful or the atom pang otherwise. (If you find this strange, it's because *pang* is Swedish for *bang*, as in "crash, bang, it failed.") If it worked, the nodes should now be connected. You can check this by running nodes() again on all three nodes. On a, you should see that it now knows b, and vice versa. On c, you should still see an empty list, because it hasn't been in touch with the other two yet:

```
(b@mybox.home.net)2> nodes().
['a@mybox.home.net']
```

If this step fails for you even if your nodes are on the same machine, it could be that you're trying to use fully qualified names but the DNS hasn't been properly set up. For example, on a PC connected to a home LAN, you may end up with a node name like 'a@mypc.home.net', even though the address mypc.home.net can't be resolved by the DNS. (You can use a tool like the normal command-line ping to see if the name is usable or not.) If your nodes can't connect, then restart them using –sname instead of –name and try again.

   Next, connect b to c, and call nodes() again:

```
(b@mybox.home.net)3> net_adm:ping('c@mybox.home.net').
pong
(b@mybox.home.net)4> nodes().
['a@mybox.home.net','c@mybox.home.net']
```

No surprises: b knew a already, and now it also knows c. Running nodes() at a and c as well, you see that the cluster has become fully connected:

```
(a@mybox.home.net)4> nodes().
['b@mybox.home.net','c@mybox.home.net']
```

```
(c@mybox.home.net)3> nodes().
['b@mybox.home.net','a@mybox.home.net']
```

As a last experiment, kill the b node (for example, by entering q().; see section 2.1.4), and look at what happens on the remaining a and c nodes:

```
(a@mybox.home.net)5> nodes().
['c@mybox.home.net']
```

```
(c@mybox.home.net)4> nodes().
['a@mybox.home.net']
```

They're still in contact, even though the node that originally introduced them is gone. If you restart b and connect it to either a or c, the cluster will again contain all three nodes.

But how does all this work—in particular if the nodes are supposed to be able to be running on separate machines?

8.2.3 *How Erlang nodes find each other and communicate*

Look at the processes running on your system, and try to find the one called EPMD. For example, on a UNIX-like operating system, you can run ps:

```
$ ps ax | grep -i epmd
  758    ??  S   0:00.00 /usr/local/lib/erlang/erts-5.6.2/bin/epmd -daemon
```

EPMD is the Erlang Port Mapper Daemon. Whenever you start a node, the node checks that EPMD is running on your local machine and starts it otherwise. EPMD keeps track of which nodes are running on the local machine and what ports they have been assigned. When an Erlang node on one machine wants to talk to a remote node, the local EPMD talks to the EPMD on the remote machine (by default using TCP/IP on port 4369) and asks if it has a node by that name up and running. If so, the remote EPMD replies with the port used for communicating directly with the remote node. But EPMDs never try to locate each other automatically—communication must always be triggered by one node looking for another.

> **Advanced node discovery**
> Systems exist that allow you to find and connect Erlang nodes through network multicast, broadcast, and other clever means. If you're running Erlang in a cloud environment like EC2 where you add and remove computers on demand, you may want to look into these. One project that has been receiving some attention recently is nodefinder, at http://code.google.com/p/nodefinder/.

Note that Erlang's default distribution model is based on the assumption that all the machines in the cluster are running on a trusted network. If that isn't the case, or if some of the machines need to talk to the outside world, then communication over the unsafe network should be done using direct TCP (or UDP or SCTP) with a suitable protocol for your application, as you did with the RPC server in chapter 3. Alternatively, you can tunnel the traffic via SSL, SSH, or IPsec, or even configure the Erlang distribution layer to use SSL or another carrier protocol (see the Erlang/OTP SSL library and ERTS user guides for details).

In a typical production environment, you have a number of machines on a trusted network and one or more Erlang nodes that communicate with the outside world via an Erlang web server like Yaws, MochiWeb, or the standard library `inets` `httpd`. You may also be running other protocols on certain ports. Apart from that, nothing can access your network from the outside. Still, it would be foolish to have no security at all, if only to avoid human error. Erlang's distribution uses a system of magic cookies for authorization; and apart from firewalls, the most common reason for failing to connect nodes is an incorrectly set cookie. The next section will explain how this works.

8.2.4 *The magic cookie security system*

Assuming you've managed to start a node at least once, look in your home directory. (On Windows, this is probably C:/Documents and Settings/<username>, C:/Users/<username>, or whatever %HOMEDRIVE%%HOMEPATH% happens to expand to.) You should find a file named .erlang.cookie. If you open this file with a text editor, you'll see a long string. This is your automatically generated cookie. You can check this by running the following command from the shell on an Erlang node:

```
(b@mybox.home.net)1> auth:get_cookie().
'CUYHQMJEJEZLUETUOWFH'
```

The string returned should be the same one you see in the .erlang.cookie file. An Erlang node doesn't allow traffic from other nodes unless they know the magic cookie. When a node starts, it reads the .erlang.cookie file if it exists and uses the string found there as its magic cookie. (If you edit the file and change the string to something else, and then restart the node and rerun the previous command, you should see that the modified cookie is used.) If the node doesn't find a cookie file, it instead creates a new file containing a randomly generated string—that's how the file got there in the first place. Try deleting the file and restarting the node: you should see the file appear again with a fresh random string.

By default, a node assumes that all other nodes it wants to talk to are using the same cookie as itself. When you start several nodes on a single computer, as you did earlier (using the same user account and home directory), all of them use the same cookie file, and so they're allowed to communicate with each other. If you want nodes on two different machines to communicate, the easiest way is to copy the generated cookie file from one machine to the other, ensuring that they're equal but still sufficiently hard to guess. Preferably, nobody except the owner should have read access to the cookie file.

This security model guards against basic attacks—for example, if you've started an Erlang node on a computer with no firewall, an attacker won't be able to easily guess

> **Connecting multiple computers**
>
> If you have two computers with Erlang installed (the more, the merrier), and they're connected over the network, you can now try to repeat what you did in section 8.2.2. First, ensure that the cookie file is the same on both; then, start at least one node on each machine, and try to connect them using `net_adm:ping/1`.

your cookie—but more importantly, it also guards against human error. Suppose you have two separate clusters of Erlang nodes running on your network, and you don't want them to accidentally join to form a single fully connected cluster (for example, if there's a bandwidth bottleneck between them). By using different cookies, you can guarantee that members of the two separate clusters won't accidentally be connected by a `net_adm:ping(...)` or similar.

For more complex setups, you can programmatically set the cookie with the built-in function `set_cookie(Node, Cookie)`. This allows you to configure a node so that it uses specific cookies for talking to specific other nodes. In principle, each node in the cluster can have a different cookie, but in practice the system of having the same cookie file contents is the most common.

Next, let's make your nodes chat to demonstrate what you can do with message passing in distributed Erlang.

8.2.5 *Sending messages between connected nodes*

We went over the basics of message passing using ! and `receive` in chapters 1 and 2. In the chapters after that, you've also been sending messages through API functions such as `gen_server:cast(...)`. We now look at ways of passing messages between nodes. Make sure nodes a, b, and c are started and connected as before. (For added thrills, run them on separate computers.) Working through the following examples should help you get your mind around how easy distribution can be in Erlang.

The first thing we demonstrate is how to talk to a process that is registered under some known name on the remote node. Enter the following on node b (recall that an expression isn't complete until the terminating period character, even if you press Enter after each line):

```
(b@mybox.home.net)2> register(shell, self()).
true
(b@mybox.home.net)3> receive
(b@mybox.home.net)3>     {From, Msg} ->
(b@mybox.home.net)3>       From ! {self(), "thanks"},
(b@mybox.home.net)3>       io:format("Msg: ~p~n", [Msg])
(b@mybox.home.net)3> end.
```

At the first prompt, you register the shell process locally under the name `shell`. (See section 2.13.3 if you need a reminder about process registration.) The registration returns `true`, indicating that it worked. After that, you enter a `receive` expression; after you enter the last line and the period, the shell doesn't print another prompt—it's executing the receive and will wait until a message matching {From, Msg} arrives. You expect From to be a process identifier that lets you reply to the sender, and Msg to be any data. When you get such a message, you send a quick reply that includes your own process identifier, and then you print the received Msg. Only when all that has finished can you enter further expressions in this shell, so you leave it alone for now.

Next, do the same thing on node c. This will leave you with both b and c waiting for messages. Now, switch to node a, and enter the following:

```
(a@mybox.home.net)2> lists:foreach(fun(Node) ->
(a@mybox.home.net)2>                     {shell, Node} ! {self(), "hello!"}
(a@mybox.home.net)2>                  end,
(a@mybox.home.net)2>                  nodes()).
```

You use the higher-order function lists:foreach/2 to iterate over the list of connected nodes as given by nodes(), which should contain b and c in this case. For each node, you send a message of the form {self(), "hello!"} to a destination specified by the tuple {shell, Node}. This is a form of destination we didn't mention in section 2.13.3; it means the message should be sent to the process registered under the name shell on the specified node. If you said shell ! {...}, it would refer to a process registered on the local node a, and that isn't what you want here.

If you now look back at your other two nodes, they should each have received a message, sent you a reply, and printed the message as you instructed them to do. The result should look like this on both nodes:

```
Msg: "hello!"
ok
(b@mybox.home.net)4>
```

Note that in the receive, you bound the variable From to the sender's pid. You can inspect it by entering it in the shell:

```
(b@mybox.home.net)4> From.
<5135.37.0>
```

This shows a text representation of the process identifier. From the first number, you can tell that it comes from another node—for local pids, this is always zero. Note that you used this pid to send a reply back to the sender with a straightforward From ! {...}. The destination node is encoded in the pid. (Don't think too much about the actual numbers—they're temporarily assigned and have no deeper meaning.) If you do the same thing on node c, you should see the same representation of From as on b.

What happened with the replies? Simple—they're waiting for you in the mailbox of the shell process on node a. First, inspect its process ID:

```
(a@mybox.home.net)3> self().
<0.37.0>
```

You should see that its middle number is the same as those in the From pids on the other nodes. However, the first number is zero, which indicates that the process it refers to resides on the local node. Now, look in the mailbox on a:

```
(a@mybox.home.net)4> receive R1 -> R1 end.
{<5316.37.0>,"thanks"}
(a@mybox.home.net)5> receive R2 -> R2 end.
{<5229.37.0>,"thanks"}
```

(Make sure you use different variables for the two receives—otherwise, the second one will never match.) Note that the pids of the senders are both remote, as indicated by their first numbers being nonzero. Interestingly, they both have the same middle number as the shell process on a. This is because the initial shell process tends to be started at the same point in the boot sequence on all nodes. If the shell process on one node has crashed and been restarted, it will have a different number. For example, try entering 1=2. on a, and then call self() again, and you'll see it change: even in the Erlang shell, processes are used to make the system fault tolerant. (A crashed shell process loses its mailbox contents, but variable bindings are preserved.)

As you can see, distributed communication is straightforward, and it doesn't get any more complicated from here on. This is the heart and soul of it, and the rest is sugar on top. There is one more important thing to learn before you start to play with distributed programming for real, and that is how to control other nodes remotely from your local console.

8.2.6 *Working with remote shells*

Erlang's location transparency is nicely demonstrated by its rather remarkable ability to run shells remotely. After all, when you start a normal Erlang shell, you get an Erlang process that talks to the input and output streams of your console window. This communication is also built on message passing, and the shell process doesn't care much whether it's running on the same node as the console it's connected to. As a consequence, it's easy to start a shell process that runs on the remote node and does all its work there, but that is connected to the console of your local node.

This remote shell feature is supported directly in the job control interface of the Erlang shell. Recall from section 2.1.4 that if you press Ctrl-G in the shell, you get a prompt that looks like this:

```
User switch command
 -->
```

Try this on node a now. If you enter h or ? at the prompt, you see this help text:

```
c [nn]              - connect to job
i [nn]              - interrupt job
k [nn]              - kill job
j                   - list all jobs
s [shell]           - start local shell
r [node [shell]]    - start remote shell
q                   - quit erlang
? | h               - this message
```

We explained how job control works in section 2.1.5, but we didn't show how to use the r command. By now, you can probably guess. You'll use node a to start a job on node b. The nodes don't even need to be previously connected, so you can try restarting b for this exercise if you like. On a, enter the following:

```
--> r 'b@mybox.home.net'
-->
```

The r command takes a node name as an argument and starts a remote shell job on that node, like the s command starts a new local job. Make sure to use single quotes around the node name if it has dots in it (as it does here). Just as when you use the s command, you don't see any immediate effects. Let's use the j command to inspect the list of currently running jobs:

```
--> j
  1   {shell,start,[init]}
  2*  {'b@mybox.home.net',shell,start,[]}
-->
```

Job 1 is your old local shell, but look at job 2: it says it's running on node b. The next step is to connect to that job, which you can do by entering c 2—or, because the * marker shows that it's now the default job, it's enough to enter c:

```
--> c
Eshell V5.6.5  (abort with ^G)
(b@mybox.home.net)1>
```

Now look at that prompt. You're running on node b! This means you can execute any command on b as if you were sitting in front of b's console, even if machine b is in another room or on the other side of the planet. This includes any kind of maintenance work such as killing and restarting processes manually, compiling and upgrading code, or monitoring and debugging. This is pretty powerful stuff, but with great power comes great responsibility. It's equally possible to bring down a node this way.

It's often the case that you have a long-lived node running on some machine, and you want to perform operations on it. To do so, you start a new temporary node on

---

Quit with care when leaving a remote shell

When you're finished with your remote shell session and ready to quit, your fingers may find themselves typing the shell shortcut q(). Stop! Don't press Enter! That command is short for init:stop(), which *shuts down the node where the command is executed*: that is, the remote node. Probably every Erlang programmer has been burned by this at one time or another. The Ctrl-G and Ctrl-C (Ctrl-Break) escapes are safe to use, because they always work within the context of your local node. Use Ctrl-G followed by Q, or Ctrl-C (Ctrl-Break on Windows) followed by A, to shut down the local node and leave the remote node running.

your local machine; from that, you connect remotely to the other node. This way, when you're done with the maintenance, there's usually no reason to keep the temporary node running: you can press Ctrl-C twice (on UNIX-like systems, or Ctrl-Break followed by A on Windows). Doing so kills the temporary node abruptly, taking the remote job with it. If instead you want to continue running locally, press Ctrl-G, and from there connect back to your initial shell session, kill the remote job, or switch back and forth between them. The actual interactions taking place when you run a remote shell are shown in figure 8.5.

You now have a solid basis for working with distributed Erlang. We have covered the distribution model and how to start nodes and connect them, the security model and setting up cookies, sending messages between nodes, and working with remote shells. What you've learned here will serve you well as you move forward into using these features in your system. But before we go back to the Simple Cache application in the next chapter, let's build something interesting as an exercise in order to drive these points home.

Suppose you have a bunch of different services running in your Erlang cluster, distributed over the network. How does one service locate the other services that it would like to use? Wouldn't it be neat if you had a resource discovery system that could handle such things for you automatically, so you could move things around in the cluster more easily?

You may be thinking: "Resource discovery is a hard problem that will take at least 10,000 lines of code sprinkled with weird things like AF_INET and SOCK_DGRAM." Don't worry—you're learning Erlang, and that means you can put something reasonably powerful together without too much effort.

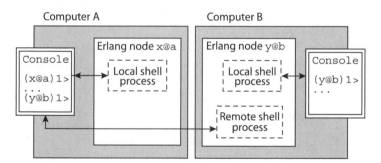

Figure 8.5 How remote shells work. Even though the remote shell process is running on computer B, it's connected to the console on computer A in exactly the same way as the local shell process on A. Thanks to the location transparency in Erlang, there is little difference between the two cases.

8.3   *The nuts and bolts of resource discovery*

The simplistic approach to networked applications is that you hardcode the locations of all the resources on the network. When things are added, relocated, or removed (for any number of reasons including scaling up, reorganizing, replacing failed instances, or code upgrades), this hardcoded configuration must be altered manually. If you've been a good software engineer, you probably have all these settings in a configuration file or database. If you've been lazy and entered it in the source code, you have to edit and recompile your modules. In either case, this manual process is both slow and error prone, and it often leads to confusing setups over time as things are moved around and reconfigured.

Instead of all this hardcoding, you can use *resource discovery* to let providers and consumers of services find one another without needing prior knowledge of the system layout. In this section, you'll build a resource discovery application that functions a bit like the yellow pages. Each node in the cluster runs a local instance of this application. Each such instance discovers and caches information about the available resources in the cluster. This distributed, dynamic approach makes the system flexible and powerful for a number of reasons:

- *No single point of failure*—It's a peer-to-peer system.
- *No hardcoded network topology*—You can add resources where you want them.
- *Easier scaling*—You can add more resources as needed.
- *Ability to run many services in a single node*—Discovery is location transparent and works just as well with only one node (particularly good for testing).
- *Easier upgrades*—You can bring down old services and start new ones dynamically. Removed services become unregistered, and new ones are discovered as they come online.

With dynamically discoverable resources, life gets easier all the way from development to production (especially in production). Before we move on to implementation, let's first make it clear what we're talking about.

8.3.1   *Terminology and taxonomy*

We need to introduce a few concepts so we can discuss them in a consistent way. These concepts are fairly universal, although they may be named differently in other literature and implementations. Resource discovery is all about enabling the relationship between producers and consumers of resources. For this purpose, it needs to track available resources offered by producers, as well as the requirements of consumers: in other words, a list of "I have" and "I want" for each participant. The "I have" items must be concrete resources that can be used or addressed directly, whereas the "I want" items only need to indicate the type of resource being sought so that a matching resource instance can be found. Table 8.1 shows the terminology we use.

Let's examine these concepts in a little more detail.

Table 8.1 Resource discovery terms and definitions

Term	Definition
Resource	A concrete resource (e.g., a fun) or a reference to a concrete resource (e.g., a pid).
Resource type	A tag used to classify resources.
Resource tuple	A pair of a type tag and a resource.

RESOURCE

A resource is either a specific, concrete resource that you can use directly, such as a fun or a chunk of binary data, or a reference to a concrete resource, such as a pid, a file handle, an ETS table handle, or similar. In general, you'll be storing mostly resource references in your system, rather than the concrete resources themselves.

RESOURCE TYPE

A resource type identifies a certain kind of resource. For example, an instance of the Simple Cache application can publish itself as being a resource of type simple_ cache. There can be many resource instances of the same type in an Erlang cluster, and it's assumed that they all have the same API no matter how they're implemented. A consumer that announces that it's looking for resources of the type simple_cache will be told about all resources of this type that have been published somewhere in the cluster.

RESOURCE TUPLE

A resource tuple is a pair of a resource type and a resource. If you have a resource tuple, you have everything you need to know in order to use the resource. The type indicates what sort of thing the resource is and how you may access it or talk to it. You may publish any resources you have through the discovery system in the form of resource tuples, so that anyone who understands the type tag can locate those resources and use them.

With this terminology straightened out, let's get to the implementation of this system. It isn't trivial—distributed applications rarely are—but you should be able to follow what's going on. We start by explaining the algorithm.

8.3.2   *The algorithm*

Let's say you start with two connected nodes, a and b (which are already synchronized), and now a third node c joins the cluster. The problem you have to solve is how to synchronize c with the other nodes. Suppose that both a and b have local resource instances of types x and y (we refer to the specific instances as x@a, and so on). Furthermore, both a and b would like to know about resources of type z. (For example, z could be a logging service needed by applications running on a and b.) Node c has a local resource of type z, and it's looking for one or more resources of type x. c doesn't care about resources of type y.

To get in sync with the other nodes, the resource discovery server on c sends messages to a and b informing them what resources it has locally. The resource discovery servers on nodes a and b receive these messages and cache the information about the resource z@c, which matches their local "I want" lists. They then both respond by sending information about their local resources back to c, which caches the information about the resources of type x and discards all information about the resources of type y. (You can think of it as a game of "I'll show you mine, if you show me yours!") Figure 8.6 illustrates these interactions.

Please make sure you read this explanation carefully before you move on the next section. It will be much easier to follow the implementation if you understand the algorithm.

Next, let's begin implementing the bare-bones resource discovery system, which you can take to the moon after you've read the rest of this book.

8.3.3   *Implementing the resource discovery application*

You'll implement all of this on the Erlang message-passing level. There are certainly other ways to do it, using techniques like network multicast and broadcast, but they are beyond the scope of this book. To keep this exercise simple and focus on the problem, you'll use a single module without any supervision or logging. (At erlware.org, you can find a much more fully featured version of resource discovery written as a multimodule OTP application, as you've been doing in the previous chapters.)

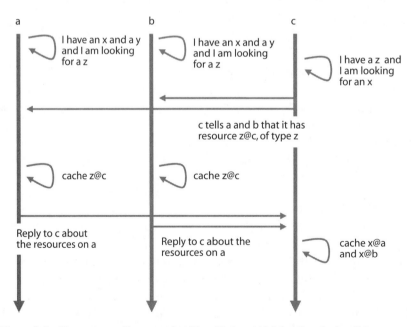

Figure 8.6   The resource discovery algorithm. Node c is joining the cluster; it has a resource of type z, which both a and b need, and it's looking for a resource of type x.

THE MODULE HEADER

It should come as no surprise by now that this module implements the `gen_server` behaviour. Apart from application-specific API functions such as `trade_resources/0`, the following header section should look familiar:

```erlang
-module(resource_discovery).

-behaviour(gen_server).

-export([
        start_link/0,
        add_target_resource_type/1,
        add_local_resource/2,
        fetch_resources/1,
        trade_resources/0
   ]).

-export([init/1, handle_call/3, handle_cast/2, handle_info/2,
        terminate/2, code_change/3]).

-define(SERVER, ?MODULE).
```

At the end of the header section, you define your state record:

```erlang
-record(state, {target_resource_types,
                local_resource_tuples,
                found_resource_tuples}).
```

It has three fields: `target_resource_types` is the "I want" part. This is a list of resource types that you're looking for. `local_resource_tuples` is the "I have" part. This is where you list, in the form of resource tuples, all resources that exist on the local node. Finally, `found_resource_tuples` is the place where you cache information about discovered resource instances matching your wanted list (even if they reside on the local node).

STARTING THE SERVER AND STORING INFORMATION

Next, you get working on your API functions. The first in the list is `start_link/0`, and its implementation is standard boilerplate from the previous chapters:

```erlang
start_link() ->
    gen_server:start_link({local, ?SERVER}, ?MODULE, [], []).
```

As usual, you register the server process locally so it can be easily found by name, even from a remote node. After `start_link()`, the next natural function to implement is the `init/1` callback that is called on startup:

```erlang
init([]) ->
    {ok, #state{target_resource_types = [],
                local_resource_tuples = dict:new(),
                found_resource_tuples = dict:new()}}.
```

This defines your initial server state: the `target_resource_types` field is initially an empty list, whereas `found_resource_tuples` and `local_resource_tuples` are empty dictionaries (associative arrays), using the standard library `dict` module.

This means you've implemented the necessary pieces to start your server. Let's now add a couple of the API functions. These operate in a similar way, so you implement them together here. Both are asynchronous casts that cause new data to be stored in the server state:

```
add_target_resource_type(Type) ->
    gen_server:cast(?SERVER, {add_target_resource_type, Type}).

add_local_resource(Type, Instance) ->
    gen_server:cast(?SERVER, {add_local_resource, {Type, Instance}}).
```

These functions are for adding to the "I want" and the "I have" lists, respectively. The first adds a resource type to the "I want" list. The second adds a resource instance that is present on the local node and marks it as being of the given type. As a point of style, note that the tuple you send has the form {Tag, Data} in both cases, even when Data has multiple fields as in {Type, Instance}. An alternative would be to pass a triple {Tag, Field1, Field2}, but for the sake of consistency it's better to make all the protocol messages be tagged 2-tuples rather than use a mix of tuple sizes.

Because these both use gen_server:cast/2, you add a couple of clauses to the handle_cast/2 callback in order to implement the server-side functionality. Let's look at the add_target_resource_type case first:

```
handle_cast({add_target_resource_type, Type}, State) ->
    TargetTypes = State#state.target_resource_types,
    NewTargetTypes = [Type | lists:delete(Type, TargetTypes)],
    {noreply, State#state{target_resource_types = NewTargetTypes}};
```

First, you pick out the current target resource types from the server state. Then, you take the resource type you've been handed and prepend it to the current list, first performing a delete so that you avoid duplicate entries. (The lists:delete/2 function leaves the list unchanged if it finds no such element.)

The add_local_resource case is similar:

```
handle_cast({add_local_resource, {Type, Instance}}, State) ->
    ResourceTuples = State#state.local_resource_tuples,
    NewResourceTuples = add_resource(Type, Instance, ResourceTuples),
    {noreply, State#state{local_resource_tuples = NewResourceTuples}};
```

After picking out the current local resources, you store the new resource instance under the specified type, and you put the bulk of this operation in an internal utility function add_resource/3 that looks like this:

```
add_resource(Type, Resource, ResourceTuples) ->
    case dict:find(Type, ResourceTuples) of
        {ok, ResourceList} ->
            NewList = [Resource | lists:delete(Resource, ResourceList)],
            dict:store(Type, NewList, ResourceTuples);
        error ->
            dict:store(Type, [Resource], ResourceTuples)
    end.
```

As usual, internal functions like this should be placed last in the module. You're using the standard library `dict` module here to map a resource type to a corresponding list of resources (so you can have multiple resources per type), as shown in figure 8.7.

If an entry for the key already exists, you read its current value so that you can add to the list and write it back; you do a delete as well to ensure that each resource occurs in the list at most once. If there was no previous entry for the key, you create a new one with a single resource in the list.

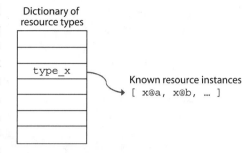

Figure 8.7 Dictionary (associative array) mapping resource types to lists of known resources

FETCHING AND TRADING INFORMATION

The next API function on the list is `fetch_resources/1`:

```
fetch_resources(Type) ->
    gen_server:call(?SERVER, {fetch_resources, Type}).
```

This function is a synchronous call, asking for a list of all the resource instances you're looking for and know about for a given resource type. To implement this, you add a corresponding clause to the `handle_call/3` callback:

```
handle_call({fetch_resources, Type}, _From, State) ->
    {reply, dict:find(Type, State#state.found_resource_tuples), State};
```

You call `dict:find/2` to look up `Type` in the current resources. This yields either `{ok, Value}` or `error`, which happens to be what you want the `fetch_resources/1` function to return, so there's no need to massage the result—you can pass it straight back.

The real heavy lifting of resource discovery is done by the last of the API functions:

```
trade_resources() ->
    gen_server:cast(?SERVER, trade_resources).
```

This API function is a simple cast to trigger the resource trading: it sends a single atom `trade_resources`, which is handled by the `handle_cast/2` clause shown next. The code in this clause and the one following drives all the communication illustrated in figure 8.6:

```
handle_cast(trade_resources, State) ->
    ResourceTuples = State#state.local_resource_tuples,
    AllNodes = [node() | nodes()],
    lists:foreach(
        fun(Node) ->
            gen_server:cast({?SERVER, Node},
                            {trade_resources, {node(), ResourceTuples}})
        end,
        AllNodes),
    {noreply, State};
```

The `trade_resources` message tells the local resource discovery server to broadcast messages asynchronously to each of the resource discovery servers on all the connected nodes in the Erlang cluster (including the local node itself, for a nice symmetry that lets you update your local list of matching resources without any additional code). This is made simple by the fact that the processes are all registered under the same name on their respective nodes.

Using `cast` between servers

In this code, you see an example of using `gen_server:cast/2` to communicate between two different `gen_server` processes. Being asynchronous, it continues immediately after posting the message. Using the synchronous `gen_server:call/3` for such purposes is generally a bad idea: doing so would make this server block until the remote server replied—and if the remote server was busy trying to call this server, you'd have a deadlock on your hands.

These broadcast messages have the form `{trade_resources, {ReplyTo, Resources}}`, where `ReplyTo` is the node name of the sender (given by `node()`), and `Resources` is the entire data structure (a `dict`) that holds the current resource tuples that the sender is publishing. Note that you don't need to worry about the receiving process mucking up your local data structure, because message passing is strictly by copy, and because Erlang allows you to send any data in messages—there's no need to rewrite or marshal the data—you can include the dictionary as it is in the message.

When a node receives one of these broadcast messages, it's handled by the following `handle_cast/2` clause:

```
handle_cast({trade_resources, {ReplyTo, Remotes}},
            #state{local_resource_tuples = Locals,
                   target_resource_types = TargetTypes,
                   found_resource_tuples = OldFound} = State) ->
    FilteredRemotes = resources_for_types(TargetTypes, Remotes),   <-| Checks for wanted resources
    NewFound = add_resources(FilteredRemotes, OldFound),   <-- Adds to known resources
    case ReplyTo of
        noreply ->
            ok;
        _ ->
            gen_server:cast({?SERVER, ReplyTo},            <-| Replies to sender
                            {trade_resources, {noreply, Locals}})
    end,
    {noreply, State#state{found_resource_tuples = NewFound}};
```

First, you need a bunch of different fields from the current state, so you use a slightly complicated pattern to extract these immediately in the clause head. Note that the pattern has the shape `#state{...}=State`, which means it's an alias pattern: it both matches and assigns a name at the same time. It's common style to write the name on the right side of the equals sign, because doing so puts the visual focus on the shape of the data, but the pattern can also be written `State=#state{...}`.

Next, you check to see if any of the sender's resources are on your "I want" list. Those whose types match are then added to your local set of known resources. After that, you only have to reply to the sender (the resource discovery process on the node identified by the `ReplyTo` field). The reply has the same shape as the broadcast message, but instead of the sender's node name it uses the atom `noreply` to indicate that no further reply is needed—otherwise, messages would bounce back and forth forever. After the process that broadcast the original trade messages has received and handled all replies, it has the same information as the others.

The following internal utility functions were used earlier. The first is a simple iteration to call the `add_resource/2` utility function you defined previously, but for a list of resource tuples. The second is more complicated and goes over a list of types (using `lists:foldl/3`), building a total list of all resources you know about for the given types:

```
add_resources([{Type, Resource}|T], ResourceTuples) ->
    add_resources(T, add_resource(Type, Resource, ResourceTuples));
add_resources([], ResourceTuples) ->
    ResourceTuples.

resources_for_types(Types, ResourceTuples) ->
    Fun =
        fun(Type, Acc) ->
            case dict:find(Type, ResourceTuples) of
                {ok, List} ->
                    [{Type, Instance} || Instance <- List] ++ Acc;      <──┐
                error ->                                          **Creates list**
                    Acc                                             **of pairs** │
            end
        end,
    lists:foldl(Fun, [], Types).
```

For each type in the list, this code looks up the list of resources for that type and transforms it (using a list comprehension; see section 2.9) into a list of pairs where each individual resource instance is marked up with the corresponding type. This list of pairs is then added to the accumulated list. (Note that you build on the left to avoid quadratic behaviour, even if the list is expected to be fairly short; see section 2.2.5.) This creates a final list that can easily be passed to `add_resources/2` afterward, as you did earlier.

FINAL WORDS

This algorithm is fairly straightforward when you get your mind around it. Although it's a bit on the simple side, it covers most of what is needed for resource discovery. The main thing that is obviously missing is the ability to automatically trigger resource trading at strategic places in your system (for example, within the supervision hierarchy) so you don't have to call `trade_resources/0` manually. We get back to this in the next chapter.

Because the node-to-node protocol depends only on asynchronous messages and doesn't strictly depend on getting answers from all the other nodes, the system should be fairly resilient to failures. The worst that can happen is that nodes suddenly disappear due to crashes, reboots, or network problems, and in that case the stored information can get out of sync (you didn't add any automatic cleanup of resources that lived on nodes that have vanished).

One simple thing you can do to improve the stability of the cluster, which we leave as an exercise for you (you should be able to do it by now), is to implement a process that periodically tries to ping every node it has ever seen, as well as trigger resource trading, in order to overcome intermittent contact problems or crashes that may cause nodes to disconnect. When that's done, you have a reasonable guarantee of a healthy cluster. When you design a system on top of resource discovery, it's important to understand what sort of guarantees you have; in this case, it depends on how long you expect it to take to repair a disconnected network and on the frequency of your automated node reconnection.

Using the techniques for distributed programming in Erlang that you were shown in the earlier parts of this chapter, you've built a system that can be used to let your programs automatically discover additional services. This removes the need for hard-coded knowledge about network topology and the locations of services within the cluster. In less than 100 lines of code, you've opened the door to building systems that are extremely dynamic and easily scalable. In the next chapter, you'll put this code to real use.

8.4   *Summary*

In this chapter, we've covered a number of different topics, all of them important aspects of distributed programming in Erlang:

- Location transparency and communication by copying
- Erlang nodes and clustering
- Access control using cookies
- Communicating between nodes
- Working with remote shells
- Putting distribution to work: implementing a basic resource discovery system

What you've learned here opens up all kinds of possibilities for your programming. We hope this chapter has sparked some real creativity by showing what can be accomplished in short order with distributed programming in Erlang.

In the next chapter, you'll take this knowledge—as well as the code you've written—and apply it to the task of making your Simple Cache application a suitable session store, essentially taking it from a standalone entity on a single machine to a cluster of caches that can work together to help the Erlware folks provide an even better experience for their users.

Adding distribution to the cache with Mnesia

9

This chapter covers

- Choosing a strategy for distributing the cache
- An introduction to Mnesia, the built-in database in Erlang
- Using Mnesia to distribute the cache over multiple nodes

Your cache application is operationally sound as of chapter 7, and chapter 8 should have brought you up to speed on distribution in Erlang. You'll need it right away. Members of the team at Erlware have been working on adding login functionality and sessions to the site: this will allow authors to update packages, tweak documentation, and change availability of their packages. You've been asked to add some features to your cache to make it suitable for storing sessions in order to support this new functionality.

The site is fronted by a stateless load balancer, so any of the available web servers could be called on to load a page. This means the session information needs to be available to all servers that participate in serving the web application. The problem is that currently your cache is local to the node it runs on and knows nothing about other caches that may be running on the other web servers. A simplified view of the current architecture is shown in figure 9.1.

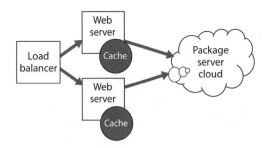

Figure 9.1
The current, simple architecture of the cache application. Each cache is local to the server it runs on. Because the load balancer distributes work between the servers, the caches need to become distributed as well if they're to store the session data.

Right now, if you stored session information in the caches, a user might log in on one web server, but because of the load balancer, the next page the user loaded might be served from a different web server. This server wouldn't be able to recognize the user because it couldn't find their session in the local cache. Allowing the caches to share information across instances would solve this issue.

9.1 Distributing the cache

You're being asked to make the cache application store the session data in such a way that you can ask any of the cache instances to return the current session state for any session key regardless of which server it was last saved on. It's no longer sufficient to store only data that is specific to the local web server; you need to make a distributed cache, where each instance is aware of the others. This means you first must think about how they should exchange this information between them.

9.1.1 Choosing a communication strategy

When you're designing a distributed program, there are two main flavors of communication to consider: asynchronous and synchronous. We talked briefly about this in section 1.1.3. With *asynchronous communication*, the sender immediately proceeds without waiting for any kind of confirmation or answer. With *synchronous communication*, the sender becomes suspended until a reply is received (even if that reply is just "thanks, I got it"). Erlang's basic form of message passing is asynchronous, because it's the most straightforward and flexible form: it's a better match for distributed programming in general, and you can always implement synchronous communication as a pair of asynchronous request/reply messages (as gen_server:call/3 does).

But just because the primary form of communication is asynchronous, it doesn't mean you can't structure your program around other paradigms. In this section, we discuss how the choice of communication strategy affects what kind of systems you can build and what properties you can expect from those systems.

ASYNCHRONOUS COMMUNICATION
Asynchronous communication is sometimes described as "fire and forget" or "send and pray." When the message is on its way, the sender is free to do something else. If the process at the other end is expected to answer, the sender will check for the reply later, as illustrated in figure 9.2. Usually, getting a reply within a specific time

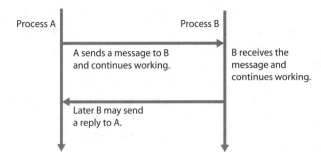

Figure 9.2
Asynchronous fire-and-forget communication: the sender isn't blocked and can go on working immediately after the message has been posted. Any reply will be sent back separately.

isn't necessary for the sender to be able to continue with its own work, or at least some of it.

This is a good basic form of communication for computer systems because it implies very little in terms of overhead. There is nothing to check, scan, verify, time, or otherwise care about. This means that it's fast, and it generally lends itself to the creation of simple and intuitive systems. We recommend that you strive to use this type of communication, except when you obviously can't.

To give a concrete example of the kind of situation where this strategy works well, consider the postal service. You may want to send a letter to your grandmother. You write it, put it in an envelope, put a few stamps on it, and drop it in the mailbox; you're done and can go about your own business the second the letter leaves your hand. You're fairly confident the message will get to her, but it may not; either way, it won't impede your activities for the day. This is nice, because if your grandmother doesn't get the message, or if she reads it much later and responds next month, you aren't stuck waiting that whole time. In other words, this system gets work done even in the face of unexpected events, if the involved parties know to behave accordingly.

SYNCHRONOUS COMMUNICATION

With synchronous communication, every message requires a reply (or at least an acknowledgment that the message was received). The sender becomes suspended until the reply arrives and can't do anything else meanwhile. Another term for this is *blocking communication*, because the sender is said to be blocked while waiting for the reply. A typical synchronous exchange of information is shown in figure 9.3.

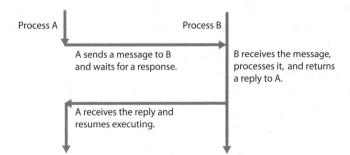

Figure 9.3
Synchronous, blocking communication: the sender is suspended until the reply arrives. Even if the reply isn't strictly needed, the pause will be at least as long as the time required for the round trip.

The obvious drawback is that the sender isn't able to perform any further work until it gets a response (which in a distributed environment takes at least twice the time it takes to traverse the network between the computers). On the other hand, a clear benefit is that systems can be easily synchronized around an activity.

Let's say a harried businessman walks into a government office because he has a ticket on his car. If he doesn't get it cleared, his car may be towed and impounded the second he parks it somewhere outside of the government parking lot where it's currently safe. He walks up to the desk and asks the clerk to please clear the violation, and he hands her a check. In contrast to the earlier mailbox example, this fellow isn't finished—he can't just leave and drive back to work. Instead, he must wait in the office for the desk clerk to process the payment and tell him the violation is clear. As soon as he receives the receipt, he can leave the office and impatiently get back to work, ensured that the system is in a known state.

For synchronous communication to be practical, it needs to support timeouts. The fellow in the government traffic authority office needs a maximum waiting time so that he doesn't sit in the office until he dies of thirst—at some point, he must give up waiting and either consider the operation a failure or take his chances and assume that it worked. If he decides it was a waste of time (that is, he never got a receipt, and the clerk seems to be gone for the day), he could return another day or

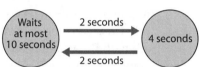

Figure 9.4   Synchronous communication with timeout. The maximum waiting time was 10 seconds, and the total time for the exchange was 8 seconds: 2 to get there, 4 to handle the request, and 2 to get back again.

perhaps try some other workaround to solve the problem. Figure 9.4 illustrates a call within the bounds of a timeout.

The reason for this little digression is that you need to know what kind of system your cache should be: Do you need to guarantee certain synchronized states at certain moments? Do you need to know that when a piece of data is inserted into or deleted from the system, all instances of the cache will reflect the new state as soon as the call to delete or insert has returned? Maybe you don't strictly need your system to be synchronized that way. Perhaps it can be more asynchronous, so that, for example, starting a delete operation and returning before all nodes have reported back is fine. The decision has a significant impact on how you code the solution. Before you start adding distribution to the cache, you need to look at your options and how they will affect the result.

9.1.2   *Synchronous versus asynchronous cache*

As we explained, both approaches have benefits and drawbacks. That is of course true of every decision you make when writing software; but in this case, the choice between an asynchronous and a synchronous approach will profoundly affect the way you implement distribution in your cache.

ASYNCHRONOUS CACHE

Suppose a person were to log in to the site, make a request for another page a second later, but find there was no record of their being logged in. If this wasn't a show-stopper, then you could potentially use nonblocking communication on inserts into the cache. Don't get us wrong—just because you didn't guarantee the state of the system when the insert operation returned wouldn't necessarily mean that inserts would fail frequently or be slow—it would just mean you wouldn't provide an iron-clad guarantee. Basically, the system as a whole could temporarily be in an inconsistent state, and there would be a small probability that someone might observe this once in a while.

In Erlang, an asynchronous message-based design is simple to implement. Recall from the previous chapter that you can make Erlang nodes form a cluster. The simplest asynchronous design builds on the fact that all cache nodes belong to the same cluster. That makes it easy to broadcast a message to each and every cache in the cluster, as you did with the resource discovery example in chapter 8. An operation on any of the caches can send an insert or delete message to all the cache instances in the cluster.

Consider the login sequence:

1. The user logs in to the site.
2. A session is created on the web server.
3. The web server calls `simple_cache:insert()`.
4. The insert function sends an insert message asynchronously to all known nodes and returns immediately.
5. The web server informs the user that they're logged in.
6. The cache instances on the other servers receive and process the insert messages.

The communication pattern is depicted in figure 9.5. This gives you a *weak consistency* among the caches: they aren't all guaranteed to have received and processed the message yet, even though the client has already been told that they're logged in.

This couldn't be any simpler. Assuming that communication between the caches is faster than the user can request another page, everything works seamlessly. The big advantage of this solution is that it operates in a straightforward way (which is always a good thing) and requires very little code to implement.

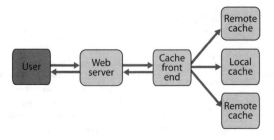

Figure 9.5
Asynchronous cache interaction: as soon as the messages to all the cache instances have been sent, the operation returns to the caller and reports that the operation is done, even though the remote caches won't be up to date until they have processed the message.

Unfortunately, the people in charge at Erlware feel that it would be unacceptable for even a single user of the site to get a "not logged in" message right after having successfully logged in—even if it would typically happen only when there is an unusually high load on the system. This means you need to consider a different strategy.

SYNCHRONOUS CACHE

Suppose instead that you want verification that your messages have been received and data has been inserted by all instances of the cache before you tell the user that they're logged in. The new sequence of events looks like this:

1   The user logs in to the site.
2   A session is created on the web server.
3   The web server calls `simple_cache:insert()`.
4   The insert function blocks until all cache instances have finished inserting the data.
5   The web server informs the user that they're logged in.

This communication pattern is shown in figure 9.6.

The guarantees here are different from the asynchronous case. In this case, you can be sure the user won't be told they're logged in until all caches have been handed a copy of the session data. This implies that the insert function must receive verification from all of the caches before it can proceed.

You can implement this in several different ways. The first is to do it as naively as we described it, using `gen_server:call/2` to send the insert messages synchronously to each of the nodes, one at a time, and return only when the last node has been updated. But if you had N remote nodes, the entire operation would then take at least N times the minimum time needed for a single such round trip over the network. That kind of latency is something you want to avoid. (Note, though, that the minimum latency when gathering the replies is the time it takes for the slowest cache to respond—every synchronous solution is limited by this, no matter how it's implemented.)

Another way would be to get serious about efficiently implementing distributed transactions and start reading up on things like two-phase commit protocols. That would probably be overkill: you'd quickly be on a slippery slope toward writing a full

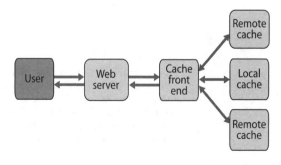

Figure 9.6
Synchronous cache interaction: the cache front end blocks on the insert operation until all the individual caches have reported that they have been successfully updated. Only then does the web server inform the user that they're logged in.

distributed database. If that's the direction you're heading, perhaps you should begin looking for an existing solution in the Erlang/OTP libraries instead.

9.1.3 *If you only had a distributed table...*

Recall from chapter 6 (figure 6.5) that your cache is structured in such a way that you're using processes as storage elements to hold the actual stored data, and you have a table that maps each key to the process identifier of the corresponding storage element. It's only this table of mappings that you need to distribute between the caches. Because of Erlang's location transparency, you don't need to copy the data between the nodes: assuming an efficient network between the web servers, fetching some data from a storage process on another of the servers will still be much faster than calling up the original package servers. Hence, the storage-element processes can stay on the node where they were created, as long as all nodes have access to the key-to-pid mapping. Figure 9.7 illustrates the relation of the table to the cache instances and the storage elements.

All you need to do is solve the problem of distributing the table. As it happens, Erlang/OTP already provides a neat solution to this problem: a distributed database called Mnesia. This seems to fit the bill perfectly. Armed with this information, you run the rudimentary design by the Erlware guys, who love it and tell you to go ahead. (Of course, you wouldn't implement something without stakeholder approval.)

To make this scheme even more interesting, you'll also use the resource discovery system that you constructed in the previous chapter to keep track of the cache nodes, which will let you add and remove nodes on the fly. If that sounds like a lot, you're right. You need to get moving, and the first step is a discussion of Mnesia and how it works.

9.2 *Distributed data storage with Mnesia*

Mnesia is a lightweight, soft real time, distributed, replicated, transactional data store. It's great at storing discrete chunks of Erlang data, particularly in RAM. Mnesia is native to Erlang and stores Erlang data as is—you never need to rewrite your data in any particular format just so you can put it in the database. This makes it the obvious

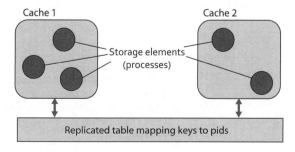

Figure 9.7
Two cache instances sharing a replicated table that maps keys to process identifiers. Erlang's location transparency makes it easy to access the processes regardless of which node they live on; only the table needs to be distributed over both nodes.

first choice when it comes to picking a database for your application, as long as you know its limits.

Mnesia was never designed to replace SQL-style databases or manage hundreds of gigabytes of persistent data distributed over several dozens of computers; and although there are stories of this being done, we recommend against aiming for that kind of usage. But Mnesia is fantastic at smaller numbers of replicas and smaller units of data. It's a good choice for reasonable amounts of persistent (disk-backed) data and great for runtime data that needs to be shared between processes, in particular if you need to distribute the data among multiple nodes for reasons of fault tolerance or efficiency. The key-to-pid mappings you want to implement are a good example of this.

> **How Mnesia got its name**
>
> When the Mnesia database was first created, the developer in charge of the project had a wry sense of humor and decided he would like to call it Amnesia. Management quickly informed him that there would be no database named Amnesia in Ericsson's product line. The developer then chopped off that pesky *A*, giving us Mnesia instead. This is a good name: mnesia is the Greek word for *memory*.

The idea of bringing up a fault-tolerant, replicated data store within minutes may be overwhelming at first. But the best way to learn is by doing, and in this section you'll create a real-world, working Mnesia database. This should make you familiar enough with the basics that you then can go on and apply it to your cache application in section 9.3.

9.2.1   Creating a project database

To get started with Mnesia, you'll create a database that can be used to store the information about the projects on an Erlware repository server. This basic version will hold information about users and which projects they own. The information will be split up over a few tables. Figure 9.8 illustrates the relationships between the data you wish to model. As you can see, the User and Project tables, which have two columns each, are linked together by the Contributor table.

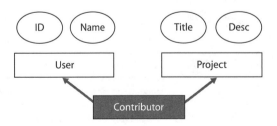

Figure 9.8
Data model for the project database. The Contributor table links the User and Project tables by connecting user IDs to titles of projects the users are involved in. Both user IDs and project titles are unique identifiers in the database.

In Mnesia, plain Erlang records are used to define the table entries. The following listing shows the records you'll use for this example.

Listing 9.1   Project database record definitions

```
-record(user, {
               id,
               name
               }).
-record(project, {
                  title,
                  description
                  }).
-record(contributor, {
                      user_id,
                      title
                      }).
```

These record definitions will be used to create your tables a bit later in this section. Before you get to that point, you have to do some preliminary work. During the course of creating this database, you'll do the following:

- Initialize Mnesia
- Start your node
- Create a schema
- Start Mnesia
- Create database tables
- Populate the tables you've created
- Perform some basic queries on the data

Let's get started with initializing Mnesia.

9.2.2   Initializing the database

Before you can do anything else, you must initialize Mnesia. This involves writing some basic information to disk. First, you need to bring up an Erlang node that is configured to write Mnesia information to a particular location in the filesystem.

STARTING THE NODE

The first thing you need to do when using Mnesia is to start the Erlang node like this:

```
erl -mnesia dir '"/tmp/mnesia_store"' -name mynode
```

This tells Mnesia to store its data in the specified directory. (Note the single quotes needed on the command line in order to preserve the double quotes around the string.) You also tell Erlang to start in distributed mode, using the -name option, so you can begin working with replication in Mnesia right away. (Use -sname instead of -name if that works better for you.) After the node has started, you need to create an initial empty schema on all the nodes that you want to involve in the replication.

CREATING THE SCHEMA

A database *schema* is a description of the tables that currently exist, plus any necessary details about those tables. For the most part, you don't need to think about this—it's what Mnesia uses to keep track of its data. Naturally, if the database is to be distributed, all the involved nodes must have their own copies of the schema, so that they all know the general structure of the data. To make it possible to shut down Mnesia or the entire Erlang node and restart it later without losing the database information, the schema needs to be stored on disk, in the directory you specified with the -mnesia dir "..." option. (It's also possible to have one or more nodes—even all of them—store their data in RAM only, including the schema; but right now you want a persistent, disk-based database.)

In this simple example, you'll only create the schema on your local node:

```
(mynode@erlware.org)1> mnesia:create_schema([node()]).
```

If the command was successful, you now have an empty schema on your node. The command can fail if one of the nodes in the list can't be contacted, if Mnesia is already running on one of the nodes, or if there is a previously existing schema on one of them. (In the last case, you can use the function mnesia:delete_schema (Nodes) to purge the old schema—but think twice before you do this: it makes any existing tables unreadable.)

With the schema in place, all you need to do is start the Mnesia application.

STARTING MNESIA

To start Mnesia manually, you can call mnesia:start(). When Mnesia is running, you can call mnesia:info() to get general information about the database, such as how many tables it contains and how many nodes it's connected to:

```
(mynode@erlware.org)2> mnesia:start().
ok
(mynode@erlware.org)3> mnesia:info().
---> Processes holding locks <---
---> Processes waiting for locks <---
---> Participant transactions <---
---> Coordinator transactions <---
---> Uncertain transactions <---
---> Active tables <---
schema          : with 1         records occupying 422      words of mem
===> System info in version "4.4.8", debug level = none <===
opt_disc. Directory "/tmp/mnesia" is used.
use fallback at restart = false
running db nodes   = [mynode@erlware.org]
stopped db nodes   = []
master node tables = []
remote             = []
ram_copies         = []
disc_copies        = [schema]
disc_only_copies   = []
[{mynode@erlware.org,disc_copies}] = [schema]
2 transactions committed, 0 aborted, 0 restarted, 0 logged to disc
```

```
0 held locks, 0 in queue; 0 local transactions, 0 remote
0 transactions waits for other nodes: []
ok
```

This comes in handy when you're working with a live system, to check that you have full connectedness and that everything is correctly configured.

Now that you've initialized the database system, you can move on to the application-specific code, starting with creating the tables you'll use.

9.2.3   *Creating the tables*

Although it's possible to create tables directly from the Erlang shell, doing so would be a bit ugly because the support for using records in the shell is limited. Instead, you'll write a small module, shown in listing 9.2, that does this job for you. This also ensures that you can easily do it again if you need to start over. As usual, we've left out the source code comments in order to save space—you wouldn't release real code looking like this. For simplicity, we repeat the record definitions from listing 9.1; they should typically be kept in a separate header file included by the module.

> **Listing 9.2   Mnesia table-creation module**

```
-module(create_tables).

-export([init_tables/0]).

-record(user, {
          id,
          name
          }).

-record(project, {
          title,
          description
          }).

-record(contributor, {
          user_id,
          project_title
          }).

init_tables() ->
    mnesia:create_table(user,
        [{attributes, record_info(fields, user)}]),
    mnesia:create_table(project,
        [{attributes, record_info(fields, project)}]),
    mnesia:create_table(contributor,
        [{type, bag}, {attributes, record_info(fields, contributor)}]).
```

As you can see, tables are created with the function `mnesia:create_table(Name, Options)`, where `Options` is a list of `{Name, Value}` pairs. The main option that you almost always need to supply is `attributes`, which assigns names to the fields of the records that will be stored in the table. Without it, Mnesia assumes you'll only have two fields in your records, named `key` and `val`, respectively. This is of course rarely the

> **Mnesia tables and Erlang records**
>
> To Mnesia, a table is just a bunch of tagged tuples. This is exactly what Erlang's records are (see section 2.11), but Mnesia can't know that a table has anything to do with your `-record(...)` declaration of the same name. You need to set up this connection yourself. (Sometimes, it can be useful *not* to be forced to have a connection between a table and a record, even if they have the same name.)
>
> You could hardcode the names, as in `{attributes, [title, description]}`; but it's better to use `record_info(fields, RecordName)` to list the field names, in case you change the record declaration later. Note that `record_info/2` isn't a real function—it will be resolved at compile time (just like the # syntax for records) and can't be called at runtime or from the Erlang shell.

case, so you should supply your own field names. But it illustrates one point: no matter what you name them, *the first field of the record is always the primary key*.

Only specifying the `attributes` option means that the table will get the default settings for all other options. These are as follows:

- The table is both readable and writeable.
- The table is stored in RAM only (the storage type is `ram_copies`).
- The records stored in the table must have the same name as the table.
- The table type is `set`, which means there can be no more than one entry per key.
- The load priority is 0 (the lowest).
- The `local_content` flag is set to `false`.

Of these, the most important to understand are the table type and the storage type. We explain the table type first and get back to the storage type after you create the tables.

THE DIFFERENT TYPES OF MNESIA TABLES

We mentioned in section 2.14.2 that ETS tables can be of different types. Mnesia tables are similar, but the options are slightly different: a table can be a `set`, an `ordered_set`, or a `bag`. As with ETS tables, a `set` treats keys as unique—if you insert a record with the same primary key as an existing entry, the new record overwrites the old. In contrast, a `bag` can contain multiple records with the same key, as long as they differ in at least one field—inserting the exact same record twice has no effect.

An `ordered_set` table behaves the same as a `set`; but whereas `sets` and `bags` are implemented using hash tables, an `ordered_set` keeps all the records stored in the order of their primary keys. This is useful if you need to be able to easily traverse all the entries in order (a hash-based table has no useful ordering).

Note that you've made your Contributor table into a `bag`:

```
mnesia:create_table(contributor, [{type, bag}, ...])
```

This allows the table to hold many different records for the same user ID key, for users that happen to be contributors on multiple projects.

STORAGE TYPES FOR TABLES

The following example shows the result of compiling the module and running the init_tables() function, and then calling mnesia:info() again to check that the tables have been created as expected:

```
(mynode@erlware.org)4> c(create_tables).
{ok,create_tables}
(mynode@erlware.org)5> create_tables:init_tables().
{atomic,ok}
(mynode@erlware.org)6> mnesia:info().
---> Processes holding locks <---
---> Processes waiting for locks <---
---> Participant transactions <---
---> Coordinator transactions <---
---> Uncertain transactions <---
---> Active tables <---
contributor  : with 0       records occupying 312     words of mem
project      : with 0       records occupying 312     words of mem
user         : with 0       records occupying 312     words of mem
schema       : with 4       records occupying 752     words of mem
===> System info in version "4.4.8", debug level = none <===
opt_disc. Directory "/tmp/mnesia" is used.
use fallback at restart = false
running db nodes   = [mynode@erlware.org]
stopped db nodes   = []
master node tables = []
remote             = []
ram_copies         = [contributor,project,user]
disc_copies        = [schema]
disc_only_copies   = []
[{mynode@erlware.org,disc_copies}] = [schema]
[{mynode@erlware.org,ram_copies}] = [user,project,contributor]
5 transactions committed, 3 aborted, 0 restarted, 3 logged to disc
0 held locks, 0 in queue; 0 local transactions, 0 remote
0 transactions waits for other nodes: []
ok
```

❶ **Creating tables worked**

❷ **Active tables**

❸ **Tables of type ram_copies**

❹ **Schema is of type disc_copies**

As you can see, init_tables() ran without error ❶. mnesia:info() shows that you now have four active tables ❷ as opposed to one previously (the schema is always one of the tables). You can also see that your application's tables are of the default ram_copies type ❸. This means they're only stored in memory, which offers the highest performance, but the data isn't persistent and will be lost in case of a crash or restart.

The schema is of the type disc_copies ❹, which means it's written to disk for persistence and will survive restarts; these tables are also fully mirrored in memory for fast read access. Finally, as you can see on the line after that, you have no tables of type disk_only_copies—as the name indicates, these are only stored on disk, and accesses are a lot slower than for the other types. Furthermore, the ordered_set table type currently isn't supported for tables that are kept on disk only.

A table can have different storage types on different nodes: for example, it could be kept on disk on one node but only in RAM on all other nodes. This configuration can even be altered at runtime, so you can switch a table from RAM-based storage to disk-based or vice versa on one or more nodes, without stopping the system. But typically, you only need to decide on a storage type when the tables are initially created.

Now that you've created your tables with the proper settings, the next logical step is to make it possible to insert some data. To do this, you'll add a little code to the create_tables module.

9.2.4   *Populating the tables*

To make it straightforward for others to insert data without knowing too much about the actual tables, you'll hide these details behind a couple of API functions. This also makes it possible to do some consistency checks on the data before it gets inserted in the database. For example, you'll only add users if they're contributors to some project, and you won't allow adding a user for a project that doesn't exist. The code for inserting users and projects is shown in the following listing.

Listing 9.3   Data-insertion functions

```
insert_user(Id, Name, ProjectTitles) when ProjectTitles =/= [] ->
    User = #user{id = Id, name = Name},
    Fun = fun() ->                                        ❶ Writes user
            mnesia:write(User),                              record to table
            lists:foreach(
              fun(Title) ->
                [#project{title = Title}] = mnesia:read(project, Title),
                mnesia:write(#contributor{user_id = Id,
                                          project_title = Title})
              end,
              ProjectTitles)                        Inserts contributor record ❷
          end,
    mnesia:transaction(Fun).                               ❸ Sets up
                                                              transaction
insert_project(Title, Description) ->
    mnesia:dirty_write(#project{title = Title,
                                description = Description}).
```

Add this code to create_tables.erl. Don't forget to export the functions insert_user/3 and insert_project/2 from the module.

TRANSACTIONS

The first of these functions takes three arguments: the unique user ID of the new user you're creating, the name of the user, and a list of all the projects this user contributes to. It's important that the operations you do here to insert a user are isolated from any simultaneous accesses to the database by other processes, so you need to perform them within the context of a *transaction*. Mnesia transactions provide the usual ACID properties:

- *Atomicity*—The transaction is executed as a unit and either succeeds or fails entirely. If it fails at any point, it's unrolled without any effects on the database.
- *Consistency*—The effects of multiple transactions on the database are as if they were executed in some particular order, going from one consistent state to the next, even if some transactions in fact overlap in real time.
- *Isolation*—All transactions appear to happen as if they have the database to themselves and can't disturb each other, even if they're running concurrently. Nobody else can see the effects of a transaction until it's completely finished.
- *Durability*—If the transaction succeeds, all its changes have taken effect. For disk-backed tables, this means the information should survive a restart or a crash.

Transactions are critical for ensuring the integrity of the database across complex operations. Setting up a transaction in Mnesia is easy—you write a fun expression (taking no arguments) to do the work and pass it to `mnesia:transaction/1` ❸. In this case, you first write the user record to the User table ❶. Then, you use `lists:foreach/2` to go over the given list of projects. For each of those, you first assert (by matching the result of a call to `mnesia:read/2` against what you expect to find) that such a project exists in the Project table, before you insert a contributor record ❷. If any of these operations fails, the whole transaction is unrolled, leaving Mnesia in the same state as previously.

DIRTY OPERATIONS

Obviously, you also need a way to insert projects before you can add users. You do so with the second function in listing 9.3. In this case, you take a shortcut and use the function `mnesia:dirty_write/1`. Any Mnesia function with the prefix `dirty_` is a dirty operation that doesn't respect transactions or database locks. This means it must be used with great care.

Generally, using a dirty operation is significantly faster than setting up a transaction and performing normal database operations, and judicious use of dirty operations can speed up your application a lot. Be warned, though—if you haven't thought through the consequences properly, you may end up with inconsistent data. Dirty reads are usually less problematic than dirty writes; but whenever you're in doubt, use transactions! (For this application, you expect that nothing else will be seriously affected by the sudden insertion of a project record, even if it overwrites a previous one.)

INSERTING DATA

It's time to enter some data in your tables. Recompile the module, and run the following commands in the Erlang shell:

```
(mynode@erlware.org)7> create_tables:insert_project(simple_cache, "a simple
    ➥cache application").
ok

(mynode@erlware.org)8> create_tables:insert_user(1,martin,[simple_cache]).
{atomic, ok}
```

Project

title	description
simple_cache	"a simple cache application"

User

id	name
1	martin

Contributor

user_id	project_title
1	simple_cache

**Figure 9.9
Mnesia table contents after entering
some data. In the User and Contributor
tables, you use a numeric user ID as
key, whereas in the Project table, the
key is the project title as an atom. Each
entry in the Contributor table refers to
corresponding entries in the User and
Project tables.**

This should give you a single project record, user record, and contributor record in each of the corresponding tables. The database now has the content shown in figure 9.9.

Next, let's look at some ways you can extract and view the data in order to prove that it's in fact there.

9.2.5   *Do some basic queries on your data*

We already sneaked in a `read` access in the `insert_user/3` function in listing 9.3. Because that's within a transaction, you can use the normal `mnesia:read/2` operation. Outside of a transaction, you can use dirty operations to read from the database, as in the following example from the Erlang shell:

```
(mynode@erlware.org)9> mnesia:dirty_read(contributor, 1).
[{contributor, 1, simple_cache}]
```

The `read` and `dirty_read` functions return a list of matching records—in this case, all records with the key 1 in the Contributor table. If no such records are found, the result is an empty list. Furthermore, recall that you had made the Contributor table a `bag`. That means if you insert more than one contributor record for user 1, the read operation returns all of them in the list. In contrast, for a normal table of type `set`, you know that a read must return either an empty list or a list with a single element.

USING SELECT WITH MATCH SPECIFICATIONS

In addition to looking up records based on the primary key, other operations for searching offer a bit more flexibility. The following example shows how to use `mnesia:select/2` to pull potentially many records from the `user` table:

```
mnesia:transaction(
  fun() ->
    mnesia:select(user, [{#user{id = '$1', name = martin}, [], ['$1']}])
  end)
```

The first argument to `select/2` is the table to search, and the second argument is a list of so-called *match specifications*. These can be complicated beasts, but for simple cases they're fairly straightforward. Each match specification is a 3-tuple {Head, Conditions, Results}. Head is an Erlang term representing a pattern, where atoms (single-quoted) of the form '$1', '$2', ..., are used to represent variables. In the previous example, you're searching for #user records whose name field is the atom martin and whose id field can be anything ('$1'). The Conditions part lets you specify additional constraints for a match, but often it's just left as an empty list, as in this case. The Results part, finally, lets you express what kind of terms you want generated for each match; here, you can use the corresponding '$1' and so on, and they will be replaced by the actual values from the match.

In addition to these numbered variables, the following atoms also have special meaning:

- '_' *(in* Head *part only)*—Doesn't matter; any value
- '$_' *(in* Result *and* Conditions *only)*—The entire matching record
- '$$' *(in* Result *and* Conditions *only)*—Same as '$1', '$2', '$3', ... (for all of those variables that are bound in the Head part)

When a transaction succeeds, the result has the form {atomic, Data}, where Data is the actual result of the code inside the transaction fun; in this case, the result of the call to select—a list containing a value for each matching record. Because the Results part of the previous match specification is ['$1'], you get exactly one element for each found match: the value of the id field. And because only one record in the table matches the name martin, the result of the call to mnesia:transaction/1 is

```
{atomic, [1]}
```

For tables with many fields, you often want to extract several fields from each matching record, using a Results specification such as [{'$1', '$2', '$3'}] or ['$$']. You can find many more details about match specifications in the ERTS User's Guide in the Erlang/OTP documentation.

USING QUERY LIST COMPREHENSIONS (QLC)

Finally, there is a more expressive way to query Mnesia: by using Query List Comprehensions (QLC). These are a more recent addition to Erlang/OTP and work in a slightly mysterious way. Superficially, they look like normal list comprehensions (see section 2.9 if you need a reminder), but they're wrapped in what looks like a call to qlc:q(...). This is just a marker that tells the compiler to handle these expressions specially. For this to work, the source code for the module must also contain the following line, which triggers the special QLC compilation:

```
-include_lib("stdlib/include/qlc.hrl").
```

(As a special case, the Erlang shell lets you use qlc:q(...) straight away; there's no concept of include files in the shell.) The value produced by qlc:q(...) is a query handle, whose results can be fetched through `qlc:eval(Handle)`. QLC is explained in detail in the stdlib section of the Erlang/OTP documentation (the `qlc` module).

QLC is a generic query interface to anything that is table-like, such as ETS tables, Mnesia tables, and even your own special table implementations if you make a QLC adapter for them. The function `mnesia:table(TableName)` creates a handle that represents the Mnesia table in a form that QLC can use as input. From that point on, normal list-comprehension syntax for filtering and aggregation is used. For example, to accomplish the same thing you did with the `select` function earlier, you can write

```
mnesia:transaction(
  fun() ->
    Table = mnesia:table(user),
    QueryHandle = qlc:q([U#user.id || U <- Table, U#user.name =:= martin]),
    qlc:eval(QueryHandle)
  end)
```

QLC is a considerably more elegant way to perform queries than using `select` and match specifications. This code is much more readable: basically, it says that you want a list containing the `#user.id` fields for each record `U` from the Mnesia table `user` such that `U#user.name` is equal to `martin`. You can also use QLC within transactions where reading may not be the only thing going on—QLC can be mixed with any other type of Mnesia function that belongs in a transaction.

What we've covered in this section is by no means an exhaustive explanation of what you can do with Mnesia—that would require a separate book. But it should give you enough of a foundation that you can move forward with distributing your cache based on Mnesia, and that is exactly what you'll do next.

9.3   *Distributing the cache with Mnesia*

With a decent high-level design for how to distribute the cache, and some understanding of the basics of Mnesia, you have what you need to dive into the implementation. For this cache to work properly, you need to do the following:

1 Switch from ETS to Mnesia.
2 Make the cache aware of the other nodes it must communicate with.
3 Implement resource discovery for the cache.
4 Bring the Mnesia tables into dynamic replication.

You'll deal with point 1 right away so that by the end of the next section, you won't be using ETS for your table anymore, but Mnesia.

9.3.1   *Switching from ETS to Mnesia*

Remember the `sc_store` module you implemented in chapter 6? This was the module you used to encapsulate your key-to-pid table, hiding the storage implementation from the rest of the code. Now this encapsulation will come in handy; even though you'll completely re-implement the way the data is stored, the rest of your code base won't need to be changed. The `sc_store` module (listing 6.6) contained four key functions:

- `init/0`
- `insert/2`
- `lookup/1`
- `delete/1`

First, `init/0` will set up your Mnesia table, just as it currently does for ETS. Later, you'll modify it further to encapsulate the logic required to enable replication; but for now, creating the table will suffice.

REWRITING INIT/0

The old version of `init/0` looked like this:

```
init() ->
    ets:new(?TABLE_ID, [public, named_table]),
    ok.
```

Here is the new version, after a Mnesia makeover:

```
init() ->
    mnesia:start(),
    mnesia:create_table(key_to_pid,
                        [{index, [pid]},
                         {attributes, record_info(fields, key_to_pid)}]).
```

The table is a normal `set` with unique keys, kept in RAM only. As always, you use `record_info(fields, ...)` to list the names of the attributes (the columns) of the table entries. Of course, this means you need a record called `key_to_pid`. Because this module is supposed to encapsulate all storage concerns for your cache, you define this record at the beginning of the source file, like this:

```
-record(key_to_pid, {key, pid}).
```

Note the option `{index, [pid]}` in the table definition. Indexes are extra tables that allow speedy operations on fields other than the primary key. Keep in mind when you're creating an index that it consumes additional space. Furthermore, the index is populated and kept up to date for each insertion into the primary table, which means that startup and writing become slower. It's important to be aware of these tradeoffs. In this case, the overhead of keeping an index is justified, letting you quickly find the key given a pid (and not just the other way around).

With the setup done, let's rewrite the `insert` function.

REWRITING INSERT/2

The `insert/2` function in chapter 6 worked like this:

```
insert(Key, Pid) ->
    ets:insert(?TABLE_ID, {Key, Pid}).
```

The Mnesia version is just as straightforward:

```
insert(Key, Pid) ->
    mnesia:dirty_write(#key_to_pid{key = Key, pid = Pid}).
```

Note that you're using a dirty write to update the table. The way you're using Mnesia here, as a basic key-value store, is so simple that transactions aren't needed. The main feature of Mnesia that you're after is replication, but we get to that later.

The `lookup` function is just as simple.

REWRITING LOOKUP/1

Here's the ETS version:

```
lookup(Key) ->
    case ets:lookup(?TABLE_ID, Key) of
        [{Key, Pid}] -> {ok, Pid};
        []           -> {error, not_found}
    end.
```

And here's the Mnesia version:

```
lookup(Key) ->
    case mnesia:dirty_read(key_to_pid, Key) of
        [{key_to_pid, Key, Pid}] -> {ok, Pid};
        []                       -> {error, not_found}
    end.
```

Because the table is a `set`, you can only get zero or one records as result, and a dirty read is sufficient for your purposes. It couldn't be simpler.

But there is a complication: in a distributed setting, the pid you get from the lookup could be referring to a dead process. Consider the following scenario: You have nodes a and b and you insert some data in the cache on node a. You check that you can look up that data on node b and get the correct value. You then kill node a and run the same query again on node b. What happens? The operation fails, because the pid in the Mnesia database still refers to the storage process which was located on node a, but is now dead. You need a way to invalidate entries that refer to dead processes.

The simplest solution is to introduce a check every time you pull a pid out of the database. The following function checks whether a pid refers to a process that still lives:

```
is_pid_alive(Pid) when node(Pid) =:= node() ->
    is_process_alive(Pid);
is_pid_alive(Pid) ->
    lists:member(node(Pid), nodes()) andalso
    (rpc:call(node(Pid), erlang, is_process_alive, [Pid]) =:= true).
```

With the help of this, you have only to add an extra check to the lookup function:

```
lookup(Key) ->
    case mnesia:dirty_read(key_to_pid, Key) of
        [{key_to_pid, Key, Pid}] ->
            case is_pid_alive(Pid) of
                true -> {ok, Pid};
                false -> {error, not_found}
            end;
        [] ->
            {error, not_found}
    end.
```

This solution means that stale pids are left in the Mnesia table until deleted or over-written by a new value, but they are ignored by the lookup function, so they do no harm. Take some time to think about how you could clean out stale pids in an efficient way. In what modules would you need to make changes?

This leaves the delete function to convert. It's the only challenging part of the conversion to Mnesia.

REWRITING DELETE/1

Here's the delete function before:

```
delete(Pid) ->
    ets:match_delete(?TABLE_ID, {'_', Pid}).
```

And here it is after:

```
delete(Pid) ->
    case mnesia:dirty_index_read(key_to_pid, Pid, #key_to_pid.pid) of
        [#key_to_pid{} = Record] ->
            mnesia:dirty_delete_object(Record);
        _ ->
            ok
    end.
```

① Finds entry given only pid

② Returns ok in case of errors

There are two reasonable scenarios: either the key isn't there (presumably it has already been deleted), or the key is there and you succeed in deleting it. In both cases, you want to return ok to the caller. Deleting a key should be an idempotent operation—that is, you should be able to do it over and over with the same result. If you find a key_to_pid record for the key, you delete it, and otherwise you return ok anyway **②**.

Take a close look at how you find an entry given only the pid **①**. This is how a Mnesia index is used: special index-aware functions (this one being a dirty variety) are employed to make use of existing indexes. For index_read/3, the first argument is the table name, the second is the key on which you want to index (the pid), and the third indicates which index you want to search (because a table can have several). You specify this using the index column number, which is given by the syntax #record-name.fieldname. Alternatively, you could use the name you specified when you created the table (the atom pid), but that would make the operation slightly slower. Apart from this, the function behaves like a normal read operation.

That wasn't too bad, was it? You now have a fully Mnesia-enabled cache, and you didn't have to change a single line outside of the sc_store module. Let's see if you can stay on the track of keeping things clean and simple as you tackle the next step to distribution.

9.3.2 *Making the cache aware of other nodes*

Next up, you'll make the cache aware of the other cache instances within its Erlang cluster. This will pave the way for syncing up with those instances so you can share data between them. The first thing a new cache node needs to do is join the cluster. In this section, we show a simple way to manage that. There are more advanced ways of doing it, but this tends to work well.

This simple method for automatically adding a new node to a predefined cluster is to always have two known blank Erlang nodes running. These are nodes without any user-defined code running on them (so there should be little reason for them to go down, ever). You start them as normal, giving them suitable names and setting the cookie to be used for authentication within this cluster:

```
erl -name contact1 -setcookie xxxxxxxx

erl -name contact2 -setcookie xxxxxxxx
```

Each cache node you bring up is configured to ping both of these nodes using their known names, as illustrated in figure 9.10. If either of these calls to `net_adm:ping/1` succeeds, then the node startup is allowed to proceed; if not, the node can't join the cluster, and startup fails with a crash dump.

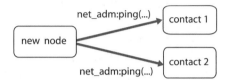

Figure 9.10   Using known, always-available contact nodes to join a cluster automatically: a simple trick that tends to work pretty well. Preferably, the nodes should run on separate physical computers.

It shouldn't be hard to decide where to add the code for this—just think about what happens when the application starts. The first thing that is called is `sc_app:start/2`, which is where you added the code to call `sc_store:init()` back in section 6.4.2. Because you want to ensure connectivity before you initialize the store, this is the place to add the code for joining a cluster.

Listing 9.4 shows the code you'll add to the `sc_app` module. Note how you use a match `ok = ...` on the result of the call to `ensure_contact()` that you added to `start/2`. This asserts that the result *must* be ok; otherwise, you get a `badmatch` exception. It's a "succeed or die" contract: either you get a connection as you intended, or the start function throws an exception and the whole application startup fails.

Listing 9.4   Making contact on application startup (sc_app.erl)

```
start(_StartType, _StartArgs) ->
    ok = ensure_contact(),                         Add this line
    sc_store:init(),                               to start()
    case sc_sup:start_link() of
        {ok, Pid} ->
            {ok, Pid};
        Error ->
            Error
    end.

ensure_contact() ->
    DefaultNodes = ['contact1@localhost', 'contact2@localhost'],
    case get_env(simple_cache, contact_nodes, DefaultNodes) of
        [] ->                                      Checks config
            {error, no_contact_nodes};             for nodes  ❶
        ContactNodes ->
            ensure_contact(ContactNodes)
    end.
```

```
ensure_contact(ContactNodes) ->
    Answering = [N || N <- ContactNodes, net_adm:ping(N) =:= pong],
    case Answering of
        [] ->
            {error, no_contact_nodes_reachable};
        _ ->
            DefaultTime = 6000,
            WaitTime = get_env(simple_cache, wait_time, DefaultTime),
            wait_for_nodes(length(Answering), WaitTime)
    end.
wait_for_nodes(MinNodes, WaitTime) ->
    Slices = 10,
    SliceTime = round(WaitTime/Slices),
    wait_for_nodes(MinNodes, SliceTime, Slices).

wait_for_nodes(_MinNodes, _SliceTime, 0) ->
    ok;
wait_for_nodes(MinNodes, SliceTime, Iterations) ->
    case length(nodes()) > MinNodes of
        true ->
            ok;
        false ->
            timer:sleep(SliceTime),
            wait_for_nodes(MinNodes, SliceTime, Iterations - 1)
    end.

get_env(AppName, Key, Default) ->
    case application:get_env(AppName, Key) of
        undefined   -> Default;
        {ok, Value} -> Value
    end.
```

Pings listed nodes ❷

Checks config for time to wait ❸

❹ **Enters wait loop**

❺ **Checks if enough nodes are connected**

❻ **Looks up configuration data**

This code is straightforward, even if it looks like a lot at first glance. The basic flow is as follows:

- Check the configuration for nodes to contact (or use hardcoded defaults).
- Ping all the contact nodes, and proceed only if you get answers.
- Check the configuration for the time to wait for other nodes to connect (or use a default).
- Wait until you see more nodes than the ones that originally answered (or you grow bored and assume you're the first proper work node to connect).

We discuss application configuration in more detail in the next chapter. For now, it's enough to show the function for looking up configuration data ❻. You wrap the library function application:get_env(AppName, Key) in a utility function get_env (AppName, Key, Default) that makes it easy to substitute a default value in case no configuration setting is found. You call this utility function first thing in ensure_ contact(), to get the list of contact nodes ❶. You also hardcode a couple of default node names for now, because you haven't set up any configuration yet.

Assuming you get a non-empty list of nodes to contact, you proceed to ensure_ contact(Nodes), where you attempt to contact all of them using net_adm:ping/1 ❷.

Note how you use a list comprehension to both ping all nodes and simultaneously collect the names of those that answer. If none of the listed nodes can be contacted, you give up. Otherwise, you do a second configuration check to find the time to wait for full connectivity ❸ (again, you hardcode a default value in case there is no configuration) and wait for further nodes to show up.

The function wait_for_nodes/2 first takes the total waiting time and divides it into a number of time slices; then, it enters a wait loop ❹. At the start of each time slice, you check whether your list of known nodes has become larger than the initial set of answering contact nodes ❺. If that is the case, you assume you now are connected to all the nodes in the cluster. Otherwise, you go to sleep for the duration of one time slice and repeat. If no other nodes turn up after the maximum wait time is up, you go on anyway (presumably, it means you're the first node in the cluster apart from the contact nodes).

> **Use configuration with care**
>
> Reading configuration settings creates functions that aren't referentially transparent: what you pass as parameters to the function isn't the only thing that decides what it will return. It's good functional programming practice not to bury such things deep in your code. Keep them at the top of the program (in the initialization part), and make them easily visible. (In this case, you only read configuration during the start/2 function.) Following this practice will make your code more manageable and more easily refactored. The more referentially transparent functions you have, the easier it is to reason about what your code does and how it will be affected if you rearrange things.

Having added this code, you know that you'll be fully connected to the cluster at the point when you start the application supervision tree (and with it, the rest of the application). The next step is to use resource discovery to find any other instances of simple_cache that may exist in your cluster.

9.3.3   *Integrating resource discovery to find other cache instances*

In this section, you'll take the resource discovery system that you built in the last chapter and integrate it into your simple cache. Because resource discovery is a generic service that can be used by any application that needs to find resource instances within an Erlang cluster, you don't want to just squeeze it in as a part of your cache application. Instead, you should pack it up as an application in its own right, and include it alongside the simple cache in your directory structure.

We don't go through the details of creating an application again—you should have seen enough of that by now to be able to do it as an exercise. As usual, you need to create the application directory structure and write a .app file, an _app module, and a _sup module (which starts the resource discovery server that you wrote in section 8.3.3). After you've done that, you should have two applications side by side, like this:

```
lib
   |- simple_cache
   |        |- src
   |        |- ebin
   |        |- ...
   |
   |- resource_discovery
            |- src
            |- ebin
            |- ...
```

You also need to specify that `simple_cache` now depends on `resource_discovery` and `mnesia`. Listing 9.5 shows an updated version of simple_cache.app that contains these dependencies as well as the event logger modules you added in chapter 7. (Compare this with the original .app file in section 6.3.2.)

Listing 9.5   Modified simple_cache.app file

```
{application, simple_cache,
  [{description, "A simple caching system"},
   {vsn, "0.3.0"},
   {modules, [simple_cache,
              sc_app,
              sc_sup,
              sc_element_sup,
              sc_store,
              sc_element,
              sc_event,
              sc_event_logger]},                       New dependencies added
   {registered,[sc_sup]},
   {applications, [kernel, sasl, stdlib, mnesia, resource_discovery]},
   {mod, {sc_app,[]}}
]}.
```

With that boilerplate out of the way, let's think about what you want to accomplish. You want to publish your local cache as available to others, and you also want to locate other cache instances in the cluster. If you recall from chapter 8 how resource discovery works, this should be easy. First, to publish the cache, you'll insert a local resource (an "I have") with the resource type `simple_cache` and the name of your node as a reference to the concrete resource. (There can be only one simple cache instance per node, so you don't need to make it any more complicated than that.) In other words:

```
resource_discovery:add_local_resource(simple_cache, node())
```

To find other caches, you insert an "I want" with the resource type `simple_cache`:

```
resource_discovery:add_target_resource_type(simple_cache)
```

The final step is to add a call to trade resources with the rest of the cluster, and wait a reasonable time for those resources to be shared (recall that your resource discovery system is very asynchronous in nature):

```
resource_discovery:trade_resources(),
timer:sleep(?WAIT_FOR_RESOURCES),
```

Predictably, this code also needs to go in the `sc_app:start/2` function, right after the call to join the cluster. This is shown in the following listing.

Listing 9.6 Modifications for resource discovery (sc_app.erl)

```
-define(WAIT_FOR_RESOURCES, 2500).

start(_StartType, _StartArgs) ->
    ok = ensure_contact(),
    resource_discovery:add_local_resource(simple_cache, node()),
    resource_discovery:add_target_resource_type(simple_cache),
    resource_discovery:trade_resources(),
    timer:sleep(?WAIT_FOR_RESOURCES),
    sc_store:init(),
    case sc_sup:start_link() of
        {ok, Pid} ->
            {ok, Pid};
        Error ->
            Error
    end.
```

Wasn't that simple? You'll now know about all the other cache instances in your cluster, and they'll know about you. The final thing you need to do is to modify your Mnesia setup so that you connect to and replicate with the other nodes in the cluster.

9.3.4 *Bringing the Mnesia tables into dynamic replication*

At last, you're going to complete the magic. Take a moment to revel in what you're about to do. Think about it: with almost no static configuration of your system—just some bootstrap code and a couple of contact nodes to get you into the cluster—you'll automatically discover all `simple_cache` instances and then replicate data across them to give you a nicely dynamic system with a high degree of fault tolerance.

Getting the nodes into replication isn't too tricky; it just requires a bit of knowledge about the way Mnesia works in a distributed context. You'll put the code that does this in `sc_store:init/0`, which can now rely on the fact that you'll at that point be connected to the cluster and will have populated the resource discovery cache (see listing 9.6). The code isn't entirely trivial, so we break it into a few parts and discuss each separately.

The previous version of `sc_store:init/0` looked as follows (see section 9.3.1), after you modified it to use Mnesia instead of plain ETS tables:

```
init() ->
    mnesia:start(),
    mnesia:create_table(key_to_pid,
                        [{index, [pid]},
                         {attributes, record_info(fields, key_to_pid)}]).
```

The new version relies on the resource discovery information and starts like this:

```
init() ->
    mnesia:stop(),
    mnesia:delete_schema([node()]),
```

```
mnesia:start(),
{ok, CacheNodes} = resource_discovery:fetch_resources(simple_cache),
dynamic_db_init(lists:delete(node(), CacheNodes)).
```

The first thing it does is to ensure that Mnesia is started and delete any existing database schema on the local node. This incarnation of the cache takes a cavalier attitude toward data and doesn't hesitate to overwrite previously used schemas or tables. This is a cache, after all: you'll keep all your data as ram_copies–including the schema. In order to delete a schema, Mnesia must not be running. (Calling mnesia:stop() is harmless if Mnesia hasn't been started.)

After that's done, init() fetches the list of all simple_cache instances the resource discovery system has found. (Recall from the previous section that you use node names to identify the instances.) This list of cache nodes should contain your local cache instance as well, so you remove that before you pass the list to the next stage: the function dynamic_db_init/1, shown in the following listing.

Listing 9.7   Initializing Mnesia depending on nodes discovered

```
dynamic_db_init([]) ->
    mnesia:create_table(key_to_pid,
                        [{index, [pid]},
                         {attributes, record_info(fields, key_to_pid)}
                        ]);
dynamic_db_init(CacheNodes) ->
    add_extra_nodes(CacheNodes).
```

This function initializes the database differently depending on whether it finds some other cache instances in the cluster. The first clause handles the case when you seem to be alone; you create the table just as you did in section 9.3.1. Because you don't call mnesia:create_schema/1 after ensuring that any previous schema is deleted, the new database schema is implicitly created and is kept in RAM only. At this point, you have a working simple_cache instance that is ready to replicate its data to any other instances that join the cluster.

If other simple_cache instances are discovered, you fall through to the second clause. In this case, you want to bring data over from the other nodes in the cluster instead. The code for doing this takes the form of a loop over the list of remote nodes, in the add_extra_nodes/1 function shown in listing 9.8.

One node must be started first

There's an important caveat here, and that is that the initial node must be started alone. If two simple_cache nodes are started simultaneously from scratch, there'll be a race condition where both may think that the other node was the first. As a consequence, no initial schema will ever be created. This can be avoided with some additional synchronization in the code, but for simplicity's sake, let's live with it for now.

Listing 9.8 Connecting to existing Mnesia nodes and replicating their data

```
-define(WAIT_FOR_TABLES, 5000).

add_extra_nodes([Node|T]) ->
    case mnesia:change_config(extra_db_nodes, [Node]) of
        {ok, [Node]} ->
            mnesia:add_table_copy(schema, node(), ram_copies),

            mnesia:add_table_copy(key_to_pid, node(), ram_copies),

            Tables = mnesia:system_info(tables),
            mnesia:wait_for_tables(Tables, ?WAIT_FOR_TABLES);
        _ ->
            add_extra_nodes(T)
    end.
```

❶ Replaces local schema with remote

❷ Tries some other node instead

This function does quite a bit but is straightforward in the end. First, you call mnesia:change_config/2 to tell Mnesia to add an extra node to the database. You need to connect to only one of the remote instances. Mnesia works in much the same way as Erlang nodes: when you connect to another Mnesia instance, you're informed about the others, and the others are informed about you. Note that in your case the new, empty node initiates the connection to a node with data on it, but that doesn't matter; Mnesia updates its list of nodes (on both sides), and nothing else happens yet. (Adding a node in this particular way should only be done with newly started nodes that are fully RAM-based and have an empty schema.)

If the connection doesn't work for some reason, you try it with one of the other nodes in the list ❷. (If you run out of nodes to try to connect to, the code crashes, causing the startup to fail, because you don't handle the case when the list of nodes is empty. This is another example of "let it crash"; there is little point in adding code for that case.)

If connecting succeeds, you first fetch the remote schema by adding a copy for the local node ❶. This replaces your temporary, empty, local schema. Then, you do the same thing for the key_to_pid table. This is the real goal you were after—allowing you to share this table across cache instances. Finally, you call mnesia:system_info(tables) to get a list of all the existing tables, and you call mnesia:wait_for_tables/2 to await a full synchronization of the contents of the newly added table before you proceed. (The extra parameter is a timeout value, after which you'll go on anyway.)

That's all, folks! There you have it: a dynamically replicating distributed cache. Go ahead and take it for a spin in the shell: start up two nodes, get them talking, insert data on one, and query it on the other. You've built a system that stores the mapping from keys to process identifiers in a replicated table. This makes it possible for any cache instance in the cluster to store such a mapping, and any instance can look up the process identifier stored for a key and talk directly to the process (no matter which node it lives on) in order to read or update the value associated with the key.

To run the code, first start a contact node or two as before, in a separate console window. For example (using the -sname flag for a cluster with short node names):

```
$ erl -sname contact1
```

Ensure that all your `.erl` files have been compiled to `.beam` files in the corresponding `ebin` directories, both for the `simple_cache` and the `resource_discovery` applications—for example, like this:

```
erlc -o ./simple_cache/ebin ./simple_cache/src/*.erl
erlc -o ./resource_discovery/ebin ./resource_discovery/src/*.erl
```

Then, start Erlang as follows:

```
$ erl -sname mynode -pa ./simple_cache/ebin -pa ./resource_discovery/ebin
```

Because the `simple_cache` application now depends on several other applications (listed in the .app file; see listing 9.5), you need to start those before you can start `simple_cache` itself:

```
1> application:start(sasl).
ok
2> mnesia:start().
ok
3> application:start(resource_discovery).
ok
4> application:start(simple_cache).
ok
```

Remember that the resource discovery will cause `simple_cache` to wait several seconds on startup. If `simple_cache` can't find the contact node, check that all nodes were started with the `-sname` flag, and change the default node names in `sc_app:ensure_contact()` to match your real host name if the alias `localhost` doesn't seem to work. (Remember to recompile the code if you modify it.)

You should be able to start several nodes in the same way (`mynode1`, `mynode2`, …), each in a separate console window, with the same applications running on them. Then try inserting a value into the cache on one node, and look it up on another. It just works.

9.4   Summary

In this chapter, you've learned the basics of using that extremely flexible distributed data store called Mnesia. You've altered your cache to use Mnesia for storage with minimal impact on the rest of the code base. You've written some simple code to make your cache automatically join an Erlang cluster. Most impressively, you've incorporated the resource discovery system that you built in chapter 8 and used it to dynamically replicate Mnesia tables across the other cache instances found in the cluster. The Erlware people will be thrilled, because they will now be able to handle session storage and not have to worry about providing a bad user experience, even when requests from the same user can be directed to different web servers at different times.

In the next chapter, you'll close the loop. You'll take this code and turn it into a real release, ready to be pushed out into production. After that, you'll truly be on the way to becoming an Erlang professional.

Packaging, services, and deployment

10

This chapter covers

- Target systems, applications, and releases
- How to define a release, and how to start it
- Packaging and installation of releases

By now, you've learned how to employ OTP behaviours, create proper OTP applications, handle logging and events, write distributed applications, and use the Mnesia database. That's no small accomplishment. Your next task is to take all your code and wrap it up in a way that makes it ready to deploy.

OTP applications provide convenient units of functionality, but only on the Erlang programming level. To build a complete standalone software service—something that runs on one or more machines on your network and communicates with your other systems and with your users—you must typically combine a number of such applications that will run on a single Erlang runtime system. In OTP, such a higher-level package is called a *release*, and the result of installing a release on some host machine is called a *target system*.

A target system generally only includes those applications that are needed for it to work as a service, as opposed to a standard Erlang/OTP distribution that contains a large number of applications, including graphical runtime tools such as those you saw in chapter 5. Minimally, a target system must contain the `stdlib` and `kernel` applications (apart from your own applications), and often the SASL application is also needed to support logging.

Before we go into details about creating releases, let's first review some aspects of applications that are of importance in this context.

10.1 Applications from a system viewpoint

OTP applications are usually active things with running processes, a distinct runtime behavior, and a discrete lifecycle. They're more like standalone software applications such as web browsers and web servers than they're like typical programming-language libraries. When you start an OTP application, you generally kick off a number of long-lived processes, some of which may potentially run for the system's entire lifetime.

An Erlang target system consists of a number of running applications. All these have similar structure and metadata and are managed in the same way.

10.1.1 Structure

All applications have the same basic structure, as illustrated in figure 10.1. The `application` behaviour encapsulates starting and stopping the application. When started, a running application has a root supervisor, which directly or indirectly manages all the other processes of the application (including any subsystem supervisors).

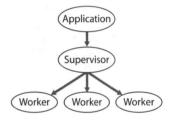

Figure 10.1 The general structure of a running application. All OTP applications are started, stopped, and managed in a uniform way. This makes it straightforward to combine them in a release.

Applications provide consistency—a single way to package and manage chunks of behavior. They have a standardized directory structure, a well-defined entry point, canonical supervision patterns, and so on. This consistency makes it possible to automate most of the steps needed to create a release from a set of separate applications.

10.1.2 Metadata

Most applications are active, not mere libraries. This means OTP needs a certain amount of information to know how an application is to be started, what other applications it depends on, and so on. This information is contained in the .app file. Your project consists of two applications at this point: `resource_discovery` and `simple_cache`. These depend, in turn, on the standard OTP applications `kernel`, `stdlib`, `sasl`, and `mnesia`.

Dependencies and transitivity

Applications usually have dependencies. For example, the `simple_cache` application is directly dependent on the `kernel` and `stdlib` applications (practically all applications depend directly on these two) as well as on the `mnesia`, `resource_discovery`, and `sasl` applications. In general, there may also be indirect dependencies. Suppose application A depends on application B, which in turn depends on application C. In that case, application A depends indirectly on application C, as illustrated in the figure, because the depends-on relation is transitive.

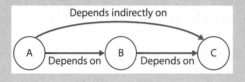

Transitivity of dependencies. Because application A depends directly on application B, which depends directly on application C, A depends indirectly on C.

The .app file for `simple_cache` should currently look like the following listing.

Listing 10.1   Application metadata: simple_cache.app

```
{application, simple_cache,
 [{description, "A simple caching system"},
  {vsn, "0.3.0"},
  {modules, [simple_cache,
             sc_app,
             sc_sup,
             sc_element_sup,
             sc_store,
             sc_element,
             sc_event,
             sc_event_logger]},
  {registered, [sc_sup]},
  {applications, [kernel, sasl, stdlib, mnesia, resource_discovery]},
  {mod, {sc_app, []}}
 ]}.
```

All of this metadata is needed for proper management of the application. One piece of information is particularly important in the context of releases: the `vsn` tuple, which specifies the current version of the application.

10.1.3   *How the system manages running applications*

Remember that the starting point for an OTP application is an implementation of the `application` behaviour, such as your `sc_app` module (which the .app file points to). This provides an interface for starting and stopping the application; but there is also an associated behaviour container, known as the *application controller*, which handles all the applications running in the system. When the application `start/2` callback function has completed the startup, it should return the pid of the newly started top-level supervisor so that the container can track it. In this way, the application behaviour is similar to the gen_event behaviour described in chapter 7: a single container manages multiple behaviour implementations (compare figure 7.1).

THE APPLICATION CONTROLLER

There is only one application controller per runtime system, registered under the name application_controller. As you can see from its low process identifier in the following example, the application controller is started early in the boot sequence of the Erlang runtime system:

```
Eshell V5.7.4  (abort with ^G)
1> registered().
[kernel_sup,global_name_server,inet_db,init,file_server_2,
 code_server,erl_prim_loader,user_drv,standard_error,
 application_controller,error_logger,kernel_safe_sup,user,
 global_group,standard_error_sup,rex]
2> whereis(application_controller).
<0.6.0>
```

The controller is also responsible for loading the .app file for the application and checking that all the applications it depends on have been started first. For each running application, a pair of application master processes are spawned by the application controller in order to isolate itself from the application code (see figure 5.3). These extra processes aren't important to you here, but it's worth knowing—in particular when debugging—that they play a part in the overall container functionality. Although the internal structure of the application behaviour container is a bit more complex than that of most other behaviours, the API provided by the application module is straightforward.

APPLICATION START TYPES

When an application is started using application:start(AppName), it gets the default type temporary. This means even if it terminates unexpectedly, the rest of the runtime system isn't affected; only a crash report is generated. But an application that is started through a call to application:start(AppName, permanent) is considered required for the target system to function: if it terminates, for whatever reason, the entire runtime system shuts down so that everything can be restarted from scratch. (The type transient can also be specified, but it behaves just like permanent for normal OTP applications.) Such a system restart can be handled automatically by an external operating system *heart process*; see the Erlang/OTP documentation of the heart module (part of the kernel application) for more details.

Now that we've highlighted the areas of applications that are of importance from a system perspective, let's talk about how you can tie these applications together as *releases* to build standalone Erlang systems.

10.2 *Making a release*

Packaging of functionality in Erlang/OTP can be viewed as a hierarchy. At the lowest level are modules, which encapsulate code. Modules are grouped into applications, which encapsulate dynamic behavior and higher-level functionality. Finally, applications are grouped into *releases*.

10.2.1 Releases

A release consists of a set of applications together with some metadata specifying how to start and manage those applications as a system. The applications in a release execute together in the same Erlang runtime system: a *target system*, stripped down to run only these applications. In this respect, a release can be seen as a service definition: the running Erlang VM becomes a system-level service, just as your simple cache is merely a service for the web server, acting like a black box from the web server's point of view.

The applications included with a release are those required for the primary functionality as well as all their direct and indirect dependencies. For example, the applications that you definitely need in your release are `simple_cache` and `resource_discovery`. Both of these depend on other applications, which may also depend on others; all of these need to be included in the release.

A release specifies which versions of those applications are required. It also has a version number of its own. For example, the release `simple_cache-0.1.4` may require applications `simple_cache-0.3.0`, `resource_discovery-0.1.0`, `kernel-4.5.6`, and `stdlib-6.0.5`, as illustrated in figure 10.2. Versioning is an important aspect of releases.

To summarize:

- A release describes a running Erlang runtime system.
- A release has a version.
- A release aggregates a number of versioned applications along with metadata on how to manage the system.
- Installing a release on a host machine produces a target system.

In the overall ecosystem of Erlang/OTP, releases are important but are surprisingly misunderstood. To show you that it isn't that complicated, you'll now create a release for the Simple Cache service.

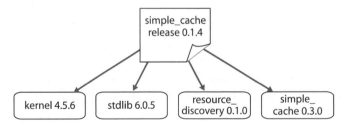

Figure 10.2   Releases and versioning. Every release has a version string, and the release contains a number of applications, each of which is also at a particular version.

10.2.2 *Preparing to release your code*

In general, you should follow these steps to create a release:

1 Decide which applications should be included.
2 Create a release metadata (.rel) file describing the release's contents.
3 Create the boot script.
4 Create a system configuration file (optional, but you typically have one).
5 Pack everything in a single package file.

We go through these steps one at a time. They're pretty easy when you know how they're done. First, you need to choose the applications to include.

You have two applications that you've developed yourself: `simple_cache` and `resource_discovery`. For a target system to run `simple_cache` as a service, it needs to contain both these applications (because `simple_cache` now uses `resource_discovery`) as well as all the other applications these two depend on, directly or indirectly: `stdlib`, `kernel`, `sasl`, and `mnesia`. Next, you need to create the .rel file.

10.2.3 *The release metadata file*

Just as you need a .app file for each application you create, containing metadata about the application as a whole, you need a *release file* with the extension .rel containing the metadata for each release. For a release, the metadata consists mainly of a list of the applications it's made up of. You also need to specify some other things, such as the version of the Erlang Run-Time System (ERTS) that you want these applications to run under, to ensure that the version on which you run the applications is the version for which they were compiled.

There is no obvious choice for where to put this release file during development; after all, it's only needed when you're about to make a release. You may want to keep it somewhere completely separate from your code. It's possible that you'll want to have several release files (with different names) for creating different release packages from the same code base. It could even be that you're creating a release from code that you've received from someone else.

Recall from section 9.3.3 that you should by now have a directory containing (at least) your two applications as subdirectories, like this:

```
lib
|- simple_cache
|    |-ebin
|    ...
|
|- resource_discovery
|    |-ebin
     ...
```

The parent directory doesn't have to be called `lib`; but naming aside, that's where you'll put the .rel file and other release-related files in this chapter. It should be your current directory when you're running the examples. In full-scale development, you'll probably want to do things differently to suit your workflow, after you know how releases work.

Listing 10.2 shows the simple_cache.rel file you'll use as the basis for creating this release. Make sure the version numbers for `resource_discovery` and `simple_cache` match those in your .app files for these applications. Depending on the version of Erlang you've installed, you may need to change the version numbers of `erts`, `kernel`, `stdlib`, `sasl`, and `mnesia` (but leave them as they are for the present).

Listing 10.2   simple_cache.rel

```
{release,
 {"simple_cache", "0.1.0"},
 {erts, "5.7.2"},
 [{kernel, "2.13.2"},
  {stdlib, "1.16.2"},
  {sasl, "2.1.5.3"},
  {mnesia, "4.4.10"},
  {resource_discovery, "0.1.0"},
  {simple_cache, "0.3.0"}
 ]}.
```

Like a .app file, the .rel file contains a single Erlang tuple, terminated by a period. It has four elements. The first is the atom `release`. This is followed by a pair containing the name of the release (as a string, not an atom) and the version. As for applications, the version string can be anything you like; but it's advisable to stick with conventional version strings, for the sake of your users as well as for third-party tools.

The third element is the ERTS version specification. This is a pair of the atom `erts` and the version of the required Erlang runtime system, as a string. Note that the ERTS version isn't the same as the version of the Erlang/OTP distribution (for example, R13B03). You can see which ERTS version you're using if you start an Erlang shell:

```
$ erl

Erlang R13B03 (erts-5.7.4) [smp:2:2] [rq:2] [async-threads:0]

Eshell V5.7.4  (abort with ^G)
1>
```

Following the text `Erlang R13B03` on the first line of output is the ERTS version—in this case, 5.7.4. Another method of finding this version number is to bring up the BREAK menu (see section 2.1.4) and select the v option:

```
1>
BREAK: (a)bort (c)ontinue (p)roc info (i)nfo (l)oaded
       (v)ersion (k)ill (D)b-tables (d)istribution
Erlang (BEAM) emulator version 5.7.4
Compiled on Tue Nov 24 11:12:28 2009
```

Update the `erts` entry of your .rel file now to match the version of your installed system.

The fourth and last element of the .rel tuple is the list of included applications and their respective versions. In this case, you list `simple_cache`, which is the main application, along with its direct and indirect dependencies: `resource_discovery`, `mnesia`, `sasl`, and even the `stdlib` and `kernel` applications. This must be a *complete* list of all the applications your target system requires. It includes not just the applications you've written but also all their direct and indirect dependencies. To find the correct version numbers for these other applications, it's easiest to wait until you run the `make_script` function in the next section and see what it reports.

The .rel file is just a high-level specification. The runtime system can't read it as it is at boot time—and even if it could, it doesn't contain enough information to start a running system correctly. It doesn't point to an ERTS executable, and it doesn't provide any information about where the listed applications can be found. This information needs to be pulled together before a real Erlang/OTP target system can be started. Next, we show you how to bundle this information with other necessary artifacts such as configuration in order to create a complete release specification that lets you start a working target system the right way.

10.2.4 *The script and boot files*

The .rel file is where it all starts, but it isn't the end of creating a running Erlang/OTP target system. The next step is to create two more files that represent a more complete specification of how to start the system. These are the .script and .boot files. The .script file contains a full specification of what will be included in applications, including paths to applications, which modules will be loaded, and other necessary information. The .boot file is a binary representation of the .script file that will be read by the Erlang runtime system when it boots.

To create these files, the first thing you need to do is start an Erlang VM that has correct paths set up to all the applications specified in the .rel file. You use the `-pa` command line flag (see section 4.3) to add code paths for all the applications that belong to your intended release and that aren't already on the default path (that is, everything except the applications included with Erlang/OTP). Following is the command line you use to start the shell with the paths to the `simple_cache` and `resource_discovery` application ebin directories. Run this from the directory where the .rel file resides:

```
erl -pa ./simple_cache/ebin -pa ./resource_discovery/ebin
```

The next step is to generate the actual boot and script files with the help of the `systools` module (part of the SASL application), like this:

```
1> systools:make_script("simple_cache", [local]).
ok
```

Running this results in the generation of two files in your current directory: simple_cache.script and simple_cache.boot. (If you instead get error messages complaining about the version numbers in the .rel file, update the file to match your local system, and run the command again.)

If you're curious, you can look at the contents of the .script file—you'll see that it looks something like this:

```
%% script generated at {date} {time}
{script,
    {"simple_cache", "0.1.0"},
    [{preLoaded, [...]},
     ...
```

It consists of a few hundred lines of Erlang terms, describing the system's entire boot process. You're not expected to understand it, but if you make changes to a .script file, you can regenerate the .boot file using `systools:script2boot(Release)`.

> **The `local` flag is mainly for testing**
>
> The `local` option passed to the `make_script/2` function stipulates that absolute paths to all applications are written in the script and boot files—meaning that if you try to start a system using this boot file, all application code must reside in exactly the place it did when the boot file was created. The `local` option is good for testing, as you're doing here, but it isn't very portable and may not be suitable for production.

You use the `local` option to `make_script/2` in order to let you easily test that you can start the system (we get to that soon), without needing to go through any installation procedure first. Without the `local` option, the generated script and boot files expect that all applications are located in a directory called lib somewhere on the filesystem, pointed out by a system variable `$ROOT`. This is suitable for a release that you want to be able to install on different host machines that don't necessarily have the same paths; but for your purpose right now, the `local` option is convenient— your applications are under development, and you haven't staged them anywhere special in the filesystem.

10.2.5 System configuration

You're almost finished creating the `simple_cache` release. The final element you need to worry about for this particular release is configuration. You may recall that in chapter 9 you added code to read configuration settings, but you temporarily fell back on the default values placed in the code (see listing 9.4). Now it's time to create a configuration file to be used with your release.

The standard name for a configuration file is sys.config. The name can be anything as long as it ends with the extension .config. Just like the .app file and the .rel file, the .config file contains a single Erlang term followed by a period. The following listing shows the sys.config file for `simple_cache`.

Listing 10.3   The sys.config configuration file

```
[
 %% write log files to sasl_dir
 {sasl,
  [
```

```
    {sasl_error_logger, {file, "/tmp/simple_cache.sasl_log"}}
  ]},
{simple_cache,
  [
   %% Contact nodes for use in joining a cloud
   {contact_nodes, ['contact1@localhost', 'contact2@localhost']}
  ]}
].
```

❶ **Path to the SASL log**

❷ **Names of contact nodes**

In a .config file, the outer term is a list of tuples. These tuples are pairs of an application name and a corresponding list of further key/value pairs, specifying options for that application. In this sys.config file, you specify for the sasl application where it should store its error log ❶ and for the simple_cache application what the names of the contact nodes are ❷ (compare with the code in section 9.3.2).

By now, you have all the necessary parts of the release, as illustrated in figure 10.3. That means you should be ready to try to start it.

10.2.6 *Starting a target system*

At this point, you have all the parts required to start the system. To do this, you need to specify two things: which .boot file to use and which .config file to use. In this case, these files are located in the root directory of the target system. This translates to the following command line, using the –sname flag for simplicity here:

```
erl –sname cache –boot ./simple_cache –config ./sys
```

Remember that you need to have at least one contact node running (see section 9.3.2) in order to start the system; their names must match either the hardcoded default in listing 9.4 or the names in your sys.config file. These nodes also need to be started using the –sname flag (not –name) or they won't be able to form a cluster with the cache node.

Running the previous command should produce an Erlang shell, meaning that the system has been successfully started. The SASL output is written to the file specified in your sys.config file, so startup is less verbose than before—you can inspect the contents of the log file to check that things are working. When you start a target system in production, you typically won't want the shell to start, and you'll generally want the

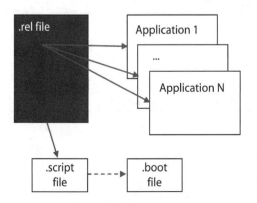

Figure 10.3
The components that make up a release. The .rel file points out the included applications and is used to generate the .script and .boot files. The sys.config file is optional but should usually be included.

system to run in the background as a daemon. (Use a remote shell from another node if you need to log in to such a system; see section 8.2.6.) All you need to do is add the flag –detached to the command line:

```
erl –sname cache –boot ./simple_cache –config ./sys –detached
```

For now, though, a shell session running in the foreground is exactly what you want, so that you can quickly prove to yourself that your release runs the things you expect. For this, you'll use Appmon (see section 5.1). Start it from the shell of the running target system, like this:

```
1> appmon:start().
{ok,<0.72.0>}
```

You should see the main Appmon window, as shown in figure 10.4.

As you can see, all the applications listed as dependencies in the simple_cache.rel file are up and running (except stdlib, which is a library application). There you have it: a running Erlang target system. Bravo!

As a variant on starting a target system, you can include the flag -mode embedded on the command line. At this point you've probably become used to how Erlang loads modules on the fly, as needed. This is the default interactive mode. But in embedded target systems, it may not be suitable or even possible to load any further code at runtime. When an Erlang system boots in embedded mode, it loads all the code according to the boot script at startup; after that, all attempts to load further modules or call modules that haven't been loaded will fail. You can read more about this in the official Erlang/OTP documentation.

You can also experiment with using the –detached flag. If you start the system this way, it runs in the background and there's no shell; but if you use the shell on one of the contact nodes, you should be able to see the detached node listed in nodes(), start a remote shell on it (see section 8.2.6), and (for example) call init:stop() to shut it down.

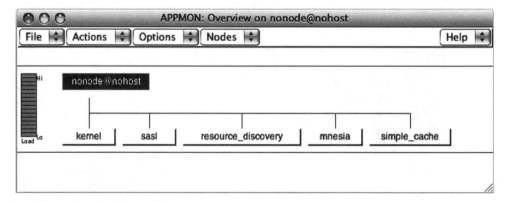

Figure 10.4 Appmon main window, showing the applications of the running release

In the next section, you'll take the release you've created and package it for easier installation and deployment.

10.3 Release packaging

Now that you've defined your release, you probably want to pack it up for easy installation, distribution, and deployment. OTP provides some helpful functionality for packaging releases, but you generally need to do some manual tweaking—it's not as simple as pressing a button (at least, not yet). For this reason, people have developed additional tools for packaging and distribution. In this chapter, though, you'll focus on creating and installing a release package using only the functionality provided by OTP.

10.3.1 Creating a release package

You create a release package using another function in the `systools` module, called `make_tar()`. If you're familiar with `tar`, you may guess that `make_tar` produces a tarball containing all the files included in the package.

> **What's a tarball?**
>
> The `tar` program is the general-purpose file archiving utility in UNIX. It's similar to `zip` but doesn't in itself compress files; it just bundles them together in a single file called a *tarball*, which can more easily be copied and untarred somewhere else. A tarball file has the extension .tar.
>
> Generally, this file is compressed as a separate pass, using the `gzip` utility. This produces a file with the extension .tar.gz or .tgz. On Windows, you can use programs such as 7-Zip to create or unpack/view tar files. Erlang supports tar files through the `erl_tar` module in the `stdlib` application.

As when you run `systools:make_script/2`, you need to start an Erlang shell with the correct paths to your applications. You should also rerun the `make_script/2` command without the `local` option to create a more realistic, location-independent boot script. Then, call `make_tar/2` with the name of the release file (without the .rel extension):

```
$ erl -pa ./simple_cache/ebin -pa ./resource_discovery/ebin

Eshell V5.7.4  (abort with ^G)
1> systools:make_script("simple_cache", []).
ok
2> systools:make_tar("simple_cache", [{erts, code:root_dir()}]).
ok
```

The `erts` option means that you want to include the runtime system as well, so that you can install the release on any compatible host machine and start it. In this example, ERTS is copied from the root directory of your current Erlang installation, which

> ### Including ERTS makes the package OS-dependent
> If you include ERTS in the package, it means you're shipping executable files that will only work on compatible operating systems. For example, executables made for 32-bit Linux won't work on a 64-bit Linux system. If you install such a package on an incompatible machine, you'll probably get a strange error message such as "erlexec: no such file or directory" when you try to start the system.

is given by code:root_dir(). If you don't include ERTS in the package, you must install it (or a full Erlang/OTP distribution) separately on the target machine, and its version must match the requirement in the release package.

   If you list what's in your current directory now, you'll see a new file called simple_cache.tar.gz. This is the compressed tarball that contains all the release files.

10.3.2 *Release package contents*

Let's look at what's inside the tarball. It should tell you what OTP cares most about. You can use the following commands on UNIX-like systems to unpack the file under a new directory called tmp:

```
$ mkdir tmp
$ cd tmp
$ tar -xzf ../simple_cache.tar.gz
```

If you don't have a separate tar utility, you can unpack the files from the Erlang shell:

```
2> erl_tar:extract("simple_cache.tar.gz", [{cwd, "tmp"}, compressed]).
```

In either case, the result should have the following structure (the version numbers will likely be different, depending on your installation of Erlang/OTP):

```
tmp
|-- erts-5.7.4
|    `-- bin
|        |-- erl.src
|        ...
|-- lib
|    |-- kernel-2.13.2
|    |    ...
|    |-- mnesia-4.4.10
|    |    ...
|    |-- resource_discovery-0.1.0
|    |    |-- ebin
|    |    |    ...
|    |    `-- priv
|    |-- sasl-2.1.5.3
|    |    ...
|    |-- simple_cache-0.3.0
|    |    |-- ebin
|    |    |    ...
|    |    `-- priv
```

```
|     `-- stdlib-1.16.2
|       ...
`-- releases
    |-- 0.1.0
    |   |-- start.boot
    |   `-- sys.config
    `-- simple_cache.rel
```

The release package always contains the two directories lib and releases. Furthermore, because you supplied the erts option to make_tar(), you also get a top-level directory named erts-<version>, with a bin subdirectory containing all the runtime system executables. In particular, you'll find an erl.src file, which is an uninstantiated version of the erl startup script (on UNIX-like systems). This file contains the string %FINAL_ROOTDIR%, and the intention is that when you install the release, you copy erl.src to erl and replace this string with the actual path of your target system.

The lib directory contains all the applications required by our release. (By default, only the ebin and priv subdirectories are included for each application.) Note that the version numbers are now included in the names of the application directories. This is so you can install multiple versions of applications (and entire releases) on top of each other and upgrade the system dynamically—or roll back a failed upgrade.

The releases directory contains the release information. It holds your .rel file as well as a subdirectory named for the release version. In that subdirectory is the boot file you created before, renamed start.boot, as well as your sys.config file. This structure allows you to keep these files around for multiple installed releases in the same root directory.

This directory layout is exactly what the Erlang/OTP installer uses: if you examine the directory where your Erlang/OTP system is installed on your computer, you'll find this same structure (although with some additional files and directories).

10.3.3 Customizing a release package

This is almost the end of the release-creation process, but not quite. You'll often want to add a little something to a release package that systools:make_tar() didn't set up for you. For example, it's common to want to include a top-level bin directory that contains some form of installation and startup scripts for the system. Let's create this bin directory under tmp and add a couple of small utility scripts (this assumes you're running a UNIX-like operating system). The first one is to be run on installation, to set up the root path of the installed release; let's call it bin/install:

```
#!/bin/sh
ROOT=`pwd`
DIR=./erts-5.7.4/bin
sed s:%FINAL_ROOTDIR%:$ROOT: $DIR/erl.src > $DIR/erl
```

Adjust the ERTS version number in the script to fit your release. Next, add a startup script named bin/simple_cache. Its contents will be similar to the command line you used to start the system in section 10.2.6:

```
#!/bin/sh
./erts-5.7.4/bin/erl \
    -sname cache \
    -boot ./releases/0.1.0/start \
    -config ./releases/0.1.0/sys \
    -detached
```

Again, adjust the version numbers as needed, and don't forget to set the executable flag on the scripts using chmod a+x ./bin/*.

A final thing you may want to do, depending on the kind of installation you have in mind, is to rename the release version subdirectory. The OTP tools generally assume that you'll only ever install a single kind of release in a specific target directory, and that directory is typically named for the release (for example, /usr/local/simple_cache); there's no need to repeat this in the name of each version subdirectory—hence 0.1.0 under releases in the previous example. But if you intend to create more fine-grained release packages that are to be combined on the same target system, you need to deviate from this scheme by renaming the version directory to have the form *ReleaseName-Version* rather than just *Version* (for example, releases/simple_cache-0.1.0 instead of releases/0.1.0). This will make it possible to install and upgrade some sets of applications independently from others without worrying about clashing directory names. As an example, you could install the Simple Cache release on top of a standard Erlang installation.

The paths in the startup script need to be changed correspondingly. Also move or copy the .rel file to the version subdirectory, so you always have the original file around even if you unpack a later release on top of this one. If you're making this kind of package, you probably don't want it to include ERTS; instead, you can make a package containing only ERTS for separate installation.

When you're happy with the contents of the release, all you need to do is re-create the tarball using the erl_tar module, as shown in the following example (assuming you're still in the tmp directory):

```
$ cd tmp
$ erl

Eshell V5.7.4  (abort with ^G)
1> erl_tar:create("simple_cache-0.3.0.tar.gz", ["erts-5.7.4", "lib",
➥ "releases", "bin"], [compressed]).
```

After running this command, you have a new package file in the tmp directory, also named simple_cache-0.3.0.tar.gz, which contains your modified release. (You can of course also pack the files using a separate tar utility if you prefer.) Having created a fully functional release package, you now need to install it somewhere on a suitable host machine and launch it.

10.4 *Installing a release*

OTP provides functionality for unpacking, installing, and upgrading releases through the release_handler module in SASL. This is a fairly complex topic, and we don't get into details here; in practice, it isn't commonly used. It can't handle installing multiple releases in the same target directory; the changes we described in the previous section for making such installations possible aren't compatible with using `release_handler`. For now, we instead explain the simple way to unpack and install a release, which is also a bit more robust.

Because you included ERTS in the package, you can unpack it in any directory on a compatible host machine—either in an empty directory or over a previously installed target system (in the case of a release upgrade)—without having Erlang/OTP installed separately on the machine. On UNIX-like systems, you can unpack the file using the `tar` utility, if you want. Alternatively, and regardless of operating system, you can use the `erl_tar` module as before:

```
$ mkdir target
$ erl

Eshell V5.7.4  (abort with ^G)
1> erl_tar:extract("simple_cache-0.3.0.tar.gz", [{cwd, "target"},
➥compressed]).
```

After that, you can `cd` into the target directory and run the bin/install script you created earlier to adjust the root path. When this is done, you should be able to use the bin/simple_cache script to start the system (make sure at least one contact node is running first):

```
$ cd target
$ ./bin/install
$ ./bin/simple_cache
```

Note that the system starts detached, and it contains only a minimum of applications. Hence, it can't run Appmon; you can start the WebTool version of Appmon (see section 5.1.2) from one of the contact nodes in order to inspect the system from a web browser.

Automated tools for packaging and installation

The process we've described in this chapter requires several manual steps. There are some alternative ways of doing packaging and installation, using some of the automated tools that exist in the Erlang community. The authors of this book are responsible for two of them, both of which are available at http://erlware.org. These are by no means standard, and they're certainly not the only tools available to manage these tasks. At the risk of plugging our own tools, we think it worthwhile to mention them because using automated tools, whether ours or others, doesn't just make life easier—it also reduces the risks of mistakes associated with manual processes.

10.5 *Summary*

We've shown you the basics of release packaging in OTP. This should give you enough information to get started using the existing tools or building custom tools based on these conventions. This is a milestone—for the longest time, releases have been seen as deep magic that only the Erlang illuminati used.

You may think, then, that your job is finished: you understand modules, you understand applications, and you understand releases. What else is there? Well, a running target system generally needs to interact with the world around it in order to be useful. This may mean speaking protocols over TCP/IP like the `tcp_rpc` server in chapter 3; but it may also involve communicating directly with other software on the same machine, perhaps written in C or Java, for reasons ranging from controlling hardware to interacting with a Java GUI such as Eclipse. Such interaction is the main topic of the third part of the book.

Part 3

Integrating and refining

Part 3 of this book covers how Erlang/OTP applications integrate with the rest of the world. To be able to pick the best tool for the job, you need some knowledge of how to code for a heterogeneous production environment. In this part, we also discuss performance and how to get the most out of your Erlang/OTP programs.

Adding an HTTP interface to the cache

This chapter covers

- Writing efficient TCP servers in Erlang
- Adding a simple text-based TCP interface to the cache
- Creating your own OTP behaviours
- Writing a basic web server
- Adding a RESTful HTTP interface to the cache

In the previous chapters, you've implemented a nice cache application. The Erlware team plans to keep enhancing it over the coming months. One of the things they recognize about the Simple Cache application is that it has the potential to be useful for projects beyond Erlware. But currently an obstacle to wider adoption is that it only has an Erlang interface, which means it can only be directly used by other applications written in Erlang.

Production environments today often contain services written in a variety of different languages. Before publishing Simple Cache as open source, you should make it useful to systems implemented in other languages. The most natural way to achieve this is to implement one or more interfaces over well-known network

261

protocols. In this chapter, you'll first implement a simple text-based protocol over TCP as a warm-up exercise, and then you'll create a RESTful HTTP interface for the same functionality.

A slight twist is in store: you'll implement the RESTful interface by writing your own scaled-down web server! This will demonstrate a number of useful programming techniques, from advanced supervision strategies to the creation of custom behaviours and the use of the efficient built-in HTTP packet-parsing routines.

In the first part of this chapter, you'll learn how to write an efficient concurrent TCP server application and implement a simple text-based interface to your cache. In the second part, you'll get a quick-and-dirty introduction to the HTTP protocol and the REST concept, and learn how to create a custom behaviour, implement a basic web server, and build a RESTful interface to the cache on top of all this.

Let's kick off this chapter with a short discussion of text-based communication and how to work efficiently with TCP sockets in Erlang.

11.1 Implementing a TCP server

Plain text is universal. As a basis for a protocol, it's simple to implement, easy to use, and easy to debug. In order to create a nice TCP/IP interface to the cache, let's start by implementing a basic text-based protocol, as simple and straightforward as possible. This will be similar to the RPC server you wrote way back in chapter 3, but with an important difference: the RPC server could handle only a single incoming TCP connection. In this chapter, you'll create the kind of industrial-strength server that every good Erlang programmer needs to know how to build. It will rely heavily on Erlang's built-in concurrency support, allowing it to handle a huge number of concurrent TCP connections.

11.1.1 A pattern for efficient TCP servers

A useful pattern for implementing a server that should handle multiple concurrent requests is to have a gen_server managed by a simple-one-for-one supervisor. Recall from section 6.3.4 that the children of a simple-one-for-one supervisor are always spawned dynamically and are all of the same type. In this case, a single gen_server child process—a handler—is initially spawned to wait on accept, listening for new connections. When a connection is established, this gen_server tells the supervisor to spawn a new handler process—a clone of the gen_server—and immediately proceeds with servicing the current connection while the clone takes over the job of waiting for the next connection.

This pattern allows for efficiently accepting connections with little or no delay between the accept and the further handling of the connection, and also with minimal delay between accepting one connection and being able to accept the next. This is very different from the way you typically work with sockets in other programming languages, but it's the most Erlang-like way. Figure 11.1 illustrates the communication and control flow in this design.

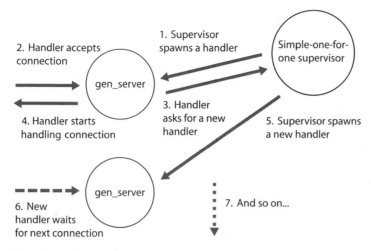

Figure 11.1   **Pattern for a highly concurrent TCP server using a simple-one-for-one supervisor. A new child process is spawned for handling each new TCP `accept` and subsequent communication with the client.**

This may seem a bit complicated, but implementing the basic framework doesn't take a lot of code, as you'll see in the following sections. (This is something of a recurring theme when you're working with Erlang.) As you may expect, the first step toward building your new TCP server is to create an OTP application to hold it.

11.1.2 *Sketching the tcp_interface application*

Because this text-over-TCP interface may be one of many external interfaces for the simple cache, it will be implemented as a separate OTP application. If you want to add, for example, text-over-UDP or an HTTP interface later on, you could follow the same pattern, and without disturbing the existing code. A release (see chapter 10) could include one, several, or none of these additional interface applications, depending on the purpose of the release.

By now, you should be familiar with the steps involved in creating an OTP application (but look back at chapter 4 if you need to check on some details). Like every application, the `tcp_interface` application needs a .app file, an application behaviour implementation module `ti_app`, and a top-level supervisor module `ti_sup`.

> **Oversimplified supervision**
>
> To keep the code as short as possible here, the top-level supervisor will be the simple-one-for-one supervisor described in the previous section. But in a more realistic application, you'd typically want to have another level of supervision above that, as you did with `sc_sup` and `sc_element_sup` in chapter 9. The HTTP server in section 11.2 will have a more solid supervision structure.

You also need a module `ti_server` for the `gen_server`-based handler processes shown in figure 11.1. When you've created the skeletons for these files, you should have a directory layout like this (in parallel with your `simple_cache` and `resource_discovery` applications):

```
tcp_interface
    |-- ebin
    |    `-- tcp_interface.app
    `-- src
        |-- ti_app.erl
        |-- ti_sup.erl
        `-- ti_server.erl
```

In the next sections, you'll implement the functionality of these modules, including all the details that make this design simple, elegant, and efficient. A few tricks and subtleties are involved, but by the end of the chapter you should be able to understand them.

11.1.3 *Fleshing out the TCP server*

As explained in section 11.2.1, in order to accept a TCP connection, you must first create a listening socket. This socket must be owned by a process that is expected to stay alive during the lifetime of the TCP server; if it dies, the socket will be closed automatically, preventing the server from accepting new connections until a new listening socket is created (for example, after restarting the application).

THE TI_APP MODULE

As a design principle, you should avoid adding code to supervisors, so a suitable place to open the listening socket in this case is in the application startup code in the `ti_app` module. From there, the socket can be handed over to the simple-one-for-one supervisor, so the supervisor can pass it on to each new handler process.

Also in the `ti_app` module, after the supervisor is done with its initialization, it must spawn the first connection-handler process as shown in figure 11.1. The implementation of `ti_app:start/2` is shown in the following listing.

Listing 11.1   The `ti_app` module

```erlang
-module(ti_app).

-behaviour(application).

-export([start/2, stop/1]).

-define(DEFAULT_PORT, 1155).

start(_StartType, _StartArgs) ->                                    ❶ Gets port
    Port = case application:get_env(tcp_interface, port) of           number
               {ok, P} -> P;
               undefined -> ?DEFAULT_PORT
           end,
    {ok, LSock} = gen_tcp:listen(Port, [{active, true}]),          ❷ Creates listening
    case ti_sup:start_link(LSock) of                                  socket
```

```
        {ok, Pid} ->
            ti_sup:start_child(),
            {ok, Pid};
        Other ->
            {error, Other}
    end.
stop(_State) ->
    ok.
```

◁─┐ **Spawns initial**
❸ **handler**

First, the module checks the application configuration (see section 10.2.5) for the port on which the server should listen ❶. If no port is specified, a default value of 1155 is used. Then, the listening socket is created ❷. After that, the supervisor is started with the socket as input. Finally, when the supervisor is running, ❸ a call to ti_sup:start_child() is made in order to have an initial ti_server process that can accept the first connection (figure 11.1).

THE ti_sup MODULE

The ti_sup module is similar to the first sc_sup module you implemented in chapter 6 (listing 6.2); both are simple-one-for-one supervisors. The main difference is that in sc_sup (later renamed sc_element_sup), the start_link function had no parameters, but the start_child function had two. In this case, start_link will take the listening socket as input, whereas no arguments are needed for the start_child function; the supervisor will already contain all it needs to start each new child. The complete source code for ti_sup.erl is shown in the following listing.

Listing 11.2   The ti_sup module

```
-module(ti_sup).

-behaviour(supervisor).

%% API
-export([start_link/1, start_child/0]).

%% Supervisor callbacks
-export([init/1]).

-define(SERVER, ?MODULE).

start_link(LSock) ->
    supervisor:start_link({local, ?SERVER}, ?MODULE, [LSock]).

start_child() ->
    supervisor:start_child(?SERVER, []).

init([LSock]) ->
    Server = {ti_server, {ti_server, start_link, [LSock]},
            temporary, brutal_kill, worker, [ti_server]},
    Children = [Server],
    RestartStrategy = {simple_one_for_one, 0, 1},
    {ok, {RestartStrategy, Children}}.
```

❶ **Supervisor init gets socket**

❷ **Socket used in child spec**

The start_link/1 function takes a listening socket and passes it on to supervisor: start_link/3 so that it ends up as input ❶ to the init/1 callback. The start_child/0 function is trivial in this case, telling the supervisor to spawn a new child of the type specified in init/1. The init/1 callback function gets the listening socket and includes it in the child spec ❷, so it becomes an argument to each new child. This short module provides a nice, OTP-compliant factory for the ti_server processes that handle the incoming connections.

THE TI_SERVER MODULE

The ti_server module is the connection handler where you accept connections on the listening socket and bind them to a dedicated socket so that you can start talking directly to the calling client over TCP. The strategy here, as illustrated by figure 11.1, is to let the simple-one-for-one supervisor keep track of the listening socket and hand it out to each new handler that it spawns. The latest spawned handler is the only one that is actively listening on the socket. As soon as it gets a connection, it tells the supervisor to start another handler to do the listening, so it can continue processing the accepted connection. After it's done that, it'll never go back to a listening state again; it'll die when its session ends. The initial version of ti_server is shown in the following listing.

Listing 11.3 Basic ti_server module

```erlang
-module(ti_server).

-behaviour(gen_server).

-export([start_link/1]).

-export([init/1, handle_call/3, handle_cast/2, handle_info/2,
         terminate/2, code_change/3]).

-record(state, {lsock}).

start_link(LSock) ->
    gen_server:start_link(?MODULE, [LSock], []).

init([LSock]) ->
    {ok, #state{lsock = LSock}, 0}.                    ❶ Sets zero timeout

handle_call(Msg, _From, State) ->
    {reply, {ok, Msg}, State}.

handle_cast(stop, State) ->
    {stop, normal, State}.

handle_info({tcp, Socket, RawData}, State) ->
    NewState = handle_data(Socket, RawData, State),    ❷ Processes
    {noreply, NewState};                                  incoming data
handle_info({tcp_closed, _Socket}, State) ->
    {stop, normal, State};
handle_info(timeout, #state{lsock = LSock} = State) -> ❸ Timeout jumps
    {ok, _Sock} = gen_tcp:accept(LSock),                  here
    ti_sup:start_child(),
    {noreply, State}.

terminate(_Reason, _State) ->
    ok.
```

```
code_change(_OldVsn, State, _Extra) ->
    {ok, State}.

%% Internal functions
handle_data(Socket, RawData, State) ->
    gen_tcp:send(Socket, RawData),
    State.
```

4 **Echoes data back on socket (for now)**

The `start_link/1` function is how the supervisor starts each handler process, passing on the listening socket. This is propagated via `gen_server:start_link/3` to the `gen_server` callback `init/1` **1**, which stores the socket in the server state and then returns, signaling a timeout of 0, using the same trick as in chapter 3 (see listings 3.4 and 3.5) to finish the startup without keeping the caller of `init/1` waiting. The zero timeout makes the new `gen_server` process drop immediately into the `timeout` clause of `handle_info/2` **3**.

At this point, the handler process has detached from the process that called `ti_server:start_link/1` and is running concurrently with any previously started handlers that haven't already finished. The handler immediately calls `gen_tcp:accept/1` on the listening socket, which blocks until the next incoming TCP connection. (It's because of this blocking call that you need to ensure that nobody else is currently waiting for this process, or you'd be holding them up as well.)

When `accept()` returns (this could happen almost immediately on a heavily loaded server, or after many months if the interface is rarely used), the first thing to do is to ask the supervisor to start another handler by calling `ti_sup:start_child()`. The new handler—a clone of this one—immediately starts waiting for the next connection on the listening socket, while the current handler process can get on with handling the connection that it has accepted.

Because the listening socket was opened in active mode (listing 11.1), and because the dedicated socket returned by `accept()` inherits this setting, all incoming data on the dedicated socket is sent directly and automatically to the handler process as a message of the form `{tcp, Socket, RawData}` **2**, just as in chapter 3. For now, all this code does is echo the incoming data back onto the TCP connection **4**. Finally, you need to handle the `tcp_closed` message from the socket to ensure that the `ti_server` process goes away automatically when the socket is closed.

This is a fair amount of detail, but you now have a general framework for a TCP server that can be reused and tailored to many different situations. For example, to provide an interface to Simple Cache, all you need to do is extend the protocol-handling aspects of the server. That's in the next section.

11.1.4 *The simple text-based protocol*

Our goal in this chapter is to make it possible to interact with the Simple Cache application over TCP so that anyone can use it regardless of what programming language they're using (or even what machine in the network they're running on). So far, you have a framework for a TCP server that doesn't do anything useful. Now, you'll implement a simple text-based protocol on top of it.

Recall from chapter 6 that the `simple_cache` API module has three exported functions: `insert/2`, `lookup/1`, and `delete/1` (listing 6.7). These are the functions you want to make available through your TCP interface.

Expressed as a grammar where | separates alternatives and `Term` stands for a constant Erlang term, the protocol for incoming calls looks like this:

```
Call -> Function ArgList
Function -> "insert" | "lookup" | "delete"
ArgList -> "[" "]" | "[" Terms "]"
Terms -> Term | Term "," Terms
```

For example:

```
insert[eric,{"Eric","Merritt"}]
lookup[eric]
```

In the other direction, the result from each request has the form

```
Result -> "OK:" Term ".\n" | "ERROR:" Term ".\n"
```

That is, either "OK:" or "ERROR:", followed by a naked term and ending with a period and a newline. For instance:

```
OK:{"Eric","Merritt"}.
```

is a reply to the request `"lookup[eric]"`, and

```
ERROR:bad_request
```

is the response to a message such as `"@*#$^!%"`.

An `insert` operation should have two arguments: the key and the associated value. The `lookup` and `delete` operations expect a key as the only argument. Note that both keys and values can be any Erlang terms.

This protocol is straightforward to use and should also be simple to parse. You can easily adapt it to use with other similar servers. It's a simple request/reply protocol, where a well-behaved client sends one request at a time and waits for a reply after each request. This effectively controls the rate of requests to each connection handler and should keep traffic at a manageable level.

Now that you've defined the format of the messages between the client and the server, you can begin implementing the actual parsing and processing of these requests.

11.1.5 *Text interface implementation*

To implement this simple text interface, you need to modify the `handle_data/3` function of the `ti_server` module (see listing 11.3). Because the TCP sockets are created in active mode for this implementation, all incoming text on the established socket for the connection will be automatically delivered as messages to the process that owns that socket—the handler process that accepted the connection. These messages will be passed to the `gen_server:handle_info/2` callback function, which is where all the heavy lifting of implementing the protocol is done. To make the code cleaner, the bulk of the message handling happens in the internal function `handle_data/3`, which previously did nothing useful except echo the data back on the TCP socket.

The new code needs to perform the following steps:

1. Parse the received line of text.
2. Interpret it as one of the three functions of the protocol.
3. Perform the requested operation.
4. Output the result back to the client.

This is shown in the following listing. It's similar to the corresponding code from chapter 3.

Listing 11.4   Simple text-based protocol implementation in `ti_server`

```
handle_data(Socket, RawData, State) ->
    try
        {Function, RawArgList} =
            lists:splitwith(fun (C) -> C =/= $[ end, RawData),
        {ok, Toks, _Line} = erl_scan:string(RawArgList ++ ".", 1),
        {ok, Args} = erl_parse:parse_term(Toks),
        Result = apply(simple_cache, list_to_atom(Function), Args),
        gen_tcp:send(Socket, io_lib:fwrite("OK:~p.~n", [Result]))
    catch
        _Class:Err ->
            gen_tcp:send(Socket, io_lib:fwrite("ERROR:~p.~n", [Err]))
    end,
    State.
```

In practice, this function could be broken down into a few helper functions, but keeping it as a single piece of code makes it easier to explain here. (Also note that this simple implementation doesn't do anything with the server state, so the function returns the `State` variable unchanged at the end.)

First, the incoming string is split at the first `[` character. If the input does contain a `[`, it's the first character in the `RawArgList` part; otherwise, `RawArgList` is empty (and parsing will fail later). The `Function` variable should contain the function name—that is, everything to the left of the `[` character.

The `RawArgList` half of the string should look like a normal Erlang list (according to the protocol you defined in the previous section). This means it can be passed through the Erlang tokenizer `erl_scan` (after you append a period character), producing a list of tokens. The token list can then be passed to the Erlang parser `erl_parse`, which results in the real argument list as a single Erlang term. This makes it easy to use the `apply/3` built-in function (BIF) to make a dynamic function call to the named function in the `simple_cache` module. Finally, the result is written back on the TCP socket for the client to read.

Many things can go wrong here; in all cases, errors are handled by the `try/catch` expression, which prints the error on the TCP socket. For instance, if the tokenization or parsing steps fail, an exception is generated because the result doesn't match `{ok, ...}`; and if calling the cache function doesn't work (perhaps the function name was wrong or just an empty string), another kind of exception is thrown.

That's the entire implementation—you now have a TCP interface to Simple Cache! If you're feeling a little underwhelmed and thinking "Was that all? It's such a small program," remember that the framework you've implemented here should easily be able to handle tens of thousands of simultaneous connections, and you can extend it in any direction you want in order to build your own industrial-strength TCP servers. You can experiment with it on your own now by starting a `simple_cache` system as in the previous chapter, but also including the path to tcp_interface/ebin, and then calling `application:start(tcp_interface)` from the system shell. (If you haven't done so already, remember that you need to write the ebin/tcp_interface.app file before you can start the application.) Call `appmon:start()` to check that all applications have been started. After both the cache and the TCP interface are running, you can connect to the system with the help of a telnet client, as you did back in chapter 3, and enter commands on the form defined in section 11.1.4.

You can try something here that the server in chapter 3 couldn't handle: have multiple simultaneous connections from two or more telnet sessions (perhaps inserting data in one session and reading it in another). You already added logging to the cache, so you should see some status messages in the Erlang console as you insert and look up data via TCP; but if you want to be able to see what's happening inside the TCP server processes themselves, you can add logging to `ti_server` as well. Finally, if you want the `tcp_interface` application to always be started as part of the system, you can include it in the release specification (see chapter 10). We leave this to you.

After this little warm-up, it's time to move on to the second part of this chapter, where you'll implement something a bit more ambitious: a RESTful HTTP interface, capable of carrying any type of payload to and from the simple cache, and allowing the cache to be integrated with any RESTful service infrastructure.

11.2   *Building a web service from the ground up*

As we mentioned at the start of the chapter, you'll implement the HTTP interface to the cache not only by designing a protocol over HTTP, but also by creating the actual HTTP server that will provide the interface. You could consider this an extreme case of Not Invented Here syndrome, but there is a method to the madness. The goal here is twofold: first, to give you a complete and robust example of a realistic TCP server, teaching you about HTTP servers and REST as a bonus (building a web server in Erlang is remarkably straightforward, as you'll see); and second, to show how you can define your own OTP behaviours—in this case, a `gen_web_server` behaviour to be used in the implementation of the HTTP interface. But before that, we need to talk a little about HTTP itself.

11.2.1 *A quick-and-dirty introduction to HTTP*

This isn't a book about HTTP, so we won't spend a lot of time explaining the protocol in detail, nor will we show how to implement a complete HTTP server. In this section, we go through some of the most important aspects of the protocol so that you'll be able to implement just enough of it in Erlang to create an efficient RESTful HTTP interface for the Simple Cache application.

To make things a little more concrete, let's use a couple of UNIX utilities to explore the HTTP protocol in a hands-on way. The first is the nc (netcat) utility, which is useful for inspecting traffic over TCP. It allows you to easily open a listening socket and inspect whatever gets sent to it. The second is the curl utility, which is a command-line HTTP client that you can use to send arbitrary requests to an HTTP server. Combining these two, you can easily see what a real HTTP request looks like.

How a GET request works

First, start nc and instruct it to listen on (for example) port 1156:

```
$ nc -l -p 1156
```

With this running in one terminal window, open another window and send an HTTP GET request to port 1156 on your local machine using curl:

```
$ curl http://localhost:1156/foo
```

Note the /foo following localhost:1156. In the first terminal window, nc prints something like this:

```
GET /foo HTTP/1.1
User-Agent: curl/7.16.3 (powerpc-apple-darwin9.0) libcurl/7.16.3
➥OpenSSL/0.9.7l zlib/1.2.3
Host: localhost:1156
Accept: */*
```

What you see is the HTTP request that curl sent. HTTP is a plain-text protocol, making it easy to read and debug. The first line specifies the request type (GET) as well as the resource (/foo) and the protocol to be used for the conversation (HTTP version 1.1). Following this initial request line come the HTTP headers; these are additional pieces of information about the request, some of which may instruct the server to do certain things in a particular way. Headers always start with a name followed by a : character. To mark the end of the header section, there is always an empty line, and then comes the message body (if any). In this case, the message body is empty.

A GET request is what your web browser normally sends to the server when you want to look at a web page—for example, when you click a link, open a bookmark, or manually type a URL in the browser's address field. The server replies by sending back the page contents.

When an HTTP server replies to a request, the first line of the reply begins with the protocol version, followed by a numeric status code and a *reason phrase* that should be a human-readable explanation of the status code (but which doesn't have to be a standard phrase and which can be expressed in a language other than English). The first digit of the status code indicates the general class of status. For example, if the requested resource can't be found, the normal reply from the server begins with

```
HTTP/1.1 404 Not Found
```

where the initial 4 means there seems to be an error on the client's side (such as asking for a resource that doesn't exist). After the first line, a reply has the same format as a request: it consists of a number of header lines, followed by an empty line and the message body. A successful request for a web page might result in a reply like the following, from a typical web server:

```
HTTP/1.1 200 OK
Date: Sat, 08 May 2010 19:09:55 GMT
Server: Apache
Content-Type: text/html

<!DOCTYPE HTML PUBLIC "-//W3C//DTD HTML 3.2 Final//EN">
<html>
 <head>
  <title>Front Page</title>
 </head>
 <body>
  <h1>Welcome</h1>
 </body>
</html>
```

In this case, the body consists of an HTML document (which is what the Content-Type header says it should be); but an HTTP request can return any kind of data depending on the nature of the resource, such as a JPEG image or a PDF document. The purpose of the Content-Type header is to help the client figure out what kind of data it received.

GET is clearly the most common kind of request. But you can make some other requests in HTTP—eight *verbs* in total—and your RESTful interface will use the PUT and DELETE verbs as well. Let's look at those before we move on.

PUT AND DELETE

To demonstrate PUT, you first need to create a small text file named put.txt containing the word *Erlang* as its only contents:

```
$ echo Erlang > put.txt
```

Next, abort the running nc and curl sessions, and restart nc as before. The -T option instructs curl to PUT a file to the given URL:

```
$ curl -T put.txt http://localhost:1156/foo
```

The output from nc looks something like this:

```
PUT /foo HTTP/1.1
User-Agent: curl/7.16.3 (powerpc-apple-darwin9.0) libcurl/7.16.3
➥OpenSSL/0.9.71 zlib/1.2.3
Host: localhost:1156
Accept: */*
```

```
Content-Length: 7
Expect: 100-continue

Erlang
```

You can see that it's similar to the previous GET request. The differences are that the initial request line now says PUT instead of GET, and that at the end of the request you see a couple of additional headers followed by an empty line and the message body (the contents of the put.txt file). The Content-Length header is 7, which refers to the six letters of the word Erlang plus a single newline character (on UNIX-like systems) that was added by the echo command when the file was created.

If you were watching the output from nc carefully as you sent the PUT request, you probably noticed that the body of the request didn't show up right away. This is due to the Expect: 100-continue header in the request. The Expect header was invented in part to make the web more efficient. When you include it in a request, the server is expected to send back a reply "100 Continue", instructing the client to proceed with sending the message body. If the server doesn't want to receive the body, it can close the connection immediately and save the client from transmitting a large amount of data to a server that's just going to throw it away. When you implement your own web server in section 11.2.3, you'll see how to handle this header.

Finally, let's look at a DELETE request. Restart nc as before, and use curl to send a DELETE request, as follows:

```
$ curl -X DELETE http://localhost:1156/foo
```

Don't worry—nothing will be deleted; nc will only show what the request looks like, which is something like this:

```
DELETE /foo HTTP/1.1
User-Agent: curl/7.16.3 (powerpc-apple-darwin9.0) libcurl/7.16.3
OpenSSL/0.9.7l zlib/1.2.3
Host: localhost:1156
Accept: */*
```

As you can see, the DELETE request looks almost exactly like the GET request, apart from the verb DELETE instead of GET on the first line. But the meaning is quite different: instead of asking for a copy of the resource /foo, this asks the server to remove that resource. Note that we aren't going into details about what a *resource* is—it's intentionally a rather abstract concept. In a plain web server, the resources are often files in the filesystem: GET means "send me a copy of the file contents," PUT means "upload a new file," and DELETE means "remove this file." But this all depends on the web server. As an interface to the simple cache, these verbs can be interpreted as operations on the cache rather than on files.

You could even use HTTP for a pizza delivery service, where GET could mean *order pizza* (if you encode your street address in the URL along with what kind of pizza, how many, and so on), PUT could mean *upload a new recipe to the menu*, and DELETE could be used to remove a recipe. All the HTTP specification talks about is "resources" and "representations of resources" (where a physical pizza delivered to your door would be a "representation" of the resource you requested). Now that you understand the basics of the HTTP protocol, let's start digging into the details of implementing the web server.

11.2.2 *Implementing a generic web server behaviour*

You'll implement this basic web server as a separate, reusable component: a new OTP behaviour. First, as with the `tcp_interface` in section 11.1.2, you need to create a skeleton for a new application alongside the applications you already have. The directory structure for this new `gen_web_server` application should look like this:

```
gen_web_server
    |-- ebin
    |    `-- gen_web_server.app
    `-- src
         |-- gen_web_server.erl
         |-- gws_connection_sup.erl
         `-- gws_server.erl
```

The `gen_web_server` will be a library application like the Erlang/OTP `stdlib`: it won't need to be started, although you can build other, active applications on top of it. This means the .app file doesn't need to include a `mod` entry to point out how to start the application, nor do you need to make an application behaviour implementation module or a top-level supervisor module here.

This is just a quick-and-dirty web server!

Don't use it in production code or think that it's a complete web server—it's not! It's a neat way to create RESTful interfaces, but at the end of the day it's just an example of how to create a custom behavior and follow sound Erlang/OTP coding practices. It doesn't handle chunking, persistent connections, and many other things you want from a real web server. Several production-quality Erlang web servers are available to choose from—if you need one, look at Yaws or MochiWeb, or use the `inets httpd` server that comes with the Erlang/OTP standard library.

Back in section 3.1.2, we said that behaviours have three parts: the container, the interface, and the implementation. Previously, you've been using existing behaviours, and you only had to provide the implementation. Now, you'll create a new behaviour with potentially many implementations, so your task is to provide the interface and the container. The container is the main chunk of reusable code, which the implementation modules will hook into via the callback functions defined by the interface. In this case, the container will be a generic web server.

The structure of the `gen_web_server` container is shown in figure 11.2. The gen_web_server.erl module is the front end that provides the API, hiding the internal details from the users of the behaviour. This module also specifies the behaviour interface.

Each instance of the `gen_web_server` container will consist of a single supervisor process that manages a number of dynamically created server processes, as in figure 11.1.

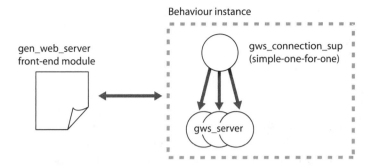

Figure 11.2 `gen_web_server` process and module layout

Because HTTP is just a text protocol over TCP, a `gen_web_server` instance works just like the `tcp_interface` application you wrote in section 11.1.3. This means each instance of the `gen_web_server` behaviour consists of a varying and unbounded number of processes. (For comparison, a `gen_server` instance only consists of a single process.) Each instance is distinct in that it manages a specific IP address/TCP port combination. But each instance can handle a large number of incoming connections on its particular port, starting a separate `gws_server` process per connection.

As in the `tcp_interface` application, the supervisor implemented by the `gws_connection_sup` module will be a simple-one-for-one supervisor, used as a factory for handler processes. The handlers are implemented by the `gws_server` module, which will be a `gen_server` similar to the `ti_server` in section 11.1.3, but requiring a lot more code in order to speak the HTTP protocol instead of the simple text protocol.

Let's start with the `gen_web_server` front-end module so you can see how simple it can be to define your own behaviour interface.

THE GEN_WEB_SERVER MODULE: DEFINING A CUSTOM BEHAVIOUR
When the compiler sees a `–behaviour(x)` declaration, it tries to call the module named x in order to find out what the interface should look like. For instance, when you say `-behaviour(gen_server)` in one of your modules, as in `ti_server`, the compiler calls `gen_server:behaviour_info(callbacks)` to get the list of callback functions that a `gen_server` implementation module should export. This means the name of a behaviour must be the same as the name of the module that defines the behaviour interface.

That module needs to export a single function called `behaviour_info/1`, whose only argument is an atom that says what kind of information is being asked for. Currently, the only such atom is `callbacks`. For any other input, the function should return `undefined`. But for `callbacks`, it should return a list of function name/arity pairs, naming the callback functions that the interface requires. To illustrate this, if you call `gen_server:behaviour_info(callbacks)` from the Erlang shell, you should get the following familiar list:

```
1> gen_server:behaviour_info(callbacks).
[{init,1},
 {handle_call,3},
 {handle_cast,2},
 {handle_info,2},
 {terminate,2},
 {code_change,3}]
2>
```

This information makes it possible for the compiler to warn you if you say that your module is implementing a particular behaviour but you've forgotten to implement (or export) some of the expected callbacks. When you define a new behaviour, you should provide this function. Listing 11.5 shows the source code for the gen_web_server module. As you can see, it contains a behaviour_info/1 function ❶ that returns a list of nine callbacks, all of which except init/1 correspond to HTTP methods like GET and POST.

Listing 11.5   gen_web_server.erl

```
-module(gen_web_server).

%% API
-export([start_link/3, start_link/4,
         http_reply/1, http_reply/2, http_reply/3]).

-export([behaviour_info/1]).

behaviour_info(callbacks) ->
    [{init,1},
     {head, 3},
     {get, 3},
     {delete, 3},                                    ❶ Defines behaviour
     {options, 4},                                      interface
     {post, 4},
     {put, 4},
     {trace, 4},
     {other_methods, 4}];
behaviour_info(_Other) ->
    undefined.

%%%====================================================================
%%% API

start_link(Callback, Port, UserArgs) ->
    start_link(Callback, undefined, Port, UserArgs).         ❷ Starts
                                                               new
                                                               instance
start_link(Callback, IP, Port, UserArgs) ->
    gws_connection_sup:start_link(Callback, IP, Port, UserArgs).

http_reply(Code, Headers, Body) ->
    ContentBytes = iolist_to_binary(Body),
    Length = byte_size(ContentBytes),                        ❸ Forms
    [io_lib:format("HTTP/1.1 ~s\r\n~sContent-Length: ~w\r\n\r\n", HTTP
                   [response(Code), headers(Headers), Length]), reply
     ContentBytes].
```

```
http_reply(Code) ->
    http_reply(Code, <<>>).

http_reply(Code, Body) ->
    http_reply(Code, [{"Content-Type", "text/html"}], Body).

%%%====================================================================
%%% Internal functions

headers([{Header, Text} | Hs]) ->
    [io_lib:format("~s: ~s\r\n", [Header, Text]) | headers(Hs)];
headers([]) ->
    [].

%% Fill in the missing status codes below if you want:
response(100) -> "100 Continue";
response(200) -> "200 OK";
response(404) -> "404 Not Found";
response(501) -> "501 Not Implemented";
response(Code) -> integer_to_list(Code).
```

The intention is that a module that implements the gen_web_server behaviour will
export all these callback functions; as each request comes in to the server, it'll be delegated to the corresponding implementation callback. For example, a PUT request
would be handled by the put/4 function in the implementation module. The init/1
callback initializes each new gws_server connection handler shown in figure 11.2,
rather than just once for the entire behaviour instance (this makes it similar to the
gen_event behaviour; see section 7.2.1). Finally, the other_methods/4 callback handles HTTP methods other than the most common ones; it could also be used to implement HTTP extensions like WebDAV.

The API provided by the gen_web_server module is simple. There are
start_link functions ❷ for starting new instances of the behaviour (either using the
default IP address for the machine or a specified IP address—useful if your machine
has multiple network interfaces). start_link also requires a callback module (as
usual for a behaviour), the TCP port to listen on, and any additional arguments
that will be passed on to the init/1 callback function for each new connection
handler. The API also includes a utility function to make it easy for implementation modules of gen_web_server to create proper HTTP replies; this http_reply
function ❸ is also called from the gws_server module to create an automatic "100
Continue" reply.

With the front end in place, the next module to implement from figure 11.2 is the
supervisor, gws_connection_sup.

THE GWS_CONNECTION_SUP MODULE
As in the tcp_interface application, the connection supervisor is a simple-one-for-one
supervisor—effectively, a factory that spawns new connection handlers on demand. A
single gws_connection_sup process will be created every time a gen_web_server
instance is started to listen on a particular port, and it will stay alive until that
instance terminates.

If you compare the code for `gws_connection_sup` shown in listing 11.6 with the code for the `ti_sup` module in section 11.1.3 (listing 11.2), you'll note that here, the `start_link` and `start_child` functions take more arguments, and the socket is being opened by the supervisor itself as part of the `init/1` function.

Listing 11.6   gws_connection_sup.erl

```
-module(gws_connection_sup).

-behaviour(supervisor).

%% API
-export([start_link/4, start_child/1]).

%% Supervisor callbacks
-export([init/1]).

%%%======================================================================
%%% API functions

start_link(Callback, IP, Port, UserArgs) ->
    {ok, Pid} = supervisor:start_link(?MODULE, [Callback, IP,
                                                Port, UserArgs]),
    start_child(Pid),
    {ok, Pid}.

start_child(Server) ->
    supervisor:start_child(Server, []).

%%%======================================================================
%%% Supervisor callbacks

init([Callback, IP, Port, UserArgs]) ->
    BasicSockOpts = [binary,
                    {active, false},
                    {packet, http_bin},
                    {reuseaddr, true}],
    SockOpts = case IP of
                    undefined -> BasicSockOpts;
                    _         -> [{ip,IP} | BasicSockOpts]
               end,
    {ok, LSock} = gen_tcp:listen(Port, SockOpts),
    Server = {gws_server, {gws_server, start_link,
                    [Callback, LSock, UserArgs]},
            temporary, brutal_kill, worker, [gws_server]},
    RestartStrategy = {simple_one_for_one, 1000, 3600},
    {ok, {RestartStrategy, [Server]}}.
```

❶ Starts first gws_server child

❷ New options for opening port

In this case, the `start_link/4` function also kicks off the first `gws_server` child process as soon as the supervisor is up and running ❶. You could also place the responsibility for doing this in `gen_web_server:start_link/4`, but this way it's guaranteed that a new `gws_connection_sup` process will always have a process that is listening on the socket, ready to handle any incoming connection.

The socket is opened using some new options ❷. First, `binary` means that incoming data is delivered as binaries, not as strings. Second, `{active, false}` means the socket is opened in passive mode. Third, {packet, http_bin} tells the socket that the incoming data is expected to be formatted as HTTP. The socket parses the text for you and sends you messages that are much easier to handle, saving you a lot of boring work and speeding up the HTTP handling. You'll see how this works when you implement the gws_server module a bit later. Finally, {reuseaddr, true} allows local port numbers to be reused sooner than they would otherwise be; without this option, the server can't be restarted (on the same port) until the OS kernel has timed out on the listening socket.

> ### TCP flow control and active/passive sockets
> Although active mode is cleaner and has more of an Erlang/OTP feel to it, it doesn't provide any flow control. In active mode, the Erlang runtime system reads data from the socket as quickly as it can and passes it on as Erlang messages to the socket's owner process. If a client is able to send data faster than the receiver can read it, it causes the message queue to grow until all available memory is used up. In passive mode, the owner process must explicitly read data off the socket, adding complexity to the code but providing more control over when data enters the system and at what rate; the built-in flow control in TCP blocks the sender automatically.

Note that we make an exception here to the rule that you don't put functionality in a supervisor. Because gen_web_server is a library application, there is no _app module in which to place this code (as in the tcp_interface application), and you'd have to add at least an extra process and probably another level of supervision in order to move this code outside of the gws_connection_sup module in a good way. That would be overkill for this book, but restructuring the program like that could make a nice exercise. Keep in mind that the listening socket must be owned by a process that stays alive during the lifetime of the server instance, so it can't be opened in the start_link/4 function in gen_web_server, nor by any of the individual gws_server processes.

There is another reason why it's excusable to keep this functionality within gws_connection_sup: in practice, it'll never be a top-level supervisor for an application. Whenever a gen_web_server container is started, it should always be as a part of an application and running under some other top-level supervisor, as illustrated in figure 11.3.

This means that if the gws_connection_sup process fails because of the additional code you added to init/1, the error will be caught by the supervisor above it. That should limit the amount of havoc it can cause in the rest of the application—although it may force the application to shut down as cleanly as possible if it doesn't succeed in restarting gws_connection_sup. This risk shouldn't be taken lightly.

Now that you understand the small but significant implementation differences between gws_connection_sup and the previous ti_sup module from section 11.1.3,

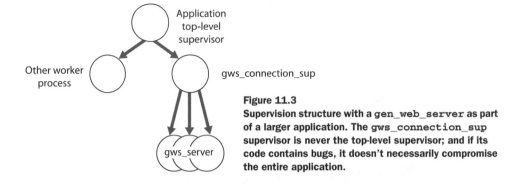

Figure 11.3
Supervision structure with a `gen_web_server` as part of a larger application. The `gws_connection_sup` supervisor is never the top-level supervisor; and if its code contains bugs, it doesn't necessarily compromise the entire application.

Fault isolation and stability of supervisors

In figure 11.3, the top-level supervisor starts two workers: one is a single process, and the other is a `gen_web_server` instance. Supervisors bring groups of processes together but also isolate them from each other. Any crashes that occur in the `gws_connection_sup` group will have no effect on the separate worker process (other than what the supervisor decides). Because of this principle, you should generally keep supervisors free from application-specific code.

A supervisor is normally highly trusted. If it fails in unexpected ways, the fault tolerance of the supervisor hierarchy is seriously weakened. This is particularly disastrous in a top-level supervisor, because if it fails, it causes a restart of the whole application—or, in the case of a permanent (required) application, a restart of the entire node.

it's time to move on to the meat of the matter: the `gws_server` module, which handles the actual HTTP connections.

THE GWS_SERVER MODULE AND THE USE OF {ACTIVE, ONCE}

Like the `ti_server` module, `gws_server` is a `gen_server` implementation. It'll handle sockets in much the same way as `ti_server`, using the same trick of returning a zero timeout from the `init/1` callback in order to defer initialization to `handle_info (timeout, State)`, which blocks on `gen_tcp:accept()` and then asks the supervisor to spawn another handler process. But there is an important difference: the way incoming data on the socket is handled.

In the `tcp_interface` application, you used the socket option `{active, true}` (see listing 11.1), which means incoming data is automatically read from the socket as soon as it's ready and is then sent as an Erlang message to the process that owns the socket. This allows you to code in a nice event-based style, but the disadvantage is that an active socket has no flow control. A client that transmits a lot of data very fast could make the server use up all of its memory just for the message queue. The `{active, false}` setting means the receiving process must read the data off the socket explicitly with `gen_tcp:read()` whenever it's ready. This makes the built-in flow control in TCP block the sender while the receiver isn't reading, fixing the out-of-memory vulnerability. The problem is that it doesn't make for a very Erlang-like programming style.

The third possibility, which you'll use here, is the {active, once} option. This puts the socket in active mode until some data is received, causing an Erlang message to be sent to the owning process, and then automatically sets it back to passive mode, which enables the flow control so that no further data is read and no messages are sent until the controlling process indicates that it's ready. Usually, it does this by setting the socket back to {active, once} and going back to waiting for the next message. The following code demonstrates a simple loop using {active, once}:

```
start() ->
    {ok, LSock} = gen_tcp:listen(1055, [binary, {active, false}]),
    {ok, Socket} = gen_tcp:accept(LSock),
    loop(Socket).

loop(Socket) ->
    inet:setopts(Socket, [{active,once}]),
    receive
        {tcp, Socket, Data} ->
            io:format("got ~p~n", [Data]),
            loop(Socket);
        {tcp_closed, _Socket} ->
            ok
    end.
```

First, you create a listening socket and use it to accept a connection, giving you a dedicated socket. After that, you enter the loop where you call inet:setopts/2 on the dedicated socket to enable {active once}, and then you sit down and wait for an incoming message from the socket. If you get some data, you handle it, knowing that the socket has been reset to passive mode, and then you loop back to reenable {active, once} before you wait for another message.

Apart from this, the real differences between the ti_server and the gws_server modules lie in the protocol handling. The former implements a simple protocol, whereas the latter will handle a subset of HTTP. The code for this module is shown in the following listing. Although it may seem like a lot at first glance, it's not that complicated.

Listing 11.7 gws_server.erl

```
-module(gws_server).

-behaviour(gen_server).

%% API
-export([start_link/3]).

%% gen_server callbacks
-export([init/1, handle_call/3, handle_cast/2, handle_info/2,
         terminate/2, code_change/3]).

-record(state, {lsock, socket, request_line, headers = [],
                body = <<>>, content_remaining = 0,
                callback, user_data, parent}).
```

❶ **Server-state record**

```
%%%=================================================================
%%% API

start_link(Callback, LSock, UserArgs) ->
    gen_server:start_link(?MODULE,
                          [Callback, LSock, UserArgs, self()], []).

%%%=================================================================
%%% gen_server callbacks

init([Callback, LSock, UserArgs, Parent]) ->
    {ok, UserData} = Callback:init(UserArgs),
    State = #state{lsock = LSock, callback = Callback,
                   user_data = UserData, parent = Parent},
    {ok, State, 0}.

handle_call(_Request, _From, State) ->
    {reply, ok, State}.

handle_cast(_Request, State) ->
    {noreply, State}.

handle_info({http, _Sock, {http_request, _, _, _}=Request}, State) ->
    inet:setopts(State#state.socket, [{active,once}]),
    {noreply, State#state{request_line = Request}};
handle_info({http, _Sock, {http_header, _, Name, _, Value}}, State) ->
    inet:setopts(State#state.socket, [{active,once}]),
    {noreply, header(Name, Value, State)};
handle_info({http, _Sock, http_eoh},
            #state{content_remaining = 0} = State) ->
    {stop, normal, handle_http_request(State)};
handle_info({http, _Sock, http_eoh}, State) ->
    inet:setopts(State#state.socket, [{active,once}, {packet, raw}]),
    {noreply, State};
handle_info({tcp, _Sock, Data}, State) when is_binary(Data) ->
    ContentRem = State#state.content_remaining - byte_size(Data),
    Body       = list_to_binary([State#state.body, Data]),
    NewState = State#state{body = Body,
                           content_remaining = ContentRem},
    if ContentRem > 0 ->
            inet:setopts(State#state.socket, [{active,once}]),
            {noreply, NewState};
       true ->
            {stop, normal, handle_http_request(NewState)}
    end;
handle_info({tcp_closed, _Sock}, State) ->
    {stop, normal, State};
handle_info(timeout, #state{lsock = LSock, parent = Parent} = State) ->
    {ok, Socket} = gen_tcp:accept(LSock),
    gws_connection_sup:start_child(Parent),
    inet:setopts(Socket,[{active,once}]),
    {noreply, State#state{socket = Socket}}.

terminate(_Reason, _State) ->
    ok.

code_change(_OldVsn, State, _Extra) ->
    {ok, State}.
```

Handles request line ❷

Handles headers ❸

❹ **End of header; body is empty**

❺ **End of header; prepare for body**

Waits for connection and starts new handler ❻

```
%%%==================================================================
%%% Internal functions

header('Content-Length' = Name, Value, State) ->
    ContentLength = list_to_integer(binary_to_list(Value)),
    State#state{content_remaining = ContentLength,
                headers = [{Name, Value} | State#state.headers]};
header(<<"Expect">> = Name, <<"100-continue">> = Value, State) ->
    gen_tcp:send(State#state.socket, gen_web_server:http_reply(100)),
    State#state{headers = [{Name, Value} | State#state.headers]};
header(Name, Value, State) ->
    State#state{headers = [{Name, Value} | State#state.headers]}.

handle_http_request(#state{callback     = Callback,
                           request_line = Request,
                           headers      = Headers,
                           body         = Body,
                           user_data    = UserData} = State) ->
    {http_request, Method, _, _} = Request,
    Reply = dispatch(Method, Request, Headers, Body,
                     Callback, UserData),
    gen_tcp:send(State#state.socket, Reply),
    State.

dispatch('GET', Request, Headers, _Body, Callback, UserData) ->
    Callback:get(Request, Headers, UserData);
dispatch('DELETE', Request, Headers, _Body, Callback, UserData) ->
    Callback:delete(Request, Headers, UserData);
dispatch('HEAD', Request, Headers, _Body, Callback, UserData) ->
    Callback:head(Request, Headers, UserData);
dispatch('POST', Request, Headers, Body, Callback, UserData) ->
    Callback:post(Request, Headers, Body, UserData);
dispatch('PUT', Request, Headers, Body, Callback, UserData) ->
    Callback:put(Request, Headers, Body, UserData);
dispatch('TRACE', Request, Headers, Body, Callback, UserData) ->
    Callback:trace(Request, Headers, Body, UserData);
dispatch('OPTIONS', Request, Headers, Body, Callback, UserData) ->
    Callback:options(Request, Headers, Body, UserData);
dispatch(_Other, Request, Headers, Body, Callback, UserData) ->
    Callback:other_methods(Request, Headers, Body, UserData).
```

7 Remembers content length for later

8 Tells client to proceed

9 Performs callback and gets results

In this gen_server, the server-state record tracks a lot of things **1**. The lsock and socket fields hold the listening socket and the dedicated socket, respectively. The request_line, headers, body, and content_remaining fields are for handling the HTTP protocol. The callback field holds the name of the behaviour implementation module, and user_data holds application-specific data to be passed to the callback module. Finally, parent holds the process ID of the gws_connection_sup supervisor.

In the tcp_interface application, there could be only one ti_sup supervisor, running under a registered name. Here, you can start many parallel instances of gen_web_server, so the gws_server processes need to be told who their particular supervisor is. This is set up in the start_link/3 function, where the pid of the caller (assumed to always be the gws_connection_sup process) is automatically passed as an argument to init/1.

The `start_link/3` function also takes a behaviour callback module, a listening socket, and some extra arguments from the user of the `gen_web_server` behaviour, all of which is passed on to `init/1`. There, you see the first interaction with the behaviour callback module provided by the user: the `UserArgs` argument is passed to the `init/1` function of the callback module (just like a `gen_server` calls your `init/1` function when it starts a new instance). This returns a `UserData` value, which is stored in the state record along with the other startup arguments.

As soon as `init/1` finishes, the new server process times out and jumps to `handle_info(timeout,...)`, where it blocks on `accept()` and then asks for a new handler, as before ❻. Note that the dedicated socket is then set to `{active, once}`, just as in the short example before listing 11.7, and that it's stored in the server-state record.

From this point on, what remains is to handle the HTTP protocol. Recall the HTTP requests you looked at earlier in section 11.2.1. For example, a PUT request with a body of "Hello!" might look like this:

```
PUT /foo HTTP/1.1
User-Agent: curl/7.16.3 (powerpc-apple-darwin9.0) libcurl/7.16.3
➥OpenSSL/0.9.71 zlib/1.2.3
Host: localhost:1156
Accept: */*
Content-Length: 7
Expect: 100-continue

Hello!
```

In general, an HTTP request has the following structure:

- The request line
- Header lines (any number)
- An empty line
- The message body

Remember the `{packet, http_bin}` option that you used when creating the listening socket in listing 11.6? This means the socket does the job of parsing this for you and sends you messages that are much simpler to handle. First, when a new request comes in, the request line is sent as a message in the following form (using the earlier PUT as example):

```
{http, Socket, {http_request, 'PUT', <<"/foo">>, {1,1}}}
```

Note that the method name is given as an atom (in single quotes). This is because it's one of the seven common methods in the HTTP specification. For other, unrecognized HTTP methods, the name is given as a binary—for example, `<<"PATCH">>`, or `<<"MKCOL">>` for the WebDAV MKCOL method.

An incoming request line ❷ is handled by storing it in the server state. After that, you need to reset the socket to `{active, once}` to allow it to read more data from the client and hand it to you as another message. Note that this is done in all clauses of the `handle_info` function where you want to continue reading from the socket.

After the request line, you generally get some headers. A socket with the {packet, http_bin} option enabled sends each HTTP header as a separate message in the following form:

{http, _Socket, {http_header, Length, Name, _ReservedField, Value}}

The handle_info clause that handles these messages ❸ does most of its work in the internal function header/3. It mainly accumulates the headers in a list in the server state, but in a couple of cases some additional work is needed. For a Content-Length header ❼, the data is stored as an integer in the content_remaining field of the state. This will be needed later to collect the body of the request. For an Expect header with the data "100-continue" ❽, an HTTP reply "100 Continue" should be sent to the client to tell it to proceed. (See section 11.2.1.) If you don't send this reply, the client will pause a couple of seconds before transmitting the body, which slows things down quite a bit.

When the empty line that signals the end of the headers is reached, the socket sends a message in the following form:

{http, _Socket, http_eoh}

If the value from the Content-Length header (stored in content_remaining) is zero at that point, you know that there will be no body following it ❹. In that case, all that remains is to process the request and send a reply. If a nonempty body is expected ❺, you need to switch the socket from {packet, http_bin} to {packet, raw}, telling it to stop parsing HTTP-specific data. After that, the incoming messages will have the usual form {tcp, Socket, Data}. For each such message, you must append the data to the body field of the state (initially an empty binary) and decrement the content_remaining counter correspondingly, until the counter reaches zero. Only then can you process the request as a whole, which is done in the internal function handle_http_request/1.

This is finally where the main interaction happens between the gen_web_server container code and the user-supplied behaviour implementation (the callback module). Previously, only the init/1 callback was called to initialize the user_data field of the server state. Now, you need to take all the information gathered about the request and dispatch to the corresponding callback function for the HTTP method.

To do this ❾, you first match out the necessary fields from the state, including the HTTP method name from the request structure. Then, you dispatch to the corresponding function in the callback module: this is expected to return the text of the HTTP reply. All that remains is to send the reply back to the client over the socket, and you're done!

Phew! That was a lot to go through, but we hope you're still with us. If you look back on the code, it's not all that bad—this is, after all, only a basic HTTP server.

But this hard work is about to pay off: the gen_web_server behaviour will make it absolutely trivial for you to implement the HTTP interface to the cache, which was the main motivation for all this if you recall from the beginning of section 11.2. It's only a matter of creating a gen_web_server behaviour implementation module with a few callback functions for interacting with the cache. But first, let's see what REST is all about and decide how the RESTful HTTP interface should look.

11.2.3 *Getting REST*

REST stands for *representational state transfer*. It's a concept that's been described as an after-the-fact summary of some of the central ideas included in HTTP. These ideas aren't limited to the HTTP protocol, but HTTP is widely supported and provides a well-known set of operations like GET, PUT, POST, and DELETE for manipulating and transferring state. These verbs also map easily to typical database CRUD operations (create, read, update, and delete), making it a simple task to design an HTTP interface to the cache.

> ### Representational state transfer
>
> The main principles of REST are that clients use a standardized interface (HTTP) for working with *representations* (documents) of resources kept on servers, referenced by global identifiers (URIs). That is, a client never gets the actual resource—which could be an abstract concept like "the current view from my window"—but gets a representation, which could possibly be offered in a number of different formats (for example, JPEG, PNG, or TIFF). Each request makes the client transfer from one state to the next, in the same way that you may click your way around a website. Often, one document contains identifiers pointing to other resources, such as the links in an HTML page.
>
> An important point is that between requests from a client, the server should never have to keep any implicit information in its state about that client: either the client holds all the necessary information, or it should be stored explicitly on the server as a resource with its own address. This last principle is perhaps the main one that prevents you from slapping an HTTP interface onto any old service and calling it RESTful.

The interaction with Simple Cache is straightforward, as a RESTful interface should be. Only three standard HTTP actions are needed: GET, PUT, and DELETE. You need to define exactly what each one means in terms of operations on the cache. The simplest is DELETE; it neither sends nor retrieves any data, apart from the resource name:

```
DELETE /key HTTP/1.1
```

This request causes a call to simple_cache:delete(Key), deleting the key from the cache. It always results in a reply "200 OK" with an empty message body.

Next, the GET action is only slightly more complicated:

```
GET /key HTTP/1.1
```

For this request, you need to call simple_cache:lookup(Key) and reply with either "404 Not Found" and an empty body if the lookup failed, or with "200 OK" and the value found in the cache as the body of the message (formatted as plain text).

Last, in a PUT request, the message body contains the value to be stored in the cache:

```
PUT /key HTTP/1.1
```

For such a request, you need to call `simple_cache:insert(Key, Body)`, and the reply to the client is always `"200 OK"` with an empty message body.

That's all there is to it. For a simple application like this, it's easy to see that the interface is indeed RESTful: it uses only basic HTTP operations to manipulate resources (entries in the cache) identified by URLs, without keeping any information about clients between requests. In the next section, you'll implement this protocol on top of the `gen_web_server` you created previously.

11.2.4 *Implementing the RESTful protocol with gen_web_server*

Like `tcp_interface` in section 11.1.2, The RESTful HTTP interface will be a separate active application `http_interface`, with an application behaviour module and a top-level supervisor. The supervisor will do one only thing: start up a single instance of the `gen_web_server` behaviour container. Here's the directory tree you should have when this is finished:

```
http_interface
    |-- ebin
    |    `-- http_interface.app
    `-- src
         |-- hi_app.erl
         |-- hi_server.erl
         `-- hi_sup.erl
```

Writing the .app file and the _app and _sup modules should be no problem for you by now. The important part is that the _sup module uses ordinary one-for-one supervision (that is, not simple-one-for-one) and starts a single, permanent child process (not temporary) via the `hi_server:start_link/1` function. Note that only the `hi_server` module will know that you're implementing the functionality on top of `gen_web_server`.

To make the port number easily configurable, you should try to read it with `application:get_env/2` in the `start/2` function of the `hi_app` module, as you did in `ti_app` in listing 11.1 (but don't open a socket here). If no configuration setting is found, the default port should be 1156, to keep it separate from the `tcp_interface` port 1155. The port number is then passed to the `start_link` function in `hi_sup` so that it can be used in the child specification for `hi_server`. (You can do the same with the IP address, if you like, or rely on the default IP address to keep things simpler for now.) We trust that you can do all this on your own.

The structure of the application is illustrated in figure 11.4. The main module of interest here is `hi_server`, which implements the actual RESTful HTTP interface based on the `gen_web_server` behaviour. This is shown in listing 11.8.

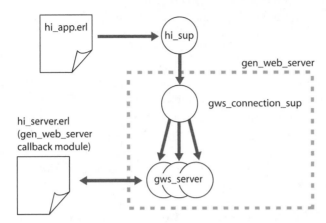

Figure 11.4
Structure of the RESTful interface application. The top-level supervisor `hi_sup` (started by `hi_app`) has a single child, which is a `gen_web_server` instance that calls back to `hi_server`.

Listing 11.8   hi_server.erl

```erlang
-module(hi_server).

-behaviour(gen_web_server).

%% API
-export([start_link/1, start_link/2]).

%% gen_web_server callbacks
-export([init/1, get/3, delete/3, put/4, post/4,
         head/3, options/4, trace/4, other_methods/4]).

%%%==================================================================
%%% API

start_link(Port) ->
    gen_web_server:start_link(?MODULE, Port, []).

start_link(IP, Port) ->
    gen_web_server:start_link(?MODULE, IP, Port, []).

%%%==================================================================
%%% gen_web_server callbacks

init([]) ->
    {ok, []}.

get({http_request, 'GET', {abs_path, <<"/",Key/bytes>>}, _},
    _Head, _UserData) ->
    case simple_cache:lookup(Key) of
        {ok, Value} ->
            gen_web_server:http_reply(200, [], Value);
        {error, not_found} ->
            gen_web_server:http_reply(404, "Sorry, no such key.")
    end.

delete({http_request, 'DELETE', {abs_path, <<"/",Key/bytes>>}, _},
       _Head, _UserData) ->
    simple_cache:delete(Key),
    gen_web_server:http_reply(200).
```

❶ **Handles GET**

❷ **Handles DELETE**

```
put({http_request, 'PUT', {abs_path, <<"/",Key/bytes>>}, _},
    _Head, Body, _UserData) ->
    simple_cache:insert(Key, Body),
    gen_web_server:http_reply(200).

post(_Request, _Head, _Body, _UserData) ->
    gen_web_server:http_reply(501).

head(_Request, _Head, _UserData) ->
    gen_web_server:http_reply(501).

options(_Request, _Head, _Body, _UserData) ->
    gen_web_server:http_reply(501).

trace(_Request, _Head, _Body, _UserData) ->
    gen_web_server:http_reply(501).

other_methods(_Request, _Head, _Body, _UserData) ->
    gen_web_server:http_reply(501).
```

❸ Handles PUT

❹ Remaining methods reply "501 Not Implemented"

That's all! The work you expended on the gen_web_server behaviour has paid off: it makes implementing a specific HTTP server like this an almost trivial exercise. Much as in a gen_server implementation module, you have the behaviour declaration, the export list for the callbacks, and some API functions for things like starting a server instance. In this case, the start_link functions want at least a port number as input, to be passed from hi_sup. Also note that an empty list is given to gen_web_server:start_link() as the UserArgs argument; this particular server implementation doesn't use it for anything.

The init/1 callback function is called by the gen_web_server for each new connection, to initialize the user_data field. The UserArgs argument that was given to gen_web_server:start_link() is passed unchanged to init/1, so in this particular implementation you expect an empty list as input. But this simple server doesn't use the user_data feature of gen_web_server for anything, so init/1 returns another empty list here.

The meat of the protocol implementation is in the get, delete, and put callbacks. You use binary pattern matching (see section 2.10.2) to strip the leading slash from the key (which is given as part of the URI). To keep this example simple, the keys and the stored data are binaries representing plain text. Other Erlang terms that may be stored in the cache aren't handled; in particular, if simple_cache:lookup(Key) succeeds, the found value is expected to be a binary, string, or IO-list, or the server can't send it back on the socket as it is.

For a GET request ❶, if the key is present in the cache, the value is returned as the body of a "200 OK" reply; otherwise, the reply is "404 Not Found" with an empty body. A DELETE request ❷ is straightforward: you delete the key and reply "200 OK". A PUT request ❸ is almost as simple, inserting the request body as the value for the key. (Note that the put callback gets Body as an argument, but get and delete don't.) The remaining HTTP methods ❹ are left unimplemented and result in a reply of "501 Not Implemented".

You could do a lot more to return a richer set of headers in the replies, but a detailed discussion about conventions for HTTP headers is beyond the scope of this book. The amount of additional information you need (or ought) to include depends largely on your application.

Let's give the HTTP-enabled Simple Cache a try. Compile the files as follows (all on one line), providing the path to the gen_web_server .beam files to erlc so the compiler can check that your hi_server module implements the gen_web_server behaviour interface correctly:

```
erlc -pa ./gen_web_server/ebin -o ./http_interface/ebin
  ./http_interface/src/*.erl
```

Start the system as described at the end of section 11.1.5 (if you like, also start the tcp_interface application), and then call application:start(http_interface) from the system shell. Check with Appmon that all applications are running as expected.

First, use curl to PUT the file put.txt (the one you created in section 11.2.1, containing the word *Erlang*) to be stored under the key xyzzy, and then look up the same key using a normal GET request:

```
$ curl -T put.txt http://localhost:1156/xyzzy
$ curl http://localhost:1156/xyzzy
Erlang
```

It's working! You can also try looking up the same key via the TCP interface, but you have to specify it as an Erlang binary

```
lookup[<<"xyzzy">>]
OK:{ok,<<"Erlang\n">>}.
```

because the HTTP interface treated all keys and data as binaries. If you feel like improving the interface, you can make it handle storing and looking up any Erlang data in the cache; or you can make it store the content-type in the cache along with the body for each PUT, so you can set the content-type correspondingly when you return each GET request.

11.3   Summary

You can now integrate the Simple Cache application with external clients through two different protocols: a custom, text-based protocol over raw TCP, and a more structured RESTful protocol over standard HTTP. Along the way, you learned some important techniques for writing a concurrent TCP server in Erlang, how to create and use a custom behaviour, and just enough HTTP to be dangerous. The work you did here has made it possible to use Simple Cache in places that aren't necessarily Erlang shops, which makes it much more useful in today's multilanguage and multiplatform production environments.

In the next chapter, we'll show you how to make Erlang interact directly with programs written in other languages, allowing tighter integration than over TCP/IP.

Integrating with foreign code using ports and NIFs

This chapter covers
- Ports, linked-in drivers, and natively implemented functions (NIFs)
- Integrating a third-party C library
- Integrating the C library using NIFs

At this point, the cache does a number of interesting things, such as log its actions, distribute across multiple nodes, and automatically connect to the cluster. It also has a RESTful HTTP interface for storing binary data, as well as a simpler text-based TCP interface for storing Erlang terms in general. Overall, the Erlware people are happy. But it would be nice if the clients who use the HTTP interface were able to store structured data in a standard way, and without doing their own marshalling and unmarshalling. The Erlware people would like you to modify the RESTful API to use the JavaScript Object Notation (JSON) format for storing and retrieving data. (See www.json.org for details. Note that in this chapter, we'll refer to JSON objects as *maps*, to be consistent with the terminology used by YAJL.)

To translate between JSON text and Erlang terms, they want you to use an open source JSON library called YAJL, which is written in C. The YAJL parser is based on SAX-style callbacks, which is useful to you because it'll allow you to build the resulting Erlang terms without having to go via an intermediate format. You can find the latest version of YAJL at http://lloyd.github.com/yajl/. You'll also find the version used in this chapter bundled with the rest of the source code for this book, at GitHub.com (search for *Erlang and OTP in Action*).

The idea is that it's better to use a well-tested library to parse a standardized format like JSON, rather than write your own parser and spend a lot of time shaking out the bugs. Furthermore, while there'll be some overhead in communication with the C library, and parsing small JSON documents won't be noticeably faster than if you used pure Erlang, it's likely that this solution will pay off when it comes to parsing large documents, perhaps containing several megabytes of Base64-encoded data. This approach also gives us the opportunity to introduce you to Erlang's general mechanisms for communicating with the world outside.

Like most programming languages, Erlang allows you to interface to code written in other languages, but its standard mechanism for doing this is a bit unusual. Most other languages have a foreign function interface (FFI) that provides a way to link with C code so it can be called from the host language. Erlang instead extends the message passing paradigm to interact with foreign code as well. To the Erlang code, the foreign code behaves much like a separate Erlang process: it can receive messages from the Erlang side and can send messages back to Erlang. On the Erlang side, it's represented by a process-like object called a *port* (see section 2.2.7).

You can also integrate with foreign code via the Erlang distribution mechanism. Using the Erl_Interface ei C library or the Jinterface Java library—both included in Erlang/OTP—it's possible to create a C or Java program that masquerades as an Erlang node. To a real Erlang node (that is, an Erlang VM running in distributed mode), the foreign program looks like another node—it has a node name and communicates using the Erlang distribution protocol. But for simple tasks, making such a *C node* (or Java node) is usually overkill. Chapter 13 will go into detail about creating a foreign node using Jinterface.

Finally, and new as of this writing, natively implemented functions (NIFs) allow you to create functions that behave just like Erlang's built-in functions (BIFs). These functions each belong to a specific Erlang module and are called like normal Erlang functions, although they're implemented in C via the erl_nif library. NIFs have minimal communication overhead; but a single bug in your NIF code can easily crash the entire Erlang VM, so they shouldn't be used willy-nilly—only when you're certain they're the right solution. We'll talk more about NIFs after we've introduced you to ports.

12.1   Ports and NIFs

Ports are the oldest and most basic form of connecting Erlang to the world outside. In their plain form, ports are simple and elegant to use, provide an important layer of isolation between your Erlang code and the foreign code, and are usually fast enough. They're also completely language neutral: the foreign program can be written in any language. Whenever in doubt, you should always start with a plain implementation using ports and then optimize later if it turns out that you need more speed.

The basic form of communication with a port is by passing messages. To pass data from Erlang to the port (and on to the foreign code connected to it), you can send a message to the port in the following form

```
PortID ! {self(), {command, Data}}
```

where `Data` is a binary or an IO-list (a possibly deep list of bytes and/or binaries). Note that you need to include the pid of the port owner process in the message; this is usually the current process, but any other process that knows both the port ID and the owner's pid is allowed to send messages to the port. (There are also a number of BIFs in the `erlang` module that allow direct manipulation of ports, regardless of ownership, but we'll stick to the message passing style here.)

When a port has data to deliver from the foreign code, it sends it asynchronously to the port owner process as a message on this form:

```
{PortID, {data, Data}}
```

The shape of the `Data` field depends on which options were used to create the port. For example, it can be either a binary or a list of bytes, and the port can be instructed to send the data in fixed-size chunks or line by line for a plain-text protocol.

Ports come in two different flavors: *plain ports* execute the foreign code as an external program running in a separate operating system process, using its standard input and standard output streams for communication with Erlang. The external program can be anything that can run as an executable under the host operating system—including shell scripts—as long as it can perform its function through stdin and stdout.

For example, running an operating system command like `echo 'Hello world!'` from within Erlang can be as simple as

```
Port = open_port({spawn, "echo 'Hello world!'"}, []).
```

(We'll talk more about opening ports in section 12.2.) The resulting message from the port will look like this:

```
{#Port<0.512>, {data,"'Hello world!'\n"}}
```

In some cases, you may need to write a small wrapper shell script or C program to adapt an existing executable program to interact with Erlang over the standard I/O, but many UNIX-style programs can be used from Erlang as is.

With plain ports, the worst that can happen is that the external program crashes and the port is closed; the Erlang VM isn't affected, allowing the Erlang code to detect and handle the situation, perhaps by restarting the external program.

The other kind of port uses linked-in drivers, often also called *port drivers*. As the name implies, a *linked-in driver* is a shared library, usually written in C, that's loaded and linked dynamically with the Erlang VM. This has the benefit of faster communication; but as with NIFs, a linked-in driver has the potential to crash or corrupt the entire Erlang VM. Communication with a linked-in driver is still byte-oriented, as with plain ports; and from the point of view of your Erlang code, both kinds of ports look the same. This means it's easy to go from a plain port to a linked-in driver when the need arises.

In this chapter, we'll talk about both variants of ports and how and when to use them. Both have their own benefits and drawbacks, and understanding these is key to choosing the right approach in the context of your system.

12.1.1 *Plain ports*

Ports are the simplest and most common way to communicate with foreign code in Erlang. They're objects with one foot in each world: one on the Erlang language side and one on the operating system side. On the Erlang side, a port is similar to a process: it's created, you can communicate with it using normal message passing, and it can die. Each created port gets a unique identifier that won't be recycled. Because ports don't execute any Erlang code themselves, each port also has an *owner*, which is a normal Erlang process; when a port receives data from the outside, it's sent to the port owner, which can decide what to do with it. The process that opens a port becomes the owner by default, but it's possible to hand over ownership to another process—for example, using the BIF `erlang:port_connect/2`. If the port owner dies, the port is closed automatically.

On the operating system side, a plain port is just another running program, which happens to be connected to the Erlang VM via its standard input and standard output. If the program crashes, Erlang can detect it and perhaps restart it or take some other action. The program lives in its own address space, and the only interaction it has with Erlang is over standard I/O. That means no matter what the program does, it can't crash the running Erlang system. Considering the unsafe nature of most foreign code, that's a big benefit, and it's one of the reasons systems written in Erlang can achieve such a high grade of stability even if they communicate with other programs. Even hardware drivers can be implemented in this way, if real-time demands aren't too great. You can see in figure 12.1 how the external code is connected to the Erlang side.

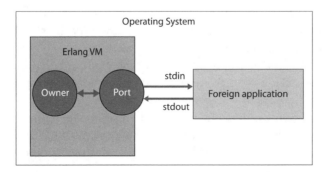

Figure 12.1
Communication between Erlang and foreign code over standard input and standard output, using a plain port. If the external program crashes, the port is closed.

Of course, there's no such thing as a free lunch. To get this level of safety, you pay a price in speed. All data that moves between the two processes must be passed as a byte stream. You may need to define your own byte-oriented protocol, with marshalling and unmarshalling of data. If you need to pass complex data, the Erl_Interface ei library provides support functions if you're writing in C. Similarly, the Jinterface library provides support for talking to a Java program. For other languages, you may need to define your own, or you may be able to use the IDL Compiler (IC) shipped with Erlang/OTP. Depending on the application and your needs, this can be complex or simple. For example, an external program for controlling a switch can have a character-based protocol where "0" means off and "1" means on.

12.1.2 Linked-in port drivers

Superficially, linked-in drivers work exactly like plain ports: the foreign code communicates with the Erlang code via byte-oriented messages. But under the hood, the mechanism through which those messages travel is different, and a linked-in driver executes in the same operating system process space as the Erlang VM. The main purpose is performance.

The drawback—and it's a severe one—is that if the port driver crashes, it brings down the entire Erlang system. This situation is made worse by the fact that port drivers are written in C, a language that leaves a lot of the error checking and resource management to the developer. Unfortunately, developers are only human, and aren't good at handling these things. In general, code written in C and other low-level languages is much less reliable; and because the code is linked directly into the Erlang VM, any error has the potential to bring down the entire Erlang system, which subverts all your fault-tolerant Erlang code. Figure 12.2 illustrates how a linked-in port driver works (compare it to figure 12.1).

Keep in mind that when you use a linked-in driver, you're trading safety for speed. You should make this trade-off only when you're sure you need the additional speed for your system. See chapter 14 for a discussion about profiling and optimization.

12.1.3 Natively implemented functions (NIFs)

NIFs are a new feature in Erlang. Although ports remain the simplest and safest solution for communicating with foreign programs, sometimes you want to make

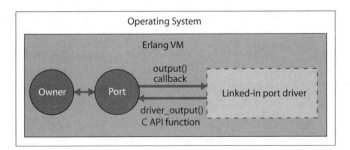

Figure 12.2
Linked-in drivers live in the same operating system process space as the Erlang VM, using a C API with callback functions and buffers for transferring the data.

something like a new built-in function with minimal overhead. With NIFs, you define a function in C in such a way that it becomes available as an Erlang function, just like a BIF. This is similar to the way foreign function interfaces work in most other languages—for example, Java and Python—so it probably looks more familiar if you have experience with such languages. Don't let that make you take the NIF approach as your first choice—consider the consequences of getting a hard system crash with no other clues than a core dump. If you do use NIFs, you may want to run your most important systems on nodes separate from the ones that run the NIF code, at least until the code has been sufficiently tested in battle.

NIFs also have another fundamental problem: the native function runs in the context of the VM thread that calls it, and the thread can't be rescheduled until the NIF has returned control to the VM. This makes NIFs suitable only for functions that execute and return quickly; long-running NIFs hold up resources for the Erlang VM scheduler.

To summarize, there are three low level mechanisms for interfacing between Erlang and other languages: plain ports, linked-in port drivers, and NIFs. All are valuable for different reasons: plain ports are a safe and easy way to hook up an external program over standard I/O, linked-in port drivers offer greater speed at the price of safety, and NIFs are an efficient but perilous way of hooking in library functions. To integrate the JSON parsing library with the Simple Cache, you'll start by making a plain port interface.

12.2 *Integrating with the parser through a port*

The task you've been given is to integrate an existing JSON parser written in C with the Simple Cache application. That means you need to connect the C library to Erlang using one of the approaches described in the previous section. This will let you have the best of both worlds: you get to use a fast library to do the parsing, while you keep the bulk of your code in Erlang. It also means you don't need to learn a lot about how to parse JSON correctly, so even if you have to spend some time on the integration, the total amount of effort should be much reduced compared to writing a parser from scratch in Erlang.

Because you want to be able to easily change the implementation from using plain ports to using a linked-in port driver or NIFs, the interface to the library should be as modular as possible. Fortunately, the API is simple: the library should take a JSON document as input, parse it, and return the resulting Erlang data structures to the caller.

As we said in section 12.1, a plain port should be the default choice unless there's good reason to use a linked-in driver or NIFs. That means you need to write an external program that reads from stdin and writes to stdout as a wrapper around the library code; and because the YAJL library is written in C, it's easiest and most efficient to write the external program in C as well. To integrate this with Erlang, you'll need some functionality on the Erlang side to create the port, send messages to it, and handle the data that comes back from the port. Let's start with this code, both because it's easier and because it will give you a better idea of how the communication will work.

12.2.1 *The Erlang side of the port*

As we said in section 12.1.1, there'll always be an associated Erlang process that owns the port, and any incoming data from the port will end up in the owner's mailbox. If the owner dies, the port gets closed. This makes port management easy; and because the theme of this book is Erlang and OTP, you should of course implement that process as a gen_server. We won't show all the code for this server, only some select bits; you've seen many examples of gen_server modules already and should be able to fill in the blanks yourself.

To match the examples in this book, the module name should be jp_server, and the server should be a locally registered process with the same name as the module. Create a basic application named json_parser to contain this module, complete with the usual jp_app and jp_sup modules, as well as a front-end API module named json_parser that calls the corresponding functions in jp_server.

THE SERVER API

We'll start with the jp_server API functions: you only need a single such function, apart from the usual start_link/0 for starting the server, and that is parse_document/1. It looks like this:

```
parse_document(Data) when is_binary(Data) ->
    gen_server:call(?SERVER, {parse_document, Data}).
```

As usual, the API function is just a wrapper for a call to a gen_server function. In this case, because you expect to receive a result, you want to use the synchronous gen_server:call/2. The Data argument should be a binary that contains the text for the JSON document you want to parse. Calling parse_document/1 makes the gen_server call its callback function handle_call/3 with {parse_document, Data} as the first argument. That's where the communication with the port will happen.

OPENING THE PORT WHEN THE SERVER STARTS

Before we show how to transmit the data to the port, let's first take care of opening the port when the json_server process is started, so there's a port to talk to in the first place. This should be done in the init/1 callback function of the gen_server. Apart from anything else you want to do in init/1, you need to call the BIF open_port/2 and store the resulting port identifier in the server state, as follows:

```
case code:priv_dir(?APPNAME) of
    {error, _} ->
        error_logger:format("~w priv dir not found~n", [?APPNAME]),
        exit(error);
    PrivDir ->
        Port = open_port({spawn, filename:join([PrivDir, "jp_prog"])},
                         [binary, {packet, 4}, exit_status]),
        {ok, State#state{port=Port}}
end
```

(This assumes you've defined the macro APPNAME to hold the name of your application—in this case, json_parser—and that you've declared a field named port in the state record in the gen_server module.) The previous code first gets the path of the priv subdirectory of your application, then appends the name jp_prog, and uses this path to launch the external C program using open_port({spawn, ProgramPath}, Options). The details of this C program will be the subject of the next section.

> **NOTE**   The normal location for external programs that are part of your application is in the priv directory (or a subdirectory thereof). You can always get the path of the priv directory of any application by calling code:priv_dir/1 with the application name.

The application directory and the code path

When you use one of the functions like priv_dir/1 in the code module, it searches your code path for the application name you specified. For instance, if you call priv_dir(foo), and the path contains a directory .../foo/ebin, the priv_dir function will return the corresponding directory name .../foo/priv. In a production system where all paths are properly set up at the start, this works fine; but when you're testing things from the Erlang shell on your own computer, you may have started Erlang with erl –pa ./ebin. That gives the system no clue as to the name of the application, so priv_dir/1 will fail to locate application foo. To get around this, you can start Erlang with erl –pa ../foo/ebin or similar.

The second argument to open_port/2 is a list of options that specify details on how the port should treat the data going back and forth between Erlang and the foreign code. In this case, you'll use the following options:

- binary specifies that the port should send you data as binaries instead of lists of bytes.
- {packet, N} tells Erlang to put an *N*-byte integer (1, 2, or 4 bytes) at the head of each chunk of data it sends to the foreign code, specifying the number of bytes that follow. This makes certain things easier for the C code later.
- exit_status says that you want to get the exit status of the external program as well as the data.

You can find more details in the Erlang/OTP documentation for erlang:open_port/2.

Now that you know the port is opened and its identifier is stored in the process state, let's move on to the code that handles the {parse_document, Msg} request.

COMMUNICATING WITH THE PORT

The following code sends a message to the port, which will transfer the data to the foreign code, and then waits for a reply:

```
handle_call({parse_document, Msg}, _From, #state{port=Port}=State) ->
    Port ! {self(),{command, term_to_binary(Msg)}},
    receive
```

```
        {Port, {data, Data}} ->
            {reply, binary_to_term(Data), State}
    end.
```

Note the use of `term_to_binary(Msg)`, which encodes the term `Msg` as binary data using Erlang's standard external transport format. This means you can send any Erlang data to the external program, which in its turn can use the Erl_Interface `ei` library to decode the data, as you'll see in the next section. (In this example, `Msg` is a binary already, sent from your `parse_document/1` API function, but the previous code can marshal any Erlang term into external format for sending over a port.)

When the external program has processed the request and sends the parsed data structure back to the Erlang side, it's delivered as a message `{Port, {data, Data}}` to the port owner: your `gen_server`, which is waiting for it. Here, you expect the incoming data to be in the same external format, so all you need to do is transform it back to an Erlang term using `binary_to_term/1`.

You may have noticed one unusual thing about the code. Normally, you want to avoid delays in the handling of a `gen_server` request; but here, it may take some time (if the document is large) before the reply comes back from the port. For this implementation, that's not a problem: the external program is made to handle only one client at a time, so there's no point in having concurrent requests to the port—it would require that you keep track of which client should receive which result. By blocking the handling of a request until communication with the port is completed, you get the `gen_server` to do the concurrency control for you (which is particularly useful if you're integrating with a hardware driver or similar). This implementation may be good for parsing one document at a time, but in this naive form it doesn't parallelize.

DETECTING FAILURE

Because you created the port using the `exit_status` option, your server will receive an out-of-band message when the external program exits. You can use this to track and manage the external program. As an example, you could restart the program by reopening the port, as follows:

```
handle_info({Port, {exit_status, Status}}, #state{port=Port}=State) ->
    error_logger:format("port exited with status ~p; restarting",
                        [Status]),
    NewPort = create_port(),
    {noreply, State#state{port=NewPort}}.
```

(This assumes you've moved the details of opening the port to a function `create_port()`.)

Another, possibly more elegant, way is to make the `gen_server` a true proxy for the external program. You can make the server a transient child of a supervisor; and if the external program exits with a nonzero status, you shut down the server with a reason other than `normal`, which causes the supervisor to restart the entire server. That way, there'll be a one-to-one relationship between process restarts and restarts of the external program, letting you take advantage of things like SASL logging and restart strategies in OTP. We won't get into those details here, but we encourage you to experiment with such a solution.

12.2.2 *The C side of the port*

The Erlang code you wrote in the previous section expects to find an executable program file named jp_prog in the application's priv subdirectory. Now it's time to create that program, and you'll do so in C. You won't need to be a C guru to understand most of this code, but you'll need a working C compiler such as gcc on your computer if you want to try it out. On Windows, you might want to use MinGW, which is a port of the gcc compiler together with a minimal set of UNIX utilities for running simple scripts and makefiles.

This C program will be a standalone executable that acts as a wrapper around the YAJL library described at the start of this chapter. It'll read a JSON document as text on the standard input stream, use YAJL to parse it, and encode it as Erlang terms with the help of the Erl_Interface ei library. These terms will then be written as a chunk of bytes back to the standard output stream. This behavior is just what the Erlang side of the port expects.

> **Using Erl_Interface or not**
>
> Note that Erl_Interface isn't the only way to implement the C side of your code. If it suits your application better—for example, if you're only going to transmit plain text or chunks of bytes in both directions and no structured Erlang data—you can use a simple byte-oriented protocol and do the encoding and decoding yourself. With Erl_Interface, you leave all that to the library and work with Erlang terms on both sides, which is a more heavyweight solution but makes it easier if you want to send complex Erlang terms back from the C code.

Remember that, usually, you don't want to mix source code in other languages with your Erlang source files in the src directory. Instead, create a separate directory named c_src to hold the C files. The following listing shows the first part of the file c_src/jp_prog.c, with some basic include statements and declarations that will be needed.

Listing 12.1   c_src/jp_prog.c: declarations

```
#include <stdlib.h>
#include <stdio.h>
#include <string.h>

#include <ei.h>                         ❶ Erl_Interface and
#include <yajl/yajl_parse.h>              YAJL header files

#define BUFSIZE 65536

static int handle_null(void *ctx);       ❷ Declares parser
static int handle_boolean(void *ctx, int boolVal);   callback functions
static int handle_integer(void *ctx, long integerVal);
```

```
static int handle_double(void *ctx, double doubleVal);
static int handle_string(void *ctx, const unsigned char *stringVal,
                         unsigned int stringLen);
static int handle_map_key(void *ctx, const unsigned char *stringVal,
                          unsigned int stringLen);
static int handle_start_map(void *ctx);
static int handle_end_map(void *ctx);
static int handle_start_array(void *ctx);
static int handle_end_array(void *ctx);
```
                                                              ❸ **Tells YAJL about**
                                                                  callbacks
```
static yajl_callbacks callbacks = {
  handle_null,
  handle_boolean,
  handle_integer,
  handle_double,
  NULL,   /* can be used for custom handling of numbers */
  handle_string,
  handle_start_map,
  handle_map_key,
  handle_end_map,
  handle_start_array,
  handle_end_array
};
```
                                                              ❹ **Tracks nested**
                                                                  data structures
```
typedef struct container_t {
  int index;     /* offset of container header */
  int count;     /* number of elements */
  struct container_t *next;
} container_t;

typedef struct {
  ei_x_buff x;
  container_t *c;
  char errmsg[256];
} state_t;
```
                                              ❺ **Holds state during**
                                                  YAJL parsing
```
#define ERR_READ          10
#define ERR_READ_HEADER   11
#define ERR_PACKET_SIZE   12
```
                                              Exit status
                                              codes

First, you need to include the header files for the Erl_Interface ei library and the YAJL library ❶ so you can use the functions and data structures that these libraries provide. Then, you have to declare the names and type signatures of the callback functions you'll implement, so you can refer to them even though you haven't implemented them yet ❷. After that, you fill in the yajl_callbacks structure with the names of your callbacks ❸, so the YAJL library can find them. One of the fields is left as NULL: it can be used to override the default callbacks for integers and doubles, for example, if you want to implement handling of numbers too large to fit into a long integer.

DATA STRUCTURES

You also need a couple of data structures of your own. First, the container_t structure ❹ keeps track of information needed to handle JSON arrays and key/value maps. Because these can be nested, you need to be able to represent containers within containers—this is what the next field is for. The count field tracks how many elements have been seen so far—for example, the parser may currently be at the fourth element of an array that is itself the value of the seventh entry in a key/value map. Last, the index field is used to fix up the encoding of the resulting data structure: when the end of an array has been seen, and you know exactly how many elements it contains, you need to go back and update the header at the start of the Erlang term you're building with the total number of elements, and the position to be back-patched is kept in the index field. You'll see how this works shortly.

The second data structure, state_t ❺, is used for the global state while the YAJL parser is running. Each YAJL callback function is given a pointer to this structure as the first parameter (called the *context* in the YAJL documentation). This is similar to the way gen_server callbacks in Erlang are passed the current state as the last parameter. Your state contains a pointer to the current container (this is NULL if the parser isn't currently inside any container) and an ei_x_buff structure, which is defined by the Erl_Interface ei library and is used for building an encoding of an Erlang data structure. (Using an ei_x_buff lets the ei library take care of dynamically allocating enough memory for the Erlang term that you're building, which makes things simpler.) It also holds a string buffer used for error reporting.

READING AND WRITING DATA

The first pieces of code you need are those that handle input and output. Recall that communication with the Erlang side will be done over the standard I/O streams and that the data packet—in both directions—will be preceded by a 4-byte integer in network byte order (big-endian) that specifies the number of bytes following it.

> **Network endianism alert**
>
> The packet header bytes are always in network byte order (big-endian), regardless of platform, so make sure your code decodes this correctly regardless of the endianness of the platform you're currently running on. In particular, don't just read the bytes straight into a uint32_t integer and assume things will work.

This convention was decided back in section 12.2.1 when you used the {packet, 4} option to open the port. On one hand, it complicates things by making it necessary to read and decode the packet length in the C side of the code; but on the other hand, it means that when you know the length of the packet, it's simple and fast to read the rest of the data. Similarly, writing data back to Erlang requires first sending a properly formed length header; but after you've done that, you can output the data in a single write operation. The following listing shows the code that handles I/O.

Listing 12.2   c_src/jp_prog.c: reading and writing

```
static void write_packet(char *buf, int sz, FILE *fd)
{
  uint8_t hd[4];
```

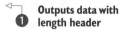 ❶ Outputs data with length header

```
    hd[0] = (sz >> 24) & 0xff;
    hd[1] = (sz >> 16) & 0xff;
    hd[2] = (sz >> 8) & 0xff;
    hd[3] = sz & 0xff;
    fwrite(hd, 1, 4, fd);

    fwrite(buf, 1, sz, fd);
    fflush(fd);
}

static size_t read_bytes(unsigned char *buf, size_t max, FILE *fd)   ◁─┐
{                                                                      │
    size_t n;                                              Reads bytes │
    n = fread(buf, 1, max, fd);                            into buffer ❷
    if ((n == 0) && !feof(fd)) {
        exit(ERR_READ);
    }
    return n;
}

static void read_packet(unsigned char *buf, size_t max, FILE *fd)   ◁─┐
{                                                                      │
    size_t n, sz;                                      Reads data with │
    uint8_t hd[4];                                     length header   ❸

    n = read_bytes(hd, 4, fd);
    if (n == 0 && feof(fd)) exit(EXIT_SUCCESS);
    if (n != 4) exit(ERR_READ_HEADER);
    sz = (hd[0] << 24) + (hd[1] << 16) + (hd[2] << 8) + hd[3];
    if (sz > max) {
        exit(ERR_PACKET_SIZE);
    }
    n = read_bytes(buf, sz, fd);
    if (n != sz) {
        exit(ERR_READ);
    }
}
```

The write_packet function ❶ outputs a number of bytes but prefixes it with a 4-byte length header in network byte order. The read_bytes function ❷ is a utility function that reads at most *max* bytes into a buffer, and the read_packet function ❸ reads an entire length-prefixed data packet. Note that if reading or writing fails, the program exits with a nonzero exit status. This is because if there's a communication error or the protocol has become desynchronized so you no longer know what's a packet header and what's raw data, it's better to give up and let Erlang restart the program. If the input stream is closed between documents, the program exits, signaling success.

RUNNING THE JSON PARSER

After a document has been successfully received from the Erlang side and resides in the input buffer, you need to initialize and run the YAJL parser on the data. This is done in the parse_json function (see listing 12.3). Note that this function takes a pointer to your state_t structure as the first parameter, so it can be passed on to YAJL, which in its turn passes it to each of your callback functions so they can access the state structure.

Listing 12.3   c_src/jp_prog.c: parsing JSON

```
static const char *parse_json(state_t *st, unsigned char *buf, size_t len)
{
  yajl_parser_config cfg = {
    1, /* allow comments */
    0  /* don't check UTF-8 */
  };
  yajl_handle yh;
  yajl_status ys;
  const char *err=NULL;

  yh = yajl_alloc(&callbacks, &cfg, NULL, st);
  ys = yajl_parse(yh, buf, len);
  if (ys == yajl_status_insufficient_data) {
    ys = yajl_parse_complete(yh);
  }
  if (ys == yajl_status_insufficient_data) {
    err = "unexpected end of document";
  } else if (ys != yajl_status_ok) {
    unsigned char *msg = yajl_get_error(yh, 0, NULL, 0);
    strncpy(st->errmsg, (char *)msg, sizeof(st->errmsg)-1);
    yajl_free_error(yh, msg);
    st->errmsg[sizeof(st->errmsg)] = 0;
    err = st->errmsg;
  }
  yajl_free(yh);
  return err;
}
```

❶ Initializes YAJL parser handle

❷ Frees YAJL handle

This function begins by creating a few things needed by YAJL: a configuration structure, a handle, and a status variable. Then, `yajl_alloc` is called to initialize the handle ❶, using your callback specification from listing 12.1, the configuration structure, and the state pointer (the context). The third argument is given as NULL for now. After the handle is initialized, you can call `yajl_parse` on the data buffer using the handle. YAJL then parses the data, using your callbacks to generate the result. After parsing, the handle needs to be freed again by calling `yajl_free` ❷.

If the return status indicates that the document seems to be incomplete, you call `yajl_parse_complete` to tell it there's no more data; and if the status is still the same, you set the return value to indicate that the document ended unexpectedly. If some other non-OK status is returned, you call `yajl_get_error` to get an error string that you need to copy into your buffer in the state structure and then release with `yajl_free_error`. That extra bit of work makes `parse_json` easy to use: if the parsing succeeds, it returns NULL, and otherwise it returns a string that explains the error.

DECODING AND ENCODING ERLANG TERMS WITH EI

With all that in place, we can now look at the code that processes a single request packet sent from the Erlang side that's been read into the input buffer. This is done in the function `process_data`, which also uses a helper function called `make_error`, both shown in listing 12.4. Up until this point, we've only been talking about reading and writing data and calling the YAJL parser, but we now need to explain a little about how Erlang terms are handled in the C code with the help of the ei library.

> **Listing 12.4 c_src/jp_prog.c: parsing a single document**

```c
static void make_error(state_t *st, const char *text)
{
  ei_x_free(&st->x);
  ei_x_new_with_version(&st->x);
  ei_x_encode_tuple_header(&st->x, 2);
  ei_x_encode_atom(&st->x, "error");
  ei_x_encode_string(&st->x, text);
}

static void process_data(unsigned char *buf)
{
  state_t st;
  st.c = NULL;
  ei_x_new_with_version(&st.x);                    ❶ Initializes
                                                      output buffer

  int index = 0;
  int ver = 0, type = 0, size = 0;
                                                   ❷ Decodes version
  if (ei_decode_version((char *)buf, &index, &ver)) {   byte of input
    make_error(&st, "data encoding version mismatch");
  } else if (ei_get_type((char *)buf, &index, &type, &size)
             || type != ERL_BINARY_EXT) {
    make_error(&st, "data must be a binary");
  } else {                                         ❸ Encodes start
    ei_x_encode_tuple_header(&st.x, 2);               of {ok, ...}
    ei_x_encode_atom(&st.x, "ok");
    const char *err;
    if ((err = parse_json(&st, &buf[index+5], size)) != NULL) {
      make_error(&st, err);
    }
  }
  write_packet(st.x.buff, st.x.buffsz, stdout);
  ei_x_free(&st.x);
}
```

The *external term format* used by erlang:term_to_binary/1 to serialize an Erlang term is the same as that used in the Erlang distribution protocol. The details of this format are documented in the ERTS User's Guide section of the standard Erlang/OTP documentation, but you don't need to know the exact byte-level representation in order to use it—the ei library helps you with decoding and encoding serialized terms. In this case, your input buffer contains the encoded term sent from Erlang to the port (see section 12.2.1). You expect this term to be a binary, containing JSON text.

Before you start decoding and parsing, you want to initialize the state structure, and in particular the ei_x_buff structure ❶ that's used to build the term to be sent back to the Erlang side. This is done with ei_x_new_with_version, which allocates a dynamic buffer and at the same time conveniently inserts a version number at the start of the buffer. Erlang's external term format requires the version of the encoding as the first byte of the data chunk—this allows different nodes and clients to be sure that they're exchanging data in a compatible way. You generally don't need to know what the current version number is; the ei functions handle this for you.

The ei decoding functions use an index variable that points into the buffer and is advanced each time a decode operation succeeds. The initial offset is zero, and the first thing you need to do to decode the input is call ei_decode_version ❷. If the version in the input buffer isn't compatible with your version of ei, the function returns a nonzero value; in that case, you generate an error term to be sent back to Erlang. If decoding succeeds, the found version number is stored in the ver variable (the actual number isn't of interest here).

The next step is to inspect the actual encoded term following the version byte. This is done in a similar way: ei_get_type returns nonzero if the data is invalid, and otherwise fills in the variables type and size to match the found term. (But it doesn't advance index: the point is only to inspect the term, not do anything with it.) If the type is ERL_BINARY_EXT, the term is a binary, as you wanted. The contents of the buffer are illustrated in figure 12.3.

At this point, you know that the encoded binary starts at buf[index]. To avoid copying the data, you can cheat a little: the documentation of the external term format says that a binary is encoded as 1 byte for the type (109) followed by 4 bytes for the size (which you've already decoded into the size variable). The actual binary data starts at buf[index+5]. This address can be given directly to parse_json, along with the size.

But before you start parsing, you need to think about what sort of value you want to return to Erlang. To allow the Erlang side to easily differentiate between successful parses and errors, you want to use the normal {ok, Result}/{error, Message} convention. This means that you'll need to start encoding the {ok, ...} tuple before you begin encoding the result data ❸.

Encoding is the reverse of decoding: you already have a dynamic ei_x_buff output buffer which automatically keeps track of the current buffer size and the offset for the next data to be encoded. To make a tuple, you call ei_x_encode_tuple_header. This inserts a header that signals "tuple start" and specifies the number of elements that follow it. (These elements may in their turn also be tuples, in a nested fashion.) In this case, you want a 2-tuple, and the first element of that tuple should be the atom ok, which you insert with a call to ei_x_encode_atom. The next encoded term becomes the second element of the tuple, and this is created by your callback functions while YAJL is parsing the data.

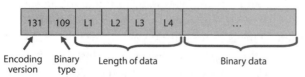

| 131 | 109 | L1 | L2 | L3 | L4 | ... |

Encoding version / Binary type / Length of data / Binary data

Figure 12.3
The external term format encoding of a binary term in the input buffer. The ei library helps you decode this so you don't have to think about the details.

The utility function make_error is used to report errors. Because you've already initialized the ei_x_buff output buffer and possibly inserted data into it, make_error starts by freeing the existing buffer and initializing a new one. It then builds a tuple {error, Message} in the same way that you made the {ok, ...} tuple, but in this case using ei_x_encode_string to create the Message term from the error string.

Finally, at the end of process_data, you write the final encoded result term (either {ok, Data} or {error, Message}) from the output buffer to the standard output stream using the write_packet function, and de-allocate the output buffer.

THE MAIN FUNCTION

Only one detail is left before we start looking at the YAJL callback functions: the main loop, shown in the following listing.

Listing 12.5   c_src/jp_prog.c: main loop

```
int main(int argc, char **argv)
{
  static unsigned char buf[BUFSIZE];
  for (;;) {
    read_packet(buf, sizeof(buf)-1, stdin);
    buf[sizeof(buf)-1] = 0; /* zero-terminate the read data */
    process_data(buf);
  }
}
```

The main function is the entry point of a C program. Its arguments are the number of arguments (argc) passed on the command line and the actual argument strings (argv), but this particular program doesn't use any arguments. Because you've moved all the real work to isolated functions, this main function is simple: it creates the buffer for input data, and then it loops forever (or until one of the functions in listing 12.2 calls exit), reading a packet from the Erlang side at a time and processing it.

ENCODING JSON DATA AS ERLANG TERMS

We now come to the last part of the C program: the implementation of the YAJL parser callback functions that will be called as YAJL parses the JSON data. For simple values like null, true/false, numbers, and strings, there's a single callback for each. For the compound JSON data structures (arrays and maps), there's one callback function for the start of the structure and another for when the structure ends.

Remember that each callback is handed a pointer to your state_t structure (the YAJL context—see listing 12.3). All the information you need to build the corresponding Erlang terms must be accessible via this structure. In C, it's tempting to start using global variables for this sort of thing; but if you do, you'll have to rewrite it later for the linked-in driver version in section 12.3, which requires that the code be reentrant.

Before you begin coding these callback functions, you need to decide how the JSON data should be represented as Erlang terms. This is shown in table 12.1.

The representation tries to follow Erlang's conventions (for instance, using the atom 'undefined' as the null value), be space-efficient (by representing JSON strings—

Table 12.1   The representation of JSON data as Erlang terms. Note that the null value translates to the atom `'undefined'`, which suits Erlang's conventions better.

JSON	Erlang `json()` representation
`null`	`'undefined'`
`true`	`'true'`
`false`	`'false'`
`42, 3.14, ...` (integers and floats)	`number()`
`"..."` (string)	`binary()`
`[x1, x2, ...]` (array)	`{ json(), json(), ... }`
`{"abc": x1, "def": x2, ...}` (map)	`[ {binary(), json()}, ... ]`

including the labels in maps—as binaries), and be unambiguous. When you see a list, you know it must be representing a map of key/value pairs and not a string or an array. When you see a tuple that isn't a key/value pair, you know it must be representing an array. Representing JSON arrays as Erlang tuples means you can easily index into the array, and uses less space than a list; but on the other hand, it requires that you convert the tuple to a list in order to add or remove elements. This trade-off seems reasonable.

Now that you know what output you should be generating, let's look at the simple YAJL callbacks first, shown in the following listing.

Listing 12.6   c_src/jp_prog.c: simple YAJL callbacks

```
static void count_element(state_t *st)
{
  container_t *c = st->c;
  if (c != NULL) ++(c->count);                    ①  Increments element count
}                                                     of current container

static int handle_null(void *ctx)
{
  state_t *st = (state_t *)ctx;
  count_element(st);
  ei_x_encode_atom(&st->x, "undefined");
  return 1;
}

static int handle_boolean(void *ctx, int boolVal)
{
  state_t *st = (state_t *)ctx;
  count_element(st);
  ei_x_encode_boolean(&st->x, boolVal);
  return 1;
}

static int handle_integer(void *ctx, long integerVal)
{
```

```
    state_t *st = (state_t *)ctx;
    count_element(st);
    ei_x_encode_long(&st->x, integerVal);
    return 1;
}
static int handle_double(void *ctx, double doubleVal)
{
    state_t *st = (state_t *)ctx;
    count_element(st);
    ei_x_encode_double(&st->x, doubleVal);
    return 1;
}

static int handle_string(void *ctx, const unsigned char *stringVal,
                         unsigned int stringLen)
{
    state_t *st = (state_t *)ctx;
    count_element(st);
    ei_x_encode_binary(&st->x, stringVal, stringLen);
    return 1;
}

static int handle_map_key(void *ctx, const unsigned char *stringVal,
                          unsigned int stringLen)
{
    state_t *st = (state_t *)ctx;
    ei_x_encode_tuple_header(&st->x, 2);
    ei_x_encode_binary(&st->x, stringVal, stringLen);
    return 1;
}
```

② Encodes JSON string as binary

③ Begins 2-tuple to hold key/value pair

All of these use the helper function count_element, which increments the element counter in the current container structure, if there is one (see listing 12.1) **①**. For example, if you see an integer while within an array, you increment the element count of the array. Apart from that, these functions are straightforward, each inserting some data into the output buffer; for example, the handle_string callback uses ei_x_ encode_binary to build a binary term containing the text of the JSON string **②**. All the callbacks return 1 to YAJL to signal "all OK, continue parsing." The one notable function is handle_map_key. This is called for the key of a key/value pair in a JSON map.

When a pair is seen, you've already started building a list to hold the pairs of the map. Each pair is a 2-tuple of the key and the value; and much as you did to encode the {ok, ...} tuple in listing 12.4, all you need to do here is insert a 2-tuple header **③**

How YAJL handles key/value pairs

Only the key part of a key/value pair has a special callback function in YAJL. There's no special callback to handle the value—the normal callbacks are used for that. If necessary, you can put a flag in the state structure to signal that the next value is part of a pair—you'll need that in section 12.3—but right now, you don't need to do anything special to encode a value that's part of a pair.

followed by the key (a binary) as the first element. You know that the next called call-back function will insert the value as the second element, completing the tuple. Simple! (Note that you don't call `count_element` when handling keys, only values, because the count should be incremented only once for the whole tuple.)

Finally, you need to implement the callbacks for handling the start and end of arrays and maps. This is a little trickier. The code is shown in the following listing.

Listing 12.7   c_src/jp_prog.c: map and array YAJL callbacks

```
static int handle_start(void *ctx, int array)
{
  state_t *st = (state_t *)ctx;
  count_element(st);

  container_t *c = malloc(sizeof(container_t));
  c->next = st->c;
  st->c = c;
  c->count = 0;
  c->index = st->x.index;

  if (array) {
    ei_x_encode_tuple_header(&st->x, 1);
  } else {
    ei_x_encode_list_header(&st->x, 1);
  }
  return 1;
}

static int handle_start_map(void *ctx)
{
  return handle_start(ctx, 0);
}

static int handle_start_array(void *ctx)
{
  return handle_start(ctx, 1);
}

static int handle_end(void *ctx, int array)
{
  state_t *st = (state_t *)ctx;
  container_t *c = st->c;
  if (array) {
    ei_encode_tuple_header(st->x.buff, &c->index, c->count);
  } else {
    ei_encode_list_header(st->x.buff, &c->index, c->count);
    ei_x_encode_empty_list(&st->x);
  }
  st->c = c->next;
  free(c);
  return 1;
}

static int handle_end_map(void *ctx)
{
```

1   Allocates, links, and initializes new container

2   Inserts dummy tuple or list header

3   Back-patches header with final count

4   Unlinks and frees container structure

```
    return handle_end(ctx, 0);
}

static int handle_end_array(void *ctx)
{
    return handle_end(ctx, 1);
}
```

The similarities between handling maps and arrays in this example are large enough that it's easier to combine the code into common `handle_start` and `handle_end` functions using a flag to select whether you're encoding an array.

   In `handle_start`, you first increment the element count of the current container—an array within an array must be counted as an element of its parent, not of itself. Then, you allocate space for a new container structure (using ordinary `malloc`), link it into the state as the new current container, and initialize its count to zero. Crucially, you also memorize the current index position of the `ei_x_buff` so you can locate this point in the output buffer later ❶. When this is done, you insert a header for a tuple or a list depending on whether you're building an array or a map, respectively ❷. Because you don't yet know how many elements the container will have, a dummy value of 1 is used for now.

   When `handle_end` is called, you know the final element count of the container. You then need to update the header you created previously with this number. You do this by calling `ei_encode_tuple_header` (or `ei_encode_list_header` for a list) with a pointer to the start of the current `ei_x_buff` buffer together with the previously saved buffer position from the container structure and the element count ❸. The `ei_encode_` functions differ from the `ei_x_encode_` functions in that they leave all the memory management to you. Hence, this call doesn't affect the current index position of the `ei_x_buff` structure—it only overwrites the old dummy header you inserted before. For the end of a list, you also need to insert the final empty list element by calling `ei_x_encode_empty_list`—this is inserted after the last encoded element of the list, not immediately after the header. The state of the output buffer at this point is illustrated in figure 12.4.

   Finally, you unlink the container structure from the state and free the memory ❹.

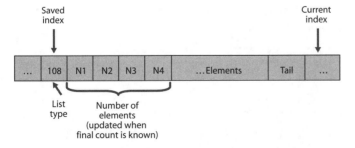

Figure 12.4   Back-patching the list header with the final length. The saved index points to the start of the list header, while the current index of the dynamic `ei_x_buff` points to the first byte after the tail of the list.

Phew! That was a lot, but we wanted to show a complete example of how to integrate a real-world library with Erlang. Fortunately, only a small part of the code needs to be modified when you implement the linked-in driver version in the next section, so the effort spent in making the code well-structured will pay off. But now, it's time to compile the code and try it out.

12.2.3 *Compiling and running the code*

You compile your src/*.erl files to ebin/*.beam files as normal. For the C code, you need to compile the file c_src/jp_prog.c to an executable file priv/jp_prog so the Erlang code that opens the port (see section 12.2.1) is able to find it and run it. We also assume here that you've written a front-end API module named json_parser that exports a function like the following:

```
parse_document(Data) ->
    jp_server:parse_document(Data).
```

To compile the C code using the gcc compiler, run the following from your command line:

```
$ gcc -o ./priv/jp_prog -I${OTPROOT}/lib/erl_interface-3.6.5/include
➥ -I${YAJLROOT}/include -L${OTPROOT}/lib/erl_interface-3.6.5/lib
➥ -L${YAJLROOT}/lib ./c_src/jp_prog.c -lei_st -lyajl
```

This assumes you've set the OTPROOT environment variable to the path of your Erlang installation (typically /usr/lib/erlang; you can call code:root_dir() in Erlang if you don't know what the path is) and the YAJLROOT variable to the path of your YAJL installation. (If you downloaded and built YAJL but didn't install it, the path will be something like lloyd-yajl-1.0.9-0/build/yajl-1.0.9/.) Note that you must both specify -I flags for the header files of Erl_Interface and YAJL, as well as -L flags for where to find the link-time library code and -l flags for the names of the libraries to link. Furthermore, the order of the source files and library files on the command line is significant.

You should now have an executable file jp_prog in the priv directory. This isn't so simple to test directly from the command line, because of the requirement that all input must be preceded by a 4-byte length header—it's easier to run it from Erlang. But in order to start jp_prog, the system must be told where to find the load-time YAJL library. If you didn't install YAJL in a standard location, you can set the LD_LIBRARY_PATH variable as follows:

```
$ export LD_LIBRARY_PATH=${YAJLROOT}/lib
```

If you're running on Mac OS X, your system uses DYLD_LIBRARY_PATH instead of LD_LIBRARY_PATH:

```
$ export DYLD_LIBRARY_PATH=${YAJLROOT}/lib
```

Then, you can start Erlang, start the json_parser application, and try parsing some JSON text. (Remember to include the directory name json_parser in the -pa flag so code:priv_dir/1 can identify the application directory; see section 12.2.1.)

```
$ erl -pa ../json_parser/ebin
...
1> application:start(json_parser).
ok
2> Doc = <<"[null, true, {\"int\": 42, \"float\": 3.14}]">>.
...
3> json_parser:parse_document(Doc).
{ok,{undefined,true,[[{<<"int">>,42},{<<"float">>,3.14}]]}}
4>
```

It works! Note that `null` has been translated to `undefined`, that the key strings in the map are represented as binaries, and that the outermost JSON array is represented as a tuple in Erlang, whereas the map is represented by a list of key/value tuples.

The integration with the C library is finally complete and works as it should. But in production, you find that when the servers are under heavy load, the marshalling and unmarshalling and the communication over pipes takes more time than you'd like. Fortunately, you can do something about that: you can convert the program to run as a linked-in driver.

12.3 Making a linked-in driver

Creating a linked-in driver should almost never be the first step you take when interfacing with foreign code. But at this point, you already have an implementation of a port connected to an external program that has been proven to be stable—it just doesn't seem to be efficient enough. It's time to consider moving to a linked-in driver.

The parser logic of your C code is already in working order, and you don't need to change it. You just need to take that logic and wrap it up in such a way that Erlang can link it in, start it, and talk to it directly. This means you'll be replacing the `main` function with a callback function that conforms to the `erl_driver` API, and creating some additional support structures and functions that are needed for linked-in drivers. But first, let's look at what makes linked-in driver code different from code in external programs.

12.3.1 Understanding linked-in drivers

As we said in section 12.1.2, linked-in drivers have the same look and feel as plain ports, but the underlying mechanism is different. A normal, external port program communicates with Erlang over standard I/O, whereas in a linked-in driver, data arrives via one or more callback functions that you define. The function may act on the data and then output a result back to Erlang. As with external programs, the same linked-in driver code can be activated any number of times for separate port instances that may have overlapping lifetimes. Because all these instances execute within the memory of the Erlang VM, possibly running as different threads, the driver code must be designed to be *reentrant*—executable by multiple simultaneous callers—and must not depend on global variables or locks.

There are two types of long-lived data in a C program or library. The first type is global variables, or *external variables* in C terminology. These are variables defined outside of any function, and they exist for the duration of the program, or as long as the library is loaded. The problem is that if there may be several concurrent callers of the code, there is still only one set of global variables, and the callers overwrite each other's data, causing corruption or crashes.

For example, let's say you want to write a simple port driver that increments a counter and returns the current value. If you don't think about reentrancy, you may use a global C variable to hold the counter. This works as long as there's only a single caller at a time. But suppose a user needs five such counters and starts five ports running the same driver code. Unfortunately, these five instances will stomp all over each other

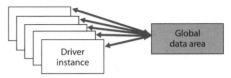

Figure 12.5   Nonreentrant linked-in driver code using shared global memory. Each driver instance tries to use the same memory area for its data, usually ending in a crash.

by incrementing the same global variable, producing odd results. This sharing of driver state is illustrated in figure 12.5.

The other type of long-lived data is dynamically allocated memory. If the library requires that each caller personally allocates the memory needed to service its call, then it doesn't matter how many simultaneous callers there are: they won't overwrite each others' working memory. This is what you want for a linked-in driver. We'll refer to this memory and its contents as the *instance-specific data*. In the example of the counter driver, if each instance has its own data area for the counter variable, you should get the behavior that users expect: for each port they open, a separate counter is maintained, and the counters don't interfere with each other. This is illustrated in figure 12.6.

You'll typically allocate this memory in the initialization phase of the driver, but you may also allocate memory dynamically as needed. Erlang's `erl_driver` API contains support functions such as `driver_alloc()` and `driver_free()` specially for managing memory in linked-in driver code.

Having discussed this, it's time to get on with the implementation. Most of the code that you wrote for the external program can be reused as-is in the linked-in driver. The only thing that needs to change is the bridge between Erlang and the C code.

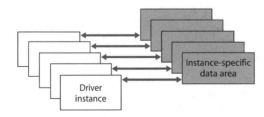

**Figure 12.6
Reentrant linked-in driver code using only instance-specific data. Each instance of the driver has its own working memory and isn't affected by the others.**

12.3.2 *The C side of the driver*

Previously, the C code was a normal standalone program with a `main` function, reading from the standard input and writing to standard output, both of which were connected to the port on the Erlang side. In the linked-in driver, the C code will run within the same address space as the Erlang runtime system, and the communication will be performed by a set of callback functions that the Erlang VM can call directly. This uses the `erl_driver` API, which is described in the ERTS Reference Manual section of the Erlang/OTP documentation.

The concrete details that we'll talk about in this section deal mostly with the bridge between the Erlang VM and the C code. Let's copy the c_src/jp_prog.c file of the previous section to a new file c_src/jp_driver.c and start modifying it. First, all linked-in driver code needs to include the erl_driver.h header file:

```
#include <erl_driver.h>
```

On the other hand, you won't need the `BUFSIZE` and the `ERR_...` definitions anymore, because no standard I/O and no exit status will be used in the linked-in driver. This also means that the functions `write_packet`, `read_bytes`, `read_packet`, and `main` can all be deleted.

Next, you'll need some new definitions for using the `erl_driver` API. These are shown in the following listing.

Listing 12.8 c_src/jp_driver.c: `erl_driver` definitions

```
static ErlDrvData drv_start(ErlDrvPort port, char *command);
static void drv_stop(ErlDrvData handle);
static void drv_output(ErlDrvData handle, char *buf, int sz);

static ErlDrvEntry jp_driver_entry = {                        ←┐  Driver entry
    NULL,                             /* init */              ❶  structure
    drv_start,                        /* start */
    drv_stop,                         /* stop */
    drv_output,                       /* output */
    NULL,                             /* ready_input */
    NULL,                             /* ready_output */
    "jp_driver",                      /* driver_name */
    NULL,                             /* finish */
    NULL,                             /* handle (reserved) */
    NULL,                             /* control */
    NULL,                             /* timeout */
    NULL,                             /* outputv */
    NULL,                             /* ready_async */
    NULL,                             /* flush */
    NULL,                             /* call */
    NULL,                             /* event */
    ERL_DRV_EXTENDED_MARKER,          /* ERL_DRV_EXTENDED_MARKER */
    ERL_DRV_EXTENDED_MAJOR_VERSION,   /* ERL_DRV_EXTENDED_MAJOR_VERSION */
    ERL_DRV_EXTENDED_MAJOR_VERSION,   /* ERL_DRV_EXTENDED_MINOR_VERSION */
    ERL_DRV_FLAG_USE_PORT_LOCKING     /* ERL_DRV_FLAGs */
};
```

```
DRIVER_INIT(jp_driver)                               Tells Erlang
{                                               ❷   about driver
    return &jp_driver_entry;
}

typedef struct {                                     Structure for
  ErlDrvPort port;                              ❸   instance-specific data
} drv_data_t;
```

This starts with declarations of the callback functions that you implement further down. After that, you need to tell the Erlang VM about your callbacks. You do so by creating and filling in an ErlDrvEntry structure with pointers to the functions you've implemented, and NULL for all the other callbacks ❶. This structure is the key to your driver code. Most of the fields are pointers to a callback function that you can implement if you want to make use of it. In this case, you only fill in the callbacks start, stop, and output. You also need to fill in one other important field: driver_name. This lets Erlang identify which ErlDrvEntry structure you're referring to when you open the port; section 12.3.4 will show how this works.

You use the DRIVER_INIT macro to register the structure with the Erlang VM. The name given as the macro argument must be the same as the one used in the structure, but without quotes. The body following the macro should return a pointer to the structure ❷.

Finally, you define the structure that holds the instance-specific driver data as showed in figure 12.6. This holds the information that your driver needs to remember from one callback invocation to the next, much like the state record in a gen_server ❸. For this example, only the Erlang port is stored here so your code knows where to send the output. Typically, you allocate memory for this structure in the start callback of the driver, which should return a pointer to the structure, cast to the special pointer type ErlDrvData. This ErlDrvData pointer is then passed as an argument from the Erlang VM to the other driver callback functions so you always have access to it.

PORT DRIVER CALLBACKS

Some of the driver callback functions are life cycle functions, like start and stop, called when a port using the driver is opened or closed. Others are called when data from the Erlang side is available. Drivers may implement over a dozen different callback functions, but fortunately, you don't have to implement all of them. Most linked-in drivers implement the start and stop functions, and possibly init, but implement only the communication functions they need.

In this example, you only need the output communication function. Note that for all except the start function, the first argument to every callback is the ErlDrvData handle returned by start.

Table 12.2 lists all the available callbacks. As you can see, there are many possibilities, although you'll probably never use all these callbacks in the same driver.

For more information about these callback functions, see the documentation for driver_entry in the ERTS Reference Manual.

Table 12.2 The available `erl_driver` callback functions. You implement only the ones that are needed for your driver and leave the rest as `NULL`.

Callback	Description
init	Called at system start-up for statically linked drivers, and after loading for dynamically loaded drivers.
start	Called when `open_port/2` is invoked.
stop	Called when the port is closed.
output	Called when output is available from some Erlang process to the port. Not used if the `outputv` callback is defined.
ready_input	Called when input is available from one of the driver's handles. Used for asynchronous I/O.
ready_output	Called when output is possible to one of the driver's handles. Used for asynchronous I/O.
finish	Called before the driver is unloaded. Only used for dynamically loaded drivers.
control	Like an `ioctl` for drivers. Called when `port_control/3` is invoked from Erlang.
timeout	Called when one of the drivers' timers triggers.
outputv	Called when someone writes to the port from Erlang. If this callback isn't defined, the `output` callback is used instead to handle writes.
ready_async	Called after an asynchronous `driver_async` call has completed.
flush	Called when the port is about to be closed and data in the driver queue needs to be flushed before `stop` can be called.
call	Much like the `control` callback, but uses Erlang's external term format for input and output.
event	Called when an event selected by `driver_event()` has occurred.

MEMORY MANAGEMENT

One thing needs to change, now that your code will be running in the memory space of the Erlang VM: you should no longer use the standard library functions `malloc` and `free` in C to manage memory. When writing a linked-in driver, you should use the `erl_driver` library functions `driver_alloc()` and `driver_free()` instead. Fortunately, the YAJL library is flexible enough that it has a mechanism for telling it which functions to use when it needs to allocate memory. All you need to do is write wrappers that can be used by YAJL around the three functions `driver_alloc()`, `driver_realloc()`, and `driver_free()`, and then fill in a structure with pointers to these functions. This is shown in listing 12.9.

> **Listing 12.9   c_src/jp_driver.c: YAJL memory-handling callbacks**

```
static void *alloc_func(void *ctx, unsigned int sz)
{
  return driver_alloc(sz);
}

static void *realloc_func(void *ctx, void *ptr, unsigned int sz)
{
  return driver_realloc(ptr, sz);
}

static void free_func(void *ctx, void *ptr)
{
  driver_free(ptr);
}

static yajl_alloc_funcs alloc_funcs = {
  alloc_func,
  realloc_func,
  free_func,
  NULL
};
```

All these functions receive a context pointer as the first argument, which you specify as the last element in the structure. (Don't confuse this with the context pointer that the other YAJL callbacks receive; they may be the same, but only if you've set them up in that way.) You won't need any context here, though, so you should leave the last field of the structure as NULL. The only remaining thing is to tell YAJL to use these alternative allocation functions. Recall that in the parse_json function, you called yajl_alloc like this:

```
yh = yajl_alloc(&callbacks, &cfg, NULL, st);
```

The argument you gave as NULL is the one used to specify the yajl_alloc_funcs structure. You now need to change this call to the following

```
yh = yajl_alloc(&callbacks, &cfg, &alloc_funcs, st);
```

and YAJL will happily use the driver_alloc functions instead of malloc.

Two more places in your code need to be changed with respect to memory management. Change the handle_start callback function

```
container_t *c = malloc(sizeof(container_t));
```

to

```
container_t *c = driver_alloc(sizeof(container_t));
```

And the handle_end function

```
free(c);
```

should now be

```
driver_free(c);
```

Using the `driver_alloc` functions instead of `malloc` ensures that the memory management is done in a thread-safe, reentrant way, using the specially tailored memory allocation routines of the Erlang VM.

SENDING DATA BACK TO ERLANG

When the linked-in driver wants to send data back to the Erlang node as output from the port to the port owner process, it uses the `driver_output` API function provided by `erl_driver`. This writes the specified buffer to the port specified in its first argument. To give the `process_data` function access to the port (stored in the instance-specific driver data structure), it should take a pointer to this data structure as a parameter. This means you need to change its definition from

```
static void process_data(unsigned char *buf)
```

to

```
static void process_data(drv_data_t *d, unsigned char *buf)
```

Then, at the end of the function body, change the call

```
write_packet(st.x.buff, st.x.buffsz, stdout);
```

to

```
driver_output(d->port, st.x.buff, st.x.buffsz);
```

By now, you're almost done with converting the code to run as a linked-in driver. Only the actual driver callback functions remain to be implemented.

THE DRIVER CALLBACK IMPLEMENTATIONS

Finally, we come to the implementation of the three callbacks you'll be using: `start`, `stop`, and `output`, shown in the following listing.

> **Listing 12.10   c_src/jp_driver.c: `erl_driver` callbacks**

```
static ErlDrvData drv_start(ErlDrvPort port, char *command)
{
  drv_data_t *d = (drv_data_t *)driver_alloc(sizeof(drv_data_t));
  d->port = port;
  return (ErlDrvData)d;
}
static void drv_stop(ErlDrvData handle) {
  driver_free((char *)handle);
}
static void drv_output(ErlDrvData handle, char *buf, int sz)
{
  process_data((drv_data_t *)handle, (unsigned char *)buf);
}
```

The first is `drv_start`, which is called when a driver instance is started—that is, when a port is opened using this driver. It creates the instance-specific data structure that the rest of the functions use and stores the Erlang port identifier in it. The pointer to this data structure is cast to the type `ErlDrvData` and returned as the result.

Next, `drv_stop` is called when the port is closed; it de-allocates the instance-specific data structure again, using `driver_free`. In a more complex linked-in driver, it's likely that your `start` callback would do things like starting threads, allocating and initializing resources, and so on. Usually, you'll then do the corresponding de-allocation of resources and tearing down of threads in the `stop` callback.

The `drv_output` function is the only communication callback used in this example. Behavior-wise, it corresponds to the `main` function in the external program in section 12.2, but the method of communication between this code and the Erlang VM has changed. Instead of using byte streams between two separate operating system processes, the Erlang VM calls this function directly, and the marshalling and unmarshalling take place in the same address space as the VM itself. There is also no need for a handler loop; the Erlang VM calls this code on demand whenever data is sent to the port, and you only have to pass a pointer to the data on to your `process_data` function, along with the pointer to the instance-specific data that you added as an extra parameter to `process_data`.

Compare your new code with the program from the previous section. Apart from the communication, the rest of the code is exactly the same. This allows you to pick the approach that works best for your application: an external program is safer but not as efficient. A linked-in driver is faster, but it has the potential to crash the entire VM. In either case, it's not too difficult to rewrite the code to use the other method, if the code is already well-structured.

12.3.3 *Compiling the driver code*

The jp_driver.c file needs to be compiled to a shared library (a *shared object* in UNIX terminology, or a *dynamic-link library* in Windows). This means you have to specify some different flags to `gcc`. From the command line, run the following:

```
gcc -o ./priv/jp_driver.so -fpic -shared -I${OTPROOT}/erts-5.7.5/include
  -I${OTPROOT}/lib/erl_interface-3.6.5/include -I${YAJLROOT}/include
  -L${OTPROOT}/lib/erl_interface-3.6.5/lib -L${YAJLROOT}/lib
  ./c_src/jp_driver.c -lei_st -lyajl
```

On Mac OS X, you need to specify the flags `-bundle -flat_namespace -undefined suppress` instead of `-shared`:

```
gcc -o ./priv/jp_driver.so
  -fpic -bundle -flat_namespace -undefined suppress
  -I${OTPROOT}/erts-5.7.5/include
  -I${OTPROOT}/lib/erl_interface-3.6.5/include -I${YAJLROOT}/include
  -L${OTPROOT}/lib/erl_interface-3.6.5/lib -L${YAJLROOT}/lib
  ./c_src/jp_driver.c -lei_st -lyajl
```

Compare this to the command line you used in section 12.2.3. Apart from the names of the source file and target file (c_src/jp_driver.c and priv/jp_driver.so, respectively), you now also need to specify the `-fpic` and `-shared` flags and the include path `${OTPROOT}/erts-5.7.5/include` for the erl_driver.h header file. The .so extension is standard for shared libraries on most UNIX-like platforms; on Windows, it's .dll.

You've now finished migrating the C side of the code to run as a linked-in driver. This mostly involved writing some wrapper code and changing the way you exchange data with the Erlang VM. Next, you need to make some adjustments to the Erlang code.

12.3.4 *The Erlang side of the driver*

A few things need to change on the Erlang side in order to use a linked-in driver. The OTP application structure will remain unchanged, but the parts of the gen_server that manage the port must be modified.

Your existing implementation of jp_server (see section 12.2.1) makes a call to open_port({spawn, Name}, Options}) where Name is the path of an executable file. The Erlang VM then takes care of starting the external program and connecting its standard input and output streams to the port, and closing the port in case the external program dies. It couldn't be simpler.

When you use a linked-in driver, the command for starting the port looks the same, but this time you're responsible for making sure that the C library has been loaded and linked. The new code for ensuring that the library is loaded and opening the port looks like this:

```
case erl_ddll:load(PrivDir, "jp_driver") of
    ok    -> ok;
    Other -> exit(Other)
end,
open_port({spawn, "jp_driver"}, [binary])
```

The primary concern here is locating the actual shared library file and loading it. As before with the external executable program, you should place the library file in the application's priv directory (or a subdirectory). This convention makes it easy to locate the directory by calling code:priv_dir(AppName); see section 12.2.1.

To load a shared library, you call erl_ddll:load(Path, Name) (note: two ds) where Path is the path to the directory of the library file, and Name is the name of the file itself *without extension* (usually .so or .dll). The filename must match the one you used in the driver_name field of the ErlDrvEntry struct. If the call returns ok, it's all right to proceed and open the port. For a linked-in driver, there's no point in using the exit_status port option (and you no longer need the handle_info callback code for handling exit status messages). Also, the {packet,N} option shouldn't be used—the erl_driver API already tells you the size of the data. Other than that, the call to open_port looks almost the same as for an external program, but the name you specify is no longer the path of a file, but a string used to identify the loaded driver.

If you've compiled the C code as described in section 12.3.3, you should now be able to test your linked-in driver implementation. The procedure for running Erlang, starting the json_parser application, and calling json_parser:parse_document/1 should be exactly the same as in section 12.2.3. Users of your parser application shouldn't notice any difference in behavior except for the increase in speed.

This completes the migration of the JSON parser from running as an external program to a linked-in driver. Instead of communicating over standard I/O, data is exchanged via API calls in C. This eliminates the passing of data across process boundaries and speeds up the communication between Erlang and the foreign code. In this case, that gives you the additional speed you need, which makes the Erlware people happy.

12.4 Implementing the parser as a NIF

NIFs are a new addition to Erlang, and they use a different approach than port-based interfaces. Like port drivers, they're based on a C API using a few callbacks; but on the Erlang side they look like normal Erlang functions and don't involve ports. The erl_nif API has its own functions for passing data structures between Erlang and C and doesn't use the external term format. This means much less code can be shared between the NIF implementation and the port driver. The advantages are speed and ease of implementation.

In this example, you'll implement the interface to the JSON parser library as a NIF. Let's get started with the Erlang side of implementing the NIF code, to get an idea of what you'll be doing.

12.4.1 The Erlang side of the NIF

When you implement the JSON parser interface as NIFs, you'll no longer need a gen_server to hold an open port—all the functionality will be provided directly from the module json_parser. There'll be no need to start the application before it can be used, and there's no supervision tree. Thus, you can get rid of the jp_app, jp_sup, and jp_server modules. The application will be a simple library application, and you can simplify the file ebin/json_parser.app to the following:

```
{application, json_parser,
 [{description, "JSON parser (using NIFs)"},
  {vsn, "0.1.0"},
  {modules, [json_parser]},
  {applications, [kernel, stdlib]}
 ]}.
```

All your Erlang code goes in the json_parser module, and you need to do only a couple of small things. First, you must implement a function that loads the shared object. This is done as follows:

```
init() ->
    case code:priv_dir(?APPNAME) of
        {error, _} ->
            error_logger:format("~w priv dir not found~n", [?APPNAME]),
            exit(error);
        PrivDir ->
            erlang:load_nif(filename:join([PrivDir, "jp_nifs"]), 0)
    end.
```

Calling erlang:load_nif(Path, LoadInfo) loads the shared library file specified by Path (without file extension), links it in, and makes the NIFs that it contains available as normal Erlang functions. The `LoadInfo` argument is passed to the `load` callback (explained in a moment) and can be used for things like version upgrade handling. In this case, just pass 0.

Second, you don't want to make your users have to call the `init()` function whenever they want to use your NIFs. That these functions are written as NIFs should be an implementation detail, invisible to users. Fortunately, you can fix that by using the module attribute `-on_load (...)` that was added to Erlang along with the `erl_nif` API. The following declaration specifies that the `init/0` function should be called automatically when the module is loaded by the Erlang VM:

```
-on_load(init/0).
```

This ensures that the NIFs are available whenever the Erlang module they belong to has been loaded, hiding the NIFness of the functions from the users.

Finally, you must provide exported stub functions for the NIFs you implement—in this case, the `parse_document/1` function:

```
parse_document(Data) ->
    erlang:nif_error(nif_not_loaded).
```

When the NIF library is loaded, the NIF implementations will override the Erlang versions.

> ### Using erlang:nif_error/1 in stub functions
> The built-in function `erlang:nif_error/1` used here has two purposes: First, if the function is called before the NIF library has been loaded, it generates a runtime error. In this respect, `erlang:nif_error/1` behaves exactly like `erlang:error/1`. Second, it indicates to code-analysis tools such as Dialyzer that the real behavior of the function (when the NIF library is loaded) isn't found by looking at the Erlang code. Without this information, Dialyzer would draw the conclusion that this function always throws an exception and would warn you that your attempts to call it won't work. For this reason, you should always use `erlang:nif_error/1` in the body of your NIF stub functions.

With that in place, all you need to do is to create the shared library priv/jp_nifs.so to be loaded by `json_parser:init()`.

12.4.2 The C side of the NIF

Start by copying the file c_src/jp_driver.c that you implemented in section 12.3 to a new file c_src/jp_nifs.c. They will have a lot in common, but a number of things need to be modified.

First, instead of including the header files erl_driver.h and ei.h at the start of the code, you must include the erl_nif.h header file:

```
#include <erl_nif.h>
```

You should also delete the functions `drv_start`, `drv_stop`, `drv_output`, and `make_error`, as well as the `jp_driver_entry` structure, the `drv_data_t` structure, and the use of `DRIVER_INIT`.

THE ERLNIFENV ENVIRONMENT

In the linked-in driver, you had to define your own data structure to hold instance-specific information. Here, the Erlang VM passes a pointer to an `ErlNifEnv` object to your C functions, and you must use this pointer as a handle in most `erl_nif` API functions that you call. (The `erl_nif` API is documented in the ERTS Reference Manual section of the Erlang/OTP documentation.) To make the handle available to the YAJL parser callback functions, you need to store it in your `state_t` structure. For reasons that will be clear later, you now also need to keep a flag in the state structure to signal whether the previous thing seen by the YAJL parser was the key in a key/value pair. Thus, you should add these two lines to your `state_t` structure definition:

```
ErlNifEnv *env;
int key;
```

Also remove the following line

```
ei_x_buff x;
```

because you'll no longer use the `ei` library for building terms. We'll get into detail about that later.

MEMORY MANAGEMENT

In the linked-in driver, you had to use the `driver_alloc` functions in the `erl_driver` library to handle memory allocation. In a NIF, you must instead use the `enif_alloc` functions provided by the `erl_nif` library. These functions need the `ErlNifEnv` as the first argument, so you have to set this up to be passed as the allocation function context. You do so in the `parse_json` function, just before you call `yajl_alloc`:

```
alloc_funcs.ctx = st->env;
```

(This overwrites the field you left as `NULL` in the `alloc_funcs` structure.)

> **NOTE** The NIF API was finalized in Erlang/OTP R14. This book describes the R13 version. The main difference is that the `enif_alloc` allocation functions no longer take an `ErlNifEnv` pointer as the first argument. If you remove this from the function calls, the code will work under R14.

Then, replace the calls to `driver_alloc`, `driver_realloc`, and `driver_free` in the YAJL memory allocation wrappers with the following corresponding calls:

```
enif_alloc((ErlNifEnv *)ctx, sz)
enif_realloc((ErlNifEnv *)ctx, ptr, sz)
enif_free((ErlNifEnv *)ctx, ptr)
```

The memory allocation in the YAJL parser callback functions must also be changed, but we'll look at that later. They'll need to be almost completely rewritten, so there's no point in making small changes to them right now.

KEEPING TRACK OF CONTAINER CONTENTS

One of the main complications with switching from the ei library to the erl_nif library is that you no longer have an ei_x_buff buffer to incrementally build the representations of arrays and maps. The erl_nif functions need to know the sizes of lists and tuples when you create them; you can't back-patch the size as you did in handle_end in listing 12.7. But there is a solution: the erl_nif functions enif_make_tuple_from_array and enif_make_list_from_array let you prepare your own C array of Erlang terms and then turn them into a tuple or list with a single call. All you need to do is manage this array while you're parsing a JSON container. For this purpose, you need to add the two fields arraysz and array to your container_t structure definition:

```
typedef struct container_t {
  int count;    /* number of elements */
  int arraysz;  /* size of elements array */
  ERL_NIF_TERM *array;  /* elements array */
  struct container_t *next;
} container_t;
```

You should also remove the index field, which is no longer required.

THE NIF IMPLEMENTATION FUNCTION

We now come to the C function that implements the NIF. The corresponding Erlang function is parse_document/1 (in the json_parser module), so name this C function parse_document_1. This function replaces the process_data function used in the previous versions of the code. The code for this, together with the declarations needed to hook the NIF into the Erlang VM, is shown in the following listing.

Listing 12.11 c_src/jp_nifs.c: NIF implementation function

```
static ERL_NIF_TERM parse_document_1(ErlNifEnv *env, int argc,
                             const ERL_NIF_TERM argv[])
{
  state_t st;                                        ① Stores NIF
  st.env = env;                                         environment in state
  st.key = 0;
  ERL_NIF_TERM term;                                 ② Sets up dummy
  container_t c = { 0, 1, &term, NULL };                top-level container
  st.c = &c;

  if (argc != 1 || !enif_is_binary(env, argv[0]))
    return enif_make_badarg(env);

  ErlNifBinary bin;                                  ③ Gets address
  if (!enif_inspect_binary(env, argv[0], &bin))         and size of data
    return enif_make_badarg(env);
  const char *err;                                   Runs parser ④
  if ((err = parse_json(&st, bin.data, bin.size)) != NULL) {
    return enif_make_tuple2(env, enif_make_atom(env, "error"),
                      enif_make_string(env, err, ERL_NIF_LATIN1));
  }
  return enif_make_tuple2(env, enif_make_atom(env, "ok"), term);
}
```

```
static ErlNifFunc json_parser_NIFs[] = {
  {"parse_document", 1, &parse_document_1}
};

ERL_NIF_INIT(json_parser, json_parser_NIFs, NULL, NULL, NULL, NULL);
```

⑤ **Lists your NIFs**

All NIF implementation functions have the same signature: they must return an ERL_NIF_TERM object (defined by the erl_nif API), and they always take three arguments. The first, env, is the ErlNifEnv pointer that we described earlier. You store this in your state_t structure for easy access ❶. The second argument, argc, is the number of Erlang arguments passed in the call to the NIF. (This makes it possible for several NIFs on the Erlang side to use the same C function for the implementation.) Finally, the arguments themselves—as many as given by argc—are passed in the array argv.

Previously, you used the ei library to construct the result term in an ei_x_buff buffer. In the NIF implementation, you need to do things differently. The return value from the NIF function should be an ERL_NIF_TERM that represents the Erlang data to be returned. To have a known location where the JSON callbacks can store this term, you need to set up a dummy top-level container_t structure made to hold a single element ❷. The element is stored in the variable term, which acts as a one-element C array; and at the end of the NIF, if all goes well you return the value in term wrapped in a tuple {ok, ...}.

Typically, you want to check that the number of arguments and their individual data types are what you expect before you get on with the real work of the NIF. In this example, the (only) argument should be a binary; if it's not, you report a runtime error by returning a special kind of ERL_NIF_TERM that raises a badarg exception.

To do the actual parsing, you need to find the JSON data embedded in the given binary, with the help of enif_inspect_binary ❸, which you pass an ErlNifBinary structure to be populated. Using the information in the ErlNifBinary, it's then easy to call the parse_json function as before ❹. If this returns an error string, you return a tuple {error, String} back to Erlang.

REGISTERING YOUR NIFS

To inform the Erlang VM about which NIFs your library publishes, you must fill in an ErlNifFunc array with the Erlang function name and arity of each NIF, and the corresponding C function that implements it ❺. You must also use the macro ERL_NIF_INIT to tell the Erlang VM about this array and to which module the functions should belong. (Note that the module name—in this case json_parser—isn't quoted.)

The last four arguments of ERL_NIF_INIT are pointers to NIF life cycle functions that you may use if you need them. (In this case, you can leave them all as NULL.) These are, in the order they occur in the ERL_NIF_INIT call, load, reload, upgrade, and unload. The load function is called when the NIF is loaded into the system, and the unload function is called just before the NIF is unloaded from the system. The reload function is called when the NIF is reloaded; and finally, the upgrade function is called when the NIF is going through a code upgrade at runtime. For this example, you don't need to use any of these.

REWRITING THE YAJL PARSER CALLBACKS

The final thing to do in order to get the JSON parser working as a NIF is to re-implement the YAJL parser callback functions. Previously, you used the `ei` library functions to encode the resulting Erlang data, but now you must instead use the functions in the `erl_nif` API, which work in a different way. This means you must rewrite most of the callback code rather than reuse what you made before. Fortunately, most of it is easily changed; the main differences are in the `handle_map_key`, `handle_start`, and `handle_end` functions.

You'll also need to change the strategy used to track the elements in container structures: instead of counting them, you'll store them in your own temporary arrays. The utility function `count_element` needs to be replaced with the more complicated function `add_element`, shown in the following listing, which takes both the state and the term to be added as input.

Listing 12.12   c_src/jp_nifs.c: add_element utility function

```
static void add_element(state_t *st, ERL_NIF_TERM t)
{
  container_t *c = st->c;
  if (c != NULL) {
    if (c->count >= c->arraysz) {                           ❶ Resizes
      c->arraysz *= 2;                                          array
      c->array = enif_realloc(st->env, c->array, c->arraysz);
    }
    if (st->key) {
      c->array[c->count-1] =                                 ❷ Handles
          enif_make_tuple2(st->env, c->array[c->count-1], t);   complete
      st->key = 0;                                             key/value pair
    } else {
      c->array[c->count] = t;           ❸ Handles other
      ++(c->count);                        elements
    }
  }
}
```

Initially, every container starts at zero elements and has a small pre-allocated array for storing elements as they're added. If the array isn't large enough for the new element, it's first resized ❶. Then, there are two possible actions depending on whether the element that is being added is the value part of a key/value pair, as signaled by the `st->key` field: If it is, then the previously inserted element was in fact the key, and you need to take it back out from the array, create a 2-tuple of the key and the value, and put that tuple back in place of the key. The element count has already been updated in this case, so you shouldn't increment it again, but the `key` flag needs to be reset ❷. If `st->key` isn't set, the operation is much simpler: you only need to insert the term at the current position in the array and increment the element count ❸.

With this mechanism in place, it becomes an easy task to re-implement the simple YAJL callbacks to use the `erl_nif` API, as shown in the following listing.

Listing 12.13   c_src/jp_nifs.c: new simple YAJL callbacks

```c
static int handle_null(void *ctx)
{
  state_t *st = (state_t *)ctx;
  add_element(st, enif_make_atom(st->env, "undefined"));
  return 1;
}

static int handle_boolean(void *ctx, int boolVal)
{
  state_t *st = (state_t *)ctx;
  if (boolVal) {
    add_element(st, enif_make_atom(st->env, "true"));
  } else {
    add_element(st, enif_make_atom(st->env, "false"));
  }
  return 1;
}

static int handle_integer(void *ctx, long integerVal)
{
  state_t *st = (state_t *)ctx;
  add_element(st, enif_make_long(st->env, integerVal));
  return 1;
}

static int handle_double(void *ctx, double doubleVal)
{
  state_t *st = (state_t *)ctx;
  add_element(st, enif_make_double(st->env, doubleVal));
  return 1;
}

static int handle_string(void *ctx, const unsigned char *stringVal,
                         unsigned int stringLen)
{
  state_t *st = (state_t *)ctx;
  ErlNifBinary bin;
  enif_alloc_binary(st->env, stringLen, &bin);
  strncpy((char *)bin.data, (char *)stringVal, stringLen);
  add_element(st, enif_make_binary(st->env, &bin));
  return 1;
}

static int handle_map_key(void *ctx, const unsigned char *stringVal,
                          unsigned int stringLen)
{
  state_t *st = (state_t *)ctx;
  ErlNifBinary bin;
  enif_alloc_binary(st->env, stringLen, &bin);
  strncpy((char *)bin.data, (char *)stringVal, stringLen);
  add_element(st, enif_make_binary(st->env, &bin));       ❶ Signals that key
  st->key = 1;                                                has been inserted
  return 1;
}
```

❶ **Signals that key has been inserted**

Note how all these functions follow the same pattern: they create an Erlang term using enif_... functions and then call add_element to insert it in the current container. Recall that you created a dummy top-level container in the parse_document_1 function (listing 12.11), so there's always a container array to hold the element. Also note how the handle_map_key function first inserts the key as if it was a normal string element and then signals that the last insertion was a key so that the next element is correctly encoded ❶.

Finally, listing 12.14 shows the new container callbacks that handle the start and end of arrays and maps. This is the last piece of code in this chapter, and it's surprisingly straightforward.

Listing 12.14 c_src/jp_nifs.c: new YAJL container callbacks

```
static int handle_start(void *ctx, int array)
{
  state_t *st = (state_t *)ctx;
  container_t *c = enif_alloc(st->env, sizeof(container_t));
  c->next = st->c;
  st->c = c;
  c->count = 0;
  c->arraysz = 32;   /* initial term buffer size */
  c->array = enif_alloc(st->env, c->arraysz);
  return 1;
}

static int handle_start_map(void *ctx)
{
  return handle_start(ctx, 0);
}

static int handle_start_array(void *ctx)
{
  return handle_start(ctx, 1);
}

static int handle_end(void *ctx, int array)
{
  state_t *st = (state_t *)ctx;
  container_t *c = st->c;
  st->c = c->next;
  if (array) {
    add_element(st, enif_make_tuple_from_array(st->env, c->array,
                                               c->count));
  } else {
    add_element(st, enif_make_list_from_array(st->env, c->array,
                                              c->count));
  }
  enif_free(st->env, c);
  return 1;
}

static int handle_end_map(void *ctx)
{
```

❶ Allocates, links, and initializes container

❷ Unlinks container from state

❸ Creates and adds Erlang list or tuple

```
    return handle_end(ctx, 0);
}

static int handle_end_array(void *ctx)
{
    return handle_end(ctx, 1);
}
```

When the start of a JSON array or map is seen, handle_start allocates a new container structure (using enif_alloc), links it into the state, and initializes it. It also allocates an initial, relatively small array to hold the elements of the container, which add_element may resize later ❶.

 When handle_end is called, the array in the container structure holds all the terms of the array or map. All that's needed is to first unlink the container so that the new tuple or list is added to the container above it ❷, create the Erlang term from the array with the help of enif_make_tuple_from_array or enif_make_list_from_array ❸, and add this term to the new current container. After that, the used container can be de-allocated.

12.4.3 *Compiling and running the code*

To compile the C code using gcc, run the following from the command line:

```
$ gcc -o ./priv/jp_nifs.so -fpic -shared -I${OTPROOT}/erts-5.7.5/include
➥ -I${YAJLROOT}/include -L${YAJLROOT}/lib ./c_src/jp_nifs.c -lyajl
```

As with jp_driver, you must use slightly different options on Mac OS X:

```
gcc -o ./priv/jp_nifs.so -fpic -bundle -flat_namespace -undefined suppress
➥ -I${OTPROOT}/erts-5.7.5/include
➥ -I${YAJLROOT}/include -L${YAJLROOT}/lib ./c_src/jp_nifs.c -lyajl
```

Like the port driver code, this must be compiled to a shared library as you did in section 12.3.3, the differences here being the names of the source and target files and the fact that you don't need to include or link with erl_interface. With the file priv/jp_nifs.so in place, the code from section 12.4.1 should now be working. As we noted in that section, everything needed to interface with the JSON library is now contained in the json_parser module, which should have been set up to automatically load your NIF library when the module is loaded. You no longer need to start the application in order to use the NIF functions, as the following example illustrates:

```
$ erl -pa ../json_parser/ebin
...
1> Doc = <<"[null, true, {\"int\": 42, \"float\": 3.14}]">>.
...
2> json_parser:parse_document(Doc).
{ok,{undefined,true,[{<<"int">>,42},{<<"float">>,3.14}]}}
3>
```

That concludes this chapter. You've seen three separate ways of interfacing Erlang with foreign code, each with its advantages and disadvantages. For NIFs, one of the disadvantages is concurrency: a call to a NIF will block the scheduler that calls it, until the

NIF returns. If you're running a typical Erlang system with one scheduler per CPU, it means one of your CPUs is prevented from running other Erlang processes until the NIF call finishes. NIFs are best suited for straightforward library calls that finish quickly. Whether they're a good choice for the JSON parser depends on your system requirements: parsing large documents could degrade the responsiveness of your system, although the throughput is likely to be very good.

12.5 *Summary*

In this chapter, we've looked at three fundamental methods of communicating with foreign code from Erlang. The use of an independent external program connected to a port is by far the preferred solution from a safety standpoint, and many existing UNIX-style programs can be usefully called as they are without any additional C programming, but in some cases speed may be of the essence. When you're convinced that something faster is needed, you may decide to use either a linked-in driver or NIFs, depending on your further requirements—for example, whether you need to perform asynchronous I/O from within the C code.

But programming in C isn't for everyone, and these days a lot of code is written in Java. It would be neat if you could talk to that code directly instead of going via a C layer. In the next chapter, we'll look at a different form of communication with foreign code: Java nodes.

13
Communication between Erlang and Java via Jinterface

This chapter covers

- Using Jinterface to communicate with Java programs
- Building a bridge between Erlang and the HBase database
- Integrating HBase with the Simple Cache application

In the previous chapter, we talked about interfacing between Erlang and foreign code via Erlang's *ports*. That's a useful and general approach, but it isn't the most convenient route to take for every form of interaction. In this chapter, we talk about a different kind of interface, where the foreign code masquerades as an Erlang node and communicates over the Erlang distribution protocol (see chapter 8). Fortunately, the Erlang language implementers have already done a lot of the heavy lifting, providing solid libraries in C and Java to make this relatively easy.

After you rounded out your cache in part 2 of this book and made it suitable for use in enterprise environments, other people and organizations picked it up and started using it for their own projects. One of those groups needs to make the data persistent, rather than keep it in memory-resident Mnesia tables. Their requirement is to preserve all the data they insert into the cache more or less forever. You could switch the Mnesia tables to be disk resident, but it doesn't feel like the right solution for a potentially huge data store. To help them out, you instead decide to add the ability to store the cached objects in an external HBase cluster.

In this chapter, we first outline how the connection to HBase will look. Then, you'll learn how Jinterface works and implement a basic Java node example. In the rest of the chapter, you'll build on those principles to implement a bridge between Erlang and Java, allowing you to store Erlang terms in an HBase table and retrieve them. Finally, you'll integrate this bridge with your Simple Cache application.

HBase

HBase is a database from the Hadoop project (http://hadoop.apache.org/hbase/). It's based on Google's Bigtable database design, and it offers a fast and reliable store for big data sets. Integrating with HBase allows your users to rely on its robust and well understood storage and distribution model and makes it possible for them to store as much data as they want.

Interaction with the HBase system works along these lines: when the cache gets a lookup request, it checks to see if the data is already present in the Mnesia table. If so, it returns the data directly; otherwise, it tries to pull the data from HBase, inserts it in Mnesia, and then returns it. When it gets a write request, the cache writes both to HBase and to Mnesia. Users of this version of the cache use it basically as a fast, memory-resident cache in front of a reliable backing store. The following figure illustrates this relationship.

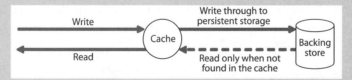

The cache as a front end to a persistent storage. Reads access only the cache, if possible, but writes are always performed on the backing store as well.

You can integrate HBase with Erlang in a number of ways, including accessing the HBase RESTful API over HTTP. Here, you'll make the HBase Java API accessible via Jinterface—a Java library that allows an application written in Java to behave as a node in an Erlang cluster.

This is a book about Erlang and OTP, not about Java and HBase. Consequently, we give you enough information to get a working HBase node up and running as a back end to your cache, but we won't go into details about HBase itself or the Java language.

13.1   Integrating Erlang with Java using Jinterface

Before we dive into HBase and the integration code, let's first look at Jinterface. Jinterface is a library written in Java that makes the Erlang distribution layer available to Java programs. It doesn't do this in an idiomatic Java way, but exposes the Erlang distribution model with as little modification as possible. For our purposes, coming from Erlang to Java, this is a good thing: nearly every Erlang construct has a matching Java class, from nodes and mailboxes to more granular objects like tuples and atoms. Let's go through the most important classes and talk about how they map to Erlang.

13.1.1   The OtpNode class

The Erlang distribution model is based on interconnected nodes. In the Jinterface library, the node concept is represented by the `OtpNode` class. A node object provides the means of connecting to and interacting with other nodes (which may or may not be real Erlang nodes). Just like a normal Erlang node, a node implemented with Jinterface has a node name and optionally an authentication cookie (see section 8.2.4). To start a node in Java, all you need to do is create an object instance of the `OtpNode` class (the following is Java code):

```
OtpNode node = new OtpNode("myJavaNode");
```

It's as simple as that. If the name string contains an @ character, it's used as it is for the full node name: for example, `"myNode@frodo.erlware.org"`. Otherwise, an @ character and the local hostname are added, forming a short name such as `myNode@frodo`. (Recall that Erlang clusters require that all connected nodes use either short names or long names, corresponding to the –sname and –name command-line flags, respectively.) In section 13.1.4, we'll show what you need to do to compile this code.

   If you also want to set a cookie for authorizing connections (see section 8.2.4), you just pass that as an extra argument when you create the node:

```
OtpNode node = new OtpNode("myJavaNode", "secretcookie");
```

`OtpNode` is an interesting class that hides all of the underlying communication, connection handling and so on from you, making it a relatively simple task to hook up your Java code to an Erlang cluster. Next, to do anything with the node, you need to create a mailbox.

13.1.2   The OtpMbox class

Mailboxes are used to interact with other nodes in the cluster. They behave like Erlang's process mailboxes, but they don't belong to any process. In the Jinterface model, a mailbox identifier serves the same purpose as an Erlang process identifier from a communication perspective only—as an address where you can send messages. Jinterface allows you to manage Java threads in any way that you like and gives you direct access to the mailbox abstraction so that your threads can communicate via messages as they please.

You create a mailbox by asking an `OtpNode` object to manufacture one for you. Mailboxes can be created with or without a name. A mailbox with a name is registered on the local node (that is, the Java node) in the exact same way as a registered process on an Erlang node. This means you can send messages to the mailbox using its name, just as for a registered Erlang process. If a mailbox doesn't have a name, you need to know its pid or have a direct reference to the mailbox object in order to interact with it. The following example shows how to create a named mailbox:

```
OtpMbox named_mbox = node.createMbox("myNamedMbox");
```

Creating an anonymous mailbox is even simpler:

```
OtpMbox anon_mbox = node.createMbox();
```

When you have a mailbox, you can use it to send and receive messages. The two fundamental API methods you'll use here are the `send` and `receive` methods of the `Otp-Mbox` class. There are several variations of these methods, but we leave it to you to study the Javadoc documentation to find out more (see www.erlang.org/doc/apps/jinterface/java/).

Sending and receiving data between Java and Erlang of course requires that you marshal the data to and from the native Erlang format. Fortunately, Jinterface provides the tools you need for that.

13.1.3 *Mapping Erlang data structures onto Java*

All data that you want to pass as messages between nodes needs to be represented using the type-mapping classes that Jinterface provides. These classes, listed in table 13.1, are a direct representation of the Erlang data types in Java. All are subclasses of `OtpErlangObject`.

Table 13.1 Java classes in Jinterface for representing Erlang data

Erlang type	Java class
Atom	`OtpErlangAtom`, `OtpErlangBoolean`
Binary, bitstring	`OtpErlangBinary`, `OtpErlangBitstr`
Fun	`OtpErlangFun`, `OtpErlangExternalFun`
Float	`OtpErlangDouble`, `OtpErlangFloat`
Integer	`OtpErlangInt`, `OtpErlangLong`, `OtpErlangShort`, `OtpErlangChar`, `OtpErlangByte`, `OtpErlangUShort`, `OtpErlangUInt`
List	`OtpErlangList`, `OtpErlangString`
Pid	`OtpErlangPid`
Port	`OtpErlangPort`

Table 13.1   Java classes in Jinterface for representing Erlang data *(continued)*

Erlang type	Java class
Reference	`OtpErlangRef`
Tuple	`OtpErlangTuple`
Term	`OtpErlangObject`

The best way to understand how to use these classes is to go through some examples. Take, for instance, the following Erlang term:

```
{some_atom, "Some string", 22}
```

Let's map this onto Java and send it to your named mailbox from the anonymous mailbox. Unfortunately, the Java side of things is more verbose:

```
OtpErlangAtom    anAtom  = new OtpErlangAtom("some_atom");
OtpErlangString aString = new OtpErlangString("Some string");
OtpErlangInt     anInt   = new OtpErlangInt(22);

OtpErlangTuple aTuple =
  new OtpErlangTuple(new OtpErlangObject[]{anAtom, aString, anInt});

anon_mbox.send("myNamedMbox", aTuple);
```

As you can see, the mapping between Erlang and Java is very direct. The main thing to remember is that compound objects like tuples and lists must be built up incrementally from individually mapped objects.

Now, let's take a quick look at transforming data in the other direction, from Erlang into normal Java objects. Suppose you receive the message from the named mailbox (and for simplicity, that you know its structure already, so you don't need to analyze it first):

```
OtpErlangObject msg = named_mbox.receive();

OtpErlangTuple t = (OtpErlangTuple) msg;

String theAtom   = ((OtpErlangAtom)   t.elementAt(0)).atomValue();
String theString = ((OtpErlangString) t.elementAt(1)).stringValue();
int    theInt    = ((OtpErlangInt)    t.elementAt(2)).intValue();
```

The `receive()` method returns the first message in the mailbox or blocks until a message arrives. The result is an `OtpErlangObject`, which you typically cast to some more specific type. As long as you know what you expect to receive, it's not too difficult to convert the Jinterface representation to native Java data. (Exactly what you want to convert it to depends on what you'll do with the data; that part is up to you.)

Remember that your goal is to create an interface between Simple Cache and HBase using Jinterface, as shown in figure 13.1. For that, you need to understand how to communicate between Erlang and Java. The next two sections will go through a complete example, first from the Java side and then from the Erlang side.

Figure 13.1
The ultimate goal of this chapter: making it possible to use HBase tables from Simple Cache via Jinterface and the HBase Java API

13.1.4 *Message-handling example in Java*

The following example code will expect to receive a 2-tuple with a name string and the pid of the sender, and reply with a similar tuple containing a greeting and the pid of the mailbox, as shown in figure 13.2.

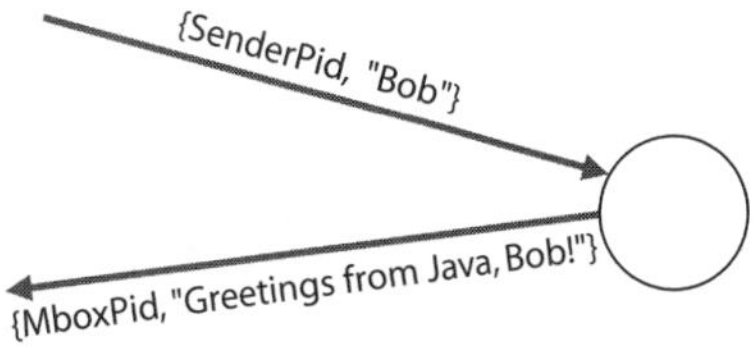

To hold this code, you'll create a source file named JInterfaceExample.java. Before you get started on the code, let's see how to compile it.

Figure 13.2 Communication pattern for the Jinterface example. When receiving a message with a name string, the Java code replies to the sender with a greeting.

COMPILING A JAVA PROGRAM

Java programs (.java files) are compiled with javac to form .class files. Just as erl uses the –pa flag to add locations to the search path, java and javac use the –cp (class path) flag. In Java, you need to give the correct search path for .class files both when you're compiling a program and when you're running it. (The Erlang compiler only needs this path to check behaviour declarations, which is useful but not required.)

You need to tell javac where it can find the Jinterface library that came with your local installation of Erlang/OTP. The path to this library looks something like /usr/local/lib/erlang/lib/jinterface-1.5.1/priv/OtpErlang.jar. Try to find the corresponding OtpErlang.jar file on your computer before you read on.

When you know the path, you can run javac with the following arguments:

```
$ javac -cp /path/to/OtpErlang.jar JInterfaceExample.java
```

If all goes well, that should produce a file named JInterfaceExample.class in your current directory. If the command fails with a "javac not found" error, you probably don't have a Java Development Kit (JDK) installed on your machine. Download and install one from http://java.sun.com/, and then check that javac is found in your system's search path and that the JAVA_HOME environment variable points to the directory where Java was installed.

THE JAVA EXAMPLE CODE

The OTP Jinterface library code belongs to the package com.ericsson.otp.erlang. To use it, your JInterfaceExample.java file must start by importing this package:

```
import com.ericsson.otp.erlang.*;
```

Next, you need to declare the JInterfaceExample class that the code will belong to:

```
public class JInterfaceExample {
  // all the rest of the code goes here
}
```

All of the following code goes between those two { and } characters. First comes the main() method, which is the entry point when you start the program. It creates a class instance and calls its process() method, passing on the argument strings from the command line:

```
public static void main(String[] args) throws Exception {
  if (args.length != 3) {
    System.out.println("wrong number of arguments");
    System.out.println("expected: nodeName mailboxName cookie");
    return;
  }
  JInterfaceExample ex = new JInterfaceExample(args[0],args[1],args[2]);
  ex.process();
}
```

Then, you need two member fields, one for the node and one for the mailbox:

```
private OtpNode node;
private OtpMbox mbox;
```

The node initialization happens in the JInterfaceExample constructor. It looks like this:

```
public JInterfaceExample(String nodeName, String mboxName, String cookie)
throws Exception {
  super();
  node = new OtpNode(nodeName, cookie);
  mbox = node.createMbox(mboxName);
}
```

First, it creates a node with the given node name and security cookie. Then, it uses the node object to create the named mailbox.

Finally, the real work happens in the process() method, shown in the following listing. It handles the incoming messages and sends responses.

Listing 13.1   Jinterface message-handling example

```
private void process() {
  while (true) {
    try {
      OtpErlangObject msg = mbox.receive();
      OtpErlangTuple t = (OtpErlangTuple) msg;                  Deconstructs tuple ❶
      OtpErlangPid from = (OtpErlangPid) t.elementAt(0);
      String name = ((OtpErlangString) t.elementAt(1)).stringValue();
      String greeting = "Greetings from Java, " + name + "!";
      OtpErlangString replystr = new OtpErlangString(greeting);
      OtpErlangTuple outMsg =
        new OtpErlangTuple(new OtpErlangObject[]{mbox.self(),
                                                 replystr});
      mbox.send(from, outMsg);                                         Creates
    } catch (Exception e) {                                     response tuple ❷
        System.out.println("caught error: " + e);
    }
  }
}
```

This method consists of an endless loop `while (true) {...}` whose only purpose is to process incoming messages. If something goes wrong, it prints the error and continues. Messages are expected to be in the form of a 2-tuple with the pid of the sender and a name string. The code deconstructs the tuple ❶ and creates the reply string. Then, a response tuple is created ❷, containing the greeting as well as the pid of the mailbox. Finally, the response is sent back to the originator of the incoming message. All this uses the same basic constructs that we showed you in the previous section.

When you've entered the code in the file JInterfaceExample.java and successfully compiled it, it's time to get the example up and running.

13.1.5 *Talking to the Java node from Erlang*

As we explained in section 8.2.3, Erlang nodes find each other via the EPMD daemon. Nodes based on the Jinterface library are no exception, but Jinterface doesn't start EPMD by itself. Whenever you start an Erlang node, however, it makes sure EPMD is running on the host machine. This is the simplest approach to solving this problem: start an Erlang node before you start any Jinterface-based code. (Even if that Erlang node is stopped again, EPMD will keep running on the host machine until it's killed or the machine reboots.)

Let's start a normal Erlang node using –sname and with the cookie `secret`:

```
$ erl -sname erlangNode -setcookie secret

Eshell V5.7.4  (abort with ^G)
(erlangNode@frodo)1>
```

Next (in another terminal window), get the Java node up and running so you can connect to it from Erlang. Getting this to work is the first major step toward integrating your Simple Cache application with the HBase Java API.

The command line for starting the Java node should look much like the following (all of it on one line), except for the path to the .jar file, which you should change to match the path on your local machine:

```
java -cp .:/path/to/OtpErlang.jar JInterfaceExample javaNode
➥theMailbox secret
```

As with `javac`, the `-cp` flag adds locations to the class search path. (Note in particular that you also add the current directory `"."` here, so that `java` will find your JInterface-Example.class file.) Next comes the name of the class that contains the `main()` method that should be called—in this case, `JInterfaceExample`. The remaining arguments are passed on to `main()`; they represent the node name, the mailbox name, and the cookie the Java node should use.

When the Java program has been started, the nodes should be able to find each other and communicate directly over the Erlang distribution protocol, as shown in figure 13.3.

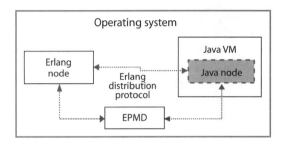

Figure 13.3
An Erlang node and a Java node running on the same machine, using the same EPMD daemon to find each other, and communicating over the Erlang distribution protocol

You can now go back to the Erlang node in the other terminal window and play around:

```
(erlangNode@frodo)1> net_adm:ping(javaNode@frodo).
pong
(erlangNode@frodo)2> {theMailbox, javaNode@frodo} ! {self(), "Eric"}.
{<0.39.0>,"Eric"}
(erlangNode@frodo)3> receive {Mbox, Msg} -> Msg end.
"Greetings from Java, Eric!"
(erlangNode@frodo)4> Mbox.
<5569.1.0>
(erlangNode@frodo)5> Mbox ! {self(), "Martin"}.
{<0.39.0>,"Martin"}
(erlangNode@frodo)6> receive Tuple -> Tuple end.
{<5569.1.0>,"Greetings from Java, Martin!"}
```

From the Erlang side, the Java node behaves just like any other Erlang node, and you use plain message-passing to communicate with it. Note that you use the form {Name, Node} ! Message to send the message to a mailbox registered under a specific name on a specific node without knowing its unique identifier (see section 8.2.5). After you get the first reply from the Java side, you can also use the returned identifier to send further messages.

Now that you understand the basics of communicating with a Java node from Erlang, you can begin implementing the interface between your Simple Cache and HBase. The first step is to install HBase and configure it to work as a backing store for the cache.

13.2 *Installing and configuring HBase*

Before you move on to implementing the actual interface, it's just as well to set up HBase first so you can start testing it immediately when you're done. This section will give a quick introduction to installing and configuring HBase, without going into details. The main thing you need to do is set up the tables needed for storing the cache data. But first: installation.

13.2.1 *Downloading and installing*

You can download HBase from http://hadoop.apache.org/hbase/. It comes as a single tarball file (see section 10.4.1) that you can unpack in a suitable location. You also need to download and unpack the Hadoop Common distribution, found at http://hadoop.apache.org/common/, in order to compile the code in this chapter. The class path to `javac` must include both the hbase-<version>.jar and hadoop-<version>-core.jar files found in these packages.

HBase has one non-obvious requirement: you must have an SSH server (`sshd`) running on your system. On many Linux-based laptop and desktop installations, `sshd` isn't installed by default, and you'll need to install it manually (preferably using the standard package manager for your system). Under Windows, you may want to install OpenSSH for Windows; or if you're using Cygwin, you can set up a Cygwin `sshd` service.

After you've downloaded the HBase tarball, you can unpack it like this:

```
$ tar -xzf hbase-0.20.3.tar.gz
```

After that, you can start up HBase from the directory where you unpacked it. Change directory to the unpacked HBase installation, and run the start script:

```
$ cd hbase-0.20.3
$ ./bin/start-hbase.sh
```

At this point, HBase will connect back to your local machine via SSH to gather certain bits of information that it needs. It may ask you for your password a couple of times.

NOTE If HBase startup fails with the error "Java could not be found," you must edit the conf/hbase-env.sh file and add an `export JAVA_HOME` line that points to your JDK installation path.

When the start script finishes, you can move on to configuration.

13.2.2 *Configuring HBase*

For your current needs, you don't have to do a lot of configuration. You just have to start an HBase shell and create a table that you can use to store the cache data. You start the shell like this (note the space between `hbase` and `shell`):

```
$ ./bin/hbase shell
```

After a couple of seconds, you're presented with some information about your version of HBase, and you get a prompt. The table you want for the cache should hold mappings from unique identifiers to chunks of binary data. The HBase command for creating such a table looks like this:

```
HBase (main):001:0> create 'cache', {NAME => 'value'}
0 row(s) in 2.3180 seconds
HBase (main):002:0> exit
```

This creates a table (a map; see the HBase documentation for details) named `cache` with a single field called `value`. HBase stores everything as binary data, so you don't need to specify the types of the fields as you do in most relational databases.

That wasn't so hard, right? Now that you've configured HBase, it's finally time to begin working on the interface that will let you access it from your Simple Cache application.

13.3   *Building the bridge between Simple Cache and HBase*

The bridge between Erlang and HBase that you'll create here is fairly specific to its intended use as a back end for your cache—it isn't a general HBase binding. That keeps down the amount of work required. Still, it'll be a well-structured solution; and to make things a little more interesting, it'll use a thread pool to handle requests asynchronously.

The bridge will have four major components, as shown in figure 13.4.

- *Erlang code*—Consists of the API functions `put`, `get`, and `delete`, in the module `sc_hbase`. Much as for a `gen_server` implementation, these functions are wrappers around a simple message-based protocol.
- *Java class HBaseConnector*—Implements these operations by talking directly to the HBase Java API, hiding most of the gory details.
- *Main Java class HBaseNode*—For the Java node. Much like the example code in section 13.1.4, it handles incoming requests from the Erlang side and dispatches them.
- *Java class HBaseTask*—Handles each request in its own thread. Uses `HBase-Connector` to perform the requested function, and sends a reply back to the Erlang client.

In the rest of this section, you'll implement these components one at a time in this order. The first is the easiest: the Erlang code, which also defines the protocol that'll be used between Erlang and Java. Let's get started.

13.3.1   *The Erlang side: sc_hbase.erl*

Remember that the purpose of all this is to realize the plan described at the start of this chapter and illustrated in figure 13.1. For each main database operation that Simple Cache performs, a corresponding operation must be made against HBase. These operations are insert, lookup, and delete.

Toward this end, the Erlang HBase API consists of a single module named `sc_hbase` in the `simple_cache` application, with the three functions `put`, `get`, and `delete`. The protocol messages sent to the Java node consist of tuples containing a

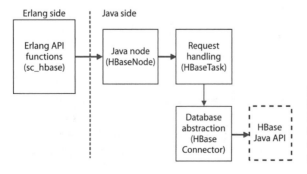

Figure 13.4
Components of the Erlang-HBase bridge: a single module on the Erlang side and three classes on the Java side in order to get a good separation of responsibilities

request tag (put, get, or delete), the pid of the sender, a reference to uniquely identify the request, the database key in question, and (optionally) a value (for put). This protocol should also be easy to handle from the Java side.

All these API functions take the name of the Java node as their first argument. They assume that the mailbox on the Java node is registered under the name hbase_server. (You could start multiple HBase-serving Java nodes with different names; but the mailbox name represents a known entry point, so it seems suitable to hardcode it as part of the protocol.) Having decided this, the implementation of sc_hbase:put/3 is straightforward:

```erlang
put(Node, Key, Value) ->
  Ref = make_ref(),
  {hbase_server, Node} ! {put, self(), Ref, term_to_binary(Key),
                          term_to_binary(Value)},
  receive
    {reply, Ref, ok} ->
      ok
  after 3000 ->
      {error, timeout}
  end.
```

Converts key and value to binaries

The reference created with make_ref() ensures that the receive expression only accepts a reply to this particular request—no stray messages can confuse it. Also note that you convert both the keys and the inserted values to binaries on the Erlang side using term_to_binary/1; this simplifies the Java side, making it oblivious to what kind of data you're storing and what the keys are. (To HBase, keys and data are just sequences of bytes anyway.) Finally, if there is no reply from Java, the operation times out.

The get function is even simpler. It only needs to take the binary value it gets in the reply from Java and convert it back into a term. If not_found is returned instead of a binary, get returns {error, not_found}:

```erlang
get(Node, Key) ->
  Ref = make_ref(),
  {hbase_server, Node} ! {get, self(), Ref, term_to_binary(Key)},
  receive
    {reply, Ref, not_found} ->
      {error, not_found};
    {reply, Ref, Binary} ->
      {ok, binary_to_term(Binary)}
  after 3000 ->
      {error, timeout}
  end.
```

Converts binary back to term

Finally, delete looks much like get, but it always returns ok:

```erlang
delete(Node, Key) ->
  Ref = make_ref(),
  {hbase_server, Node} ! {delete, self(), Ref, term_to_binary(Key)},
  receive
```

```
    {reply, Ref, ok} ->
        ok
    after 3000 ->
        {error, timeout}
    end.
```

That's all. (Remember to add sc_hbase to the list of modules in the simple_cache.app file.) The most important part is the protocol that these functions define: both the request tuples and the expected replies.

Now, let's turn to the more complicated Java side of the HBase bridge. First, you'll make a small wrapper layer around the core interaction with the HBase system: the HBaseConnector class.

13.3.2 *The HBaseConnector class*

Having implemented the Erlang API functions, it seems like a good idea to next implement the corresponding basic functions on the Java side—the rightmost component in figure 13.4—so that you afterward can focus on connecting those two endpoints. The HBase Java API is a general database API and can be somewhat baroque, but all you need here is a way to perform the three operations put, get, and delete, as defined in the previous section. You'll create a class HBaseConnector that implements these operations, so the rest of the code doesn't have to know anything about HBase.

> ### Where to put Java or C code
> To keep the Java code separate from the Erlang code in your application, it's customary to create a separate directory java_src for the .java files, rather than putting them in the src directory. (For C code, the directory name should be c_src.) Compiled C and Java files (DLLs, executables, .class files, .jar files, and so on) are usually placed under the priv directory so they can be shipped along with the release without including the source files.

Create the directory simple_cache/java_src, and then create a new source file HBase-Connector.java in that directory. Because this class will need to access the HBase Java API, you must import the corresponding libraries. You'll also need to use the -cp flag to point out the hbase-<version>.jar file (found in the directory of your unpacked HBase distribution) and the hadoop-<version>-core.jar file (where you unpacked the Hadoop Common distribution), both when you compile the Java code and when you run it later. The source file begins with the following magic words:

```
import org.apache.hadoop.hbase.HBaseConfiguration;
import org.apache.hadoop.hbase.client.*;
import java.util.NavigableMap;
```

Then, define the HBaseConnector class and its constructor:

```
public class HBaseConnector {
  private HTable table;
```

```
public HBaseConnector() throws Exception {
    super();
    table = new HTable(new HBaseConfiguration(), "cache");

}

// the rest of the code goes here
}
```

◁─┐ **Passes
   configuration
   object**

Note that to keep things as simple as possible, the Java classes in this chapter all belong to the empty package. When you compile them, you can keep the generated .class files in the java_src directory for now, along with the sources.

The `HBaseConnector` class has a single member variable `table`, which holds an `HTable` object (a part of the HBase Java API) that provides access to an HBase table. The `HTable` class is highly configurable, and its constructor requires an `HBase-Configuration` object as input. For your purposes here, the default configuration will do nicely, so you only have to pass a fresh configuration object to its constructor along with the name of the database table you want to access (the table named `cache` that you created back in section 13.2.2).

With the initialization complete, you now need to create the `get`, `put`, and `delete` methods. Recall that the HBase table you created is a simple mapping from keys to binary values. First, the `get` method retrieves a value from the database:

```
public byte[] get(byte[] key) throws Exception {
    // Throws NullPointerException if key is not found
    Result result = table.get(new Get(key));
    NavigableMap<byte[], NavigableMap<byte[], byte[]>> map =
        result.getNoVersionMap();
    return map.get("value".getBytes()).get("".getBytes());
}
```

The value is retrieved using the HBase API. Via the `table` object, you perform a `get` request by passing a `Get` object that describes the entry you're interested in. Note that the `key` argument and all other parameters sent to HBase are passed as byte arrays. HBase sees everything you store as sequences of bytes, and makes no assumptions about the types of the data. Any time you interact with HBase, it must be via byte arrays; this is one reason for making a wrapper around the API.

The `get` method returns a `Result` object that you can use to retrieve the actual value from the database. To do that, you need to create a `NavigableMap` object to describe the data to HBase and allow you to access it. Finally, you can fetch the result through the map. All this can be a bit confusing: you take the `NavigableMap` and call its `get` method with the name of your field (as bytes). That gives you another `NavigableMap` object that contains the different values, identified by their domains. In this case, you'll specify an empty domain when you insert objects into HBase, so you need to do the same thing when you retrieve them. Passing an empty byte array to the second `get` finally gives you the byte array representation of the value identified by the key.

The `put` method is simpler, doing basically what `get` does but in reverse:

```
public void put(byte[] key, byte[] value) throws Exception {
  Put put = new Put(key);
  put.add("value".getBytes(), "".getBytes(), value);
  table.put(put);
}
```

You first create a `Put` object, specifying the bytes of the key. Next, you add the value to the `Put` object, specifying the key name and an empty domain, both as byte arrays. Then, you use the `table` object to `put` the value into HBase.

The `delete` method is the simplest of the three:

```
public void delete(byte[] key) throws Exception {
  Delete del = new Delete(key);
  table.delete(del);
}
```

First, you create a `Delete` object with the key you want to delete, and then you pass that to the `delete` method of the `table` object. That's all.

Now that you have a way to perform the basic database operations you need, it's time to move on to the core part of the Java node: the `HBaseNode` class, which connects the Java side to the Erlang side in figure 13.4.

13.3.3　*Java message handling*

The main framework of the Java node looks a lot like the communication example in section 13.1.4. It receives requests as Erlang messages, analyzes and deconstructs them, and processes the requests. To make it more interesting and more asynchronous, it processes each message in a separate Java thread rather than handling only one request at a time. Java isn't like Erlang when it comes to concurrency, so starting a new thread for each request would be too inefficient. Instead, the code uses a thread-pool class provided by the Java standard library. Fortunately, most of the complexity of multithreading is handled by the libraries.

As in the example code, a class represents the main entry point of the node. This initializes the Java node and the mailbox for incoming requests. The node then enters a loop, receiving messages from the mailbox. For each message, it enqueues a task object that processes the request in a separate thread and performs the database

> **Communication bottlenecks**
>
> One thing to be aware of in the current design of this system is that although it uses a thread pool (see listing 13.2), it has only a single `OtpMbox` object. This constitutes a bottleneck for incoming requests. For the purposes of this application, it's acceptable; but it may not be for more demanding applications. Many of the approaches you'd take in Erlang to address the same problem can be used here as well.

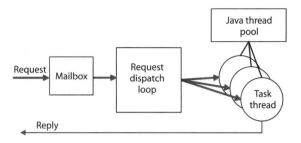

Figure 13.5
Requests are handled in separate threads via a Java thread pool. This makes it possible to process multiple requests simultaneously, increasing the throughput of the system.

operation. After the action is complete, it sends a response back to the caller that originated the request. The flow of data and control is illustrated in figure 13.5.

The main entry point to your Java node is the HBaseNode class (in a new source file java_src/HBaseNode.java). The following listing shows its class definition and constructor and the main method. Compare this to the JInterfaceExample class in section 13.1.4. Here, the mailbox name is fixed, so the constructor takes only two arguments.

Listing 13.2 The HBaseNode class

```
import com.ericsson.otp.erlang.*;                          ← Necessary for using
import java.util.concurrent.*;                         ❶ ExecutorService

public class HBaseNode {
  private HBaseConnector conn;
  private ExecutorService exec;
  private OtpNode node;
  private OtpMbox mbox;

  public HBaseNode(String nodeName, String cookie)
  throws Exception {                                     ❷ Instantiates
    super();                                                HBaseConnector
    conn = new HBaseConnector();              ←
    exec = Executors.newFixedThreadPool(10);   ←           Creates Java
    node = new OtpNode (nodeName, cookie);      ❸        thread pool
    mbox = node.createMbox("hbase_server");
  }

  public static void main(String[] args) throws Exception {
    if (args.length != 2) {
      System.out.println("wrong number of arguments");
      System.out.println("expected: nodeName cookie");
      return;
    }
    HBaseNode main = new HBaseNode(args[0],args[1]);
    main.process();
  }

  // the rest of the code goes here
}
```

In addition to the setup that you did in the JInterfaceExample constructor, you're also creating an instance of the HBaseConnector ❷, which sets up a connection to the HBase server on your local machine, and you create the Java thread pool ❸ that will be used to dispatch requests. (The `ExecutorService` class is provided by the Java standard library. To use it, you need to import some things ❶ from the `java.util.concurrent` package.)

Next, the `main()` method is just like the one in the `JInterfaceExample` class, except that in this case, you don't need the mailbox name as a command-line argument. As before, the main loop of the program is in the `process` method, shown in listing 13.3. This is an endless loop that waits for incoming messages, much like an Erlang/OTP `gen_server`. Each new message is extracted from the mail queue, analyzed, and dispatched to a new `HBaseTask` object in order to be processed. (Note that this code isn't responsible for sending a reply to the caller.)

Listing 13.3 `HBaseNode.process()`

```
// message format: { Action, FromPID, UniqueRef, Key [, Value] }
private void process() {
  while (true) {
    try {
      OtpErlangObject msg = mbox.receive();                      Decomposes message ❶
      OtpErlangTuple t = (OtpErlangTuple) msg;
      String action = ((OtpErlangAtom) t.elementAt(0)).atomValue();
      OtpErlangPid from = (OtpErlangPid) t.elementAt(1);
      OtpErlangRef ref = (OtpErlangRef) t.elementAt(2);
      byte[] key = ((OtpErlangBinary) t.elementAt(3)).binaryValue();
      byte[] value;                                              Creates HBaseTask ❷
      HBaseTask task = null;                                               object
      if (t.arity() == 5 && action.equals("put")) {
        value = ((OtpErlangBinary) t.elementAt(4)).binaryValue();
        task = new HBaseTask(mbox, conn, from, ref, action, key, value);
      } else if (t.arity() == 4 && action.equals("put")) {
        task = new HBaseTask(mbox, conn, from, ref, action, key, null);
      } else if (t.arity() == 4 && action.equals("delete")) {
        task = new HBaseTask(mbox, conn, from, ref, action, key, null);
      } else {
        System.out.println("invalid request: " + t);
        continue;
      }
      exec.submit(task);                                         Submits HBaseTask
    } catch (Exception e) {                                  ❸  object to thread pool
      System.out.println("caught error: " + e);
    }
  }
}
```

If a message has the wrong format, it's handled by printing the error information to the standard output. (Without a properly formed request tuple, you don't know who the sender is, so you couldn't send a reply even if you wanted to.) For a more production-ready implementation, you should use a proper logging service like log4j; but for the purposes of this example, this solution is sufficient.

As in the `JInterfaceExample` code, the message is first decomposed ❶, extracting the message elements and casting them to the types you expect. If something goes wrong, the exception is caught and printed, and the code loops to handle the next message in the queue.

The incoming request tuple may have four or five elements. A `get` or `delete` message will only have four elements, but a `put` message will have five. In the latter case, an `HBaseTask` object is created with a valid data field; in the former case, the `HBaseTask` object has a `null` value as data ❷. If the arity of the tuple is anything other than four or five, an error message is printed, and the next message is handled instead.

Message decomposition in Java versus Erlang

Take a moment to think about how you decompose a message in a language like Java, compared to using a language with pattern matching like Erlang. In Java, it takes almost 10 lines of code to decompose this simple tuple and decide what to do. The corresponding code in Erlang would be

```
case Message of
  {Action, From, Ref, Key} -> ...;
  {Action, From, Ref, Action, Key, Value} -> ...;
end.
```

The difference in clarity and brevity is significant. This isn't to pick on Java in particular, but to underline the power of declarative programming. Concise code tends to have fewer bugs because it's easier to see right away that it's correct.

Finally, if everything works out and an `HBaseTask` object is created to hold the data, it's submitted to the thread pool ❸ in order to process the request asynchronously while the main loop handles more messages. `HBaseTask` is the last of the components in figure 13.4 that you need to implement, and it's not complicated.

13.3.4 The HBaseTask class

All the interesting things happen in the `HBaseTask` class, shown in listing 13.4. It implements the `Runnable` interface in the Java standard library, which means it must have a `run` method that provides the main entry point. In this case, `run` only analyzes the requested action and dispatches to the appropriate handler method. (At this point, the request tuple from the Erlang node has already been decomposed to a form you can easily use.) If the request is a `get`, it's handled by the `doGet` method, `put` is handled by `doPut`, and `delete` by `doDelete`.

Listing 13.4   The HBaseTask class

```
import com.ericsson.otp.erlang.*;

public class HBaseTask implements Runnable {
  private OtpMbox mbox;
  private HBaseConnector conn;
```

```
        private OtpErlangPid from;
        private OtpErlangRef ref;
        private String action;
        private byte[] key;
        private byte[] value;

        public HBaseTask(OtpMbox mbox, HBaseConnector conn,
                         OtpErlangPid from, OtpErlangRef ref,
                         String action, byte[] key, byte[] value) {
          super();
          this.mbox = mbox;
          this.conn = conn;
          this.from = from;
          this.ref = ref;
          this.action = action;
          this.key = key;
          this.value = value;
        }

        public void run() {
          try {
            if (action.equals("get")) {
              doGet();
            } else if (action.equals("put")) {
              doPut();
            } else if (action.equals("delete")) {
              doDelete();
            } else {
              System.out.println("invalid action: " + action);
            }
          } catch (Exception e) {
            System.out.println("caught error: " + e);
          }
        }

        // the rest of the code goes here
      }
```

The methods doGet, doPut, and doDelete perform the requested actions. Any exceptions that occur in these methods are caught and handed by the run method, which then sends an error reply back to Erlang. Let's start by looking at doGet:

```
private void doGet() throws Exception {
  OtpErlangObject result;
  try {
    result = new OtpErlangBinary(conn.get(key));
  } catch (NullPointerException e) {
    result = new OtpErlangAtom("not_found");
  }
  OtpErlangTuple reply = new OtpErlangTuple(new OtpErlangObject[] {
                            new OtpErlangAtom("reply"), ref,
                            result
                         });
  mbox.send(from, reply);
}
```

This gets the value for the given key and sends it back to Erlang as a binary (or sends an atom `not_found` if the lookup fails). Note how the `HBaseConnection conn` object makes it easy to retrieve the value, making this part of the code completely independent of the details of the HBase API. Next, here's the `doPut` method:

```
private void doPut() throws Exception {
  conn.put(key, value);
  OtpErlangTuple reply = new OtpErlangTuple(new OtpErlangObject[] {
                          new OtpErlangAtom("reply"), ref,
                          new OtpErlangAtom("ok")
                        });
  mbox.send(from, reply);
}
```

Again, `doPut` is a mirror image of `doGet`, inserting the value into HBase for the specified key. In this case, a simple `"ok"` is sent back to Erlang as the result. Finally, `doDelete` is similar:

```
private void doDelete() throws Exception {
  conn.delete(key);
  OtpErlangTuple reply = new OtpErlangTuple(new OtpErlangObject[] {
                          new OtpErlangAtom("reply"), ref,
                          new OtpErlangAtom("ok")
                        });
  mbox.send(from, reply);
}
```

That concludes the Java side of the implementation. You should now have a working Java node that provides an interface to HBase for the basic operations `get`, `put`, and `delete`. The only thing left is integrating it with the Simple Cache application.

13.4 *Integrating HBase with Simple Cache*

To make the Simple Cache application use your shiny new Erlang-HBase bridge to store cache data in an HBase table, you need to modify the `lookup`, `insert`, and `delete` functions of the cache so they interact with HBase, as outlined at the start of the chapter. Because you made the code for the cache so well-structured, the only file you need to change is the front-end module simple_cache.erl, as illustrated by figure 13.6. This file should still look much as it did back in listing 6.7 (section 6.4.3), apart from the calls to `sc_event` that you added in chapter 7 to support logging.

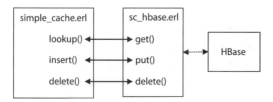

**Figure 13.6
Integrating the sc_hbase.erl module with the
`simple_cache` application. Each of the
`lookup`, `insert`, and `delete` API
functions of the cache need to be modified to
also communicate with HBase.**

First, define the name of the HBase Java node so that you only have a single place to change if you want to rename it later. At the top of the file, after the export declaration, add the following line:

```
-define(HBASE_NODE, 'hbase@localhost').
```

(The node name should be made a proper configurable parameter of the `simple_cache` application, but we leave that as an exercise for you.) After that, you can move on to modifying the access functions. Not a lot needs to be done; only the `lookup` function requires more than a single line of code.

13.4.1 Lookup

First, you must modify `simple_cache:lookup/1` to look up an entry in HBase if it can't find the entry locally (and only then). The new version is shown in the following listing. As before, it relies on `try/catch` to handle errors and report `not_found`, including if the calls to `fetch` and `get` return something other than `{ok,...}`.

Listing 13.5   The new `simple_cache:lookup/1`

```
lookup(Key) ->
    sc_event:lookup(Key),
    try
        case sc_store:lookup(Key) of               Tries local
            {ok, Pid} ->                           lookup
                {ok, Value} = sc_element:fetch(Pid),
                {ok, Value};
            {error, _} ->                          Tries to
                {ok, Value} = sc_hbase:get(?HBASE_NODE, Key),   fetch from
                insert(Key, Value),                HBase
                {ok, Value}
        end
    catch
        _Class:_Exception ->
            {error, not_found}
    end.
```

If the local lookup fails, the function tries to look up the key in HBase. If it's found, the entry is inserted in the cache to make the lookup faster next time. If the HBase lookup fails, the match against `{ok, Value}` fails, and the `try` expression handles it.

That was the hard part; modifying the `insert` and `delete` functions is much simpler.

13.4.2 Insert

All that `simple_cache:insert/2` needs to do is make sure each entry that's inserted in the cache is also inserted into HBase. The new version looks as follows:

```
insert(Key, Value) ->
    case sc_store:lookup(Key) of
    {ok, Pid} ->
        sc_event:replace(Key, Value),
```

```
        sc_element:replace(Pid, Value);
    {error, _Reason} ->
        {ok, Pid} = sc_element:create(Value),
        sc_store:insert(Key, Pid),
        sc_event:create(Key, Value)
    end,
    sc_hbase:put(?HBASE_NODE, Key, Value).
```
|‾ **Inserts into**
 ◁__| **HBase as well**

The only thing added here is a call to `sc_hbase:put/2` when a new value is inserted into the system. The HBase interface doesn't require different approaches depending on whether the key already existed, so you need to add only a single line. But it should be done after the corresponding entry is created in the cache, to avoid a race condition where a simultaneous lookup operation might find that the key isn't yet in the cache but can be retrieved from HBase.

Finally, the `delete` function is similar to the `insert` case.

13.4.3 Delete

When a value is deleted from the cache, it must be deleted from the HBase table as well. The new version of `simple_cache:delete/1` looks like this:

```
delete(Key) ->
    sc_event:delete(Key),
    case sc_store:lookup(Key) of
    {ok, Pid} ->
        sc_hbase:delete(?HBASE_NODE, Key),
        sc_element:delete(Pid);
    {error, _Reason} ->
        ok
    end.
```
|‾ **Deletes entry**
◁__| **from HBase**
◁‾|
 __| **Deletes from**
    cache last

Note that the call to `sc_element:delete/1` must be performed after the call to `sc_hbase:delete/2`, to make sure the value isn't reinserted into the cache by a lookup operation that happens to run concurrently with the delete operation. If you remove the entry from the cache first, a lookup may still be able to find the entry in HBase and put it back in the cache before the delete operation has had time to remove it from HBase.

Assuming you've completed the three Java classes presented in this section (`HBaseConnector`, `HBaseNode`, and `HBaseTask`) and compiled them successfully, it's now time to get things up and running.

13.5 Running the integrated system

Your cache system is no longer all that simple, and you need to ensure that several things are started (and in the right order) for it to work:

- Make sure HBase is started (see section 13.2.1).
- Start one or more contact nodes (at least one on the local machine, ensuring that EPMD is also running before you try to start a Java node). For example: `erl -sname contact1 -detached -setcookie secret`.

- Start the Java node for the HBase bridge, making sure to use the same cookie as the Erlang nodes. This is described in more detail next.
- Start the `simple_cache` system (see section 10.2.6). For example: `erl –sname mynode -pa ./simple_cache/ebin -pa ./resource_discovery/ebin -boot ./simple_cache -config ./sys –setcookie secret`.
- If the nodes can't find each other, check that all of them have been started using the `–sname` flag (assuming your HBase Java node also uses a short name— that is, without any dots in the host part of the node name) and that they all use the same cookie.

Starting the HBase Java node is much like when you started the example node in section 13.1.5, but you need a number of additional Java libraries to run the code for the HBase bridge. In addition to the OTP Jinterface library, the HBase library, and the Hadoop Common library that you needed to compile the code (see section 13.2.1), you also need the following Java libraries:

- Apache Commons Logging, from http://commons.apache.org/logging/
- log4j, from http://logging.apache.org/log4j/
- Apache ZooKeeper from http://hadoop.apache.org/zookeeper/

Luckily, you can find the JAR packages for these libraries in HBase's lib directory, so you don't need to install them individually.

Of course, to find the Java .class files that you've created for the HBase bridge, the Java class path must include the simple_cache/java_src directory, or simple_cache/priv/java if you prefer to keep the generated .class files separate from the .java source files. The command line can get a bit unwieldy, but it should look something like this (all on a single line—we've had to break it here for space reasons):

```
java -cp simple_cache/java_src:/path/to/OtpErlang.jar:/path/to/
➡ hbase-<version>.jar:/path/to/hadoop-<version>-core.jar:/path/to/
➡ commons-logging-<version>.jar:/path/to/log4j-<version>.jar:/path/to/
➡ zookeeper-<version>.jar    HBaseNode hbase secret
```

Here, `hbase` is the node name, which must match the one defined by the `HBASE_NODE` macro in simple_cache.erl (section 13.4); and `secret` is the cookie string for the Java node. If you like, you can set the `CLASSPATH` environment variable for Java instead of using the `-cp` command-line argument each time. Alternatively, you can create a small shell script to run this command.

If everything goes well, you should have an HBase database, a Java node for the Erlang-HBase bridge, and a `simple_cache` Erlang target system, all up and running. You should be able to insert data into the cache and look it up again via the `simple_cache` module, and you should also be able to inspect and manipulate the HBase contents directly via the `sc_hbase` module, as in the following example dialogue:

```
Eshell V5.7.3  (abort with ^G)
(mynode@localhost)1> sc_hbase:get(hbase@localhost, foo).
{error,not_found}
```

```
(mynode@localhost)2> simple_cache:insert(foo, bar).
=INFO REPORT==== 24-Apr-2010::21:25:27 ===
create(foo, bar)
ok
(mynode@localhost)3> simple_cache:lookup(foo).
=INFO REPORT==== 24-Apr-2010::21:25:50 ===
lookup(foo)
{ok,bar}
(mynode@localhost)4> sc_hbase:get(hbase@localhost, foo).
{ok,bar}
(mynode@localhost)5> simple_cache:lookup(17).
=INFO REPORT==== 24-Apr-2010::21:27:17 ===
lookup(17)
{error,not_found}
(mynode@localhost)6> sc_hbase:put(hbase@localhost, 17, 42).
ok
(mynode@localhost)7> sc_hbase:get(hbase@localhost, 17).
{ok,42}
(mynode@localhost)8> simple_cache:lookup(17).
=INFO REPORT==== 24-Apr-2010::21:29:09 ===
lookup(17)
=INFO REPORT==== 24-Apr-2010::21:29:09 ===
create(17, 42)
{ok,42}
(mynode@localhost)9> simple_cache:lookup(17).
=INFO REPORT==== 24-Apr-2010::21:34:49 ===
lookup(17)
{ok,42}
(mynode@localhost)10> simple_cache:delete(foo).
=INFO REPORT==== 24-Apr-2010::21:29:41 ===
delete(foo)
ok
(mynode@localhost)11> simple_cache:lookup(foo).
=INFO REPORT==== 24-Apr-2010::21:29:44 ===
lookup(foo)
{error,not_found}
(mynode@localhost)12> sc_hbase:get(hbase@localhost, foo).
{error,not_found}
```

❶ Automatically caches data found in HBase

❷ Cache lookup succeeds directly

Let's walk through what happens in this dialogue. First, the lookup determines that foo isn't in HBase. You insert foo into the cache, after which you find foo both in the cache and in HBase.

Next, the lookup determines that 17 isn't in the cache. You insert $17 \rightarrow 42$ directly in HBase, after which the cache lookup finds 17 in HBase and inserts $17 \rightarrow 42$ into the cache. In the next lookup, 17 is found directly in the cache. Finally, you remove foo from the cache, after which the lookup no longer finds foo in HBase.

As you can see, everything works just as expected. Note in particular the log info message create(17,42) ❶: it shows that when key 17 isn't found in the cache, it's looked up in HBase (where it was inserted beforehand) and then automatically stored in the cache for future lookups. The following lookup operation ❷ succeeds immediately. Your external users will be pleased.

13.6   *Summary*

You should now have a working knowledge of how to use Jinterface to create a non-Erlang node in Java, interact with it, and integrate it with your system. The same techniques can be used to create a bridge to any other Java library you want to leverage.

You've almost reached the end of this book. It's been a long journey, and we hope you've learned a lot of new things: details of the Erlang language; the use of behaviours via OTP applications, supervision, logging, and event handling; distributed Erlang, Mnesia, and how to make releases; and integration with the outside world through HTTP, ports, drivers, and Jinterface. In the next chapter, we'll round all this off by looking at some techniques for measuring and improving the performance of your code.

Optimization and performance

> *There is no such thing as fast, only fast enough*
>
> —Joe Armstrong

Optimization should only be on your mind when you know you need to shave off those extra milliseconds or kilobytes. That is what the Erlware team needs to do right now. It turns out that having a repository of Erlang software available for download is something that lots of people want. With the improved speed and functionality of the site, thanks in part to the simple cache you've implemented, more and more people are hitting the erlware.org site. Efficiency is once again starting to become an issue. Throwing hardware at the problem isn't an option at the moment, so scaling up horizontally by adding machines isn't a viable approach. The Erlware team must optimize their code to save as many clock cycles as possible.

> **Martin says...**
>
> I remember the first time I met Joe Armstrong, one of the creators of Erlang, back in 2002 at a functional programming conference in the United States. He was filled with tons of great sayings and computer science maxims, some original and some quoted. Many of them stuck with me. One of my favorites was, "Make it work, then make it beautiful, then if you really, really have to, make it fast." He went on to say, "90 percent of the time, if you make it beautiful, it will already be fast. So really, just make it beautiful!"

Your code is already beautiful, which means all that's left is low-level optimization. This chapter aims to give you the tools for optimizing the code you've written in the previous chapters, so that you can assist the Erlware team. We want you to go into this chapter with an understanding that modifying your code for efficiency's sake alone—and possibly sacrificing simplicity, readability, and maintainability—should be done as a last resort and *only* after your code has been made beautiful but still isn't fast enough. This chapter is about that small percentage of cases when making it beautiful doesn't do the trick.

The only way to be successful at performance improvement in general is to be systematic. Some problems may be obvious enough that they practically jump up and wave at you; but beyond that, you need to measure, establish base lines, look for bottlenecks, optimize, and then measure again to see whether performance has improved. In this chapter, we'll discuss the tools and tricks you can employ to get the job done.

We'll begin by discussing how to be systematic about performance tuning, finding what the problem is, and knowing when you've fixed it.

14.1   How to approach performance tuning

Performance tuning has been called an art, and in many respects it is. Some people have great skill at divining bottlenecks and cleverly removing them, but that is largely a result of the intuition that comes with years of practical experience—it isn't something you can easily learn from a book. In this chapter, we'll focus on the science of performance tuning and how to go about it in a methodical manner.

The Erlware group tries to approach the performance tuning problem systematically through the steps shown in figure 14.1. Let's go through these steps in more detail.

14.1.1   Determining your performance goals

Before you begin tuning, you should know when you can say that you're finished. Your goals should have the following characteristics (known by the SMART acronym):

- *Specific*—Clearly defined in terms of, for example, CPU usage or throughput per second.
- *Measurable*—Verifiable through systematic measurement.

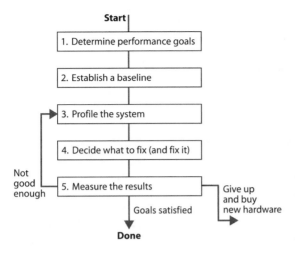

Figure 14.1
The process of performance tuning:
determine your goals, establish a
baseline, profile, optimize, measure again.
Repeat until the goals are satisfied or you
give up.

- *Attainable*—Reasonable to achieve. You should be able to expect to achieve the goals within the limits of the project; otherwise, you've set them too high to start with.
- *Realistic*—Given the current resources and motivation, if the goals are only attainable through tremendous effort by the whole team, they aren't realistic.
- *Timely*—Able to be finished in a predetermined time. Don't leave the tuning effort open ended: setting a time limit focuses your effort and helps you brush away the unimportant.

For example, based on the number of actual hits to the erlware.org website and the transaction volume generated on different parts of the system, the Erlware team decides what the goals for acceptable performance are at this time. They also look at the statistics over the last few months to see the overall trends in traffic, and they take a stab at what traffic will look like six months from now considering the company's current promotional efforts. Based on this, the team sets the goals for the current performance tuning effort.

14.1.2 Establishing a baseline

If your goals are measurable (as they should be), you can establish baselines. Run tests to find out where you currently stand with regard to the metrics for your goals. For example, what are the current CPU consumption and throughput of your system (before you do any tuning)? The broader the baseline, the easier it will be to determine the impact of any changes you make.

14.1.3 Profiling the system

If your measurements show that your goals aren't fulfilled—sometimes it turns out that you didn't have a problem to begin with, at least not where you thought—you need to find out where the time is spent (or the memory or bandwidth is used). Profile the code and look for CPU bottlenecks, memory hogs, lock contention, processes stuck waiting for I/O, or other problem points.

14.1.4 *Decide which problems to attack*

After you've identified what the main problems seem to be, you must decide which ones to attack right now. Perhaps the one that seems to be the biggest overall problem isn't worth tackling at the moment, because it would take a lot of effort (and you're not sure exactly how much you'd gain). There may be other, smaller problems that can be more easily fixed, which could let you achieve your optimization goals for now without embarking on a perilous rewrite of a core component. Pick the issues that seem likely to give the best payoff, considering that you should realistically be able to fix them within the timeframe you have. And don't try to fix them all at once: do them one at a time so that you can see which changes really affect the performance.

14.1.5 *Measure the results*

Rerun the measurements after you've changed the code, and compare to your baseline. Is the new code an improvement? (You'd be surprised how many times an "obvious improvement" to the code has no measurable effect or even turns out to be worse.) If it is, have you reached your stated performance goals? In that case, congratulations—you're finished, for now. Otherwise, go back to step 3 in figure 14.1 and keep profiling, rewriting, and measuring until your goals are achieved (or you run out of time and decide that you need to get more money and buy new hardware).

You can use many tools to measure a system's performance characteristics, from simple logging and other kinds of instrumentation of the code, to various Erlang-specific tools like `etop` and `percept` or the open source project `eper`, to external operating system–specific tools. Most of them fall outside the scope of this book. In this chapter we'll show you how to use the basic tools provided by the Erlang/OTP standard library to profile Erlang code. This is the topic of the next section.

14.2 *Profiling Erlang code*

Profiling is the most reliable method for determining where the performance bottlenecks are in your system. With practice, you can learn to spot typical gotchas and performance pitfalls by just looking at the code; but at the end of the day, tracking down performance bottlenecks usually requires profiling.

In the general sense, *profiling* means gathering statistics about the code as it's running, associating the data with corresponding points in the code. The most typical form of profiling measures where in the code the most time is being spent: those are your main bottlenecks. But time can be measured in different ways: spent CPU time tells you how much real work your program is doing, whereas wall-clock time tells how long you had to wait for the program to finish. If wall-clock time is high but CPU time is low, it means your code is spending most of the time waiting for something else (usually disk or network I/O) instead of working. If CPU time is high, you may be using a bad algorithm (perhaps with quadratic or exponential behaviour). As an approximation of the amount of CPU time spent, some simple profilers only measure the number of times each function has been called or each line of code has been executed. Other things that profilers may measure include memory usage at different points in the code, I/O usage, and the number of processes ready to run. (A program point where few or no other processes tend to be ready to execute could be a synchronization bottleneck, limiting the amount of parallelism in your system.)

Erlang/OTP puts a number of profiling tools at your disposal, including `cover` for code coverage, the `instrument` module for memory-usage analysis, and some new ones like the `percept` tool for concurrency profiling. Here, we'll cover the two main time-profiling tools included with Erlang/OTP: `fprof` and `cprof`. We'll start with `cprof`, for no other reason than that it's the easiest to use.

14.2.1 Counting calls with cprof

The `cprof` tool doesn't provide the same depth of information that `fprof` does, but it's simple and straightforward to use. `cprof` counts function calls. The main reason you'd want to use it instead of `fprof` is that it has minimal impact on the running system (the profiled code becomes about 10 percent slower). This means it's more suitable for analyzing code running live in production, if that should become necessary.

Listing 14.1 shows a small module `profile_ex` containing some code that takes a short time to run but otherwise doesn't do anything interesting. The sole purpose of the code is to give you something to profile. (The cache application is too big to use as an example and isn't particularly CPU intensive.)

Listing 14.1 Example code for profiling

```erlang
-module(profile_ex).

%% API
-export([run/0]).

run() ->
    spawn(fun() -> looper(1000) end),
    spawn (fun() -> funner(1000) end).

looper(0) ->
    ok;
looper(N) ->
    _ = integer_to_list(N),
    looper(N - 1).

funner(N) ->
    funner(fun(X) -> integer_to_list(X) end, N).

funner(_Fun, 0) ->
    ok;
funner(Fun, N) ->
    Fun(N),
    funner(Fun, N - 1).
```

The run() function spawns two processes to run in parallel: the first runs the looper/1 function, and the second runs the funner/1 function, in both cases with an argument of 1000. The looper/1 function calls integer_to_list(N) and discards the result, for each N between 1 and the original input value. The funner/1 function does much the same thing, but it uses a fun that's passed as an extra argument to the loop in funner/2.

The following Erlang shell session demonstrates how you can use cprof to profile the example module:

```
Eshell V5.7.4  (abort with ^G)
1> c(profile_ex).
{ok,profile_ex}
2> cprof:start().                                      ❶ Starts cprof
5359
3> profile_ex:run().
<0.43.0>
4> cprof:pause().                                      ❷ Stops profiling
5380
5> cprof:analyse(profile_ex).                          
{profile_ex,3006,                                      ❸ Fetches results
           [{{profile_ex,looper,1},1001},
            {{profile_ex,funner,2},1001},
            {{profile_ex,'-funner/1-fun-0-',1},1000},
            {{profile_ex,run,0},1},
            {{profile_ex,module_info,0},1},
            {{profile_ex,funner,1},1},
            {{profile_ex,'-run/0-fun-1-',0},1},
            {{profile_ex,'-run/0-fun-0-',0},1}]]}
6> cprof:stop().
5380
7>
```

After the profile_ex module has been compiled and loaded (recall that c(...) also loads the module), you call cprof:start() ❶. This enables call counting for all modules from this point on. You don't need to do anything special with the code you're profiling—no special recompilation or reloading—and the code doesn't need to have been compiled with debugging information. This makes cprof a useful tool that you can run any system and without disturbing the running applications.

Many times, you'll only be interested in the call counts of a specific module, not of all the modules in the system. For example, you could call cprof:start(profile_ex) to profile only the profile_ex module. This further limits the impact of running with call counting enabled. Right now, though, the overhead of profiling isn't a problem.

When cprof has been started and told what to profile, you run the code that you want to measure. When it's finished, you tell cprof to pause so that it stops counting calls ❷. To get the results of the profiling session, you then call cprof:analyse (profile_ex) to fetch the counts for all functions in the profile_ex module ❸.

The returned term is fairly readable as it is: the functions are listed in decreasing order of call count. You can see that the results are what you would have expected:

1,001 calls to both the main loop functions `looper/1` and `funner/2`. (The 1001th call was when the counter reached zero.) You also see that a function with the strange name `'-funner/1-fun-0-'/1` has been called exactly 1,000 times: this is the compiler-generated function that contains the code for the fun defined in the `funner/1` function. (This isn't called in the case when the loop counter reaches zero.) All the other functions are called exactly once. Note that the calls to `integer_to_list/1` don't show up. First, this built-in function (BIF) isn't part of the `profile_ex` module; and second, even if you tried to profile the `erlang` module where it belongs, the BIFs in Erlang can't be call counted by `cprof`.

Running `cprof` is an easy way to find out which functions are being called and how many times. Sometimes this says everything you need to know, but you usually want more detail. You can get this with the `fprof` tool.

14.2.2 *Profiling execution time with fprof*

The `fprof` profiler is perhaps the most valuable of the standard profiling tools. It gives you a wealth of useful information in a digestible format, and it's easy to use. It's one of the first tools to bring in when you need to diagnose performance issues. It supersedes the older `eprof` (which is still included in the distribution but is much less efficient). Both `fprof` and `eprof` are built on top of Erlang's tracing functionality, so neither requires any special compilation of the code or additional debugging information. They have much higher overhead than `cprof` and can make the code run up to 10 times slower, so they should be used with some care if you need to profile a system in production.

> **`runtime_tools` application required**
>
> `fprof` depends on `dbg`, which is part of the `runtime_tools` application (described in the Tools section of the Erlang/OTP documentation). This must be present on your system in order to use `fprof`. `runtime_tools` is included in the standard Erlang/OTP distribution, but if you've installed Erlang via a package manager, you may need to check that you also have this package. The `fprof` module, together with `cprof`, `cover`, `instrument`, and a few others, belong to the unimaginatively named `tools` application.

Running `fprof` is similar to running `cprof`. The following dialogue demonstrates how you can use `fprof` to analyze the `profile_ex` module from the previous section:

```
Eshell V5.7.4  (abort with ^G)
1> c(profile_ex).
{ok,profile_ex}
2> fprof:trace(start).          ⤶
ok                              ❶ Starts tracing
3> profile_ex:run().
<0.42.0>
4> fprof:trace(stop).
```

```
ok
5> fprof:profile().
Reading trace data...
.............
End of trace!
ok
6> fprof:analyse({dest, "profile.txt"}).
Processing data...
Creating output...
Done!
ok
7>
```

❷ Processes trace

❸ Analyzes profiling data

Instead of generating a term that you can inspect directly in the shell, this creates a file called profile.txt in your current directory. First, fprof is told to start tracing ❶. The tracing information is by default written to a file named fprof.trace, which is in a binary format, not fit for human consumption. You call profile_ex:run() as before, and after a moment or two, you stop the tracing again. Next, you must call fprof:profile() ❷ to take the trace accumulated in the file and turn it into raw profiling data. This compiled data is kept in RAM by the fprof server. You can then analyze the data by calling fprof:analyse/1 ❸, in this example telling it to output the results (in human readable format) to a file named profile.txt.

Several variations on how to start a trace and produce the final output exist, and we leave it as an exercise for you to study the documentation for fprof. It's also important to be aware of the amount of code you're actively profiling. Unlike cprof, fprof can accumulate data quickly, and if you profile large chunks of code over an extended period of time, fprof can generate gigabytes of profiling information.

But the procedure for generating the output isn't nearly as important as the ability to understand what it means, which is what we'll look at next.

INTERPRETING THE OUTPUT FROM FPROF

The output from the analysis is in the profile.txt file. As is common when you're working with Erlang, the text has the form of Erlang terms (terminated by period characters) and contains some Erlang comments (beginning with % characters). This means you can easily read it with the standard library file:consult(Filename) function and process the contents if you want to compute some statistics. The format can be a bit eye-watering at first glance, but it's not so hard to read when you know what to look for. We'll go through the important parts of the file and explain what they mean.

The file begins with a comment that says Analysis results followed by a summary of the options that were given to the analysis (useful in case you want to rerun the analysis later with the exact same options):

```
%% Analysis results:
{ analysis_options,
 [{callers, true},
  {sort, acc},
  {totals, false},
  {details, true}]}.
```

Then comes a short section that shows the total number of function calls (CNT), the total amount of time (in milliseconds) for the entire execution (ACC), and the total amount of time spent within the functions listed in this file (OWN).

```
%                                        CNT       ACC       OWN
[{ totals,                              5045,   78.976,   78.929}].
```

In other words, time spent in functions that aren't being profiled isn't included in the total OWN time. In this example, you didn't limit the profiling to any particular modules, so OWN is very close to ACC. In general, *own* time means the time spent within a particular function, not counting the time spent in calls to other functions, whereas *accumulated* time means total time spent from start to end. Time is measured as wall-clock time by default; you can change this with the cpu_time option.

After the totals, the file contains a section for each Erlang process that was involved in the trace. Every such section starts with a summary for the process, like this:

```
%                                        CNT       ACC       OWN
[{ "<0.51.0>",                          3012,undefined,   48.973},
 { spawned_by, "<0.38.0>"},
 { spawned_as, {erlang,apply,["#Fun<profile_ex.1.108254554>",[]]}},
 { initial_calls, [{erlang,apply,2},{profile_ex,'-run/0-fun-1-',0}]}].
```

This is the summary of the profiling data for one of the two processes spawned by profile_ex:run(), as you may be able to see from the initial_calls and spawned_as entries. You can also see that the total OWN time for the process is a bit more than half the total OWN time for the entire file, which makes sense: profile_ex:run() started two processes that did about the same amount of work, but one did it in a more complicated way than the other. ACC is always shown as undefined for a process.

A little further down in the file you'll find another process summary with similar initial_calls and spawned_as entries:

```
%                                        CNT       ACC       OWN
[{ "<0.50.0>",                          2011,undefined,   29.338}
 { spawned_by, "<0.38.0>"},
 { spawned_as, {erlang,apply,["#Fun<profile_ex.0.133762870>",[]]}},
 { initial_calls, [{erlang,apply,2},{profile_ex,'-run/0-fun-0-',0}]}].
```

That is of course the other process spawned by profile_ex:run(). Note that the spawned_by entry confirms that these processes had the same parent. (You also see from the numbers in the process identifiers that <0.50.0> was spawned before <0.51.0> even though they showed up in reverse order in this file.) Adding up the CNT and the OWN columns for these two processes yields just about the totals at the start of the file.

After the process summary (up to the next one in the file) come the functions called by the process, one "paragraph" (an Erlang term) per function. For example:

```
{[{{profile_ex,funner,1},                   1,   49.047,    0.025},
  {{profile_ex,funner,2},                1000,    0.000,   20.692}],
 { {profile_ex,funner,2},                1001,   49.047,   20.717},     %
 [{{profile_ex,'-funner/1-fun-0-',1},    1000,   28.217,   18.482},
```

```
{suspend,                                    1,    0.113,    0.000},
  {{profile_ex,funner,2},                 1000,    0.000,   20.692}]}.
```

Each such paragraph has one line marked with a final % character—that line shows the function that the paragraph concerns: in this case, profile_ex:funner/2. It has been called a total of 1,001 times, taking a total time of 49.047 milliseconds, of which 20.717 milliseconds were spent in this function alone. The lines above the % marker show where this function was called from: in this case, it was called once from funner/1 and 1,000 times from funner/2. Looking at the code from listing 14.1, this makes perfect sense.

The lines below the % marker show the functions that were called from this function. Again, you see that it calls itself 1,000 times, and it also calls '-funner/1-fun-0-'/1 (the autogenerated function for the fun expression in funner/1) 1,000 times. These additional calls to evaluate the fun are why the funner process performs 1,000 more calls than the looper process, as you could see in their total call counts.

Finally, you see that the process was suspended once within this function, for a duration of 0.113 ms. Process suspension is shown in this file as if it was another function call, and it even gets a paragraph of its own:

```
{[{{erlang,apply,2},                         1,   29.427,    0.000},
   {{profile_ex,funner,2},                   1,    0.113,    0.000}],
 { suspend,                                  2,   29.540,    0.000},    %
 [ ]}.
```

Here, the line that says suspend is the one marked with a % character. This paragraph says that this process was suspended once within erlang:apply/2 and once within funner/2. In all, the process was suspended for 29.540 ms. Garbage collection time is noted the same way:

```
{[{{profile_ex,'-funner/1-fun-0-',1},        6,    0.357,    0.357}],
 { garbage_collect,                          6,    0.357,    0.357},    %
 [ ]}.
```

This tells you that garbage collection for this process was performed 6 times, taking a total time of 0.357 ms.

When you know how to read these files, they aren't mysterious—in fact, they're pretty straightforward. Figuring out exactly what the numbers mean, for a particular application that you're profiling, is a different story.

An easy place to start the investigation of profile-analysis data is to look at the times for suspension and garbage collection. A process is *suspended* either when it's waiting for a message or when the scheduler puts it on hold for a while to let some other processes run. *Garbage collection* is when the runtime system is tracking down and recycling memory that was previously allocated by the process but is no longer in use. The garbage collector is also responsible for growing and shrinking process heaps as needed. A process that performs a lot of I/O operations or waits to receive messages will spend a lot of time suspended. A process that allocates a lot of temporary data will also spend part of the time doing garbage collection. Looking at suspension

> ### Caveats when reading `fprof` files
>
> The trace file contains a lot of numbers, and interpreting them can be confusing. Things don't always seem to add up. For example:
>
> - Tallying ACC times is tricky when the function is part of a complex mutually recursive operation.
> - When wall-clock time is measured, the scheduling in the operating system may affect the execution times. When this happens, it can appear that a function uses more time than it should, even when it's doing nothing. If you see something that looks unreasonable, it's best to run the profiling again and compare.
>
> Don't get hung up on trying to track down every microsecond. Look at the file as a whole, and you'll quickly be able to zero in on where the most time is spent.

and garbage collection first will quickly tell you if the differences in time spent between two processes could be due to these things.

Comparing the suspend times for the looper process with those of the funner process shown earlier, you can see that they're almost equal (32.649 vs. 29.540 ms):

```
{[{{profile_ex,looper,1},                     1,    32.224,     0.000},
  {{erlang,apply,2},                      1,     0.425,     0.000}],
 { suspend,                               2,    32.649,     0.000},     %
 [ ]}.
```

and comparing the garbage-collection times, you see that they're both very small (0.164 vs. 0.357 ms). The differences could be due to fluctuations in measurement, and in either case they're just fractions of the total execution times:

```
{[{{profile_ex,looper,1},                     6,     0.164,     0.164}],
 { garbage_collect,                       6,     0.164,     0.164},     %
 [ ]}.
```

Having ruled these things out, you can start looking at the actual functions called by each process. You saw in the paragraph for the `funner/2` function previously that a total of 20.717 ms were spent in that function alone; and it calls the function `'-funner/1-fun-0-'/1`, whose paragraph in the file looks like this:

```
{[{{profile_ex,funner,2},                  1000,    28.217,    18.482}],
 { {profile_ex,'-funner/1-fun-0-',1},   1000,    28.217,    18.482},     %
 [{{erlang,integer_to_list,1},          1000,     9.378,     9.378},
  {garbage_collect,                        6,     0.357,     0.357}]}.
```

A total of 18.482 ms is spent in the fun expression in `funner/1`, and that fun also calls out to `integer_to_list/1` for a total of 9.378 ms. These numbers add up to about 48.5 ms in all, which is near the total OWN time for the funner process (48.973 ms). That means you've accounted for where this process spends its time.

Looking at the corresponding paragraph for the `looper/1` function instead, you can see that it used 19.649 ms of OWN time, and it calls `integer_to_list/1` directly for a total of 9.505 ms (very close to the time that the funner process spent in the same function):

```
{[{{profile_ex,'-run/0-fun-0-',0},        1,    61.542,     0.021},
  {{profile_ex,looper,1},              1000,     0.000,    19.628}],
  { {profile_ex,looper,1},             1001,    61.542,    19.649},      %
  [{suspend,                              1,    32.224,     0.000},
   {{erlang,integer_to_list,1},        1000,     9.505,     9.505},
   {garbage_collect,                      6,     0.164,     0.164},
   {{profile_ex,looper,1},            1000,     0.000,    19.628}]}].
```

These numbers add up to about 29.2 ms, which again is very near the total OWN time for the looper process. Now that you've accounted for where both processes spend their time, it's also easy to see exactly where the difference lies: the use of the intermediate fun in the funner process took almost 19 ms for the 1,000 calls, or about 19 microseconds per fun call.

Looking back at the code in listing 14.1, it's easy to see that funner/1 is more time consuming than looper/1 (unless the compiler is allowed to use inlining to eliminate the use of the intermediate fun). The important thing isn't that you proved something obvious with the help of fprof, but that you've learned how to read these files and determine where the time is being spent.

With the cprof and fprof tools in your arsenal, you have a good starting point for performance analysis of your system. This will both help you assess where problems may exist in the code and, after you've fixed them, allow you to establish which of your optimizations had any measurable effect.

But sometimes even when you've found the problem points, it's not necessarily apparent why there is a problem with the code. In the next section, we'll discuss various caveats and pitfalls that you should be aware of so you can spot them in the wild.

14.3   *Erlang programming language caveats*

One of the things that make Erlang code easy to read and understand is that there is generally little hidden complexity. In most cases, the cost of performing an operation is clear and up front: there are no implicitly called object constructors and destructors, no overloaded instances of + that turn out to be copying entire objects behind your back, no virtual function table indirections, no synchronized regions, and no blocking send primitives. A call to some function can of course do almost anything, but in that case it's usually clearly documented (and if you haven't read the documentation, or there is none, you at least know that there is a point in the program where all bets are off).

That said, like any programming language, Erlang has its little caveats. We'll start this discussion by looking at some aspects of Erlang's primitive data types that you should be aware of when you're trying to make your program more efficient. The primitive data types are the most heavily used parts of the language, and proper choice of data representation and how you handle that data can make an enormous difference.

14.3.1 *Performance aspects of the primitive data types*

First, note that sizes of data types in Erlang are counted in *machine words*. This is due to the way the BEAM emulator works. On a 32-bit machine, a word is 4 bytes; on a 64-bit machine, a word is 8 bytes. Table 14.1 lists the sizes of the primitive data types.

Table 14.1   Sizes of data types in Erlang

Data type	Size in memory
Small integer (*immediate*)	1 word
Large integer (*bignum*)	3 words or more (as large as needed)
Float	4 words on 32-bit architectures, 3 words on 64-bit architectures
Atom	1 word (the name string is stored only once per Erlang node, in the so-called atom table)
Binary or bitstring	3-6 words + size of data divided by word size
Pid, port, or reference	1 word for a local process/port/reference, 5 words for a remote process/port/reference
Fun	9-13 words + 1 word per captured variable
Tuple	2 words + 1 word per element
List	1 word + 2 words per element

Let's go through some aspects of these data types with regard to efficiency. For the purposes of this discussion, funs can be regarded as a kind of tuple with some additional metadata, and pids (and ports and references) are similar to integers.

SMALL INTEGERS

Small integers require only a single word of memory, but the BEAM needs to use a few bits of that word as a tag, to be able to separate it from other things. This is illustrated in figure 14.2.

On a 32-bit machine, only 28 bits can be used for the value (including the sign bit); integers between -134217728 and +134217727 fit in one word, whereas larger integers are stored as so-called *bignums*.

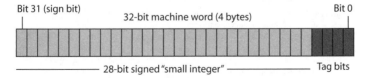

Figure 14.2   Tagged representation of small integers in the BEAM. On a 32-bit machine, only 28 bits are available for storing the integer value. Integers that require more bits are stored as bignums.

BIGNUMS

When you program in Erlang, you can use integers of any size. When they get too large to fit in a single word, the runtime system automatically changes their representation to bignums, which can be of any size (up to the available memory). The only visible difference to you is that arithmetic on large integers becomes slower than on small integers. This is sometimes noticeable when you have a tight loop that does a lot of arithmetic, and you give it some input that causes many of the operations to be done on large numbers. It may then be possible to rewrite the program to do the calculations a different way or factor out some large part of the numbers so that most of the operations involve only small integers.

FLOATS AND BOXED REPRESENTATIONS

Erlang's floats use 64-bit precision. This means they don't fit in a single word (not even on a 64-bit machine, because as we said about small integers, the BEAM also needs some bits for the tag). Therefore, floats always use what's called a *boxed* representation: first, there's one word that contains a tag and a pointer to a location on the process's heap memory where the rest of the data is stored. This word is all that's copied when you pass the float as an argument to another function or store it in a data structure. Then, the data on the heap begins with another word that describes the kind of data (float) and its size. After that comes the actual 64-bit floating-point data: two words on a 32-bit machine, or one word on a 64-bit machine. This is illustrated in figure 14.3.

Several other of the primitive data types also use a boxed representation, including bignums (which is why they need at least three words) and tuples.

ATOMS

Atoms are similar to small integers: each occurrence uses only one word of memory. The data stored in that word is an index into an atom table where the actual name string for that atom is stored. The name also uses a little memory, but it's stored only once on each Erlang node. In particular, comparing two atoms for equality is just as fast as comparing two small integers. This is what makes atoms efficient for use as

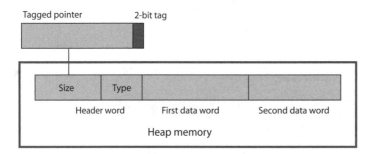

Figure 14.3   Boxed representation of values that don't fit in a single word, such as floats and bignums. The tagged pointer is the only thing that gets passed between functions or inserted in another data structure.

Creating atoms dynamically can be a memory leak

It's common for novice Erlang hackers to come up with the idea of creating atoms on the fly for various purposes: atoms with names like x1, x2, ..., x187634, and so on. This may work fine for one-shot programs that generate at most a few hundred thousand atoms and then halt the Erlang VM. But the atom table size is limited, currently to just over a million entries. When it overflows, the VM crashes with a "system limit" error. For a small standalone program, that's not a big issue, but you don't want that to happen in a long-running production system.

As an example, you may be doing this sort of thing without realizing it in a server that receives data from the outside world and transforms the data into Erlang messages. If you're converting strings in the incoming data to Erlang atoms, rather than representing them as Erlang strings or binaries, you may be open to an attack: someone could bring down your node by sending large numbers of unique strings.

labels in tagged tuples. Atoms are added to the table (if they aren't already present) when a module is loaded that contains an occurrence of the atom, or when the node receives a message from another node that contains a new atom, or when you call list_to_atom(NameString). But atoms aren't garbage collected, so unused atoms aren't removed from the table: the only way to clear the table is to restart the node.

Atoms should be used to represent mostly static sets of identifiers. Use them as much as you like, but avoid creating arbitrary atoms from untrusted data sources. You can use the BIF list_to_existing_atom(NameString) to ensure that you only convert strings to already known atoms in the system. If the name string isn't already in the atom table, this function will throw an exception.

BINARIES AND BITSTRINGS

Binaries and bitstrings (see section 2.2.2) are just chunks of bytes. Their representation is similar to bignums but is a little more complicated because several different kinds of binaries exist under the surface, even though this is invisible to you. There are two main types:

- *Heap binaries* (small) are up to 64 bytes in size. They're stored on the process's own heap, like a float or a bignum. When passed in a message between processes, the data is copied just as it is for any other Erlang data type.
- *Reference-counted binaries* (large) are stored in a separate global memory area shared by all processes, and garbage collection for these binaries is handled by reference counting. When a large binary like this is passed from one process to another within the same Erlang VM, only a pointer has to be transferred, which saves a lot of copying. This makes it possible to let one process read a large chunk of binary data from a file or a port and pass it on to a second process without wasting time on additional copying of the data. Although it's good to know that this is handled well by the system, exploiting this property for efficiency hacks is ugly and should be done only as a last resort.

The syntax for working with binaries is powerful but can be tricky to get right; and it can be hard to see how to best use it, especially if you're writing loops over binary data. One way to quickly get an idea of whether you're using binaries efficiently is to compile your code with the bin_opt_info flag—for example, by setting the operating system environment variable ERL_COMPILER_OPTIONS to [bin_opt_info]. This flag makes the compiler print additional warnings and information about how binaries are used in the code, which can be a big help.

TUPLES

Tuples are refreshingly straightforward. Keep in mind that they're read-only data structures, and updates require copying. Because records are really tuples, updating a field in a record means you're creating a new tuple: to update a record containing 10 fields, 12 words of data need to be written. On the other hand, picking out fields in a tuple or record is as fast as it can be. This means you have a trade-off between fast reads and fast updates. For data that doesn't change, a huge tuple can work as a quick-access array, but updating it is inefficient. By nesting tuples, you can build a tree structure where accesses have to go through several indirections and become slower, but updates become less costly; this is how standard libraries like the array module work.

LISTS

We've talked about how lists are represented, and things to keep in mind when you're programming with lists (see sections 2.2.5, 2.2.10, and 2.15.5, and appendix B), so we'll just mention a few points about the storage requirements for lists. Recall what we said about boxed representations earlier in the section about floats. List cells are a bit like tuples with two elements, but with an important difference from an implementation perspective: the first word, which contains the tag and the pointer to the heap where the rest is stored, has a special tag that says list cell. Because list cells always have two elements, there is no need for any additional type or size information; so whereas a tuple of two elements has a *header word* as the first word on the heap, a list cell needs no such extra word: it only consists of exactly two words on the heap, and nothing more (see figures 2.1 and 2.2 in section 2.2.10). This makes Erlang's lists efficient as a general data structure.

> ### Memory usage for strings
>
> If the elements in the list are small integers, like the character codes in a string, then the head word of each cell holds the entire element. That means a string uses exactly two words per character in the string. When you're working with relatively short strings (say, less than 10,000 characters), and you're using strings as temporary data structures, this is generally no problem. But if you store text as strings (lists of character codes) in a database or in an ETS table or other data structure in memory, you're using a lot more space than necessary. Converting the strings to binaries could shrink them by a factor of 8 (or 16 on a 64-bit machine). On the other hand, convenience should also be considered: if you have plenty of memory and it's not currently a problem for you, changing the code to use binaries everywhere may not be worth it, particularly if the code gets messier.

That concludes our discussion of the primitive data types. In the next section, we'll look at some performance aspects of Erlang's BIFs and operators.

14.3.2 *Performance of built-in functions and operators*

Erlang defines a number of operators and a number of BIFs. These are implemented directly in C code as part of the runtime system, which makes them efficient in general, but you must still consider a few performance implications and caveats. In this section, we'll bring up a few common pitfalls when using the following:

- ++
- --
- list_to_atom(CharList)
- length(List)
- size(Thing)

THE ++ OPERATOR

We talked about this in section 2.2.5 and at the end of section 2.15.5, so we'll just say it again: don't make lists grow on the right side! Also note that the ++ operator is an alias for lists:append/2, so the same warnings apply for that function.

THE -- OPERATOR

The -- operator is an alias for lists:subtract/2. It's rarely used: it deletes the elements in the right-side list from ones in the left-side list. It only deletes the first found occurrence for each element on the right side, so it can't be used to remove all occurrences from the left side unless you know how many there are. The following example demonstrates how it works:

```
1> [1,2,3,2,1] -- [2,1,2].
[3,1]
```

As you can see, only the first occurrence of 1 was removed from the left side, both 2s were removed, and the 3 wasn't affected. The order of the elements is preserved.

The issue with this function is that it uses quadratic time: it has to go over the left-side list once for each element in the right-side list. For short lists, it's not noticeable; but if the lists is long, it can be a problem. If the order of the elements isn't important, it's a much better idea to sort them first and then use ordsets:subtract/2.

LIST_TO_ATOM/1

Remember that atoms are never garbage collected, so use this function with care. It may be that list_to_existing_atom/1 is a better choice for your application; see the discussion about atoms previously in section 14.3.1.

LENGTH/1

Always remember that length(List) traverses the list to count the elements, much like the C function strlen counts the length of a string. It's a common mistake for people with a background in Java to forget this and assume it's a constant time operation—it's not! See the end of section 2.15.5 for tips on how to use pattern matching instead in some common situations.

SIZE/1

It's sometimes a source of confusion that length/1 is used for lists only, whereas size/1 works on tuples and binaries, but not on lists. The difference is that size/1 always takes constant time and doesn't need to traverse the data, so it's a very fast operation. But the fact that the size/1 function is overloaded to work both on tuples and binaries is a little unfortunate, because it counts elements in the former case and bytes in the latter. It also doesn't give any hint to someone reading the code whether a tuple or a binary is expected, and if you don't know that, then you also don't know what the resulting number stands for. These things make it harder for a tool like Dialyzer to help you find possible mistakes.

In modern Erlang code, it's recommended that you use tuple_size(T) to get the number of elements of a tuple, and either byte_size(B) or bit_size(B) to get the number of bytes or bits, respectively, of a binary or bitstring. In case of a bitstring (whose length in bits isn't evenly divisible by 8), byte_size(B) rounds upward—that is, it always returns the smallest number of bytes that can contain all the bits in B. Using these functions clarifies what you're doing and also offers important hints to the compiler and the Dialyzer tool.

Now that we've talked about BIFs and operators, we'll say a few words about the efficiency of normal, user-defined functions.

14.3.3 Functions

Using functions efficiently can sometimes be important to shave off extra microseconds when you really need that kind of performance tweaking. It's also an area where you may encounter several myths and misconceptions. We'll start with table 14.2, which shows the invocation times for the different ways in which functions can be called.

The absolute times depend on the speed of the hardware, but the relative times may also vary a bit with new releases of the compiler and runtime system. For example, it used to be (many years ago) that calling a function in another module was noticeably slower than calling a local function. Nowadays, they're almost the same. In general, you can see from table 14.2 that you don't need to worry much about function-invocation times unless you're writing extremely performance-critical code: only meta-calls are significantly slower, and they tend to be used rarely. Keep in mind

Table 14.2 Speed of function calls

Type of function call	Time
Local function: foo()	Very fast
Known remote function: bar:foo()	Almost as fast as a local function call
Unknown remote function: Mod:Func()	About 3 times slower than a local call
Fun application: F()	About 2-3 times slower than a local call
Meta-call: apply(Mod,Func,Args)	About 6-10 times slower than a local call

that if the number of arguments is fixed, the `Mod:Func(...)` form is a better choice than calling `apply/3`.

TAIL RECURSION VERSUS BODY RECURSION

We talked about tail recursion and body recursion in section 2.15.2. Like the difference between local and remote calls, it used to be that a body-recursive solution was often slower than a tail-recursive one. Due to improvements in the runtime system and compiler, the difference is much smaller these days, and an elegant body-recursive function may often be at least as fast as a tail-recursive version.

If speed is important, and you're able to implement both a tail-recursive and a body-recursive version (one of them may be much easier than the other, depending on the problem), then don't assume—measure both versions. The results may even vary between different hardware platforms, due to things like cache implementations. It also depends a lot on the size of the input (which decides the depth of recursion), so measure both for smaller inputs and for larger ones; and think about what kind you expect to see most of, and if worst-case or average-case time is most important.

CLAUSE SELECTION

When a function or fun expression has multiple clauses (or you have a `case`-, `if`-, `try`-, or `receive`-expression with multiple clauses), the compiler does its best to minimize the number of tests needed to decide which clause should be selected. It does this using an algorithm called *pattern matching compilation*, which groups and sorts clauses and splits them into a series of nested if/then/else tests. But it can only change the order in which tests are performed as long as it doesn't have any visible effect on the outcome (apart from being faster).

For example, testing whether the input is either the atom `true` or the atom `false` can be done in any order, because the alternatives are mutually exclusive: if it's one, it's not the other. The same thing goes for testing whether a list is empty or non-empty, and so on. But sometimes the alternatives overlap; for example, in the following function

```
coffee_size(N) when N < 12 -> short;
coffee_size(N) when N < 16 -> tall;
coffee_size(N) when N < 20 -> grande;
coffee_size(_)             -> venti.
```

the logic depends on the order of the tests, and switching the order of the two topmost clauses would cause every N smaller than 16 to yield `tall`, even for N smaller than 12. The compiler can only detect when it's definitely safe for it to reorder clauses, and everything that seems unsafe is left in the order that you wrote it.

The one thing you want to avoid, then, is introducing uncertainty in the middle of otherwise straightforward clauses. Take the following code as an example:

```
handle_message(stop) -> do_stop();
handle_message(go)   -> do_go();
handle_message(Msg) when Msg =:= Special -> do_special(Msg);
handle_message(report)   -> do_report();
```

```
handle_message(calc)      -> do_calculate();
handle_message(OtherMsg) -> do_error(Other).
```

This expects either one of four atoms, or some particular term `Special` (as a variable, to be given at runtime), and reports an error for all other terms. It may be that `Special` is supposed to also be an atom, but the compiler can't be sure of that. In particular, `Special` could be one of the atoms `report` or `calc`, and that means it's not allowed to move the four clauses for `stop`, `go`, `report`, and `calc` together. Instead, the best the compiler can do is to group the `stop` and `go` tests, then test for `Special`, and then group the `report` and `calc` tests. If you as the programmer know that `Special` can never be `report` or `calc`, you should manually move it below the other tests. For a simple example like this, the performance difference would be very small; but if you have many clauses with complicated patterns, it can pay off to make sure tests can be grouped properly. (Not to mention that it it's more readable and better shows the intent.)

We'll finish this chapter by discussing some efficiency aspects of processes.

14.3.4 *Processes*

Processes are the fundamental execution environment of any Erlang program. Whenever code is running, it's being executed by a process. Even if you write a library module that doesn't start any processes of its own, the code is executed by the process that called it.

As we've pointed out before, processes are cheap in Erlang. Running lots of concurrent processes is what Erlang is all about. But what you choose to do within each process can have a large impact on the overall performance of the system.

USING OTP BEHAVIOURS OR NOT

Although the actual time it takes to spawn a new process can be measured in microseconds, the initialization of an OTP behaviour-container process is a different story. When you call `gen_server:start_link()`, a number of things happen behind the scenes, including the call to the `init/1` callback function in your implementation module. As we've mentioned before, the `start_link` function doesn't return to the caller until the `init/1` callback has finished. This is in order to make the startup sequence deterministic so that when the caller gets the process ID of the new server process and is allowed to proceed, the server is fully initialized and ready to accept requests.

Sometimes, though, you want to use large numbers of processes that come and go rapidly. Take, for example, the connection-handling processes you wrote in chapter 11, such as `ti_server` in listing 11.3. These spawn a new process for every incoming TCP connection. Under heavy load, measurements will show that a lot of time is spent in process initialization. The more transient the processes, the greater the proportion of time is spent in the OTP library code. If speed becomes a major concern, it can be useful to stray from OTP behaviours and instead roll your own extremely lightweight processes with the direct use of `spawn`, having minimal overhead but also providing minimal control beyond what you implement. This sort of thing is error prone and should be left for special cases, and only after you've gained some experience programming with processes and OTP so you understand what you're giving up.

SETTING THE INITIAL HEAP SIZE

When many processes are being spawned and dying quickly, you can perform another optimization: you can make the initial heap size of each process large enough to avoid the need for garbage collection or memory allocation after the process has been started.

The default process heap size is 233 words (932 bytes on a 32-bit machine), but this grows if the process needs more space (and it can also shrink again). This automatic memory management is handy, but it has a certain cost in runtime performance. If you know how much memory your transient processes need during their brief life span, you can specify the initial heap size by using one of the spawn_opt functions to start them, like this:

```
erlang:spawn_opt(Fun, [{min_heap_size, Words}])
```

In this way, a process works as a memory region; the memory is allocated when the process starts and is reclaimed when the process dies, and no further memory management is necessary between those two points. This is illustrated in figure 14.4.

The downside is that you are constantly over-approximating how much memory is needed per process, so you may be sacrificing memory space for speed.

HIBERNATING

If you need a very large number of processes active for a long period, but most of them will only be asleep and waiting for a message that is expected to arrive at some point in the future, you should consider letting those processes go into hibernation.

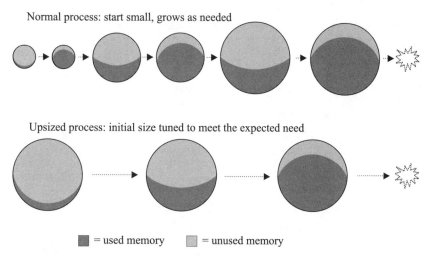

Normal process: start small, grows as needed

Upsized process: initial size tuned to meet the expected need

■ = used memory   ▢ = unused memory

Figure 14.4 Setting a larger initial heap size to avoid garbage collection and resizing for processes that perform a known, fixed amount of work in a short period of time

A process *hibernates* by calling `erlang:hibernate(Mod, Func, Args)`. When it does this, it throws away its call stack, making it forget where it is in the program. Thus, the call to `hibernate/3` never returns, and any active `catch` or `try/catch` expressions are also forgotten. It then forces a garbage collection, minimizing the amount of space allocated for the process. Finally, the process goes to sleep and stays suspended until it gets a message in its mailbox. (If the mailbox isn't empty when it hibernates, it wakes up immediately.) When this happens, the process behaves as if it had called `apply(Mod, Func, Args)`, except that it has nowhere to return to.

Hibernation minimizes the footprint of sleeping processes, allowing you to have more of them around than would otherwise be possible. This can be useful in a system that monitors a very large number of external entities.

Processes based on `proc_lib`, such as `gen_server` and other OTP behaviours, should use `proc_lib:hibernate/3` instead of `erlang:hibernate/3` to ensure that things are properly set up again with respect to the OTP libraries when the process wakes up.

And with that, we end our coverage of all things performance related.

14.4   Summary

In this chapter, you've learned some basic methodology for tuning your code: setting your goals, measuring what your system is doing, deciding which problems to attack, and confirming that your changes were effective. You've learned how to use the `cprof` and `fprof` tools to profile your code with respect to execution time, and you've been introduced to some important caveats, pitfalls, and tricks with respect to the efficiency of your Erlang code. This means you should be able to join the Erlware team in their optimization effort and make your code as efficient as it can be. Just remember to keep it beautiful.

appendix A
Installing Erlang

You can install Erlang several ways, depending on your operating system and your personal preferences. Erlang currently runs on modern versions of Windows, on Mac OS X, Linux, and most other UNIX-like operating systems, and on the VxWorks real-time operating system.

A.1 Installing Erlang on Windows

If your operating system is Windows, download and run the latest installer .exe file from www.erlang.org/download.html. This includes documentation and sets up menus and icons for starting the special `werl` shell on Windows (see section 2.1.1).

A.2 Installing Erlang on Mac OS X, Linux, or other UNIX-like systems

On Unix-like systems, you can build and install Erlang from source code, which is the best way to ensure that you have the latest version; or, on some systems, you can use a package manager such as Ubuntu's `synaptic` to automatically download and install the official Erlang package for your system—but note that this may not be the latest release of Erlang. On Mac OS X, the current version of Erlang is available in the Homebrew package manager (http://mxcl.github.com/homebrew/).

A.2.1 Compiling from source

Point your browser at www.erlang.org/download.html, and get the latest source package. After it downloads, un-`tar` the package, `cd` into the directory, and run the ./configure script. You can add a `--prefix=...` flag if you want to install to a location other than the default, which is /usr/local/lib/erlang. For example:

```
./configure --prefix=/home/jdoe/lib
```

When the code is configured properly (see the next section if you have issues), run

```
make
```

and then

```
make install
```

Note that you'll probably need to do the install step with root privileges, if you're installing to the default location. On many systems these days, that means running it as

```
sudo make install
```

After installing, you should be able to enter `erl` to start Erlang or `erlc` to run the Erlang compiler. If you install to a nonstandard location, make sure the bin subdirectory of that location is listed in your `PATH` environment variable.

A.2.2   *Resolving configuration problems*

To compile Erlang from source, some libraries and tools must be installed already on your system. Some of the more common items that may not be installed by default are

- A fully working GCC compiler environment
- Ncurses development libraries

Try installing any missing packages and run `configure` again, before you run `make`. (The exact package names may vary with your system.)

Some libraries, if missing, only cause a warning in the configure step, telling you that some Erlang applications won't be built. If you don't need these applications, you can go ahead and run `make`; otherwise, you need to install the missing packages and reconfigure. Some typical examples are

- OpenSSL development libraries
- ODBC development libraries
- Java

If you're running with some applications disabled, and you later find out that you need one of them, you can do the `./configure`, `make`, `make install` again after you get the missing packages.

appendix B
Lists and referential transparency

What is the *point* of Erlang's list data type, you may ask (in particular if you're used to languages like Java, Python, and so on, where you work a lot with arrays, buffers, and whatnot). For every element, you also need a pointer to the next one, using valuable memory, and you can't even add elements on the right side of the list! Pah!

This is all true; but in Erlang, you're never allowed to modify the value of something if it could cause someone else's data to be changed behind their back. This is the main idea behind the fancy words *referential transparency*.

B.1 A definition of referential transparency

Referential transparency is a simple concept. It boils down to this: If you get hold of a value (a *term*), and you give it a name (let's say *X*) to keep track of it for the time being, then you're *guaranteed* that X remains unchanged no matter what, even if you pass a reference to X to some other part of the program. In other words, values kept in variables (or parts of those values) are never changed behind your back. As you can see, this goes hand in hand with Erlang's single-assignment variables.

B.2 Advantages of referential transparency

The same reasoning is behind why strings are constant in Java: you don't want to be embarrassed by printing something rude instead of your intended "More tea, Vicar?" just because you happened to pass a reference to that string to another, rather naughty function, before you printed the string.

On a more serious note, there are several reasons why this is done for *all* data in Erlang:

- It makes programming a *lot* less error prone—a very important property when you have million-line projects with dozens or even hundreds of programmers involved.
- Things that used to work fine when you were running the code in a single process don't suddenly need rewriting if you want to divide the work over two or more processes: there can be no covert channels between different parts of the program that stop working when you split the code into separate processes (perhaps running on multiple machines).
- It allows the system to do creative things behind the scenes with respect to memory management and multithreading, because it knows there will be no write accesses to existing data structures.

Hence, referential transparency isn't merely a nice property enjoyed by people of a theoretical persuasion—it has important consequences for the stability and scalability of your program, not to mention for readability, debuggability, and speed of development.

B.3 *What it has to do with lists*

Getting back to lists, this referential transparency guarantee means that if you already have a list (maybe you got it as an argument to a function), you can't add elements to the end of that list, because if you did, then anybody who had a reference to it would discover that an extra last element had materialized from nowhere. That's not allowed in Erlang.

But adding to the left (using list cells) is no problem, because the original list is never disturbed—you create a new cell that points to the first cell of the original list, saying "I'm like that list over there, but with this new element added to the head."

Hence, list cells are an elegant solution to the problem of growing lists dynamically in a referentially transparent system; and the implementation is so simple that cells work very efficiently indeed. Many extremely clever people have tried (for decades) to come up with a solution that would allow both adding to the end and lower memory usage while preserving the transparency property, but those solutions have tended to be both very complicated to implement and less efficient in the general case.

index

MORE TITLES FROM MANNING

The Joy of Clojure
Thinking the Clojure Way
by Michael Fogus and Chris Houser

ISBN: 978-1-935182-64-1
400 pages
$44.99
December 2010

Clojure in Action
by Amit Rathore

ISBN: 978-1-935182-59-7
475 pages
$49.99
February 2011

For ordering information go to www.manning.com

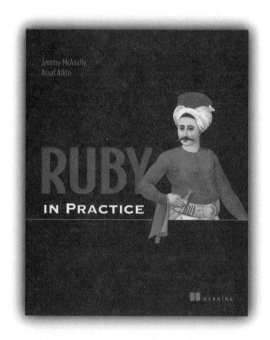

MORE TITLES FROM MANNING

Real-World Functional Programming
with examples in F# and C#

by Tomas Petricek with Jon Skeet

ISBN: 978-1-933988-92-4
560 pages
$49.99
December 2009

The Art of Unit Testing
with Examples in .NET

by Roy Osherove

ISBN: 978-1-933988-27-6
320 pages
$39.99
May 2009